MANFRIED SAVES THE DAY

A GRAPHIC NOVEL

by Caitlin Major
& Kelly Bastow

Coloring and lettering assistance by Matthew Hoddy

QUIRK BOOKS

PHILADELPHIA

This is a work of fiction. All names, places, and characters are products of the author's imagination or are used fictitiously. Any resemblance to real people, places, or events is entirely coincidental.

Library of Congress Cataloging in Publication Number:
2018949428

ISBN: 978-1-68369-108-2

Printed in China
Designed by Elissa Flanigan
Typeset in Gotham Rounded, Cubano, and Manfried
Manfried font typeset by John Martz
Production management by John J. McGurk

Quirk Books
215 Church Street
Philadelphia, PA 19106
quirkbooks.com

10 9 8 7 6 5 4 3 2 1

To Matt, Brett, and Morghan
for getting me through it
—Caitlin

To Luke, mudder, and fadder
—Kelly

Introduction

One Sunday morning I was lying in bed thinking about adopting a cat. I found a local shelter's website, which had little biographies of the cats up for adoption; the cats were all dressed in costumes, since this was around Halloween. I spent about an hour reading every one, bawling my eyes out. I wanted to adopt them all. That became the kernel of an idea that would turn into this book, which of course meant a lot of "research" (aka googling pictures of kittens in costumes).

Meanwhile, I was juggling my full-time job and promoting the first Manfried book, *Manfried the Man*. So a big part of Steve's storyline became my desperate attempt to capture how run-down and overworked I felt. Soon two sides of the book emerged: a lighthearted romp about men in a shelter, and a hard look at my work habits and how they affect the people around me. Luckily for Steve, he seems to figure it out in the end; I'm not sure if I have yet. But I did start making a monthly donation to my local cat shelter. Kelly and I encourage you to do the same.

<3 Caitlin

Cast of Characters

Meet Manfried and friends!

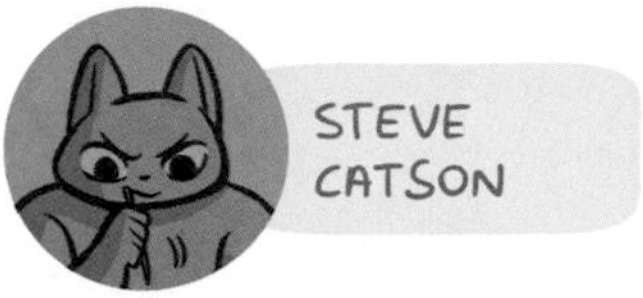
STEVE CATSON

- Up-and-coming web cartoonist
- Biggest inspiration: his pet man Manfried

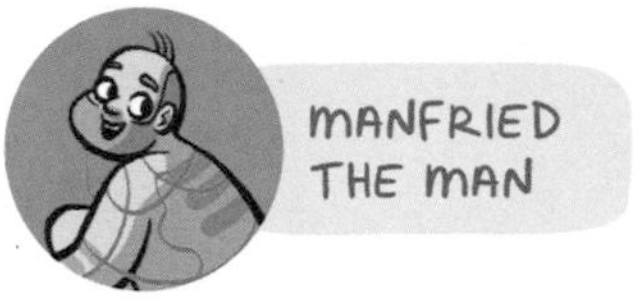
MANFRIED THE MAN

- Selfish, crabby, demanding
- Once ran away and became semi-famous*

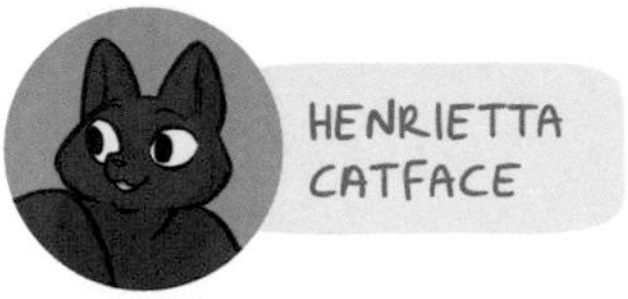
HENRIETTA CATFACE

- Owns and operates the Catlanta Man Shelter
- Is dating Steve

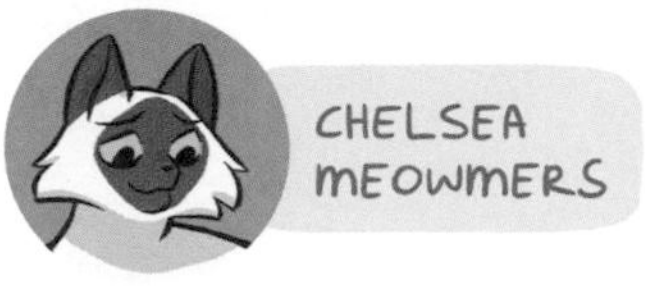
CHELSEA MEOWMERS

- Hardworking grad student
- Steve's hot-tempered neighbor

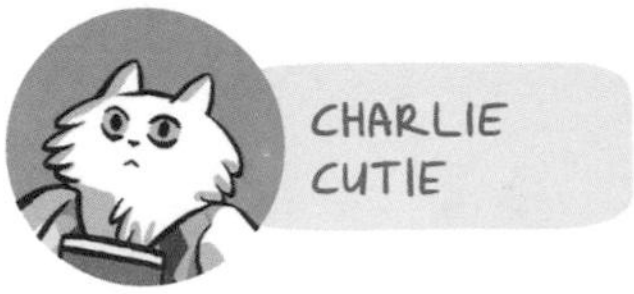
CHARLIE CUTIE

- Helps Henrietta run the Man Shelter
- Likes sweater vests

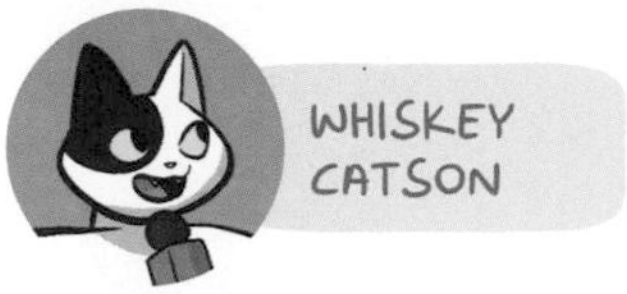
WHISKEY CATSON

- Local newscatster
- Steve's older brother

*See *Manfried the Man* (Quirk Books, 2018)

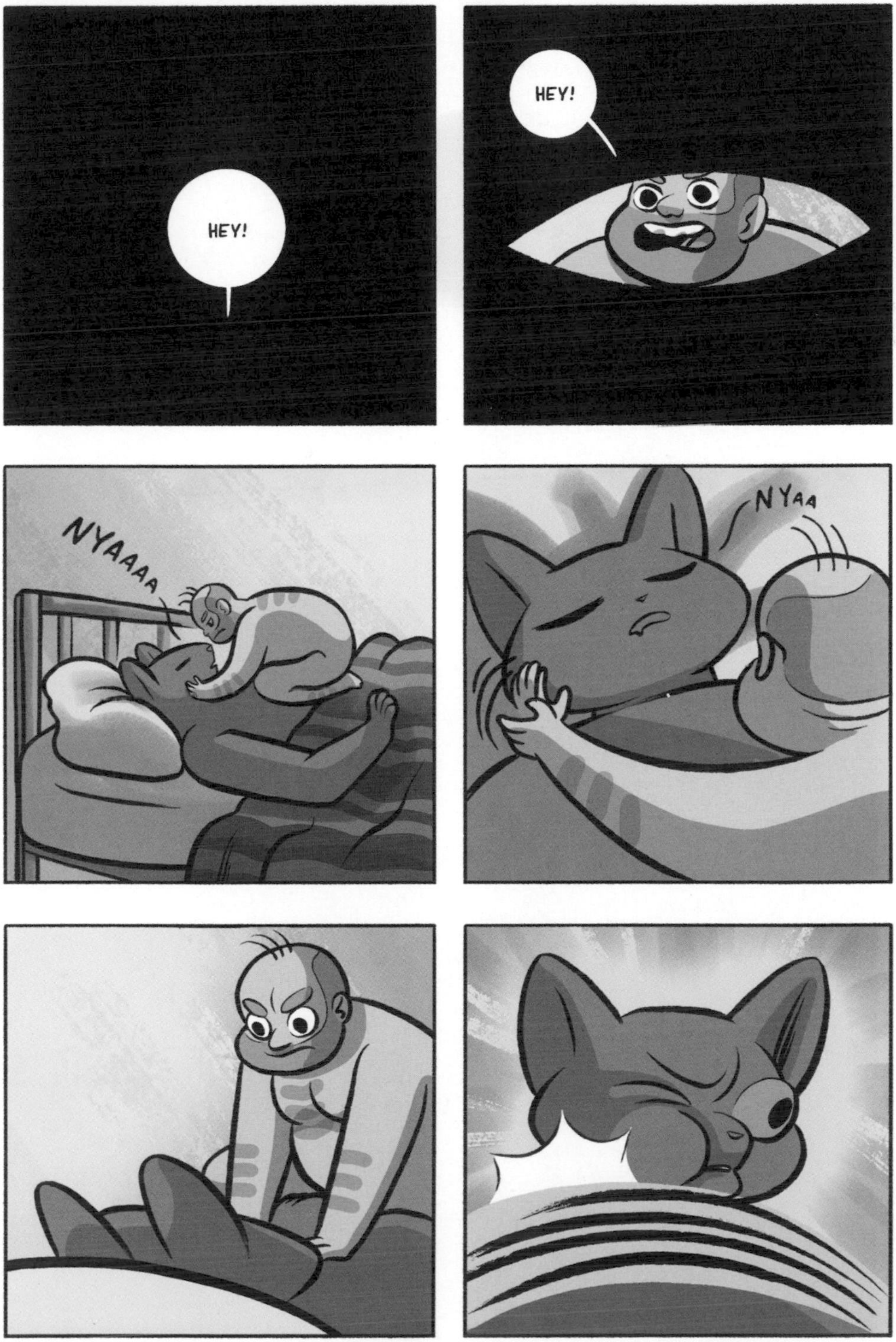
HEY!
HEY!
NYAAAAA
NYAA

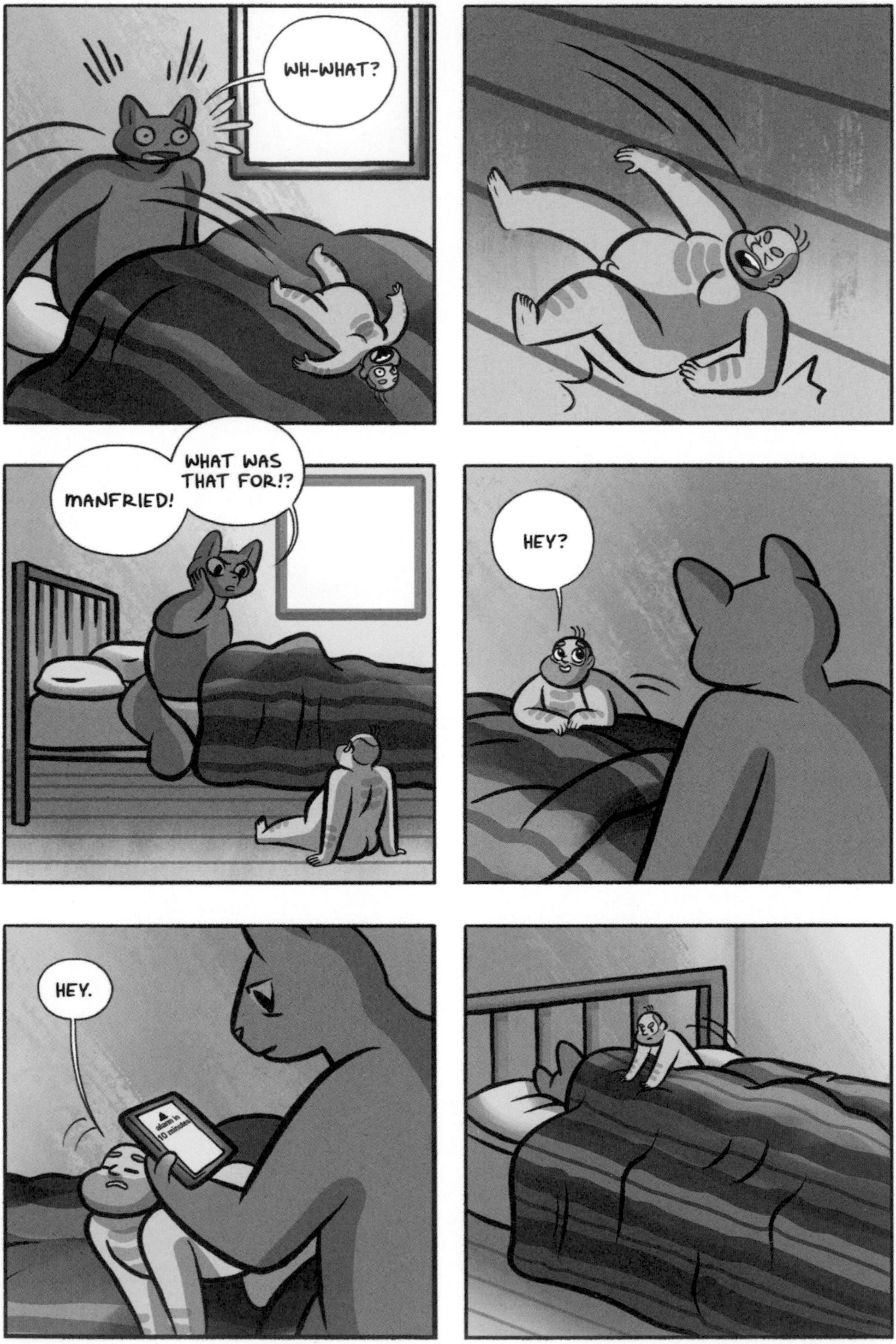
WH-WHAT?
MANFRIED!
WHAT WAS THAT FOR!?
HEY?
HEY.
alarm in 10 minutes

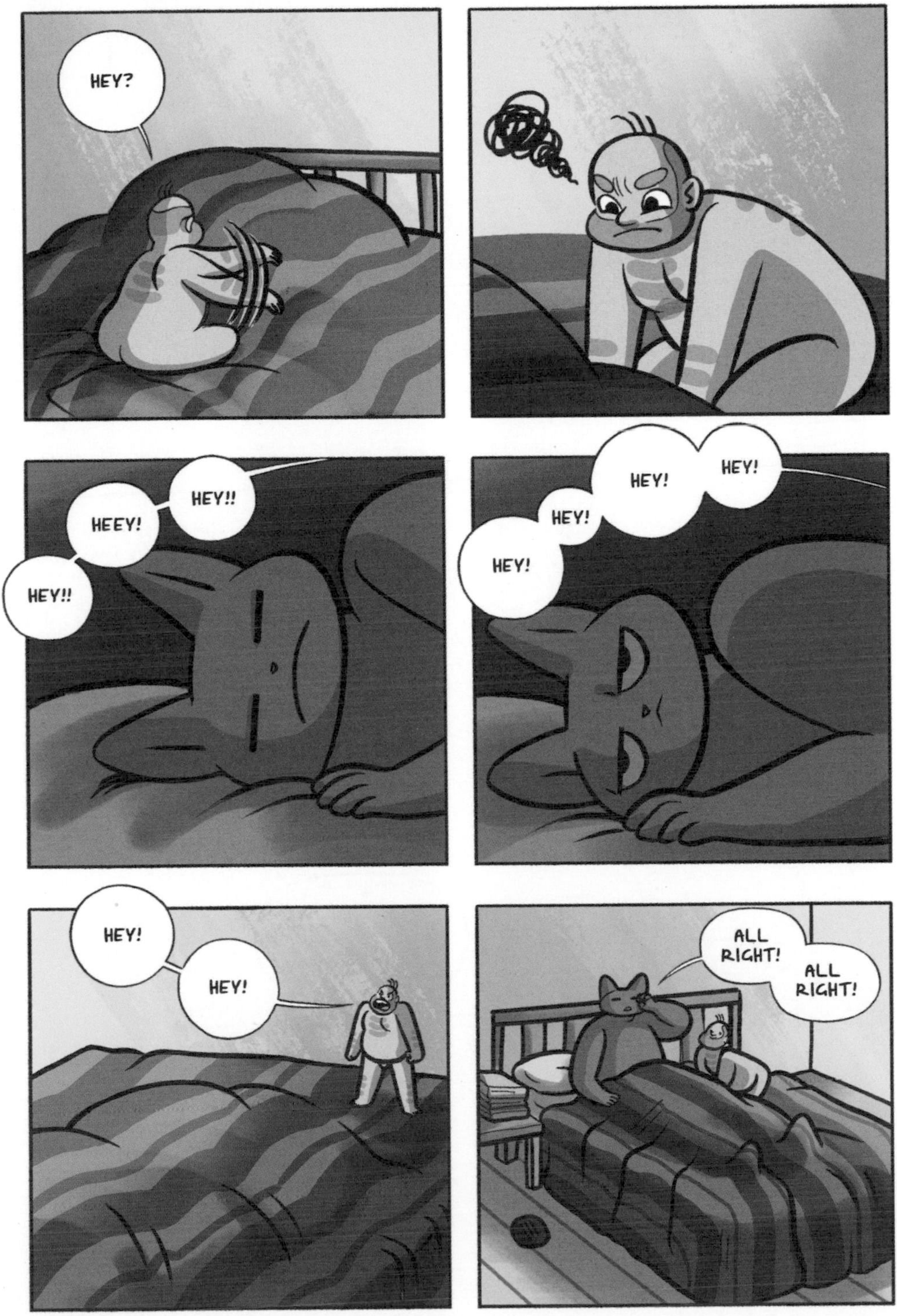
HEY?
HEY!!
HEEY!
HEY!!
HEY!
HEY!
HEY!
HEY!
HEY!
HEY!
ALL RIGHT!
ALL RIGHT!

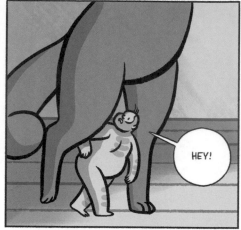

HEY!

CAN YOU NOT!?

ANYONE WOULD THINK YOU NEVER GET FED...

CHOMP CHOMP

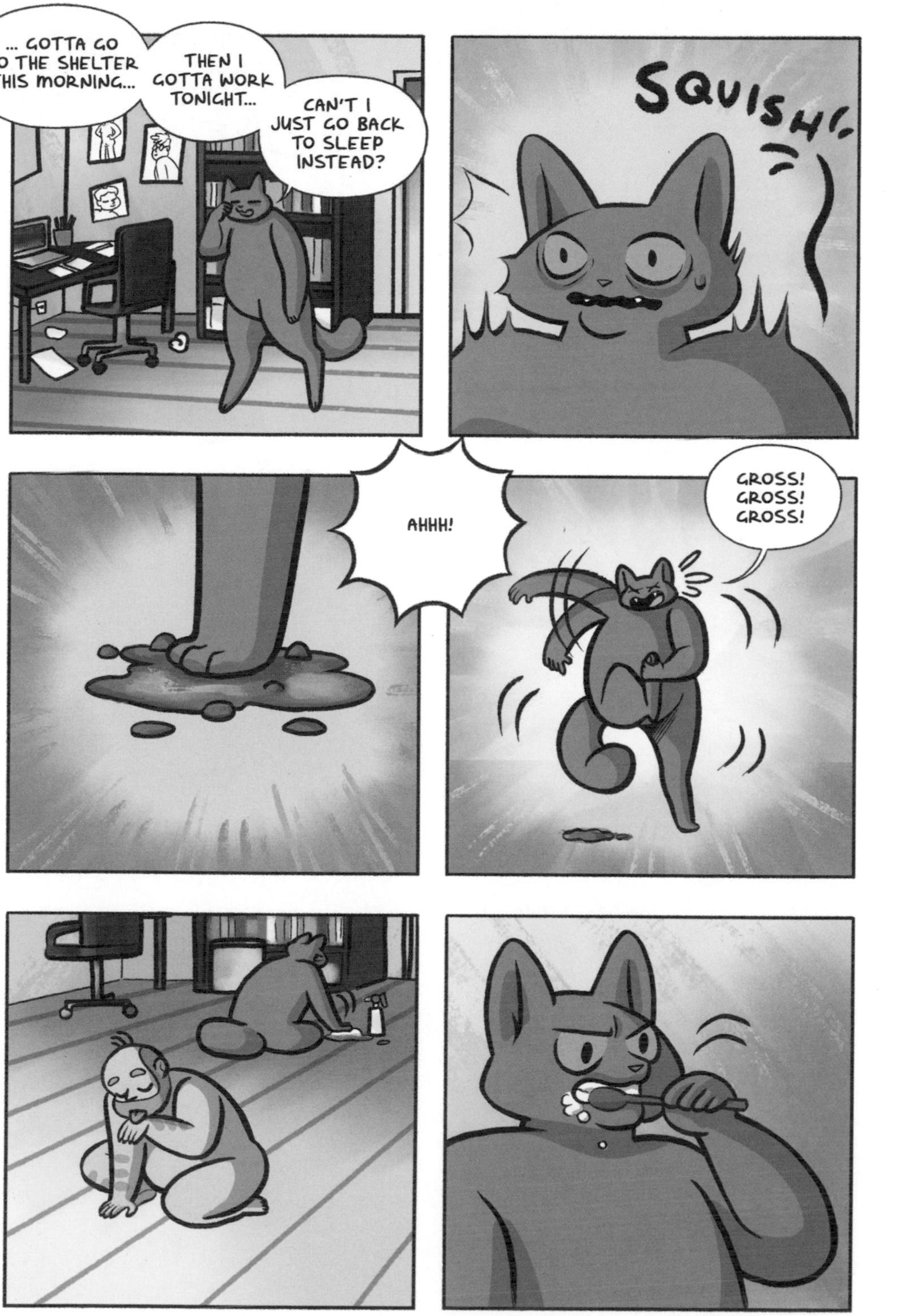
... GOTTA GO TO THE SHELTER THIS MORNING...
THEN I GOTTA WORK TONIGHT...
CAN'T I JUST GO BACK TO SLEEP INSTEAD?
SQUISH
AHHH!
GROSS! GROSS! GROSS!

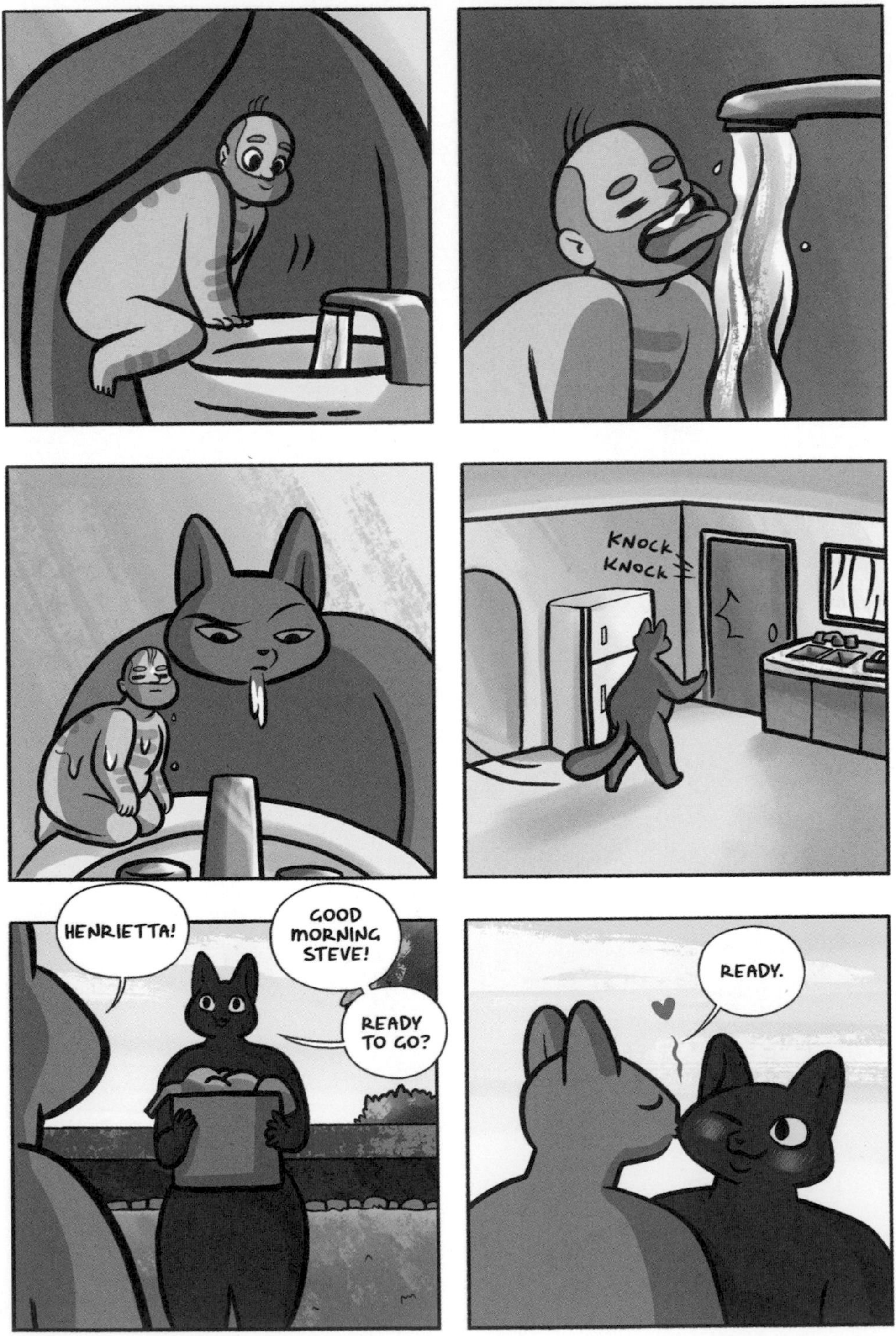

KNOCK
KNOCK
HENRIETTA!
GOOD MORNING STEVE!
READY TO GO?
READY.

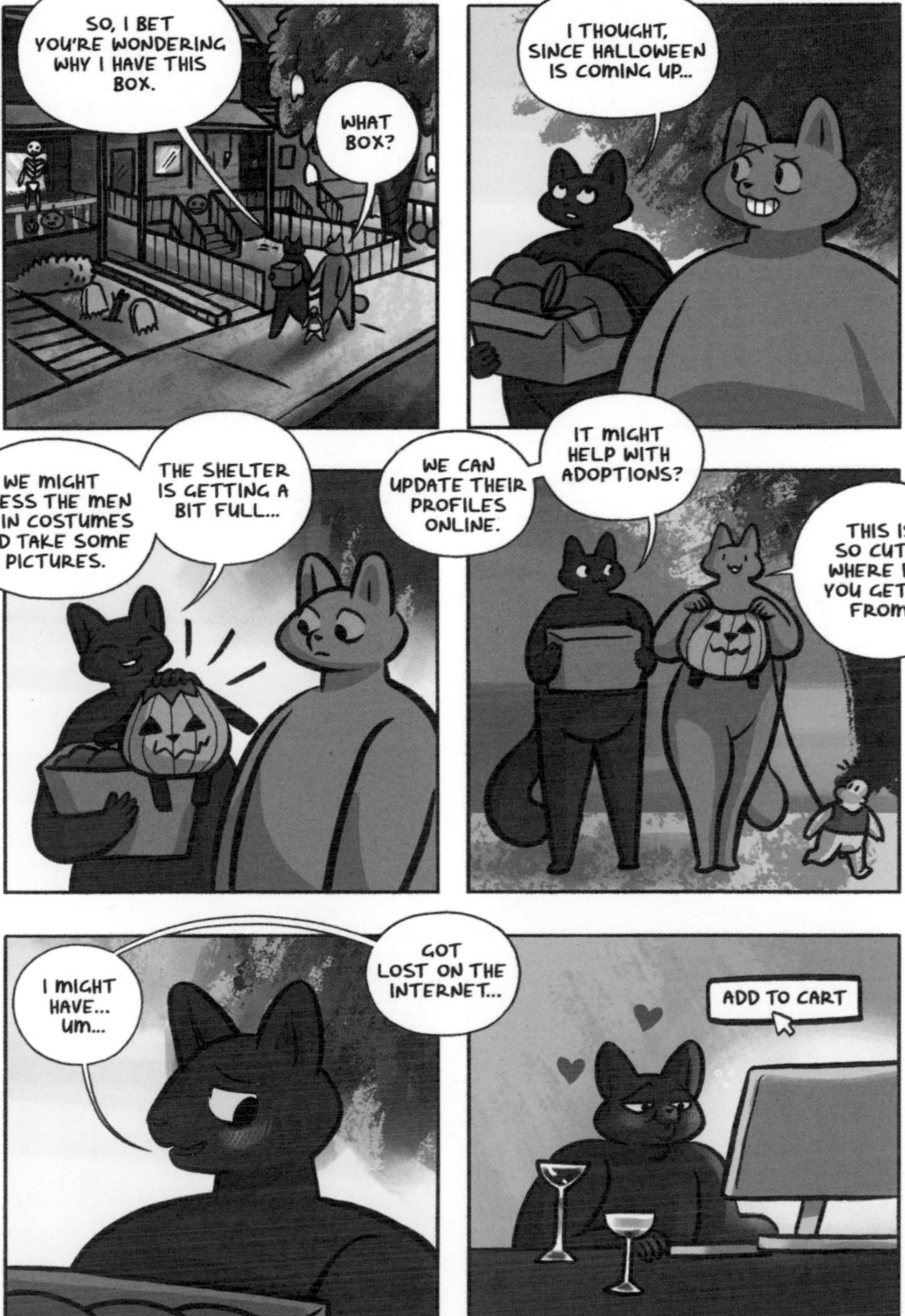
SO, I BET YOU'RE WONDERING WHY I HAVE THIS BOX.
WHAT BOX?
I THOUGHT, SINCE HALLOWEEN IS COMING UP...
THE SHELTER IS GETTING A BIT FULL...
WE MIGHT DRESS THE MEN UP IN COSTUMES AND TAKE SOME PICTURES.
WE CAN UPDATE THEIR PROFILES ONLINE.
IT MIGHT HELP WITH ADOPTIONS?
THIS IS SO CUTE! WHERE DID YOU GET IT FROM?
I MIGHT HAVE... UM...
GOT LOST ON THE INTERNET...
ADD TO CART

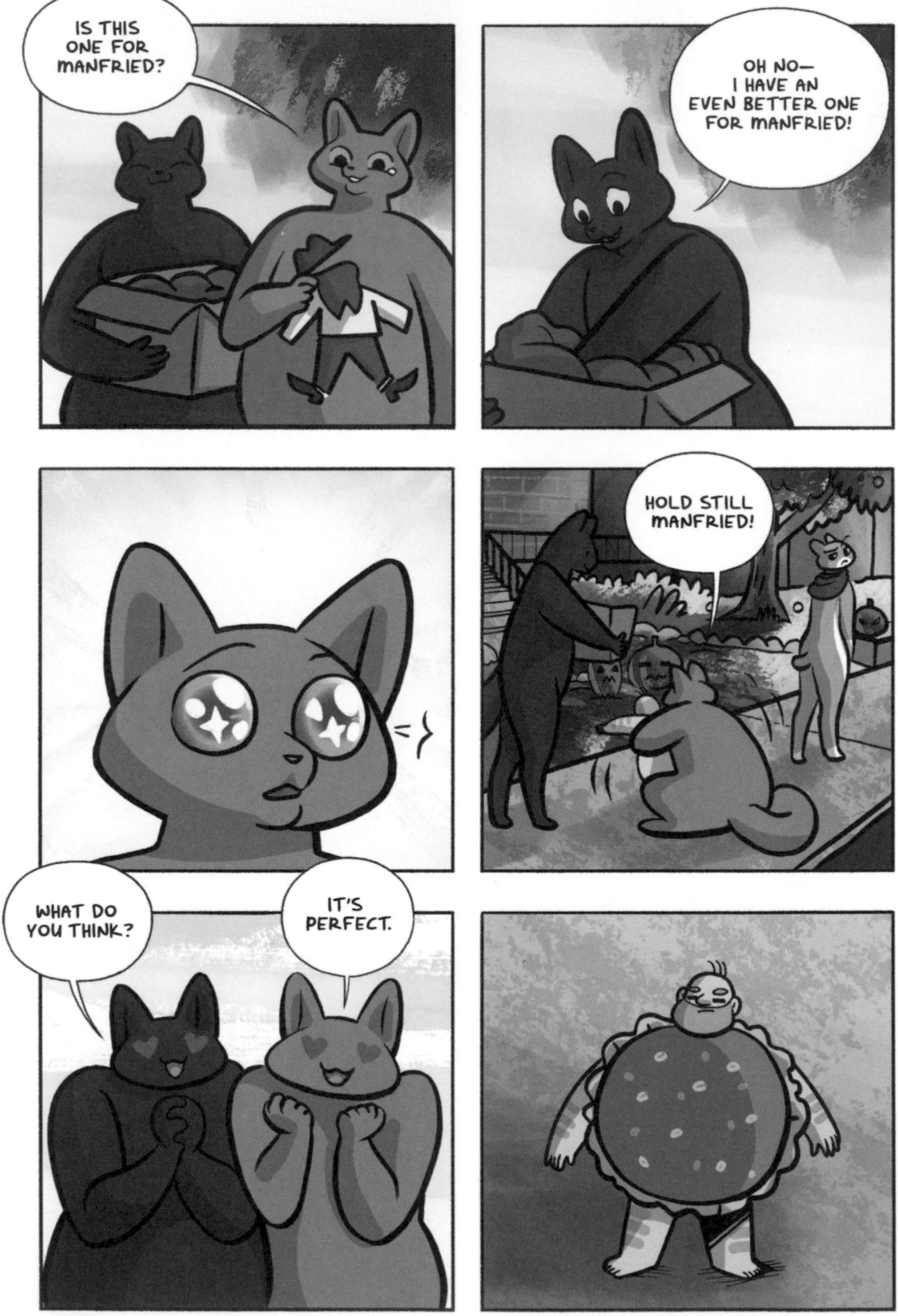
IS THIS ONE FOR MANFRIED?
OH NO— I HAVE AN EVEN BETTER ONE FOR MANFRIED!
HOLD STILL MANFRIED!
WHAT DO YOU THINK?
IT'S PERFECT.

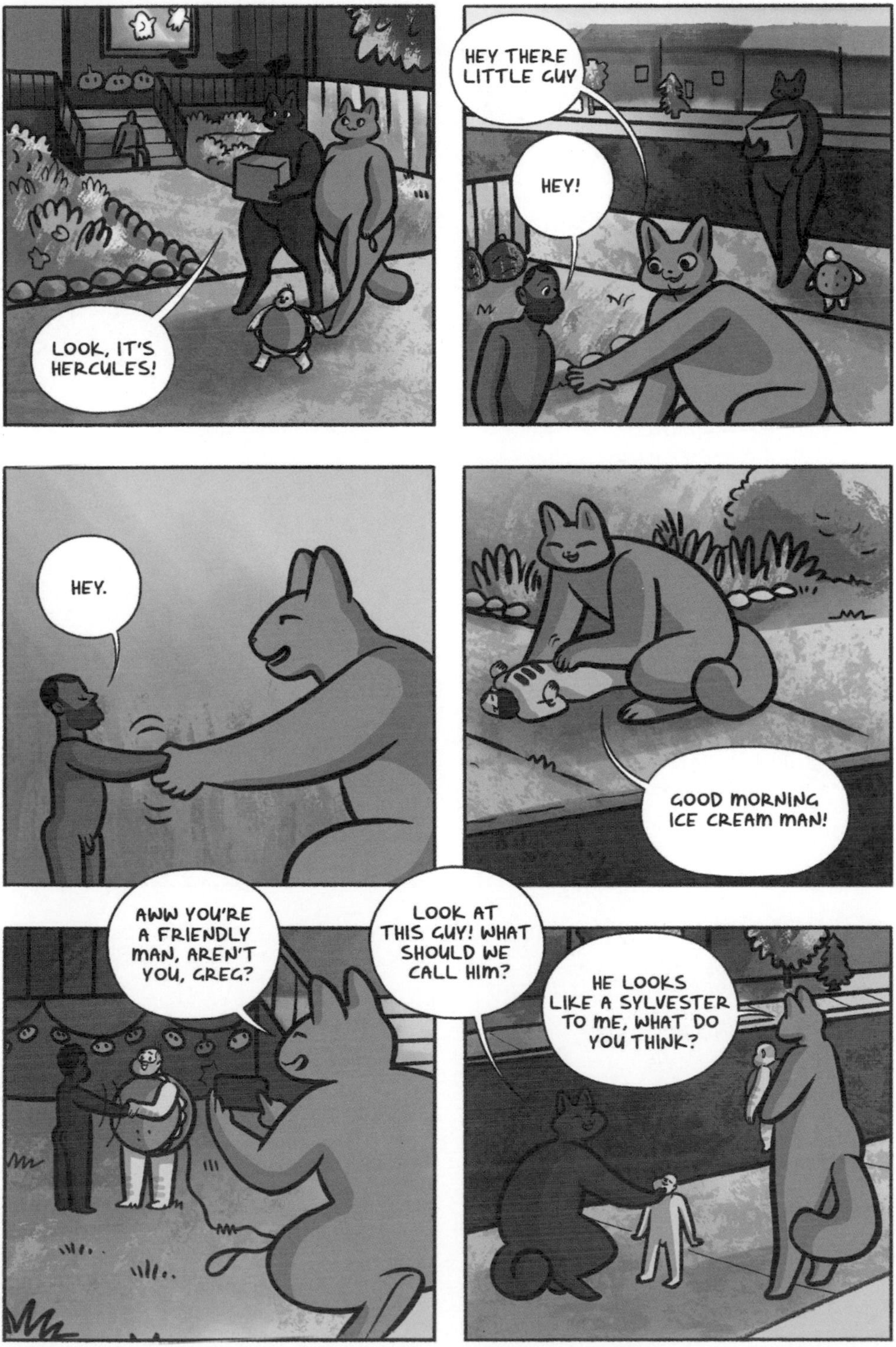
LOOK, IT'S HERCULES!
HEY THERE LITTLE GUY
HEY!
HEY.
GOOD MORNING ICE CREAM MAN!
AWW YOU'RE A FRIENDLY MAN, AREN'T YOU, GREG?
LOOK AT THIS GUY! WHAT SHOULD WE CALL HIM?
HE LOOKS LIKE A SYLVESTER TO ME, WHAT DO YOU THINK?

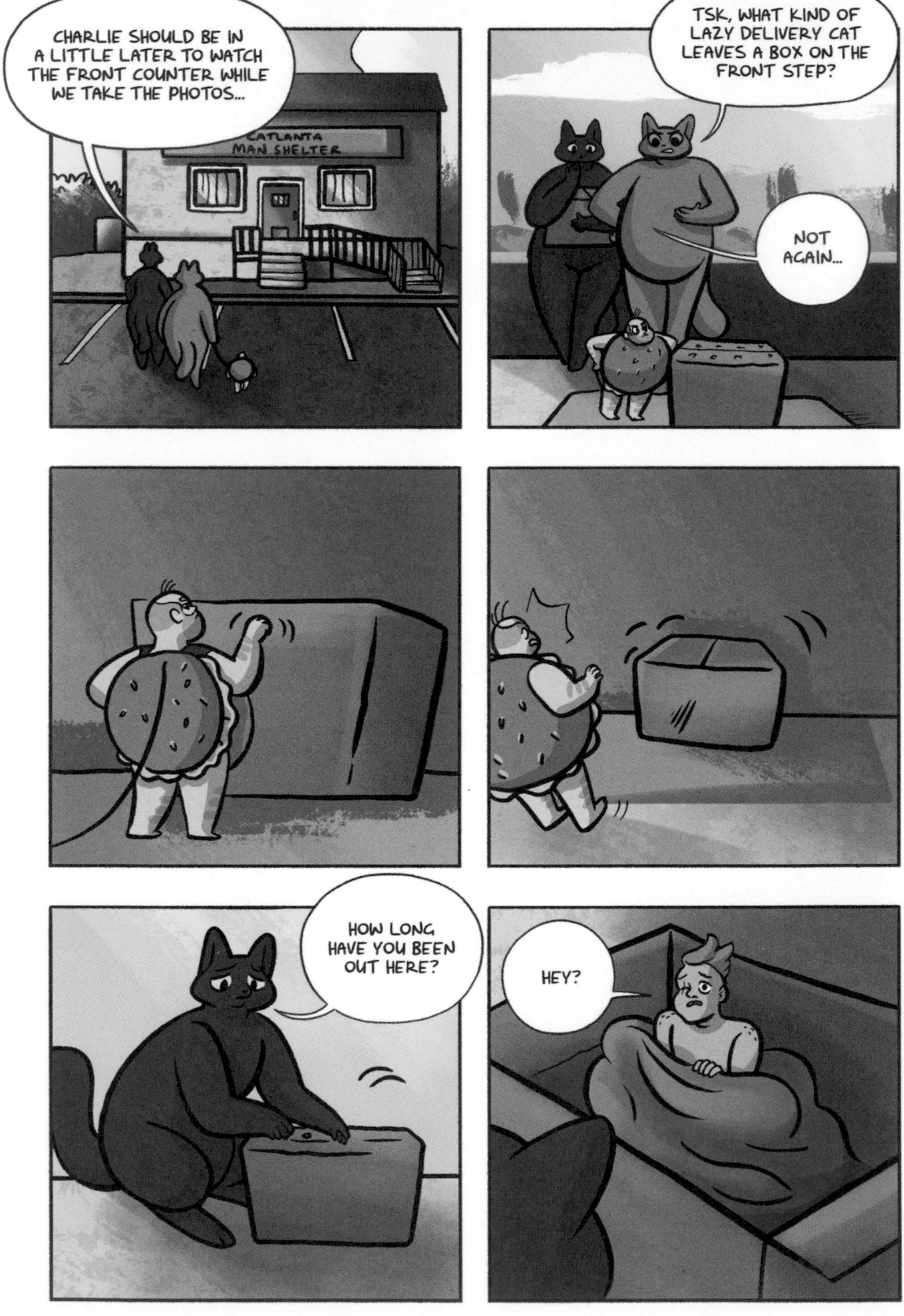
CHARLIE SHOULD BE IN A LITTLE LATER TO WATCH THE FRONT COUNTER WHILE WE TAKE THE PHOTOS...
CATLANTA MAN SHELTER
TSK, WHAT KIND OF LAZY DELIVERY CAT LEAVES A BOX ON THE FRONT STEP?
NOT AGAIN...
HOW LONG HAVE YOU BEEN OUT HERE?
HEY?

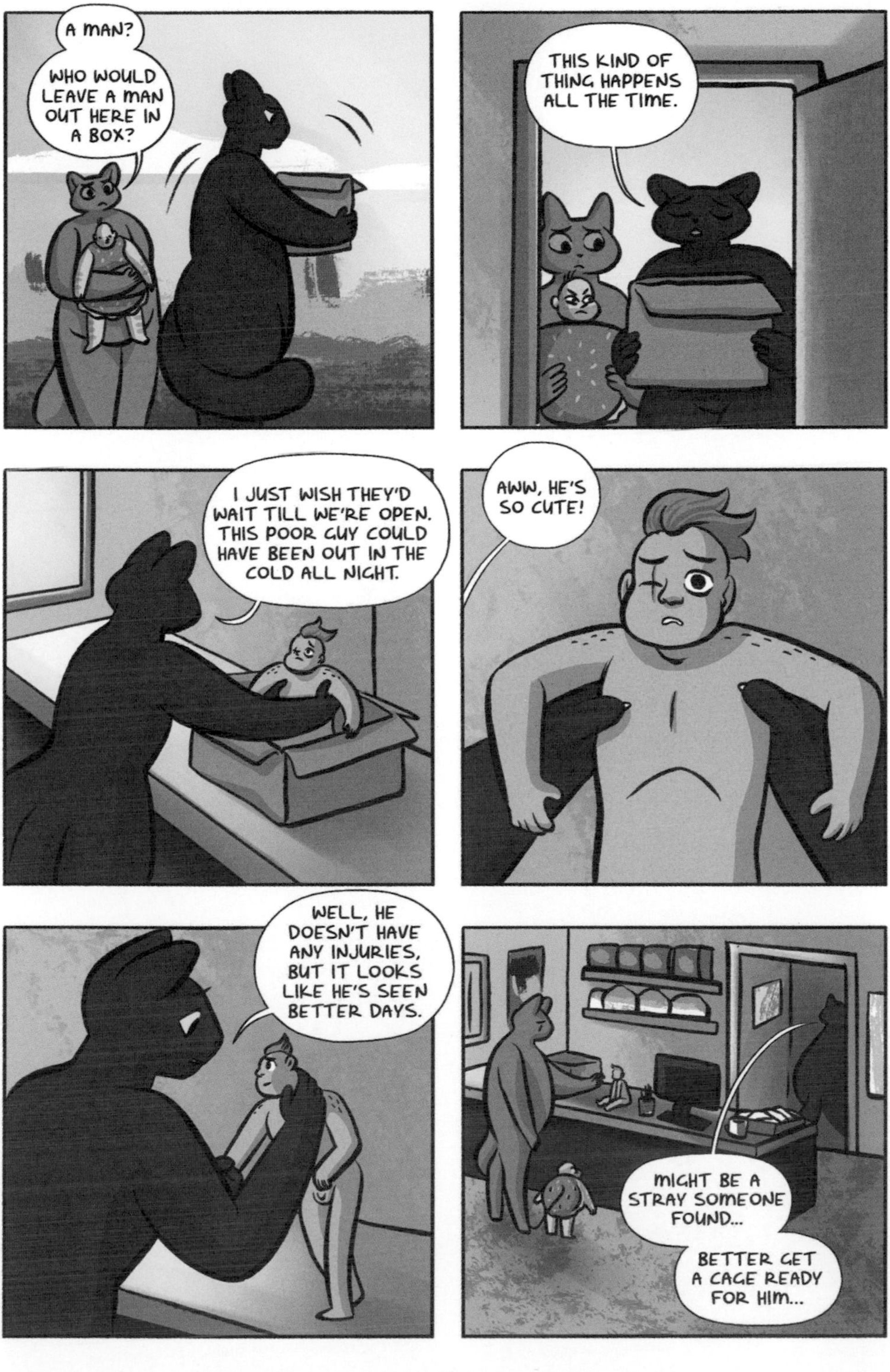
A MAN?
WHO WOULD LEAVE A MAN OUT HERE IN A BOX?
THIS KIND OF THING HAPPENS ALL THE TIME.
I JUST WISH THEY'D WAIT TILL WE'RE OPEN. THIS POOR GUY COULD HAVE BEEN OUT IN THE COLD ALL NIGHT.
AWW, HE'S SO CUTE!
WELL, HE DOESN'T HAVE ANY INJURIES, BUT IT LOOKS LIKE HE'S SEEN BETTER DAYS.
MIGHT BE A STRAY SOMEONE FOUND...
BETTER GET A CAGE READY FOR HIM...

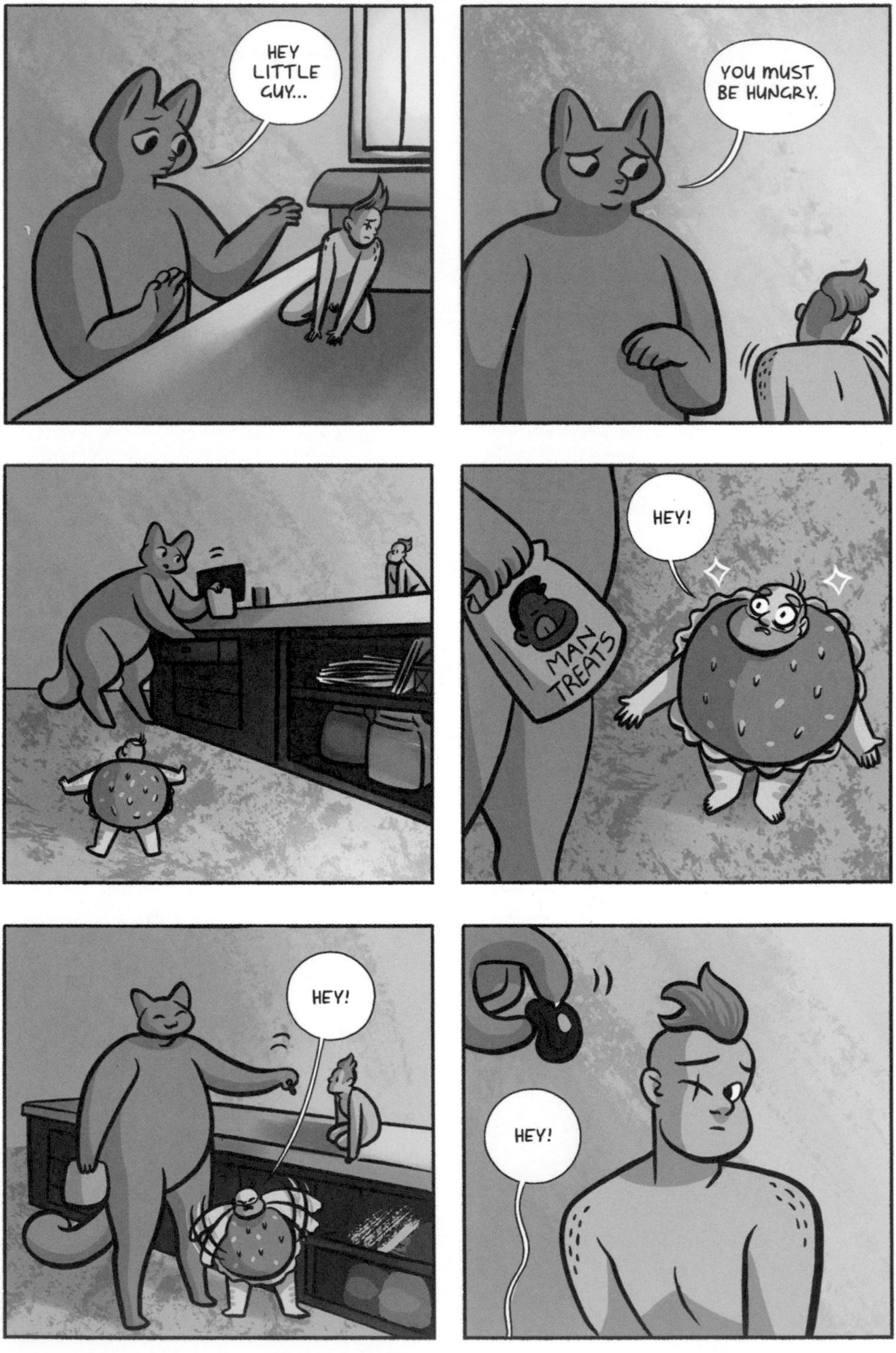
HEY LITTLE GUY...
YOU MUST BE HUNGRY.
HEY!
MAN TREATS
HEY!
HEY!

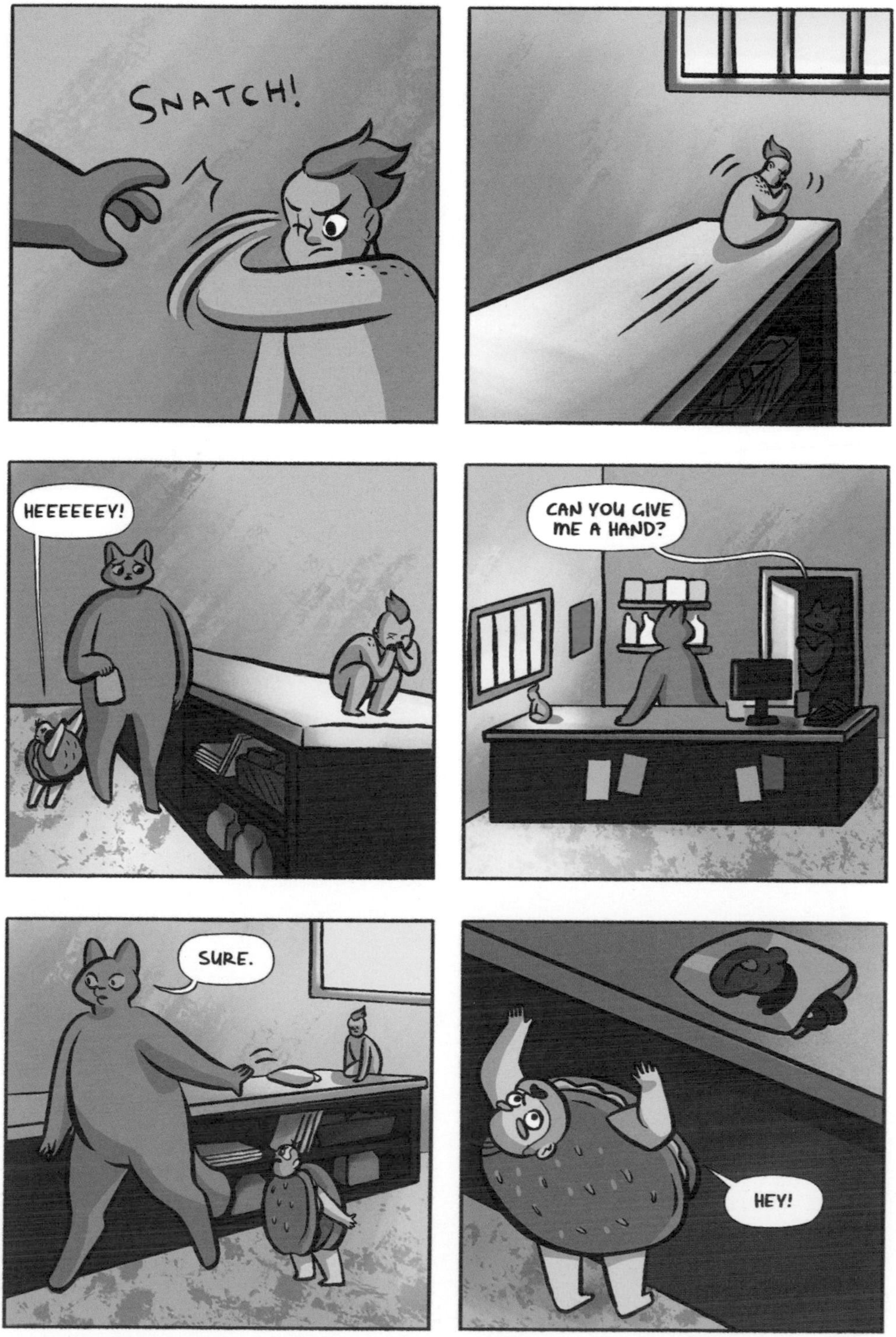
SNATCH!
HEEEEEEY!
CAN YOU GIVE ME A HAND?
SURE.
HEY!

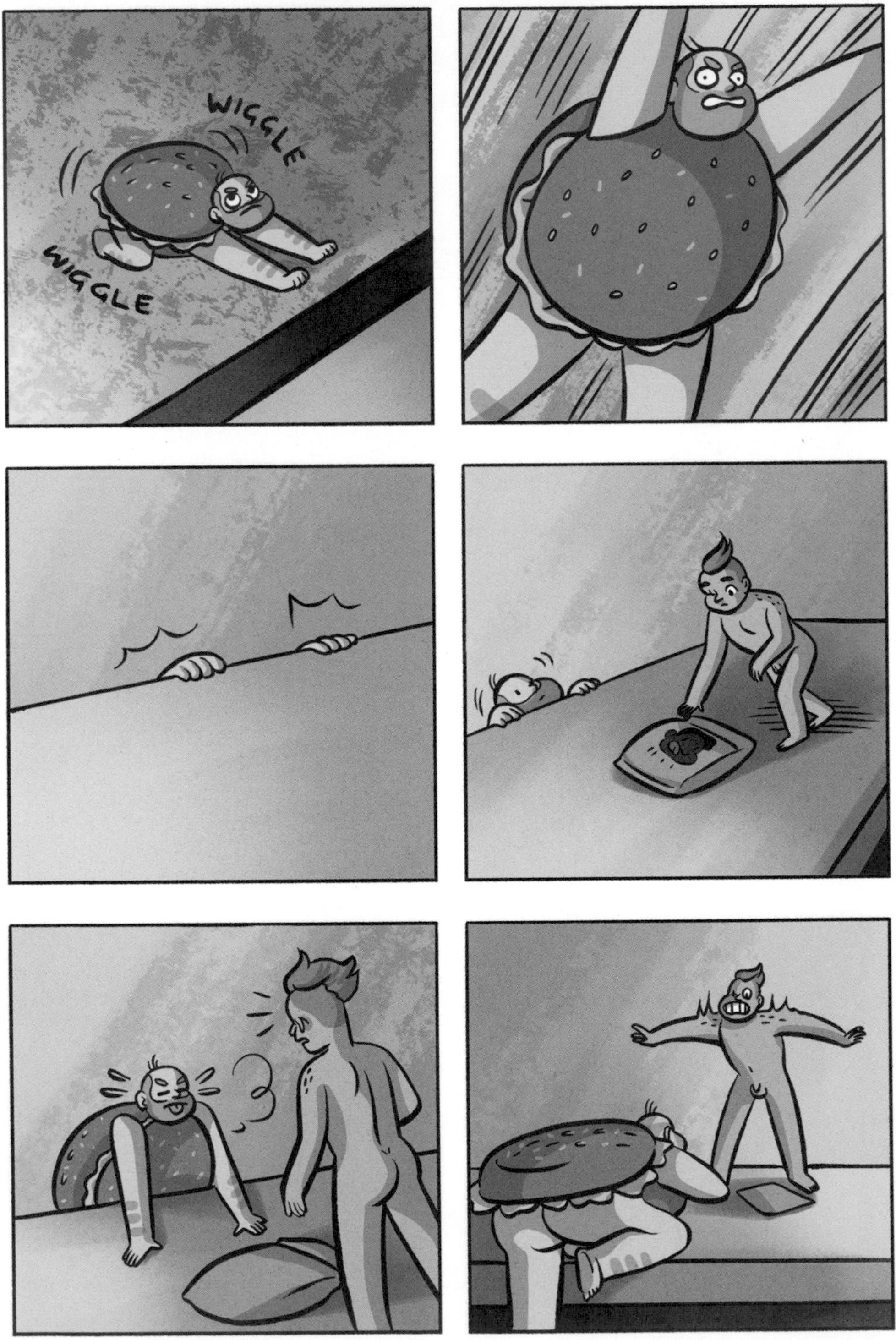
WIGGLE
WIGGLE

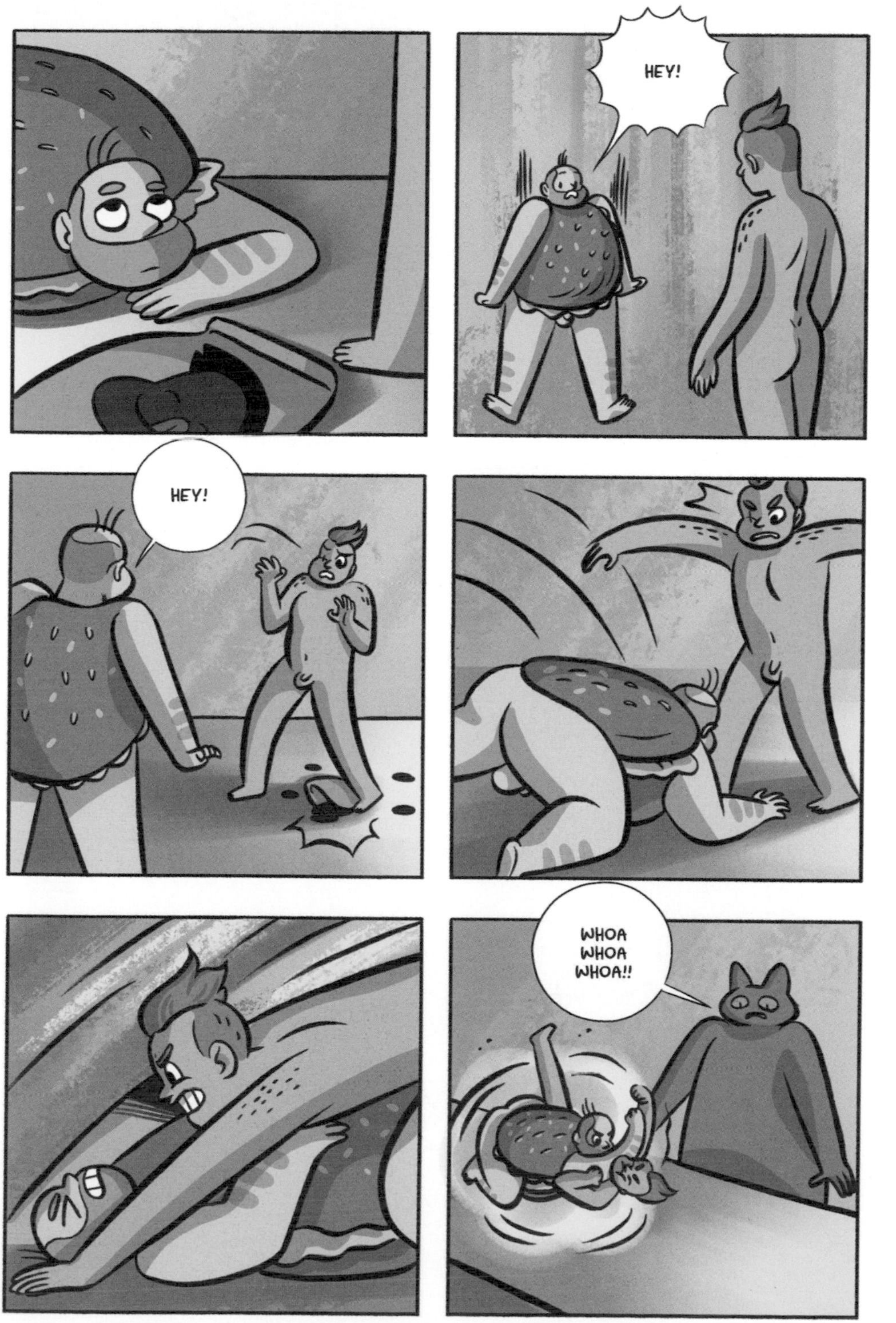
HEY!
HEY!
WHOA
WHOA
WHOA!!

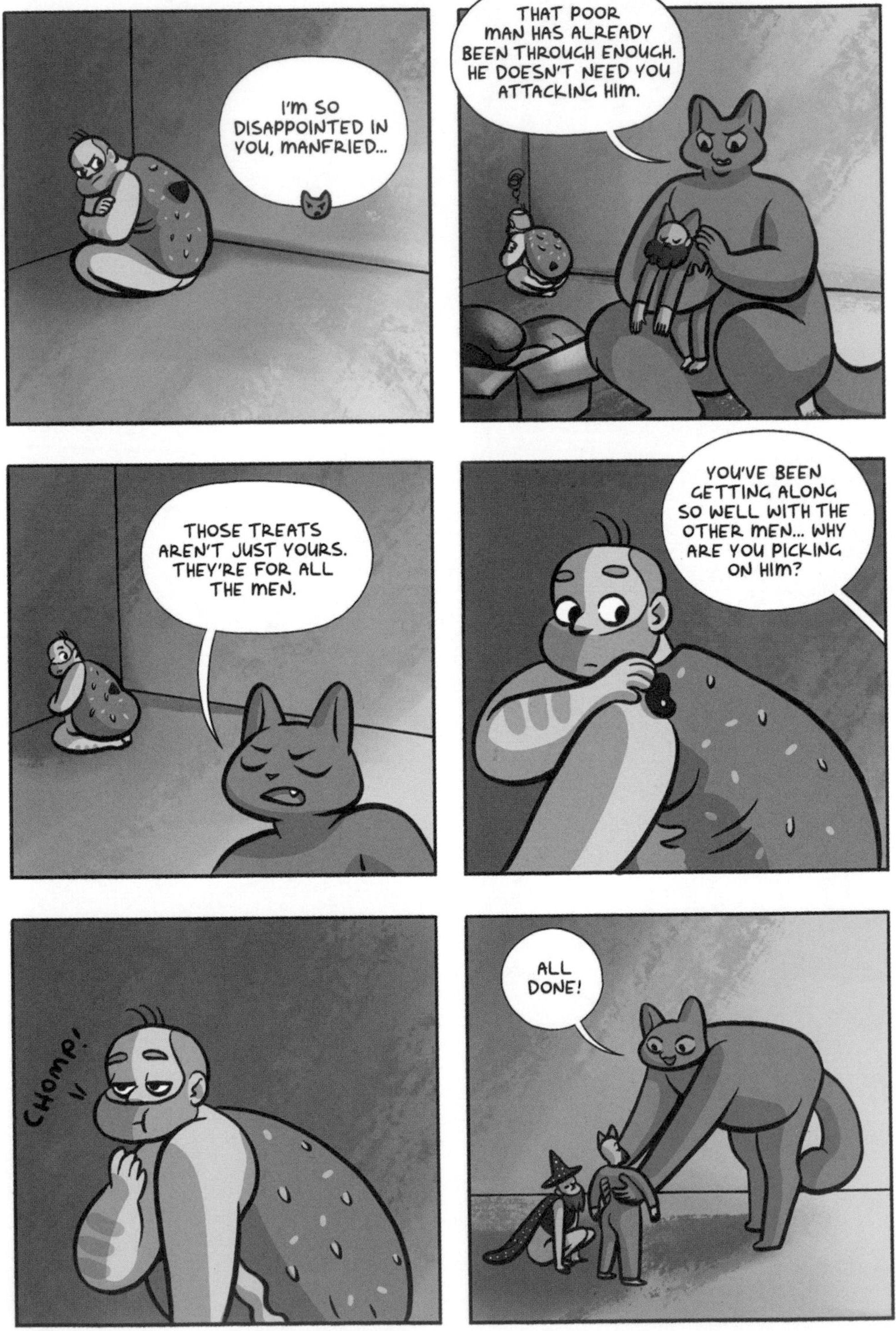
I'M SO DISAPPOINTED IN YOU, MANFRIED...
THAT POOR MAN HAS ALREADY BEEN THROUGH ENOUGH. HE DOESN'T NEED YOU ATTACKING HIM.
THOSE TREATS AREN'T JUST YOURS. THEY'RE FOR ALL THE MEN.
YOU'VE BEEN GETTING ALONG SO WELL WITH THE OTHER MEN... WHY ARE YOU PICKING ON HIM?
CHOMP!
ALL DONE!

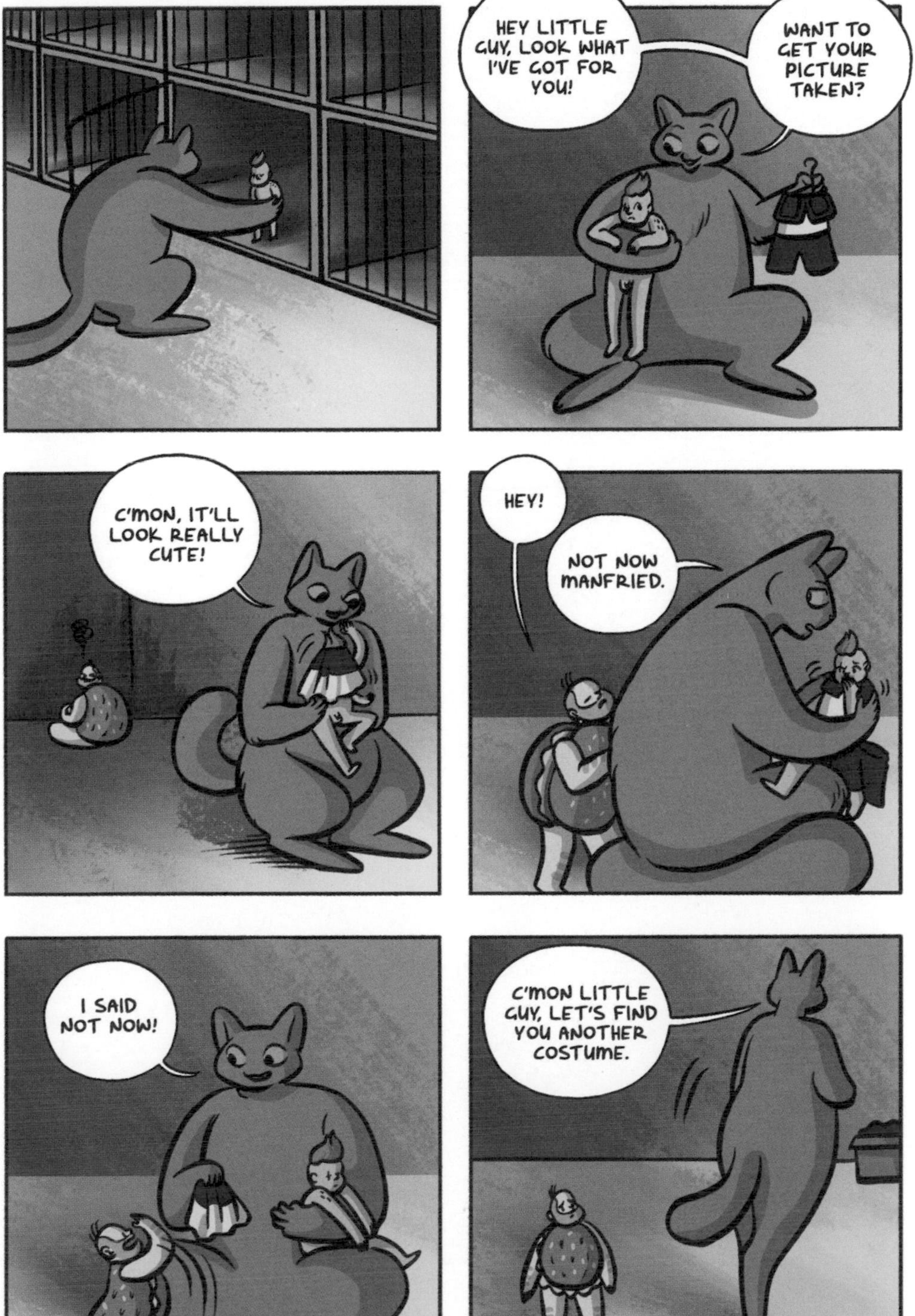
HEY LITTLE GUY, LOOK WHAT I'VE GOT FOR YOU!
WANT TO GET YOUR PICTURE TAKEN?
C'MON, IT'LL LOOK REALLY CUTE!
HEY!
NOT NOW MANFRIED.
I SAID NOT NOW!
C'MON LITTLE GUY, LET'S FIND YOU ANOTHER COSTUME.

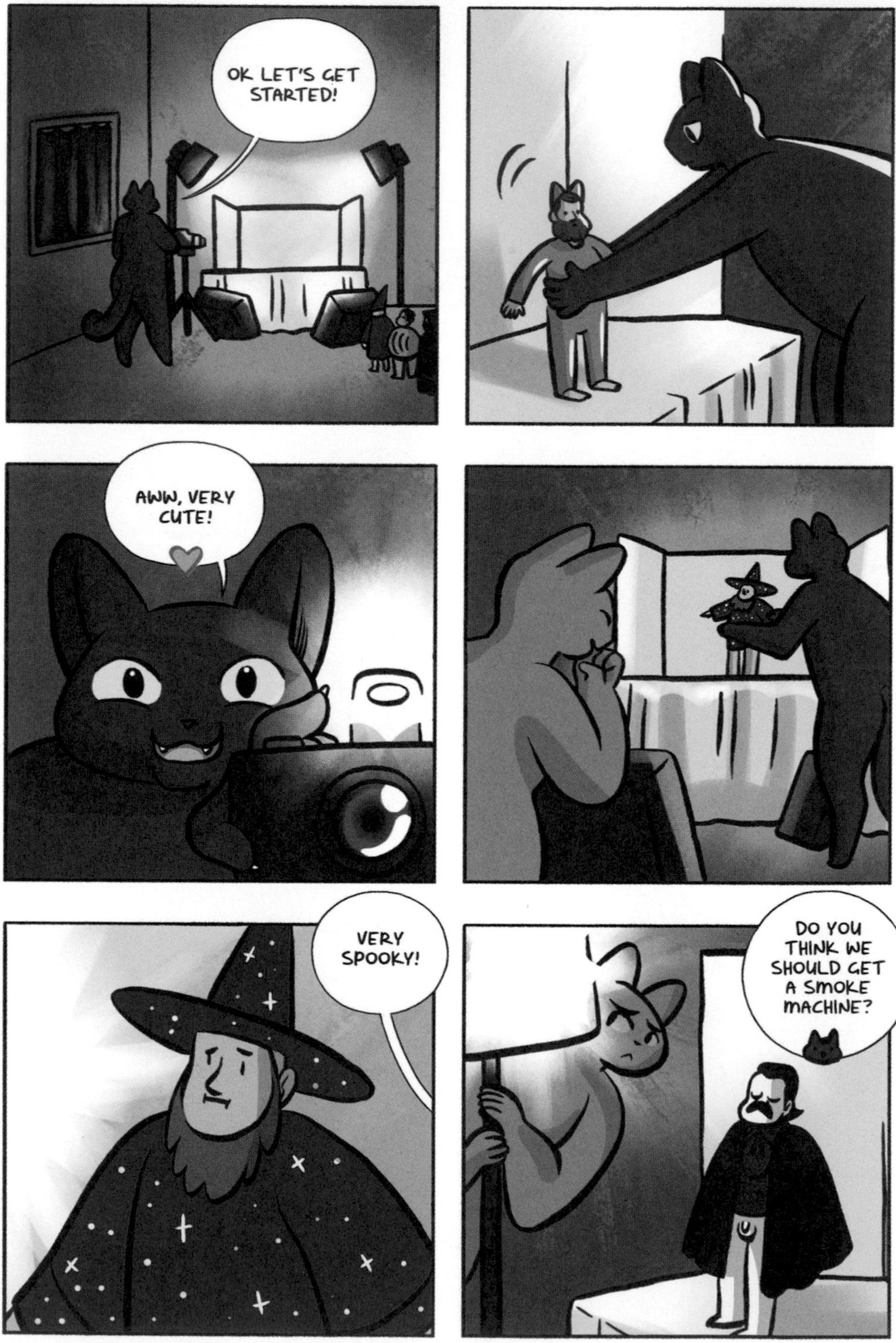
OK LET'S GET STARTED!
AWW, VERY CUTE!
VERY SPOOKY!
DO YOU THINK WE SHOULD GET A SMOKE MACHINE?

Facts about me

Age: Adult

Hair: Short

Shots up to date

Meet Professor Whiskers:

He is an older man who loves to stroll around and look for a comfy spot to relax. He is a very affectionate man, and is accepting of other men, but also quite happy with his own company.

Facts about me

Age: Teenager

Hair: Short

Shots up to date

Meet Gilbert:

Gilbert was rescued from a parking lot and is very timid. Gilbert is a little sweetie, but is still scared and will need time, patience, and TLC to help him trust. He may do better in a home that already has a tame man for Gilbert to learn from. In time he should come around and be a nice gentleman.

Facts about me

Age: Teenagers

Hair: Short

Shots up to date

Meet Ravage and Arrow: *Bonded Pair*

Ravage and Arrow are a bonded pair of brothers who were rescued from a hoarding situation. They are inseparable and love to wrestle each other, cuddle together and groom each other. They love cat attention and are both very sweet men. Ravage is the more timid one of the two and relies on his more outgoing brother Arrow to feel confident and secure.

Facts about me

Age: Adult

Hair: Long

Shots up to date

Meet Freddie:

This handsome fluff ball is Freddie. He was very afraid when he arrived at the shelter but has gained more confidence each day. He enjoys a cuddle and loves playtime with his friends. Freddie will need a family prepared to brush him most days so he does not get matted.

Facts about me

Age: Adult

Hair: Medium

Shots up to date

Meet Gomez:

Gomez came to the shelter when his owner sadly passed away. This friendly fella is about 10 years old. He would love to be a part of a real family again. He has been through a lot and would love to spend his next few years with you.

Facts about me

Age: Adult

Hair: Long

Shots up to date

Meet Prince:

Prince is very friendly with his "familiar" cats, but can be pretty shy with strangers. He loves treats, is very clean, and loves to carry his toys around with him. He uses his scratching posts, values his toys, and is very inquisitive. Prince can also be a bit of a talker and very energetic at times. Other times, he will sit by the door or window for hours and watch the world go by.

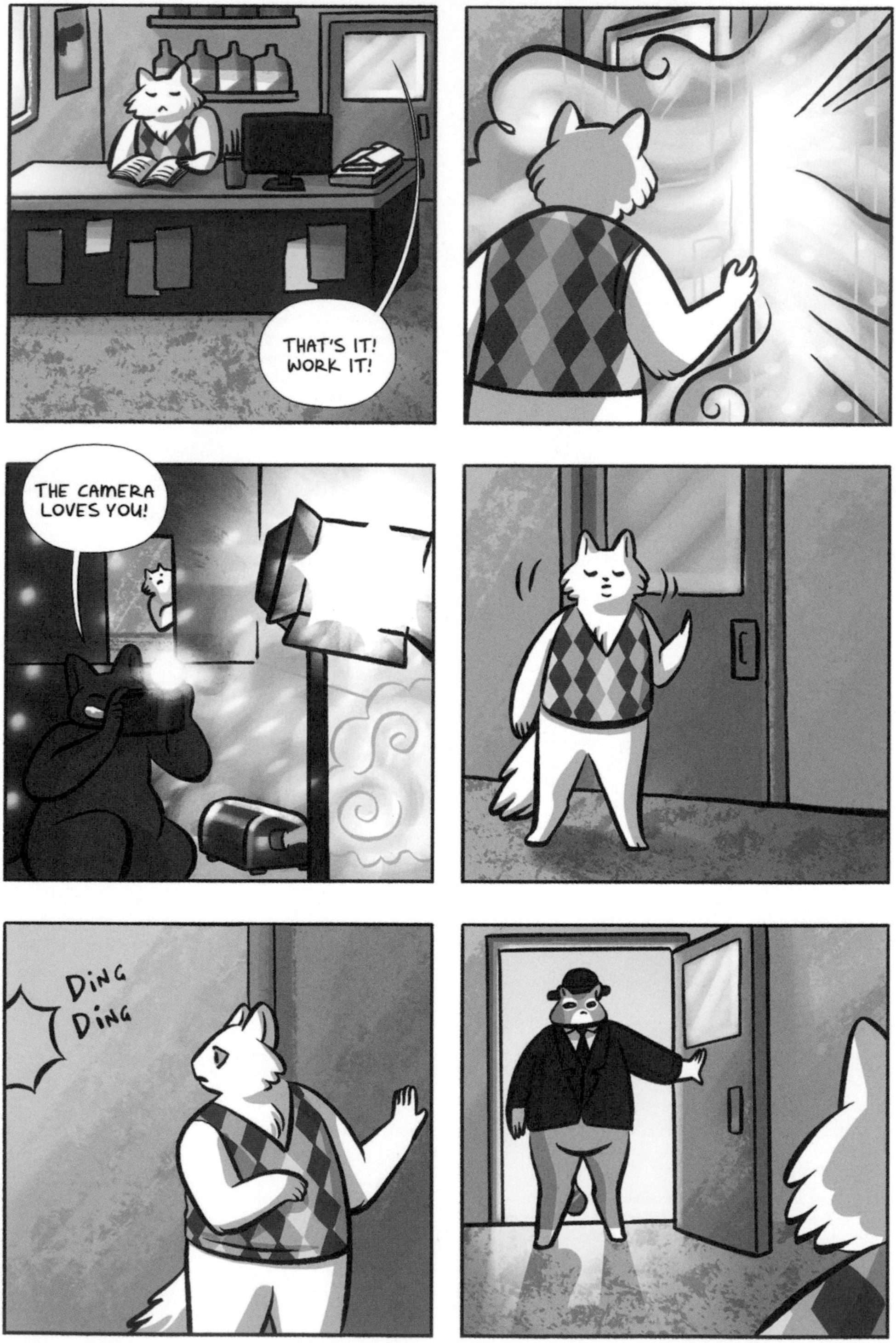
THAT'S IT!
WORK IT!
THE CAMERA
LOVES YOU!
DING
DING

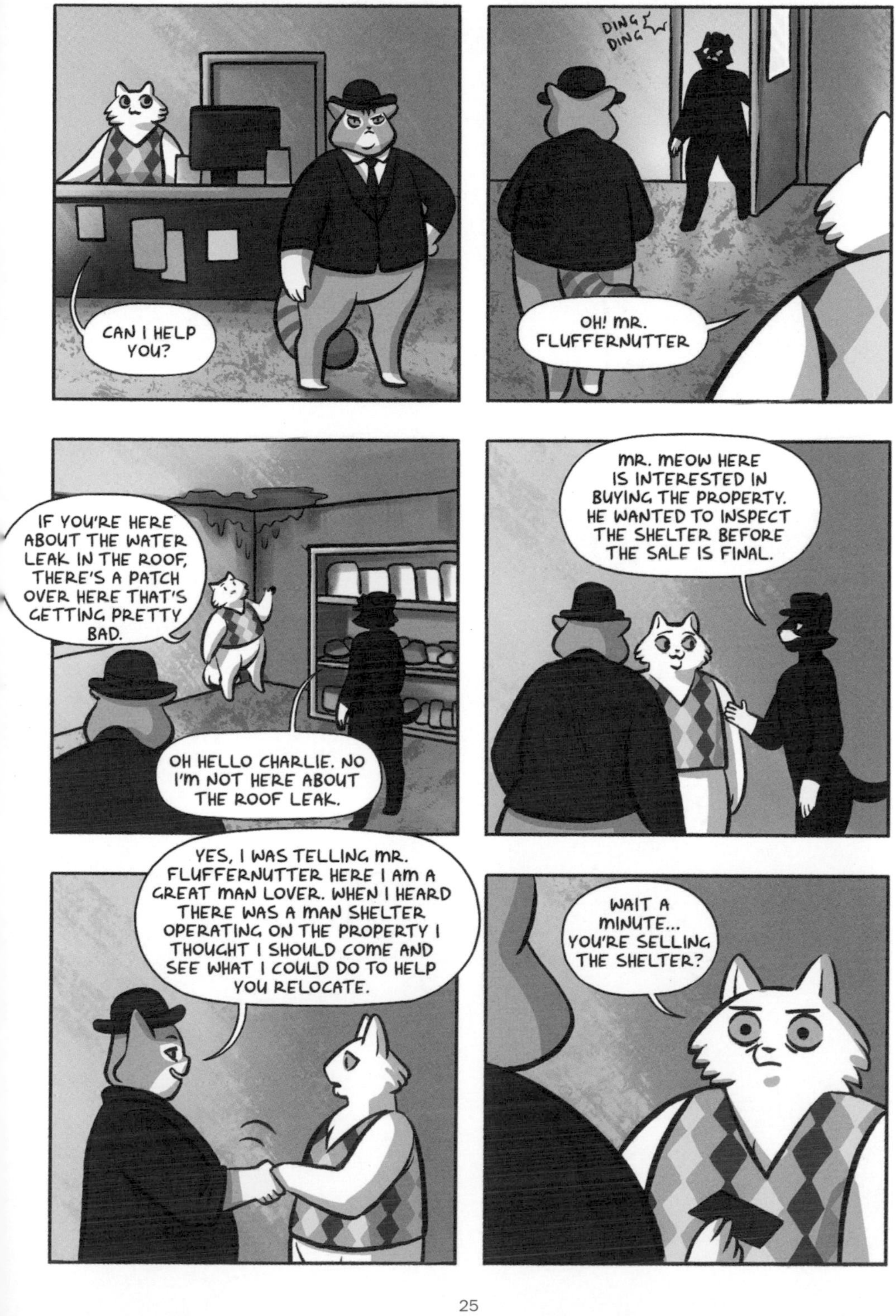
CAN I HELP YOU?
DING DING
OH! MR. FLUFFERNUTTER
IF YOU'RE HERE ABOUT THE WATER LEAK IN THE ROOF, THERE'S A PATCH OVER HERE THAT'S GETTING PRETTY BAD.
OH HELLO CHARLIE. NO I'M NOT HERE ABOUT THE ROOF LEAK.
MR. MEOW HERE IS INTERESTED IN BUYING THE PROPERTY. HE WANTED TO INSPECT THE SHELTER BEFORE THE SALE IS FINAL.
YES, I WAS TELLING MR. FLUFFERNUTTER HERE I AM A GREAT MAN LOVER. WHEN I HEARD THERE WAS A MAN SHELTER OPERATING ON THE PROPERTY I THOUGHT I SHOULD COME AND SEE WHAT I COULD DO TO HELP YOU RELOCATE.
WAIT A MINUTE... YOU'RE SELLING THE SHELTER?

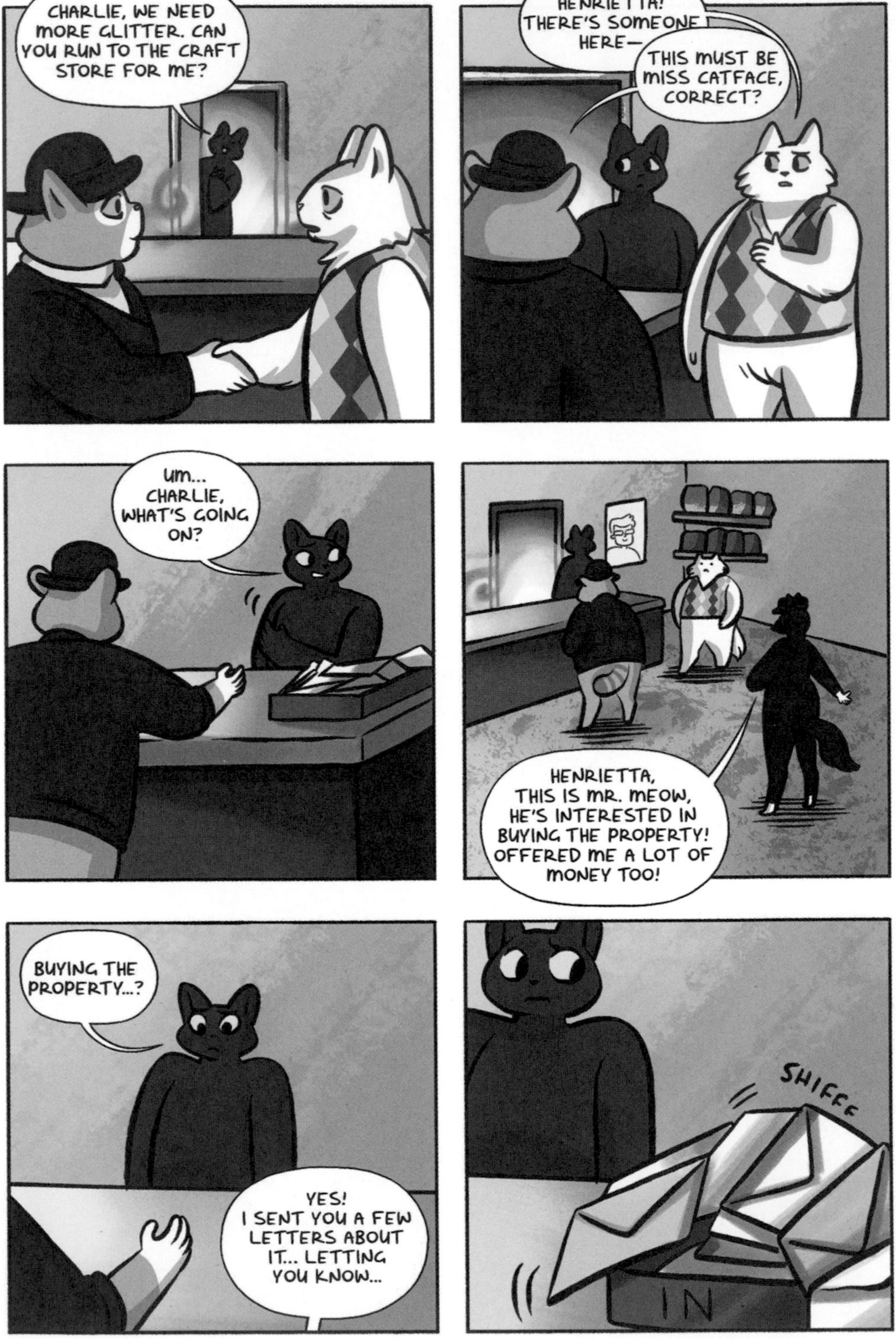
CHARLIE, WE NEED MORE GLITTER. CAN YOU RUN TO THE CRAFT STORE FOR ME?
HENRIETTA! THERE'S SOMEONE HERE—
THIS MUST BE MISS CATFACE, CORRECT?
UM... CHARLIE, WHAT'S GOING ON?
HENRIETTA, THIS IS MR. MEOW, HE'S INTERESTED IN BUYING THE PROPERTY! OFFERED ME A LOT OF MONEY TOO!
BUYING THE PROPERTY...?
YES! I SENT YOU A FEW LETTERS ABOUT IT... LETTING YOU KNOW...
SHIFFF
IN

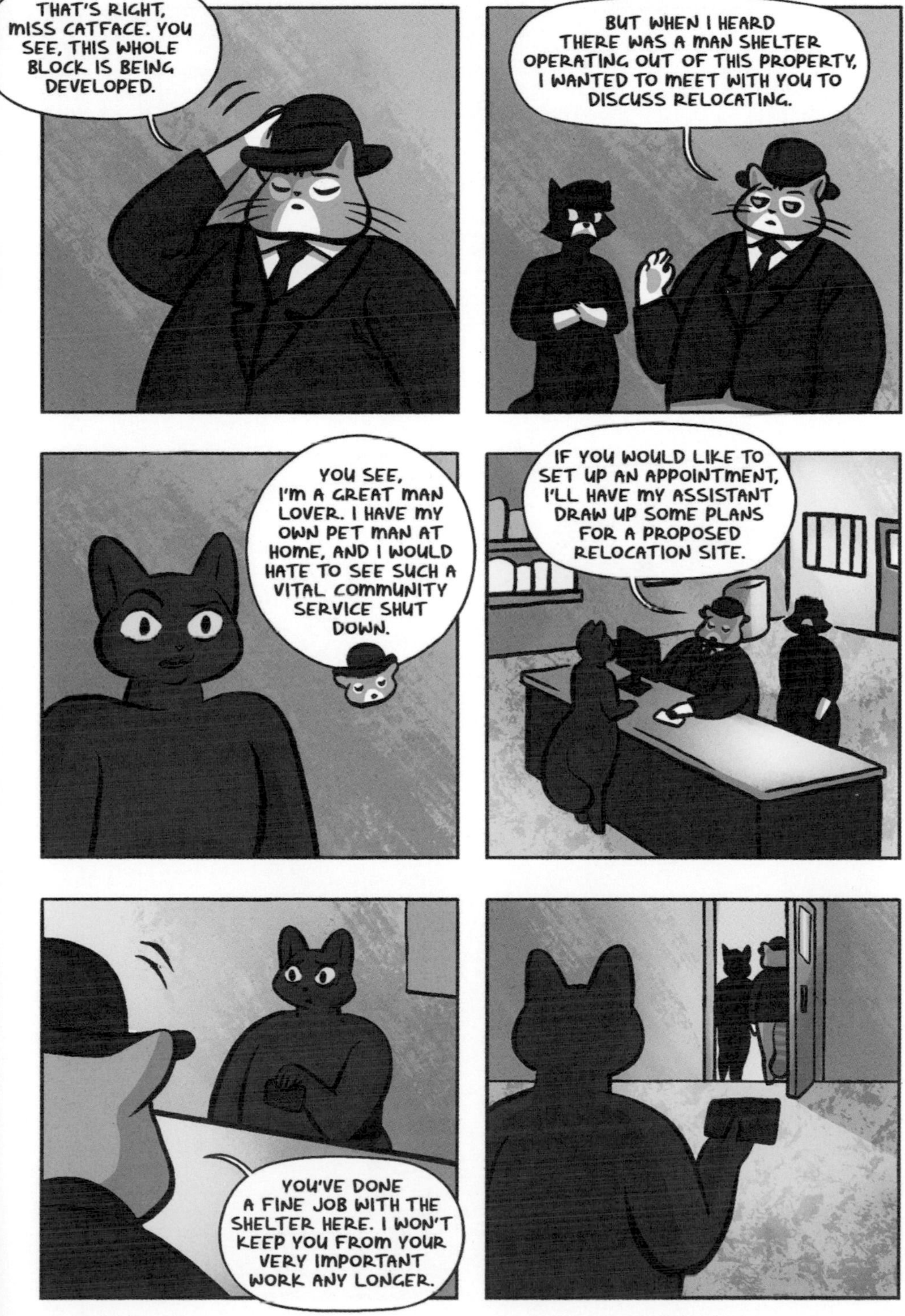
THAT'S RIGHT, MISS CATFACE. YOU SEE, THIS WHOLE BLOCK IS BEING DEVELOPED.
BUT WHEN I HEARD THERE WAS A MAN SHELTER OPERATING OUT OF THIS PROPERTY, I WANTED TO MEET WITH YOU TO DISCUSS RELOCATING.
YOU SEE, I'M A GREAT MAN LOVER. I HAVE MY OWN PET MAN AT HOME, AND I WOULD HATE TO SEE SUCH A VITAL COMMUNITY SERVICE SHUT DOWN.
IF YOU WOULD LIKE TO SET UP AN APPOINTMENT, I'LL HAVE MY ASSISTANT DRAW UP SOME PLANS FOR A PROPOSED RELOCATION SITE.
YOU'VE DONE A FINE JOB WITH THE SHELTER HERE. I WON'T KEEP YOU FROM YOUR VERY IMPORTANT WORK ANY LONGER.

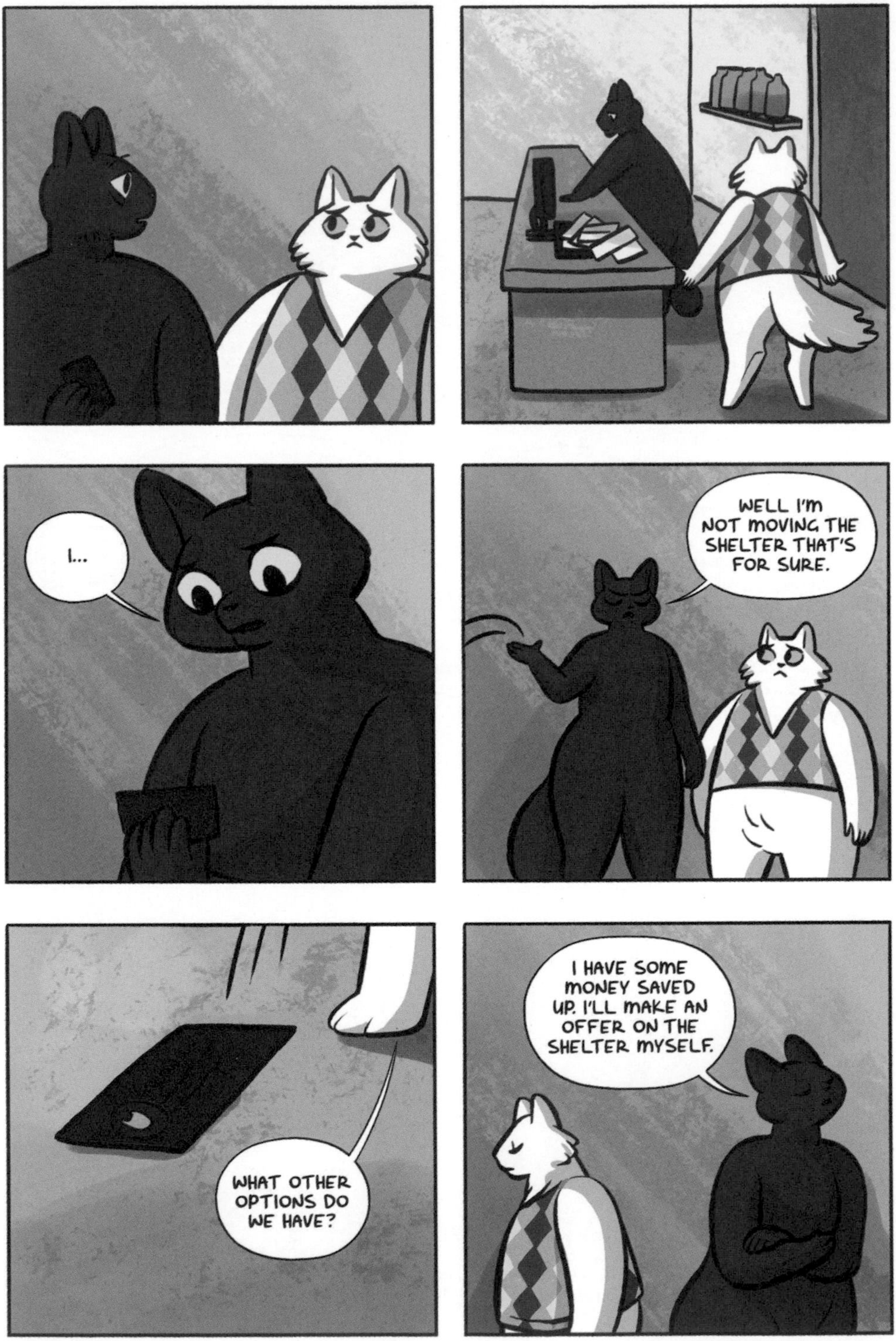
I...
WELL I'M NOT MOVING THE SHELTER THAT'S FOR SURE.
WHAT OTHER OPTIONS DO WE HAVE?
I HAVE SOME MONEY SAVED UP. I'LL MAKE AN OFFER ON THE SHELTER MYSELF.

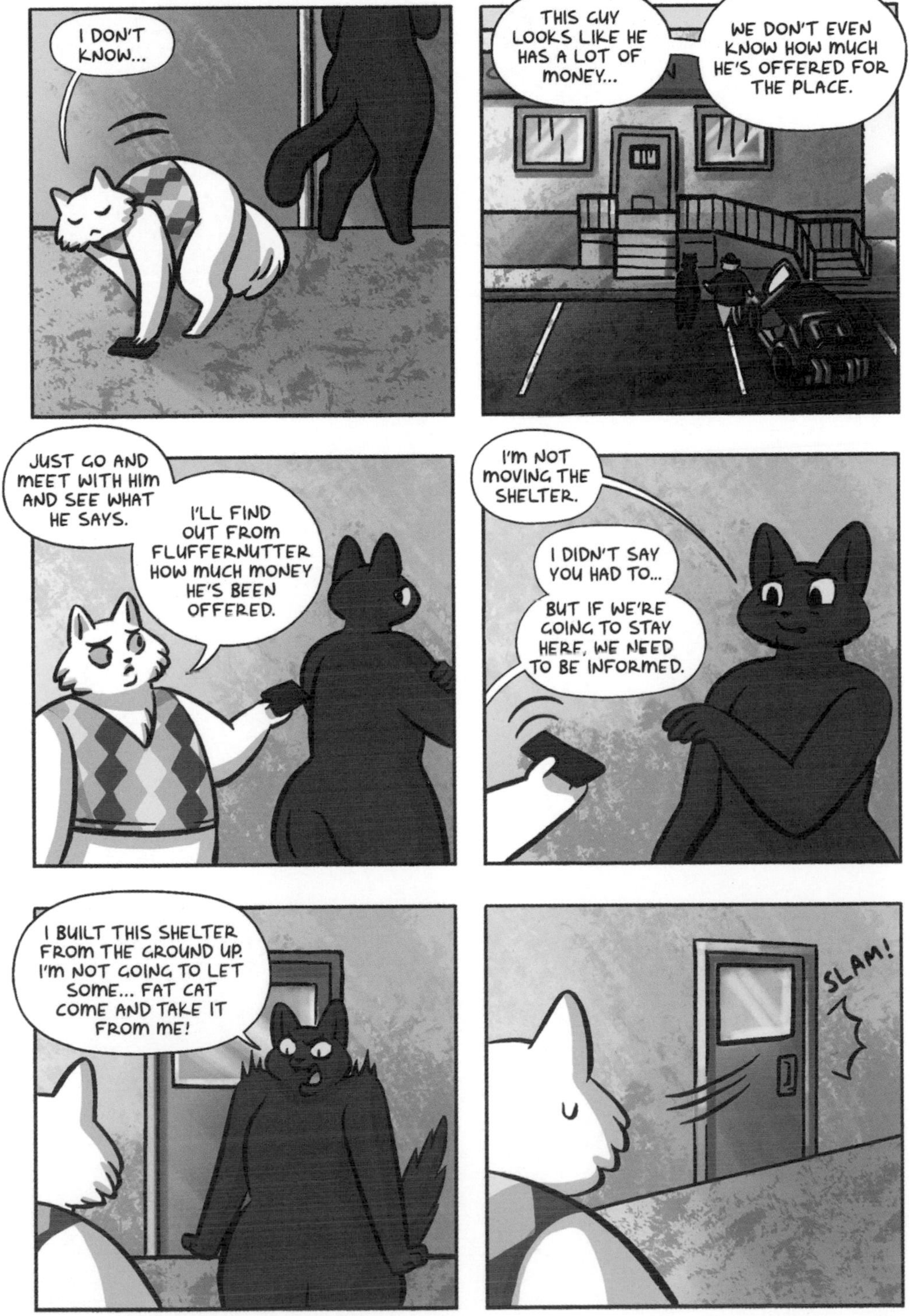

I DON'T KNOW...
THIS GUY LOOKS LIKE HE HAS A LOT OF MONEY...
WE DON'T EVEN KNOW HOW MUCH HE'S OFFERED FOR THE PLACE.
JUST GO AND MEET WITH HIM AND SEE WHAT HE SAYS.
I'LL FIND OUT FROM FLUFFERNUTTER HOW MUCH MONEY HE'S BEEN OFFERED.
I'M NOT MOVING THE SHELTER.
I DIDN'T SAY YOU HAD TO...
BUT IF WE'RE GOING TO STAY HERE, WE NEED TO BE INFORMED.
I BUILT THIS SHELTER FROM THE GROUND UP. I'M NOT GOING TO LET SOME... FAT CAT COME AND TAKE IT FROM ME!
SLAM!

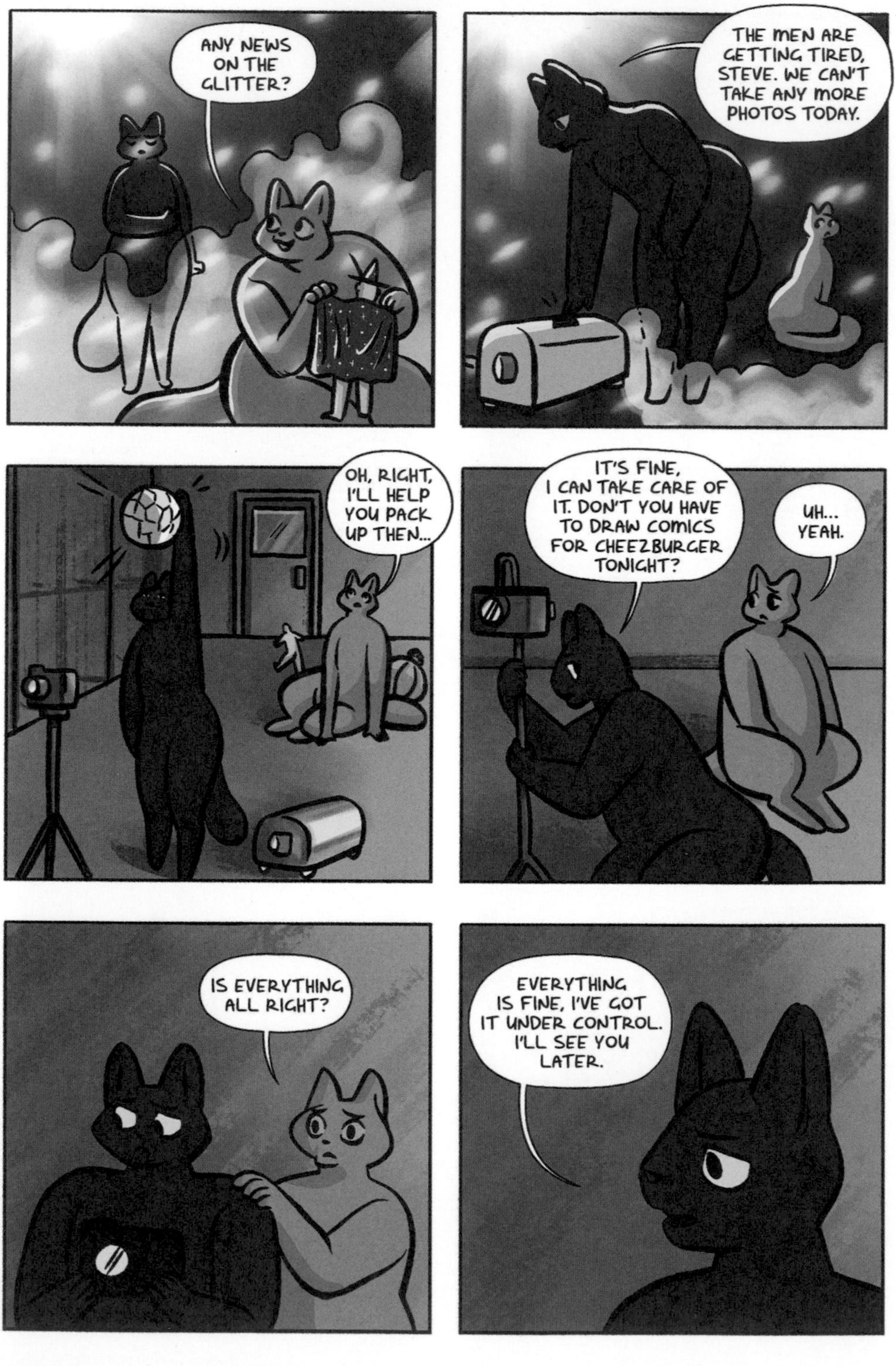
ANY NEWS ON THE GLITTER?
THE MEN ARE GETTING TIRED, STEVE. WE CAN'T TAKE ANY MORE PHOTOS TODAY.
OH, RIGHT, I'LL HELP YOU PACK UP THEN...
IT'S FINE, I CAN TAKE CARE OF IT. DON'T YOU HAVE TO DRAW COMICS FOR CHEEZBURGER TONIGHT?
UH... YEAH.
IS EVERYTHING ALL RIGHT?
EVERYTHING IS FINE, I'VE GOT IT UNDER CONTROL. I'LL SEE YOU LATER.

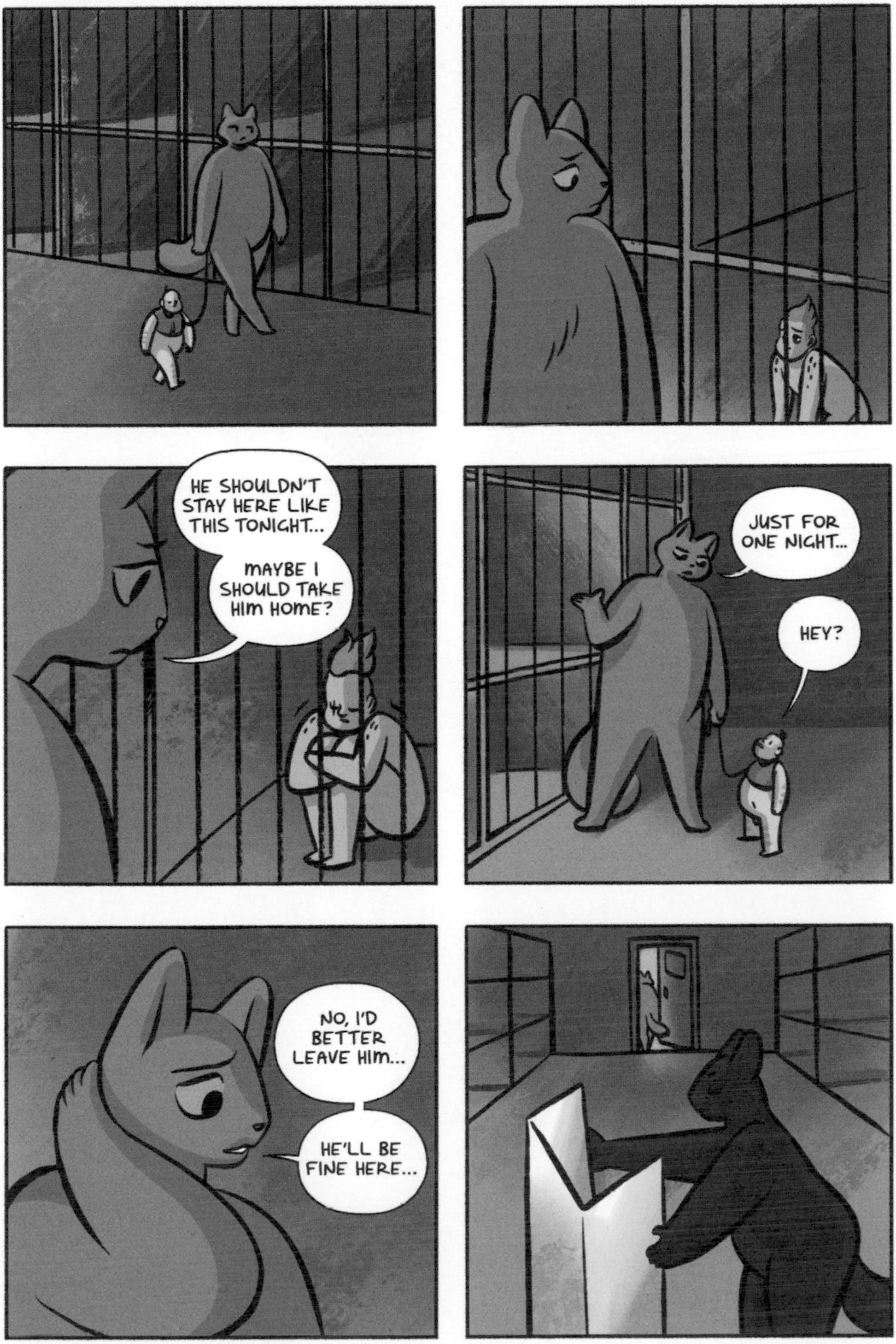
HE SHOULDN'T STAY HERE LIKE THIS TONIGHT...
MAYBE I SHOULD TAKE HIM HOME?
JUST FOR ONE NIGHT...
HEY?
NO, I'D BETTER LEAVE HIM...
HE'LL BE FINE HERE...

PART TWO

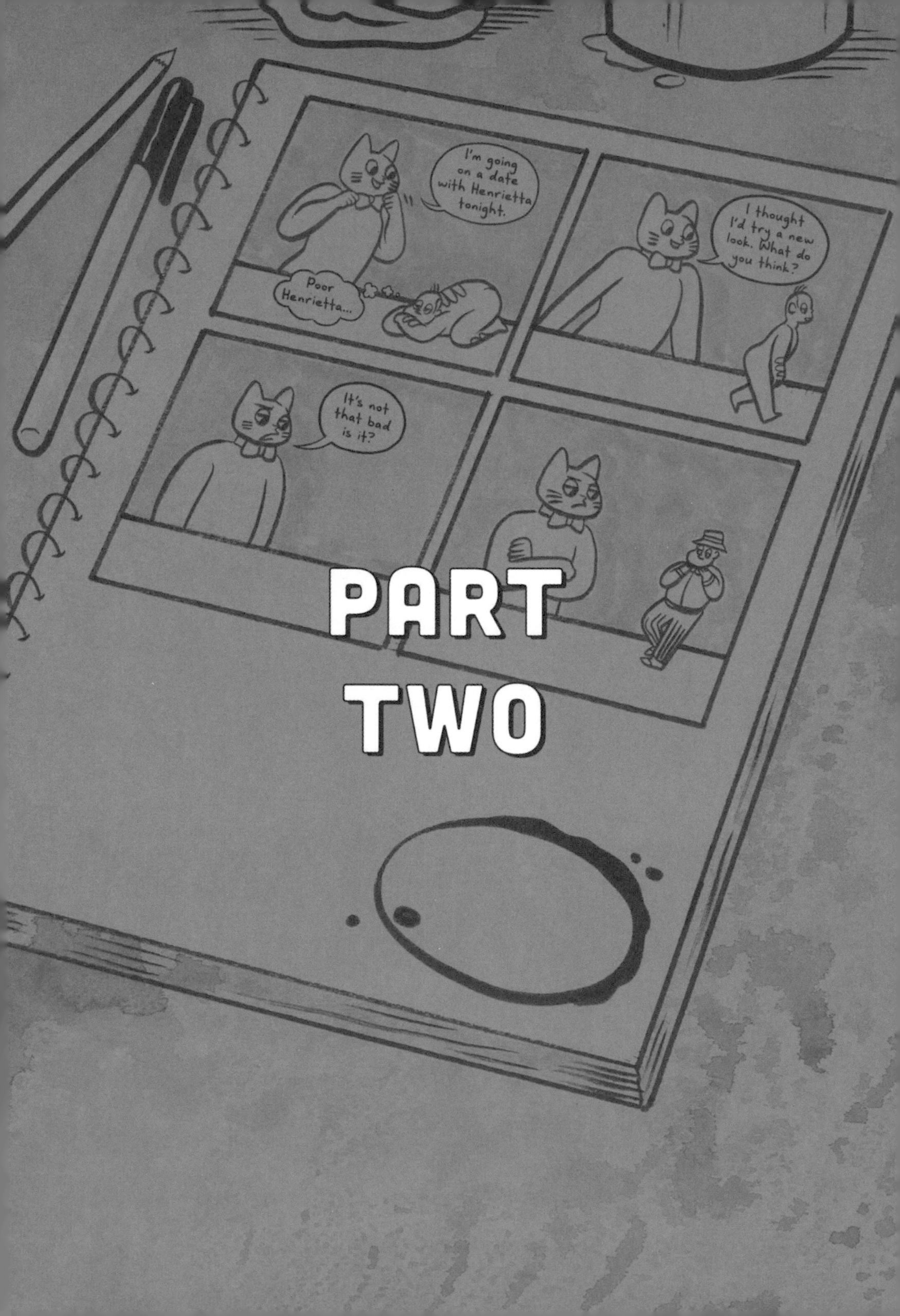
I'm going on a date with Henrietta tonight.
Poor Henrietta...
I thought I'd try a new look. What do you think?
It's not that bad is it?

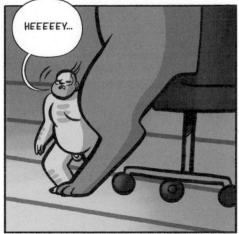

HEEEEEY...

HEEEY!

WHAT DO YOU WANT?

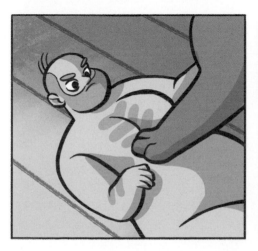

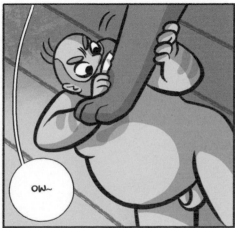

OW~

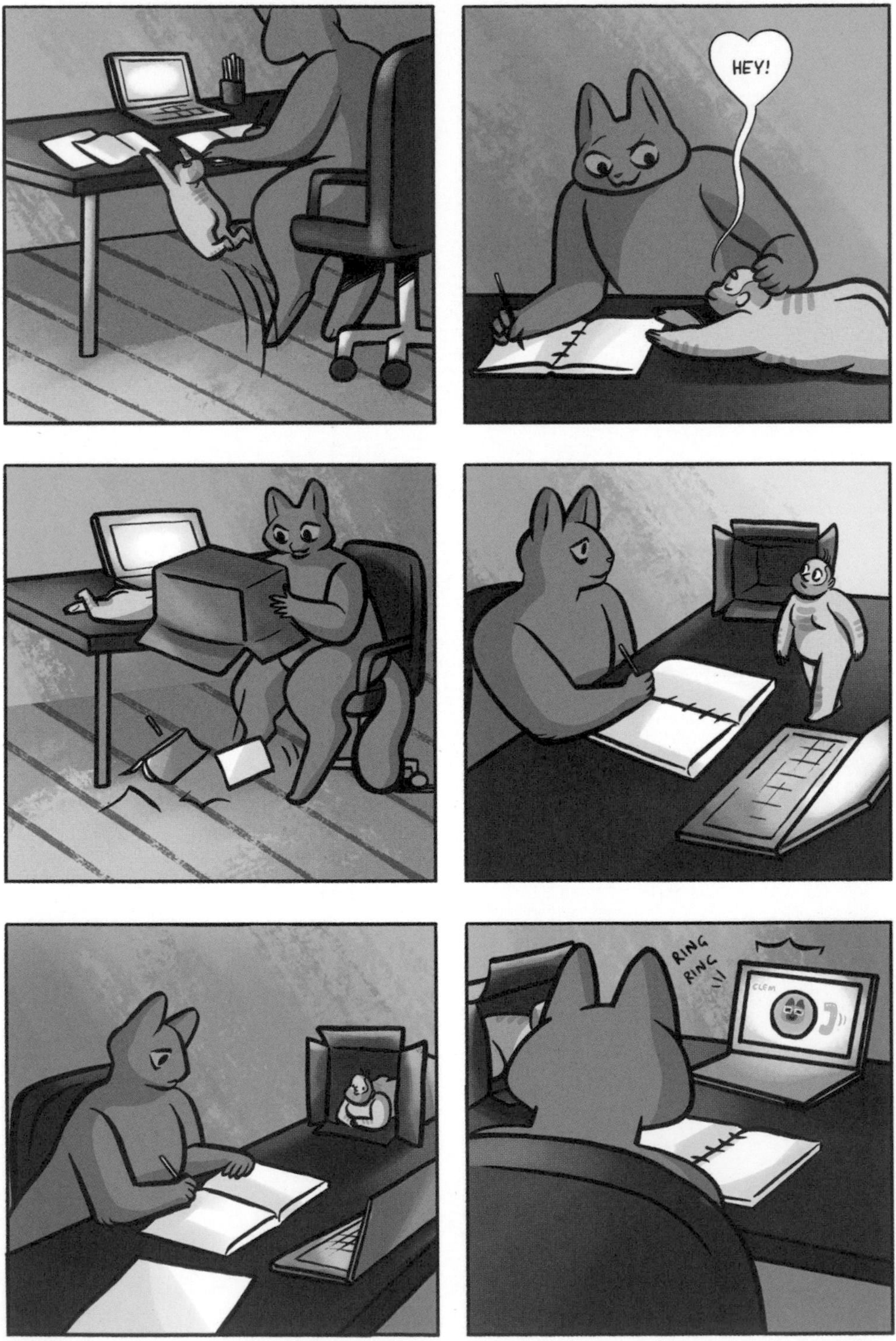
HEY!
RING
RING
CLEM

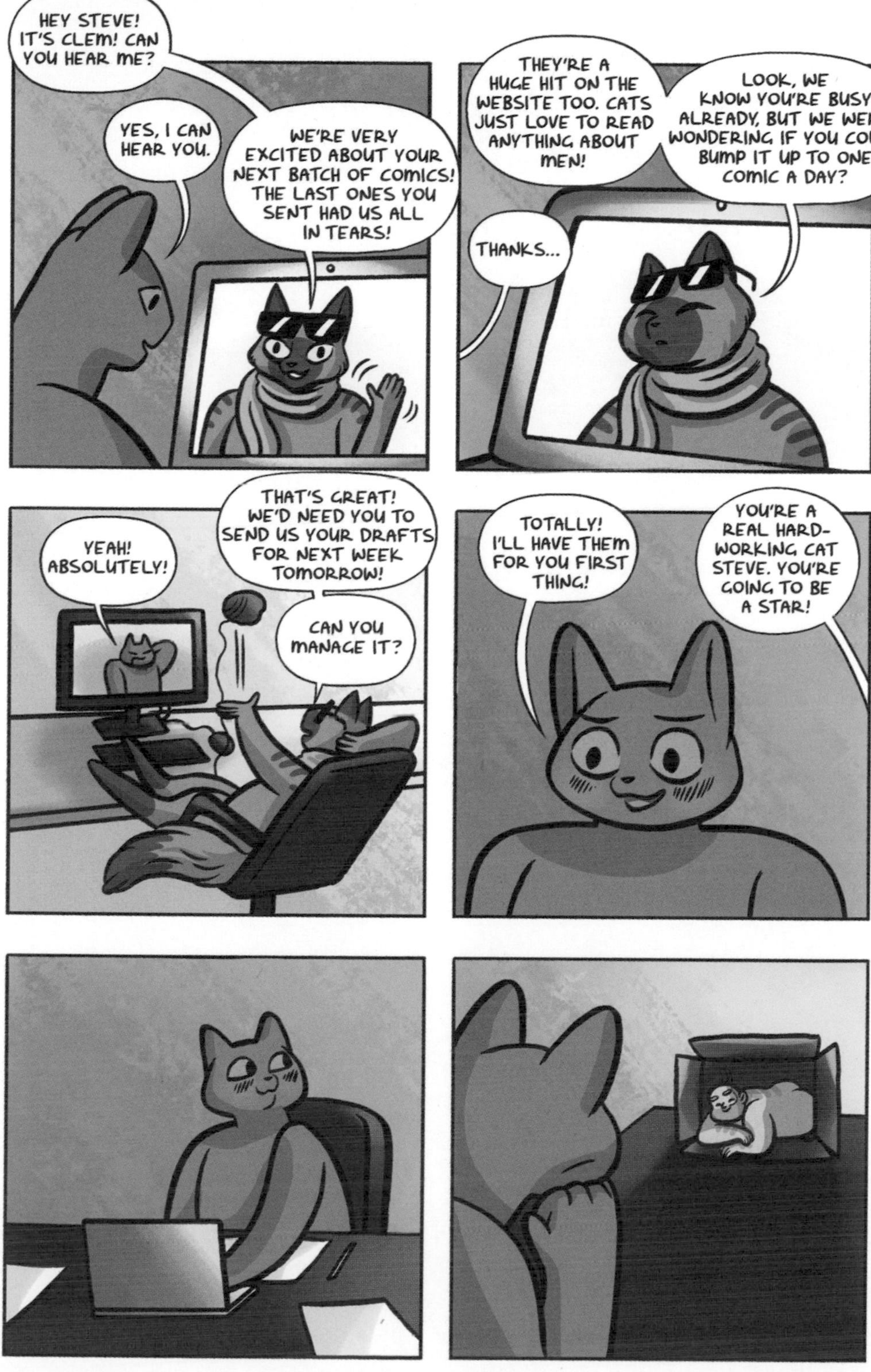
HEY STEVE! IT'S CLEM! CAN YOU HEAR ME?
YES, I CAN HEAR YOU.
WE'RE VERY EXCITED ABOUT YOUR NEXT BATCH OF COMICS! THE LAST ONES YOU SENT HAD US ALL IN TEARS!
THEY'RE A HUGE HIT ON THE WEBSITE TOO. CATS JUST LOVE TO READ ANYTHING ABOUT MEN!
THANKS...
LOOK, WE KNOW YOU'RE BUSY ALREADY, BUT WE WERE WONDERING IF YOU COULD BUMP IT UP TO ONE COMIC A DAY?
YEAH! ABSOLUTELY!
THAT'S GREAT! WE'D NEED YOU TO SEND US YOUR DRAFTS FOR NEXT WEEK TOMORROW!
CAN YOU MANAGE IT?
TOTALLY! I'LL HAVE THEM FOR YOU FIRST THING!
YOU'RE A REAL HARD-WORKING CAT STEVE. YOU'RE GOING TO BE A STAR!

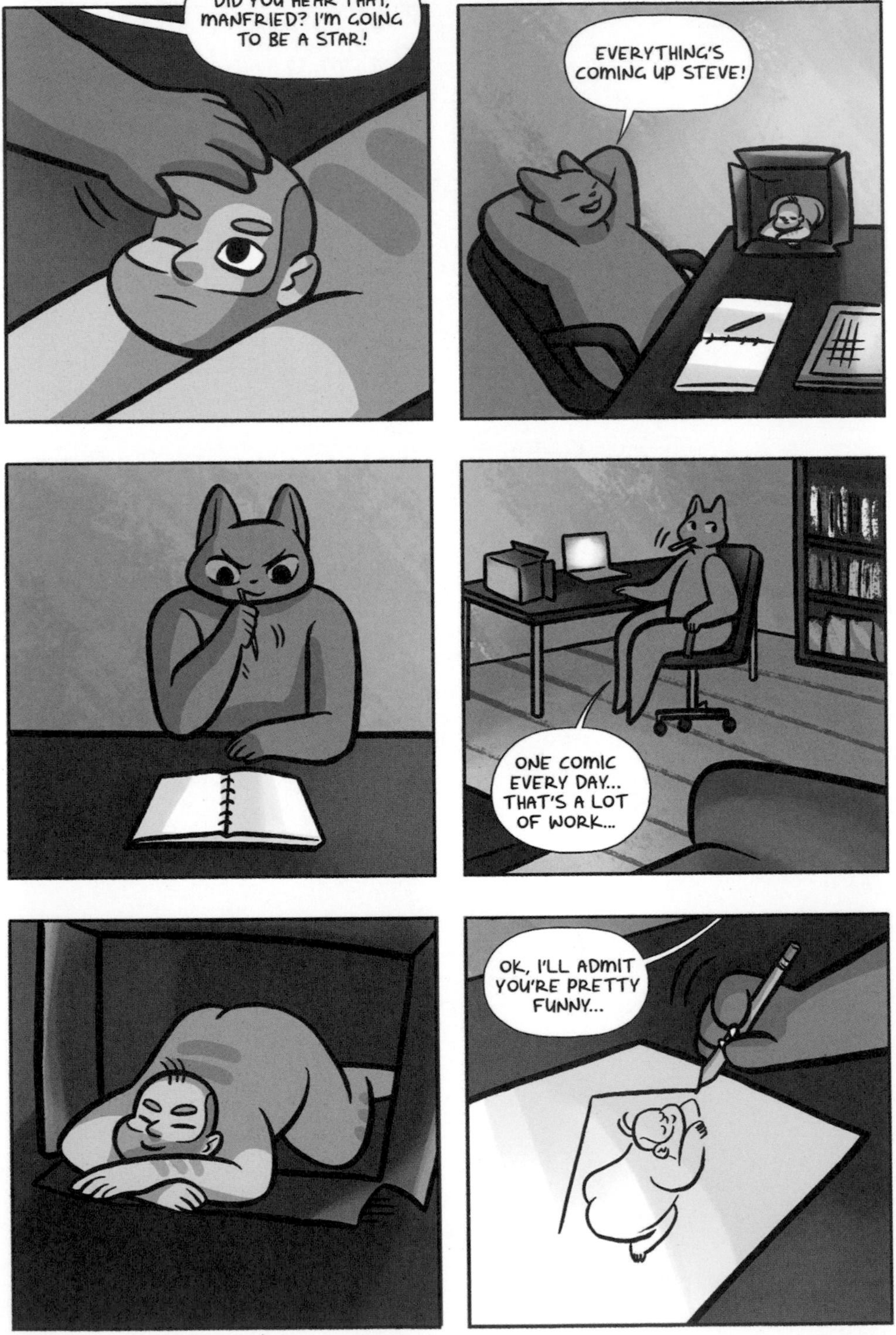
DID YOU HEAR THAT, MANFRIED? I'M GOING TO BE A STAR!
EVERYTHING'S COMING UP STEVE!
ONE COMIC EVERY DAY... THAT'S A LOT OF WORK...
OK, I'LL ADMIT YOU'RE PRETTY FUNNY...

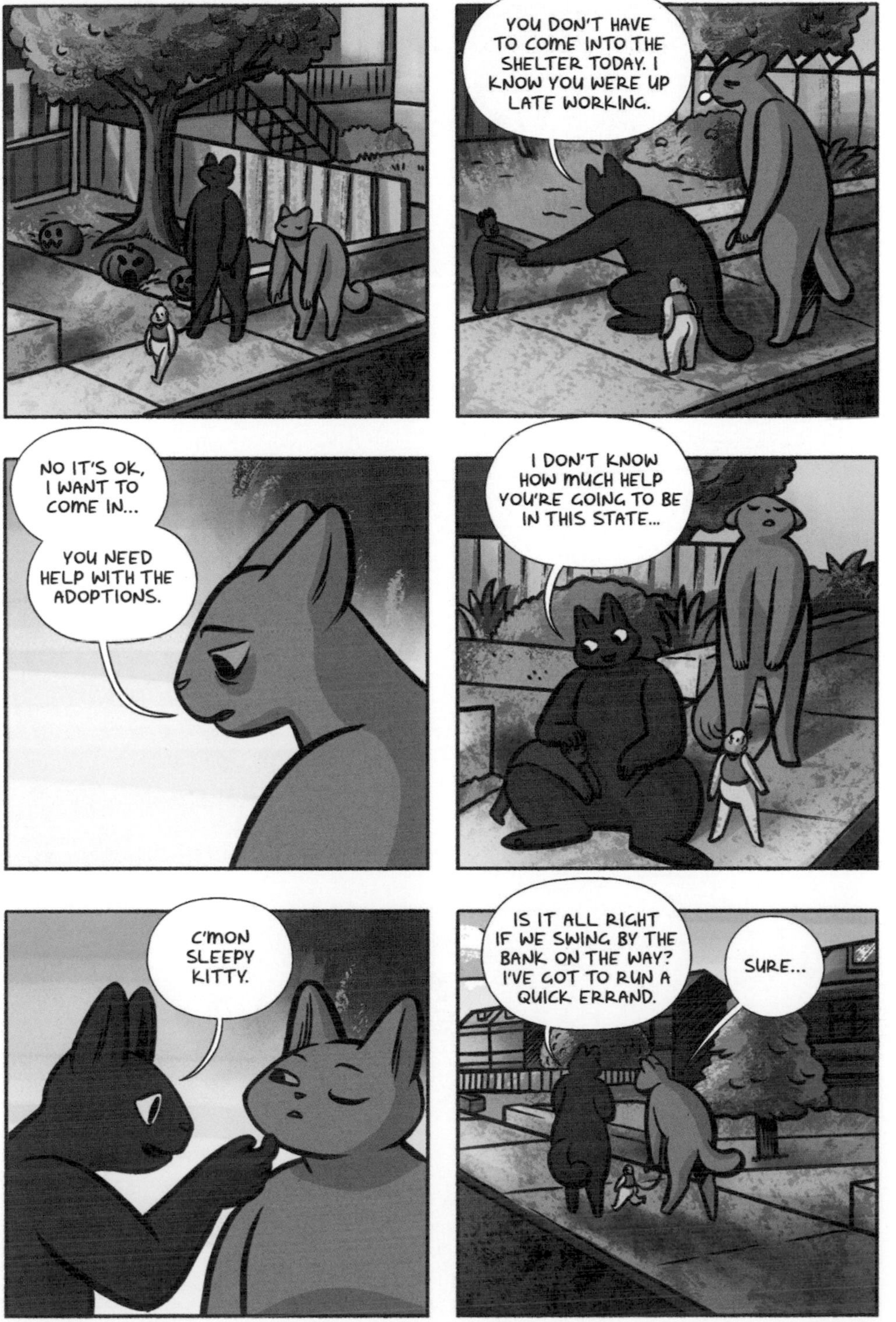
YOU DON'T HAVE TO COME INTO THE SHELTER TODAY. I KNOW YOU WERE UP LATE WORKING.
NO IT'S OK, I WANT TO COME IN...
YOU NEED HELP WITH THE ADOPTIONS.
I DON'T KNOW HOW MUCH HELP YOU'RE GOING TO BE IN THIS STATE...
C'MON SLEEPY KITTY.
IS IT ALL RIGHT IF WE SWING BY THE BANK ON THE WAY? I'VE GOT TO RUN A QUICK ERRAND.
SURE...

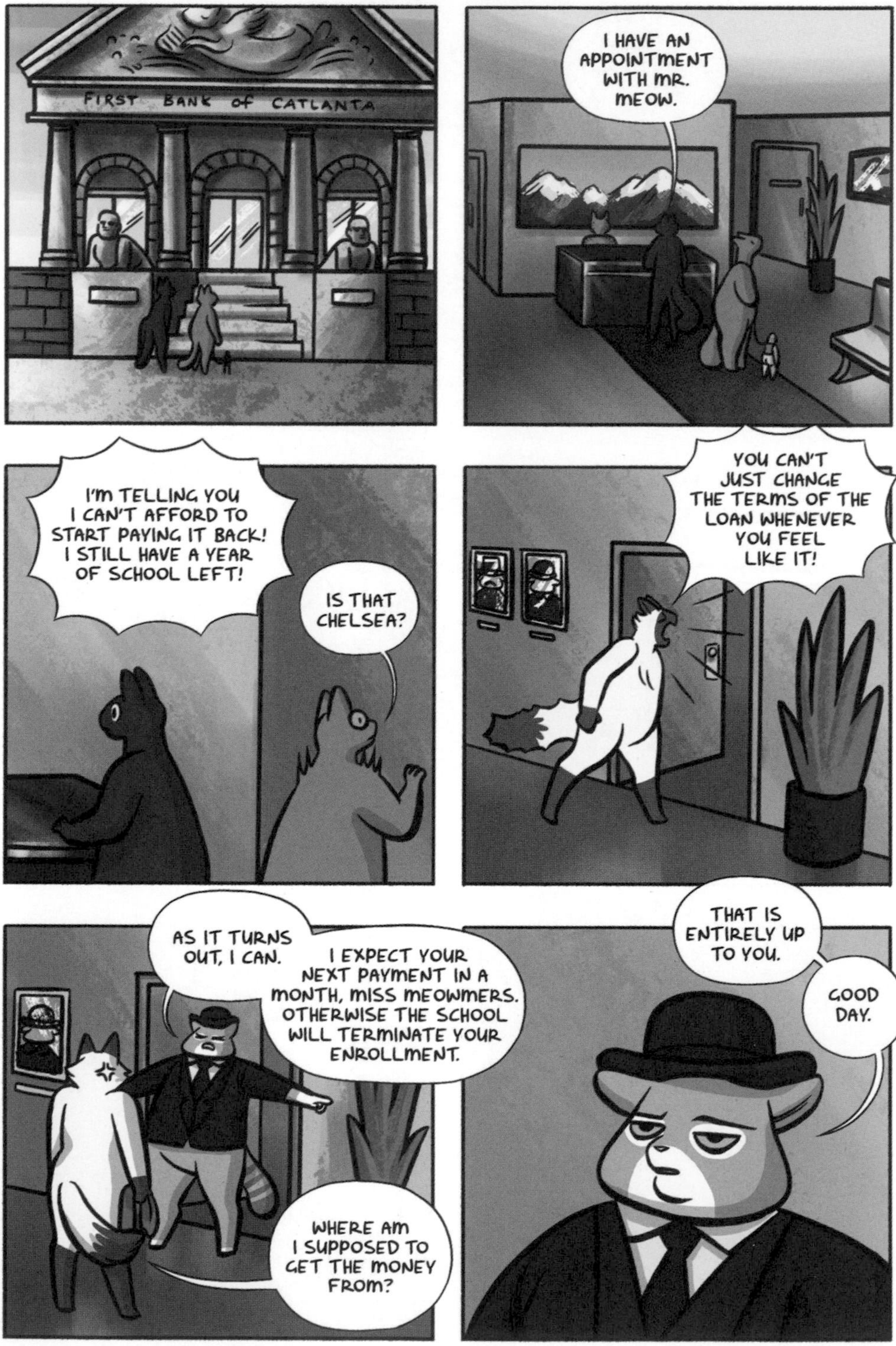
FIRST BANK of CATLANTA
I HAVE AN APPOINTMENT WITH MR. MEOW.
I'M TELLING YOU I CAN'T AFFORD TO START PAYING IT BACK! I STILL HAVE A YEAR OF SCHOOL LEFT!
IS THAT CHELSEA?
YOU CAN'T JUST CHANGE THE TERMS OF THE LOAN WHENEVER YOU FEEL LIKE IT!
AS IT TURNS OUT, I CAN.
I EXPECT YOUR NEXT PAYMENT IN A MONTH, MISS MEOWMERS. OTHERWISE THE SCHOOL WILL TERMINATE YOUR ENROLLMENT.
WHERE AM I SUPPOSED TO GET THE MONEY FROM?
THAT IS ENTIRELY UP TO YOU.
GOOD DAY.

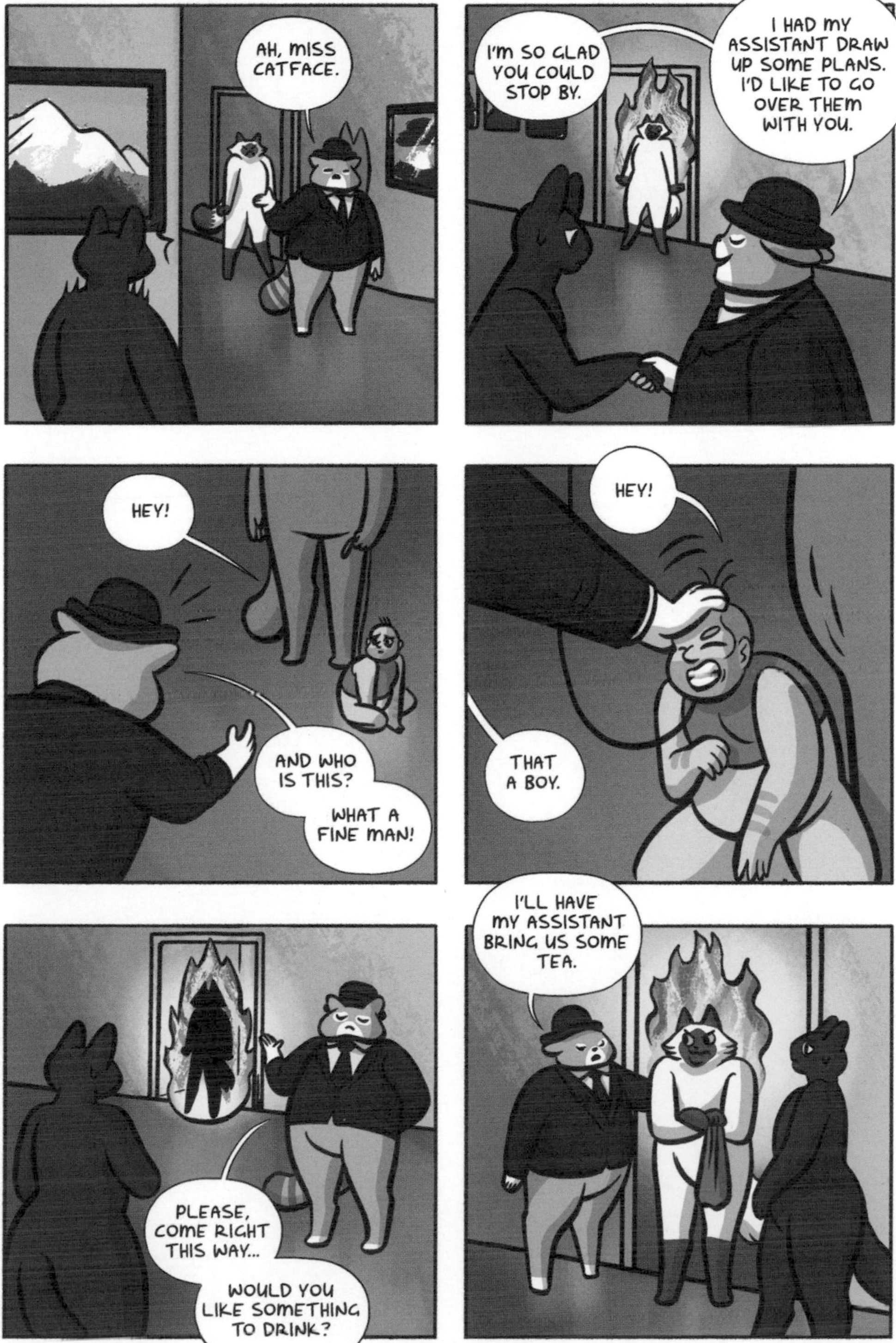
AH, MISS CATFACE.
I'M SO GLAD YOU COULD STOP BY.
I HAD MY ASSISTANT DRAW UP SOME PLANS. I'D LIKE TO GO OVER THEM WITH YOU.
HEY!
AND WHO IS THIS?
WHAT A FINE MAN!
HEY!
THAT A BOY.
PLEASE, COME RIGHT THIS WAY...
WOULD YOU LIKE SOMETHING TO DRINK?
I'LL HAVE MY ASSISTANT BRING US SOME TEA.

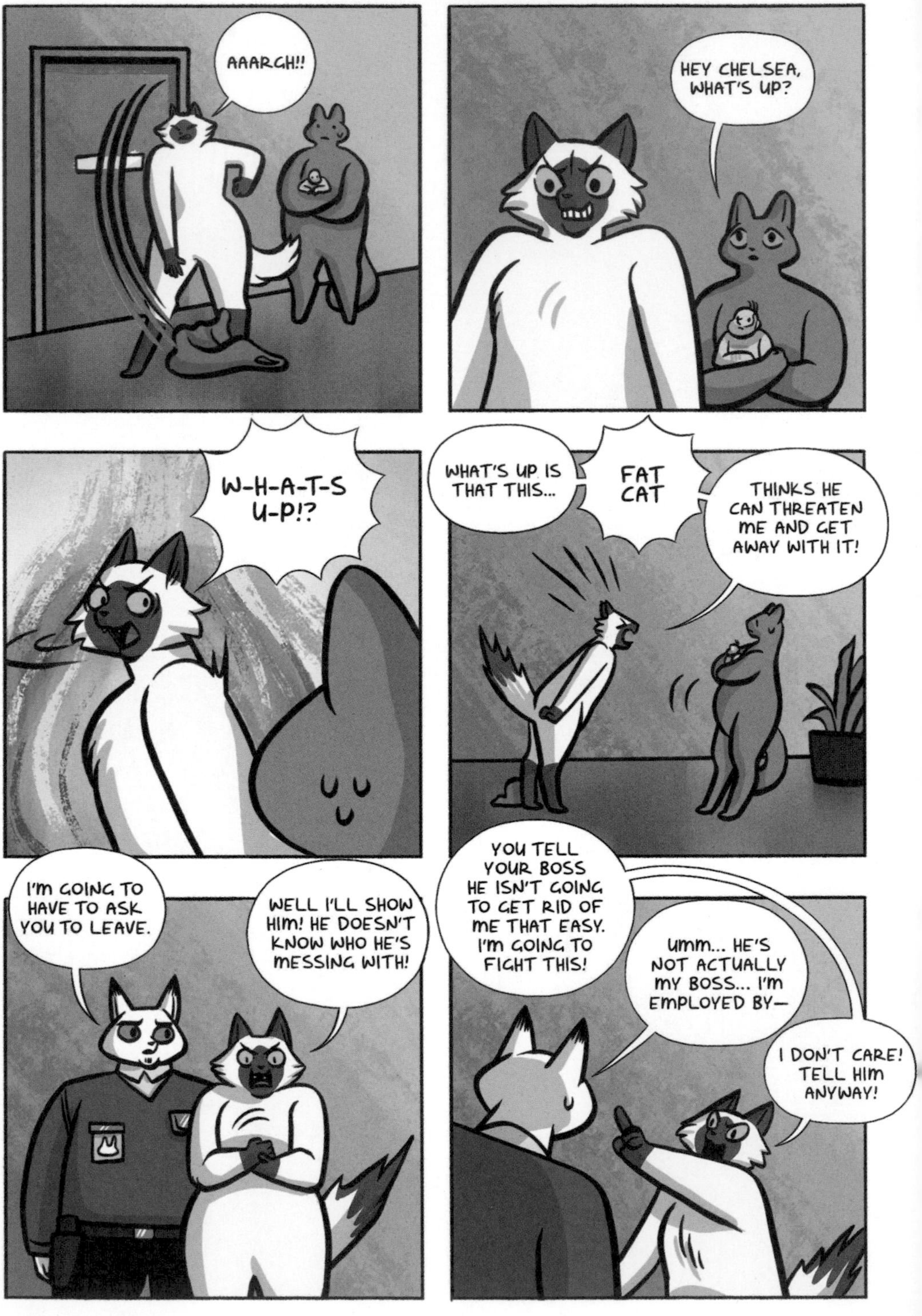
AAARGH!!
HEY CHELSEA, WHAT'S UP?
W-H-A-T-S U-P!?
WHAT'S UP IS THAT THIS...
FAT CAT
THINKS HE CAN THREATEN ME AND GET AWAY WITH IT!
I'M GOING TO HAVE TO ASK YOU TO LEAVE.
WELL I'LL SHOW HIM! HE DOESN'T KNOW WHO HE'S MESSING WITH!
YOU TELL YOUR BOSS HE ISN'T GOING TO GET RID OF ME THAT EASY. I'M GOING TO FIGHT THIS!
UMM... HE'S NOT ACTUALLY MY BOSS... I'M EMPLOYED BY—
I DON'T CARE! TELL HIM ANYWAY!

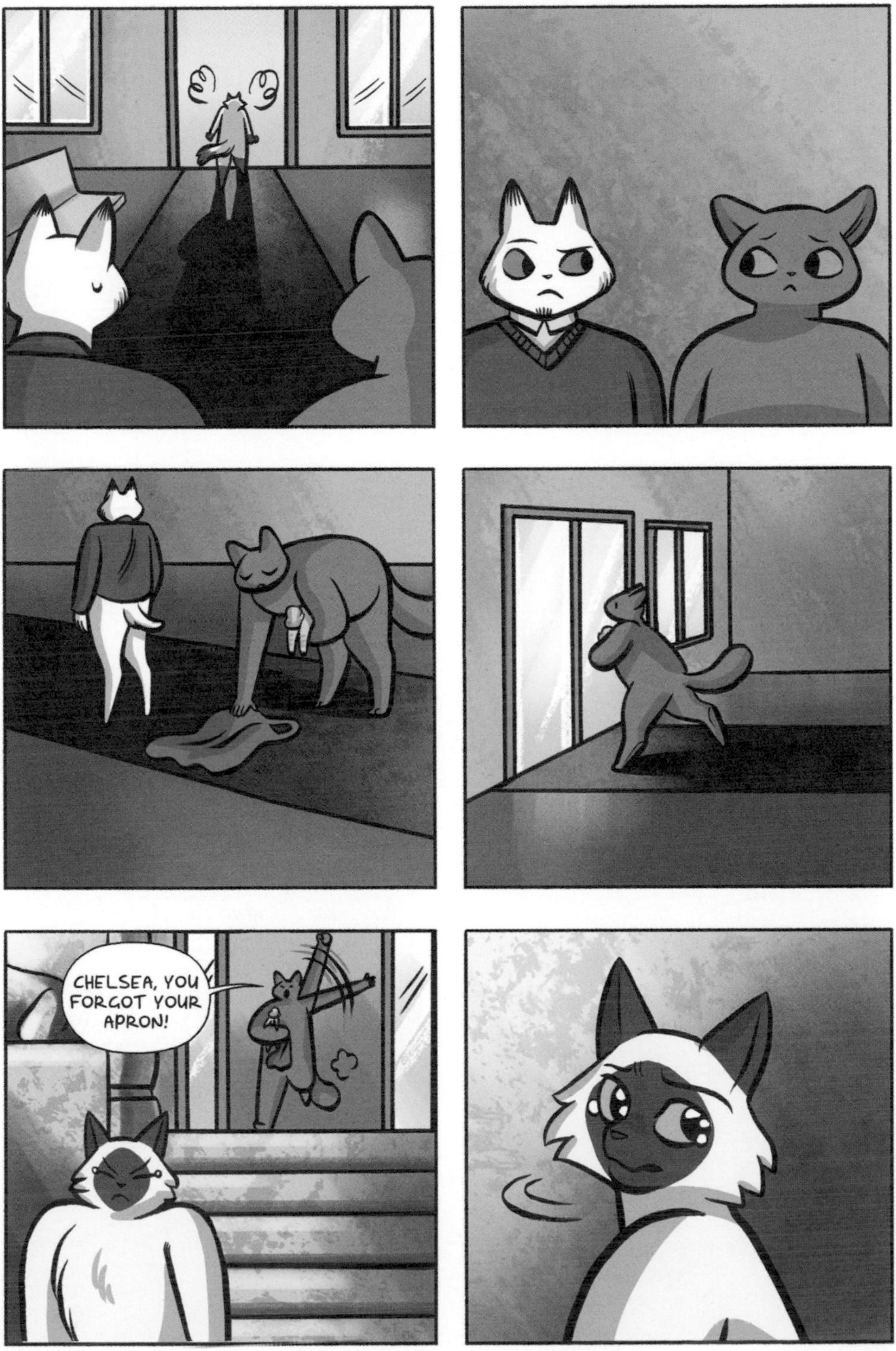
CHELSEA, YOU FORGOT YOUR APRON!

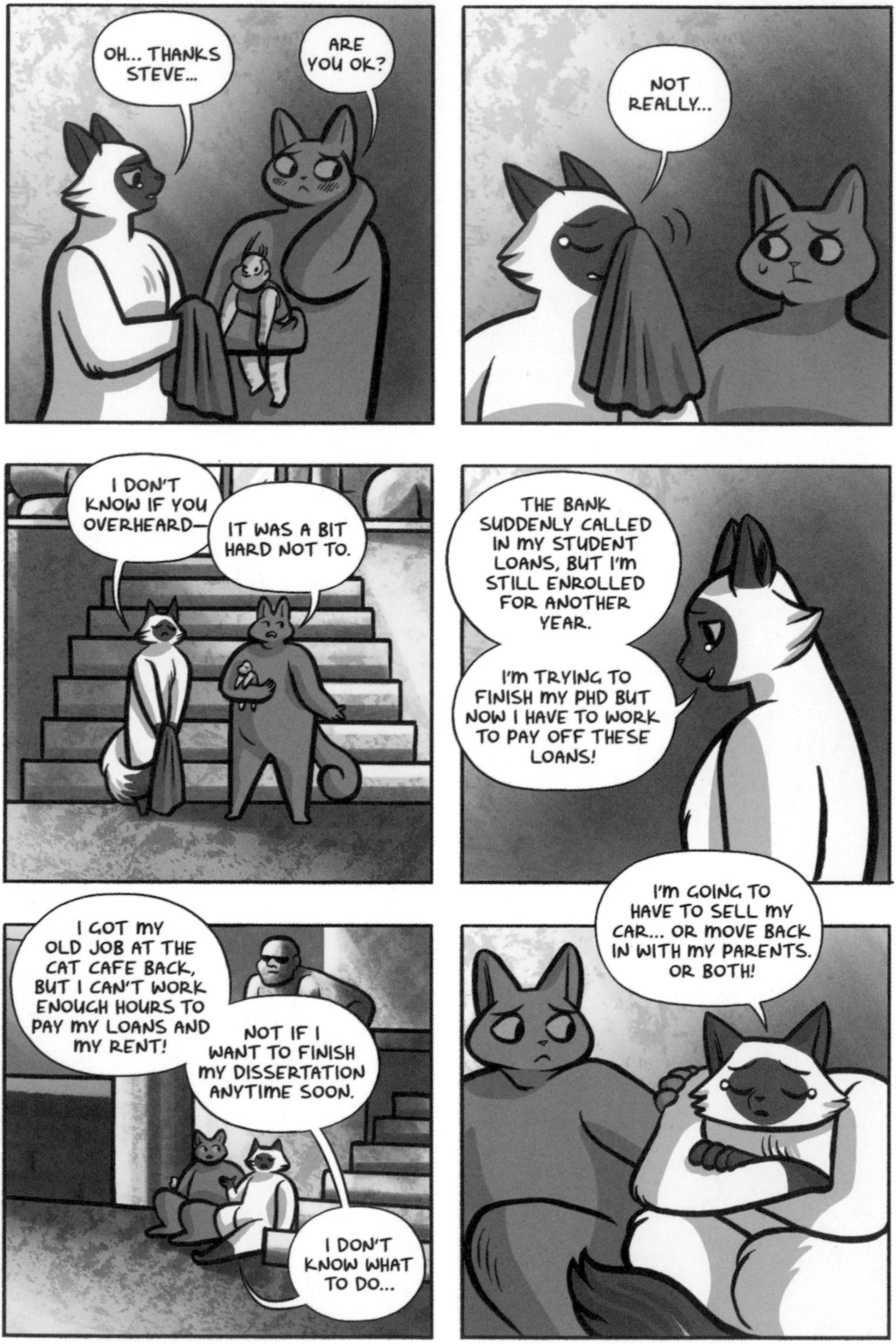
OH... THANKS STEVE...
ARE YOU OK?
NOT REALLY...
I DON'T KNOW IF YOU OVERHEARD—
IT WAS A BIT HARD NOT TO.
THE BANK SUDDENLY CALLED IN MY STUDENT LOANS, BUT I'M STILL ENROLLED FOR ANOTHER YEAR.
I'M TRYING TO FINISH MY PHD BUT NOW I HAVE TO WORK TO PAY OFF THESE LOANS!
I GOT MY OLD JOB AT THE CAT CAFE BACK, BUT I CAN'T WORK ENOUGH HOURS TO PAY MY LOANS AND MY RENT!
NOT IF I WANT TO FINISH MY DISSERTATION ANYTIME SOON.
I DON'T KNOW WHAT TO DO...
I'M GOING TO HAVE TO SELL MY CAR... OR MOVE BACK IN WITH MY PARENTS. OR BOTH!

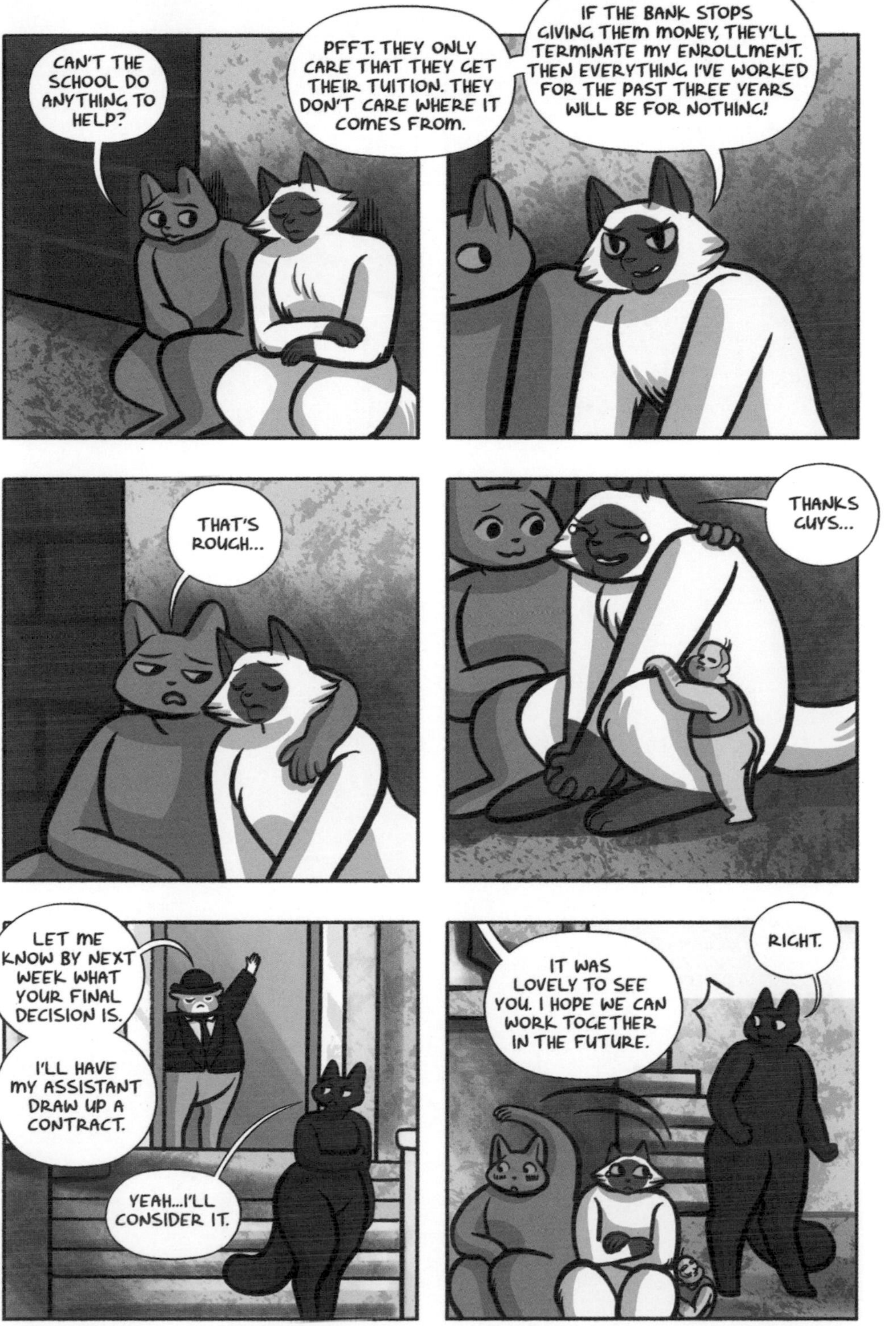
CAN'T THE SCHOOL DO ANYTHING TO HELP?
PFFT. THEY ONLY CARE THAT THEY GET THEIR TUITION. THEY DON'T CARE WHERE IT COMES FROM.
IF THE BANK STOPS GIVING THEM MONEY, THEY'LL TERMINATE MY ENROLLMENT. THEN EVERYTHING I'VE WORKED FOR THE PAST THREE YEARS WILL BE FOR NOTHING!
THAT'S ROUGH...
THANKS GUYS...
LET ME KNOW BY NEXT WEEK WHAT YOUR FINAL DECISION IS.
I'LL HAVE MY ASSISTANT DRAW UP A CONTRACT.
YEAH...I'LL CONSIDER IT.
IT WAS LOVELY TO SEE YOU. I HOPE WE CAN WORK TOGETHER IN THE FUTURE.
RIGHT.

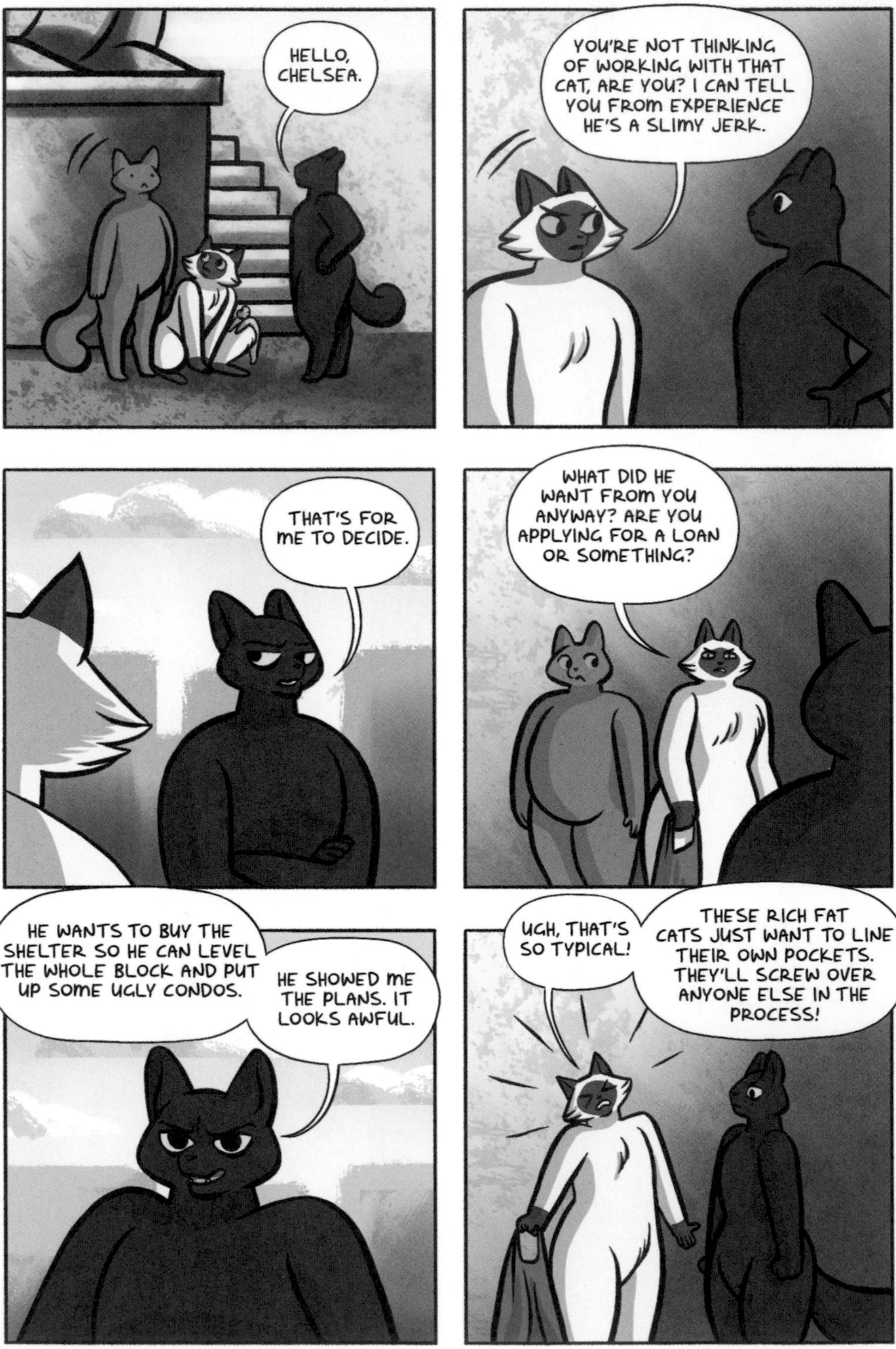
HELLO, CHELSEA.
YOU'RE NOT THINKING OF WORKING WITH THAT CAT, ARE YOU? I CAN TELL YOU FROM EXPERIENCE HE'S A SLIMY JERK.
THAT'S FOR ME TO DECIDE.
WHAT DID HE WANT FROM YOU ANYWAY? ARE YOU APPLYING FOR A LOAN OR SOMETHING?
HE WANTS TO BUY THE SHELTER SO HE CAN LEVEL THE WHOLE BLOCK AND PUT UP SOME UGLY CONDOS.
HE SHOWED ME THE PLANS. IT LOOKS AWFUL.
UGH, THAT'S SO TYPICAL!
THESE RICH FAT CATS JUST WANT TO LINE THEIR OWN POCKETS. THEY'LL SCREW OVER ANYONE ELSE IN THE PROCESS!

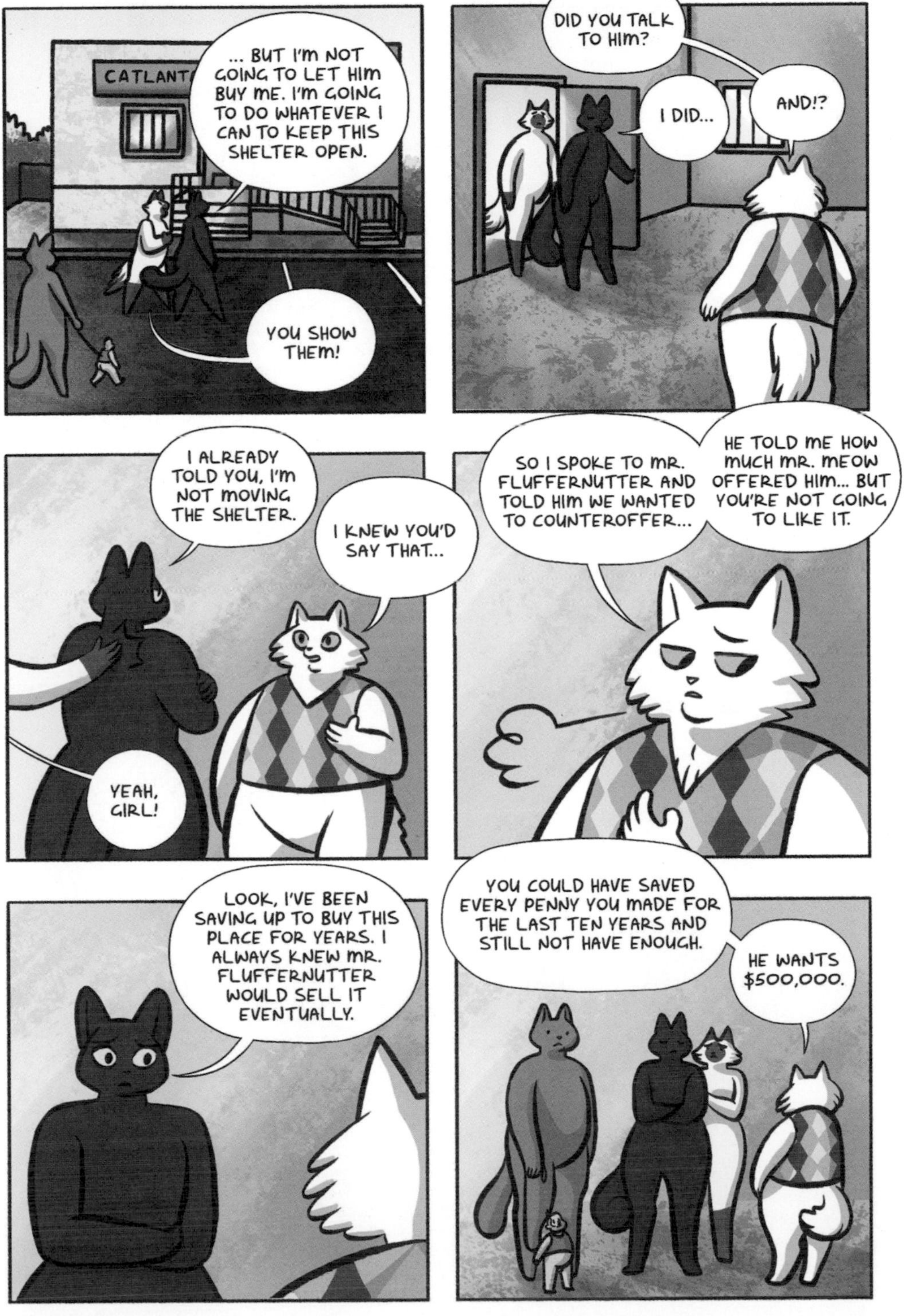
CATLANT
... BUT I'M NOT GOING TO LET HIM BUY ME. I'M GOING TO DO WHATEVER I CAN TO KEEP THIS SHELTER OPEN.
YOU SHOW THEM!
DID YOU TALK TO HIM?
I DID...
AND!?
I ALREADY TOLD YOU, I'M NOT MOVING THE SHELTER.
I KNEW YOU'D SAY THAT...
YEAH, GIRL!
SO I SPOKE TO MR. FLUFFERNUTTER AND TOLD HIM WE WANTED TO COUNTEROFFER...
HE TOLD ME HOW MUCH MR. MEOW OFFERED HIM... BUT YOU'RE NOT GOING TO LIKE IT.
LOOK, I'VE BEEN SAVING UP TO BUY THIS PLACE FOR YEARS. I ALWAYS KNEW MR. FLUFFERNUTTER WOULD SELL IT EVENTUALLY.
YOU COULD HAVE SAVED EVERY PENNY YOU MADE FOR THE LAST TEN YEARS AND STILL NOT HAVE ENOUGH.
HE WANTS $500,000.

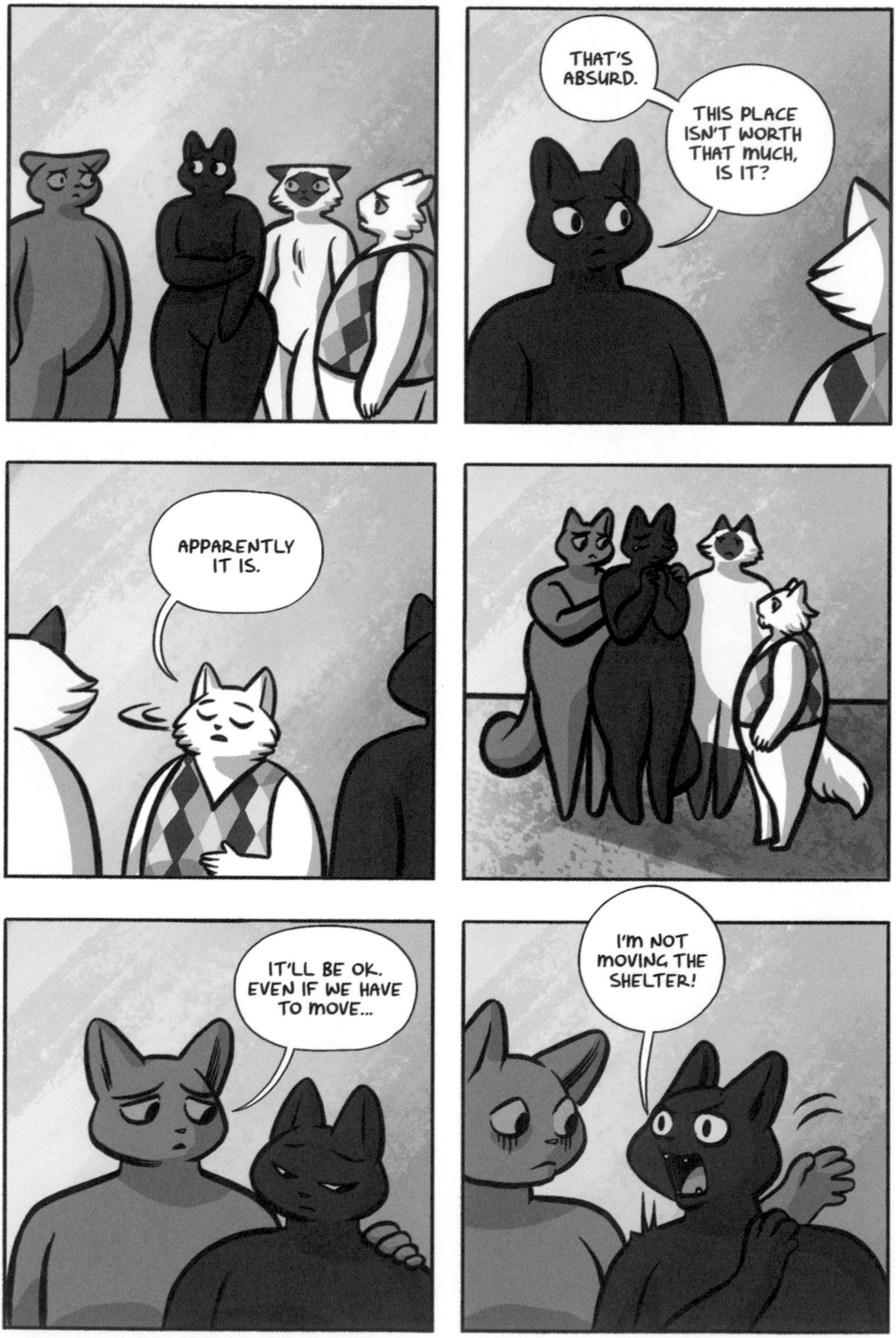
THAT'S ABSURD.
THIS PLACE ISN'T WORTH THAT MUCH, IS IT?
APPARENTLY IT IS.
IT'LL BE OK. EVEN IF WE HAVE TO MOVE...
I'M NOT MOVING THE SHELTER!

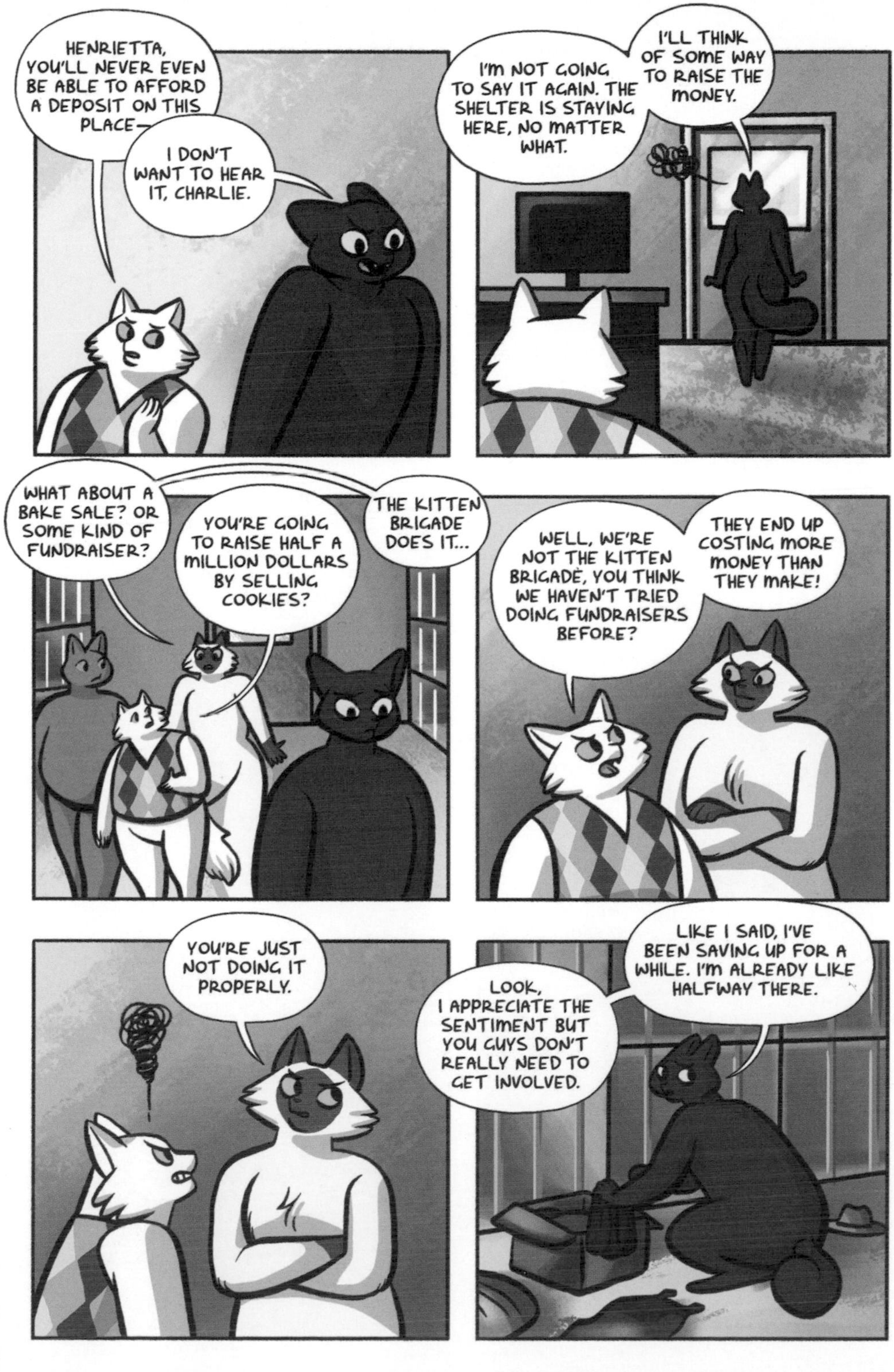
HENRIETTA, YOU'LL NEVER EVEN BE ABLE TO AFFORD A DEPOSIT ON THIS PLACE—
I DON'T WANT TO HEAR IT, CHARLIE.
I'M NOT GOING TO SAY IT AGAIN. THE SHELTER IS STAYING HERE, NO MATTER WHAT.
I'LL THINK OF SOME WAY TO RAISE THE MONEY.
WHAT ABOUT A BAKE SALE? OR SOME KIND OF FUNDRAISER?
THE KITTEN BRIGADE DOES IT...
YOU'RE GOING TO RAISE HALF A MILLION DOLLARS BY SELLING COOKIES?
WELL, WE'RE NOT THE KITTEN BRIGADE, YOU THINK WE HAVEN'T TRIED DOING FUNDRAISERS BEFORE?
THEY END UP COSTING MORE MONEY THAN THEY MAKE!
YOU'RE JUST NOT DOING IT PROPERLY.
LOOK, I APPRECIATE THE SENTIMENT BUT YOU GUYS DON'T REALLY NEED TO GET INVOLVED.
LIKE I SAID, I'VE BEEN SAVING UP FOR A WHILE. I'M ALREADY LIKE HALFWAY THERE.

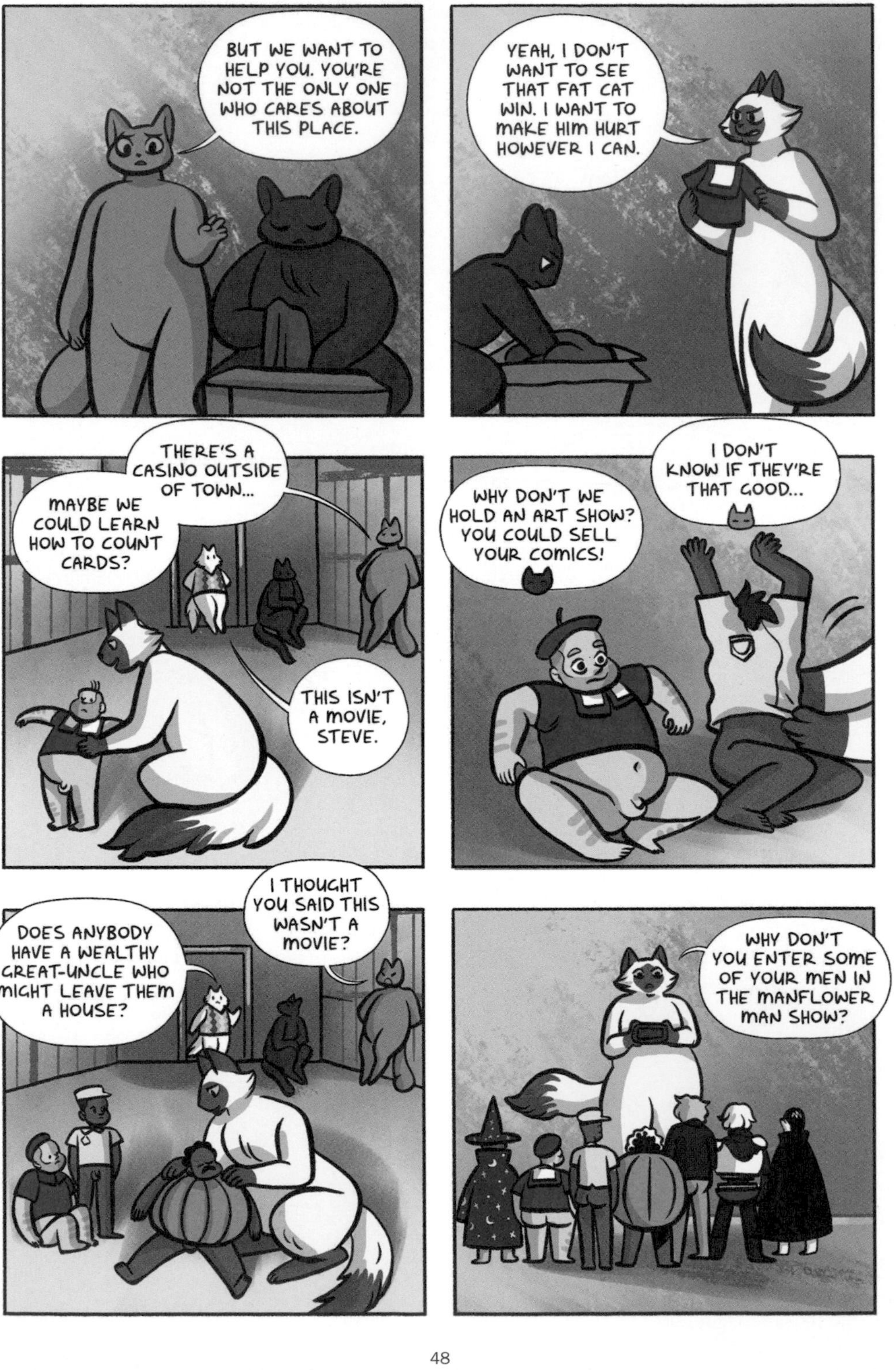
BUT WE WANT TO HELP YOU. YOU'RE NOT THE ONLY ONE WHO CARES ABOUT THIS PLACE.
YEAH, I DON'T WANT TO SEE THAT FAT CAT WIN. I WANT TO MAKE HIM HURT HOWEVER I CAN.
MAYBE WE COULD LEARN HOW TO COUNT CARDS?
THERE'S A CASINO OUTSIDE OF TOWN...
THIS ISN'T A MOVIE, STEVE.
WHY DON'T WE HOLD AN ART SHOW? YOU COULD SELL YOUR COMICS!
I DON'T KNOW IF THEY'RE THAT GOOD...
DOES ANYBODY HAVE A WEALTHY GREAT-UNCLE WHO MIGHT LEAVE THEM A HOUSE?
I THOUGHT YOU SAID THIS WASN'T A MOVIE?
WHY DON'T YOU ENTER SOME OF YOUR MEN IN THE MANFLOWER MAN SHOW?

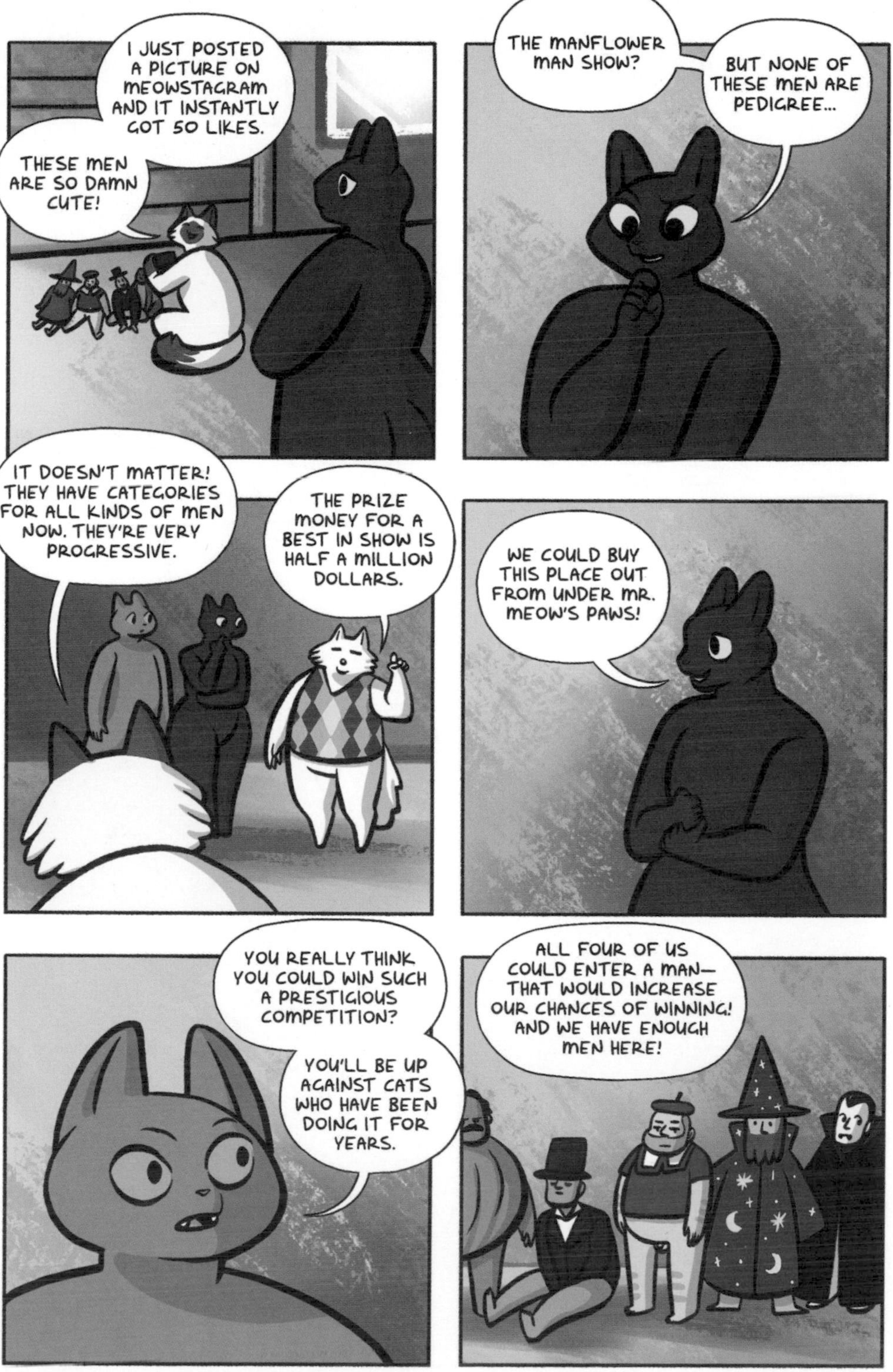
I JUST POSTED A PICTURE ON MEOWSTAGRAM AND IT INSTANTLY GOT 50 LIKES.
THESE MEN ARE SO DAMN CUTE!
THE MANFLOWER MAN SHOW?
BUT NONE OF THESE MEN ARE PEDIGREE...
IT DOESN'T MATTER! THEY HAVE CATEGORIES FOR ALL KINDS OF MEN NOW. THEY'RE VERY PROGRESSIVE.
THE PRIZE MONEY FOR A BEST IN SHOW IS HALF A MILLION DOLLARS.
WE COULD BUY THIS PLACE OUT FROM UNDER MR. MEOW'S PAWS!
YOU REALLY THINK YOU COULD WIN SUCH A PRESTIGIOUS COMPETITION?
YOU'LL BE UP AGAINST CATS WHO HAVE BEEN DOING IT FOR YEARS.
ALL FOUR OF US COULD ENTER A MAN— THAT WOULD INCREASE OUR CHANCES OF WINNING! AND WE HAVE ENOUGH MEN HERE!

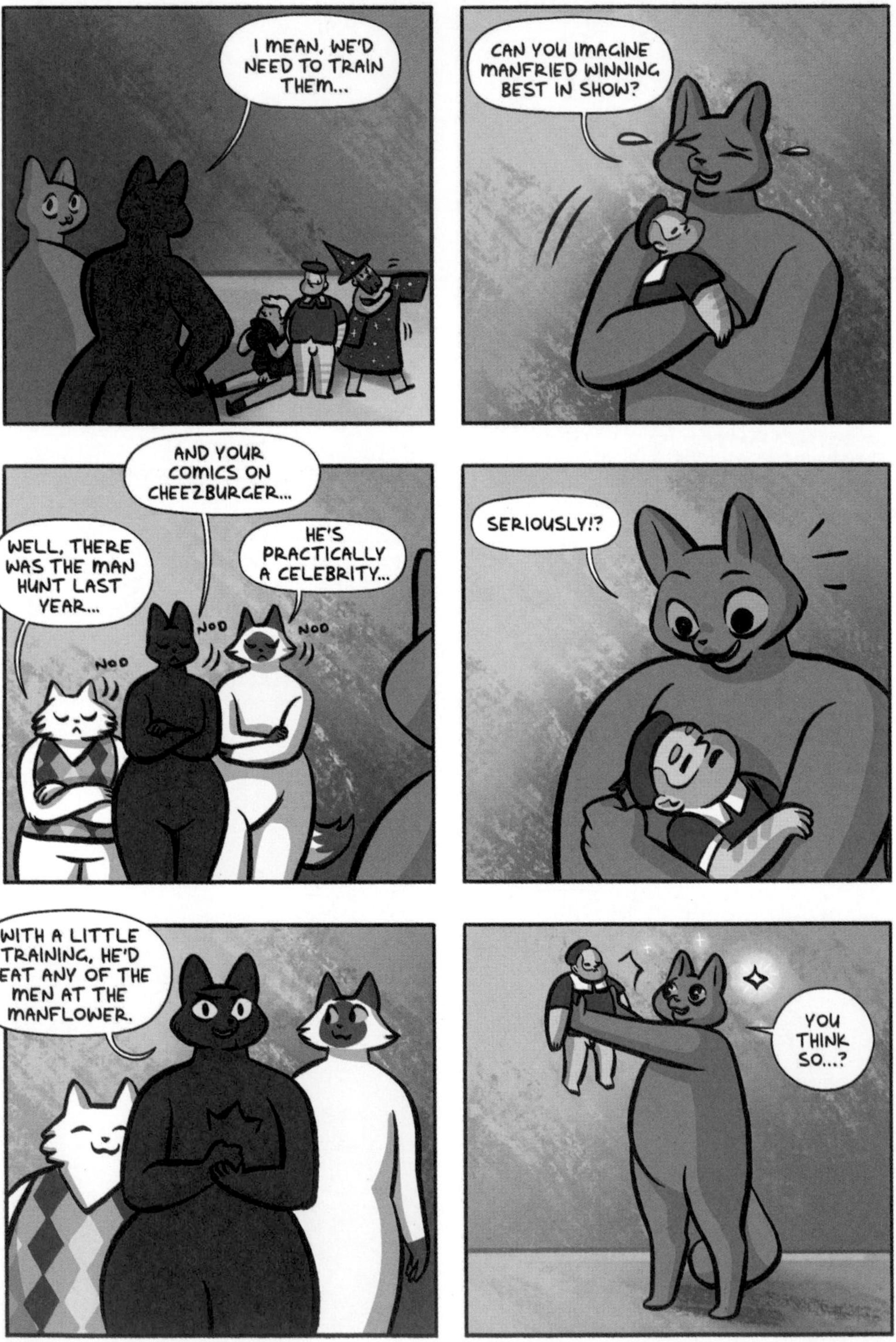
I MEAN, WE'D NEED TO TRAIN THEM...
CAN YOU IMAGINE MANFRIED WINNING BEST IN SHOW?
WELL, THERE WAS THE MAN HUNT LAST YEAR...
AND YOUR COMICS ON CHEEZBURGER...
HE'S PRACTICALLY A CELEBRITY...
NOD
NOD
NOD
SERIOUSLY!?
WITH A LITTLE TRAINING, HE'D BEAT ANY OF THE MEN AT THE MANFLOWER.
YOU THINK SO...?

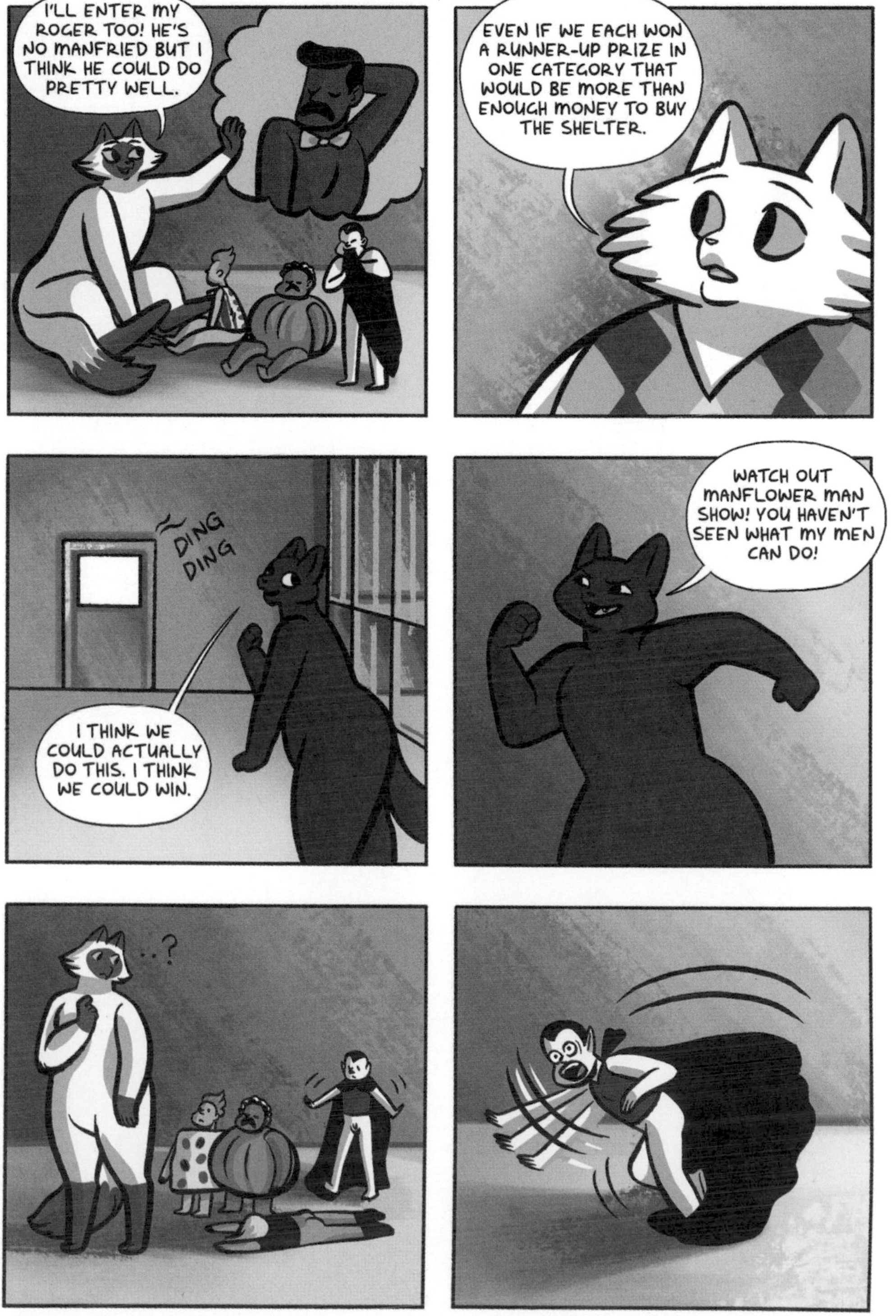
I'LL ENTER MY ROGER TOO! HE'S NO MANFRIED BUT I THINK HE COULD DO PRETTY WELL.
EVEN IF WE EACH WON A RUNNER-UP PRIZE IN ONE CATEGORY THAT WOULD BE MORE THAN ENOUGH MONEY TO BUY THE SHELTER.
DING DING
I THINK WE COULD ACTUALLY DO THIS. I THINK WE COULD WIN.
WATCH OUT MANFLOWER MAN SHOW! YOU HAVEN'T SEEN WHAT MY MEN CAN DO!
..?

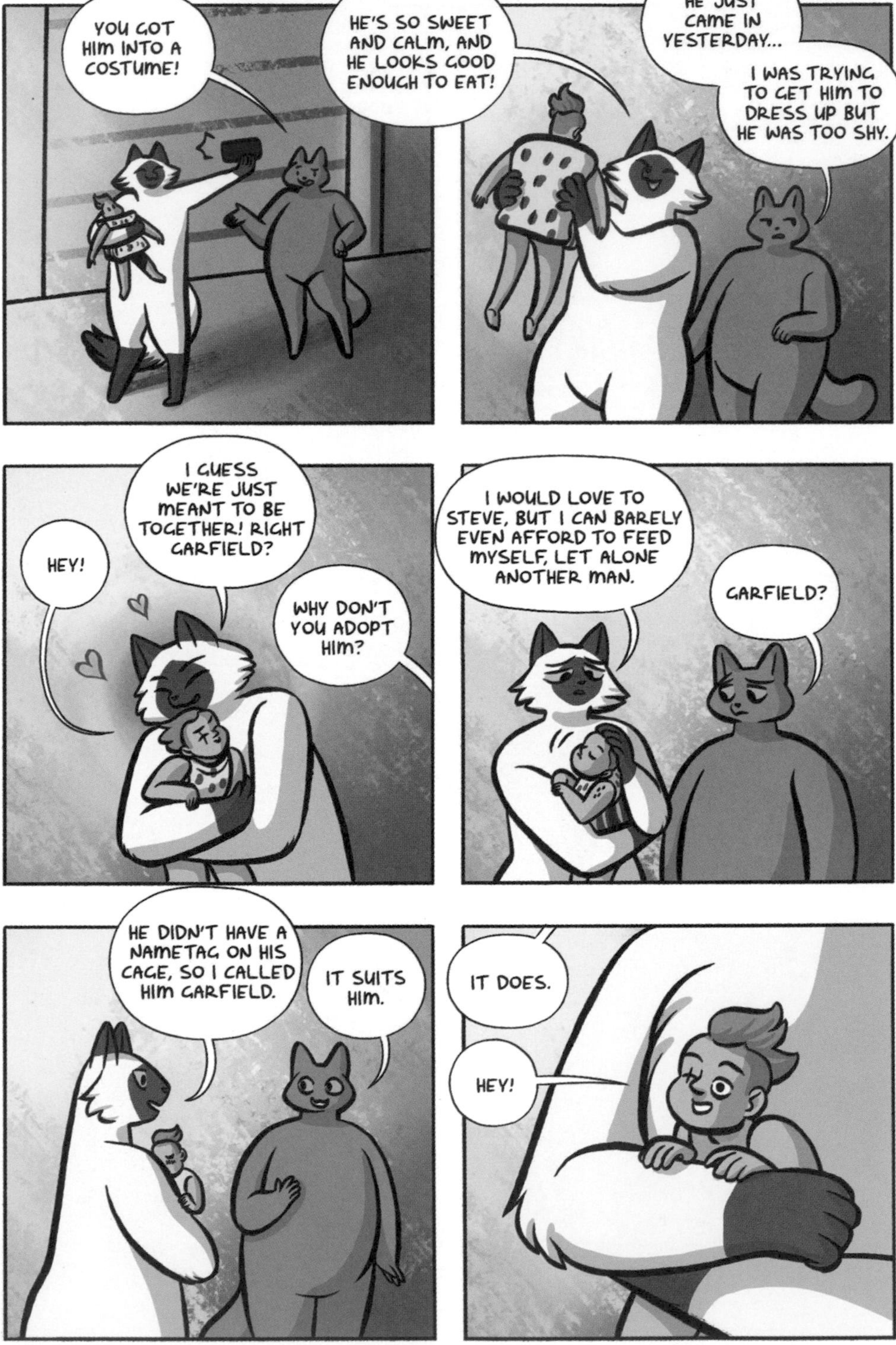
YOU GOT HIM INTO A COSTUME!
HE'S SO SWEET AND CALM, AND HE LOOKS GOOD ENOUGH TO EAT!
HE JUST CAME IN YESTERDAY...
I WAS TRYING TO GET HIM TO DRESS UP BUT HE WAS TOO SHY.
I GUESS WE'RE JUST MEANT TO BE TOGETHER! RIGHT GARFIELD?
HEY!
WHY DON'T YOU ADOPT HIM?
I WOULD LOVE TO STEVE, BUT I CAN BARELY EVEN AFFORD TO FEED MYSELF, LET ALONE ANOTHER MAN.
GARFIELD?
HE DIDN'T HAVE A NAMETAG ON HIS CAGE, SO I CALLED HIM GARFIELD.
IT SUITS HIM.
IT DOES.
HEY!

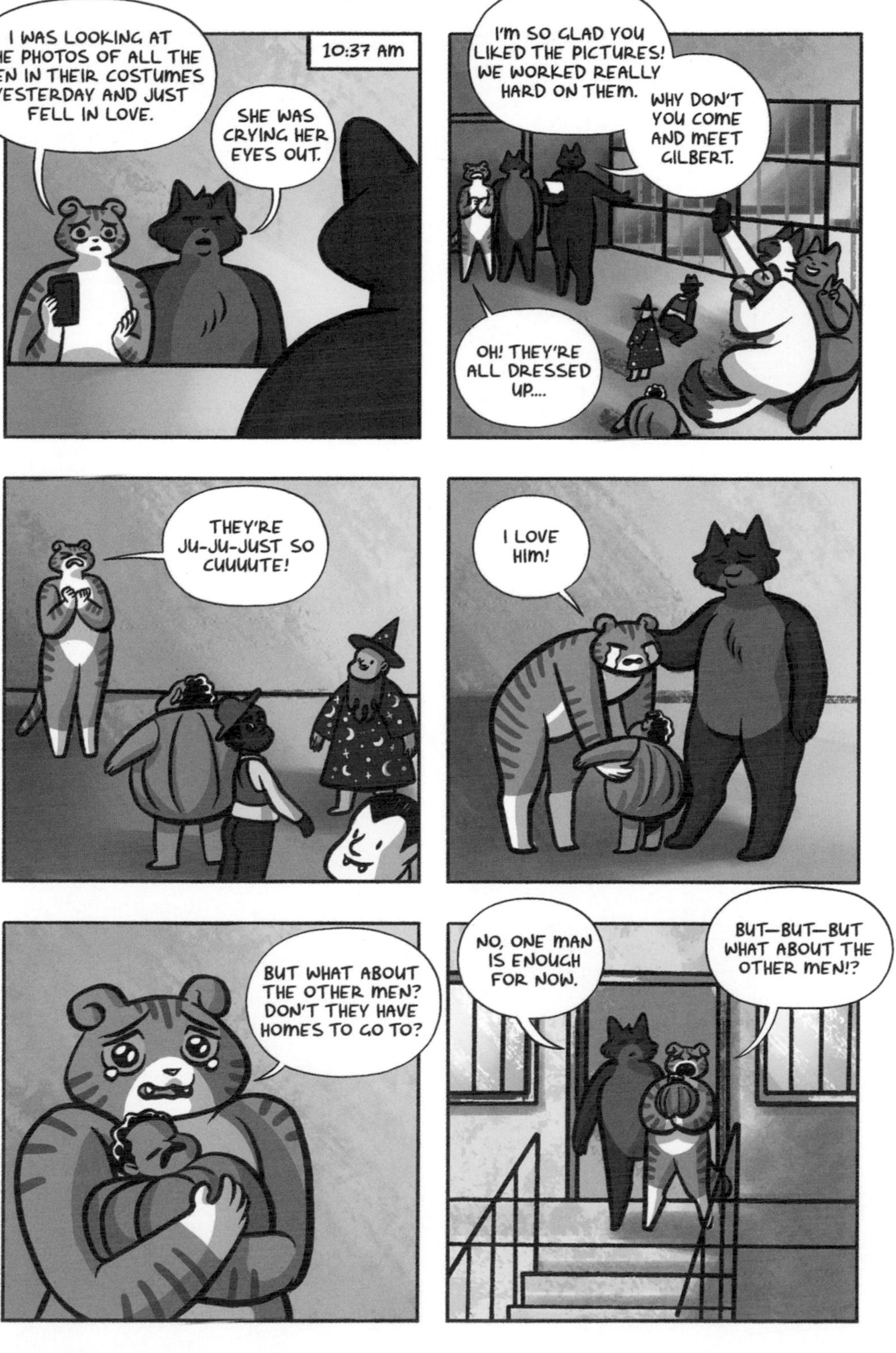

10:37 am
I WAS LOOKING AT THE PHOTOS OF ALL THE MEN IN THEIR COSTUMES YESTERDAY AND JUST FELL IN LOVE.
SHE WAS CRYING HER EYES OUT.
I'M SO GLAD YOU LIKED THE PICTURES! WE WORKED REALLY HARD ON THEM.
WHY DON'T YOU COME AND MEET GILBERT.
OH! THEY'RE ALL DRESSED UP....
THEY'RE JU-JU-JUST SO CUUUUTE!
I LOVE HIM!
BUT WHAT ABOUT THE OTHER MEN? DON'T THEY HAVE HOMES TO GO TO?
NO, ONE MAN IS ENOUGH FOR NOW.
BUT—BUT—BUT WHAT ABOUT THE OTHER MEN!?

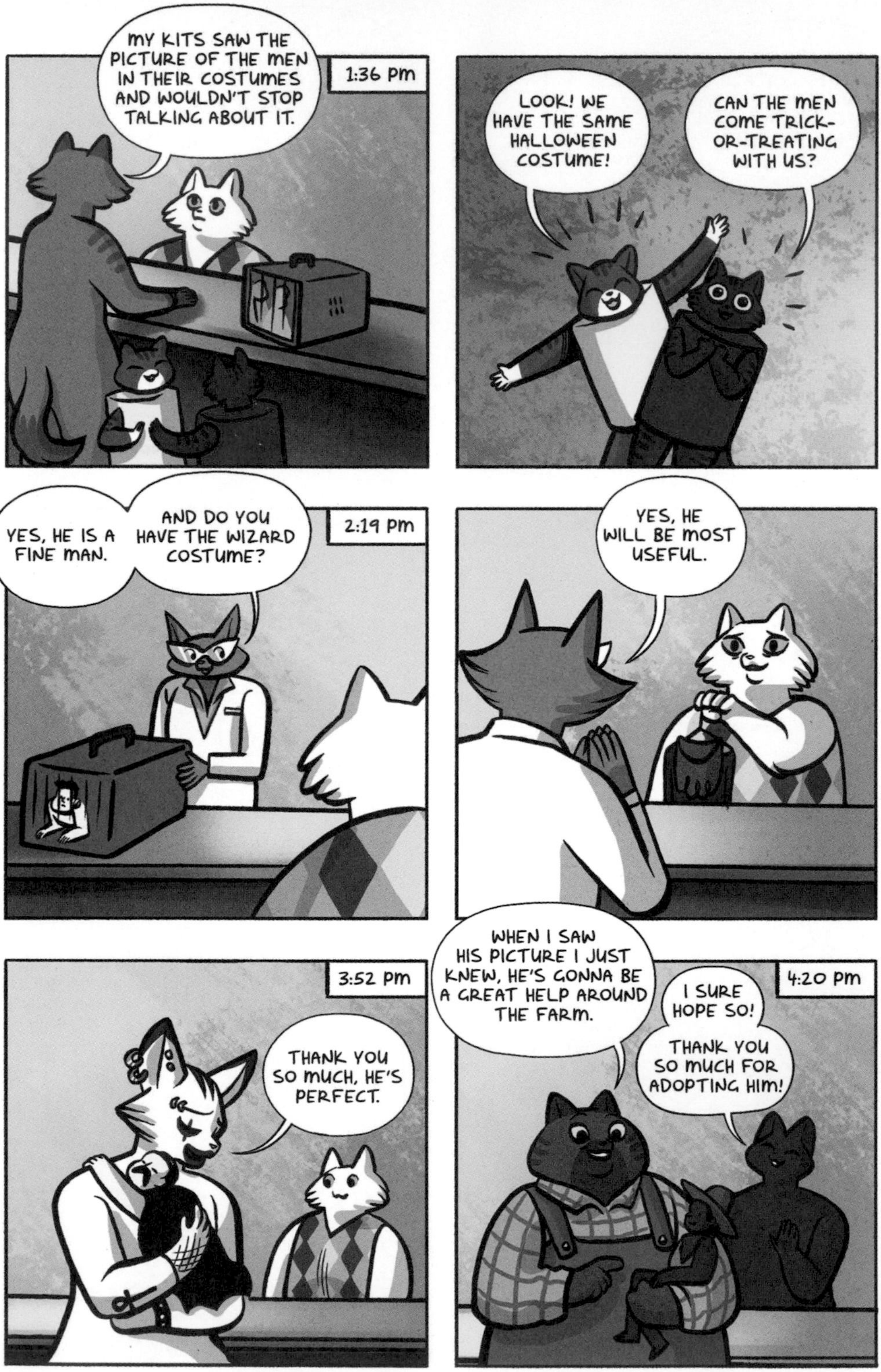

MY KITS SAW THE PICTURE OF THE MEN IN THEIR COSTUMES AND WOULDN'T STOP TALKING ABOUT IT.
1:36 pm
LOOK! WE HAVE THE SAME HALLOWEEN COSTUME!
CAN THE MEN COME TRICK-OR-TREATING WITH US?
YES, HE IS A FINE MAN.
AND DO YOU HAVE THE WIZARD COSTUME?
2:19 pm
YES, HE WILL BE MOST USEFUL.
3:52 pm
THANK YOU SO MUCH, HE'S PERFECT.
WHEN I SAW HIS PICTURE I JUST KNEW, HE'S GONNA BE A GREAT HELP AROUND THE FARM.
4:20 pm
I SURE HOPE SO!
THANK YOU SO MUCH FOR ADOPTING HIM!

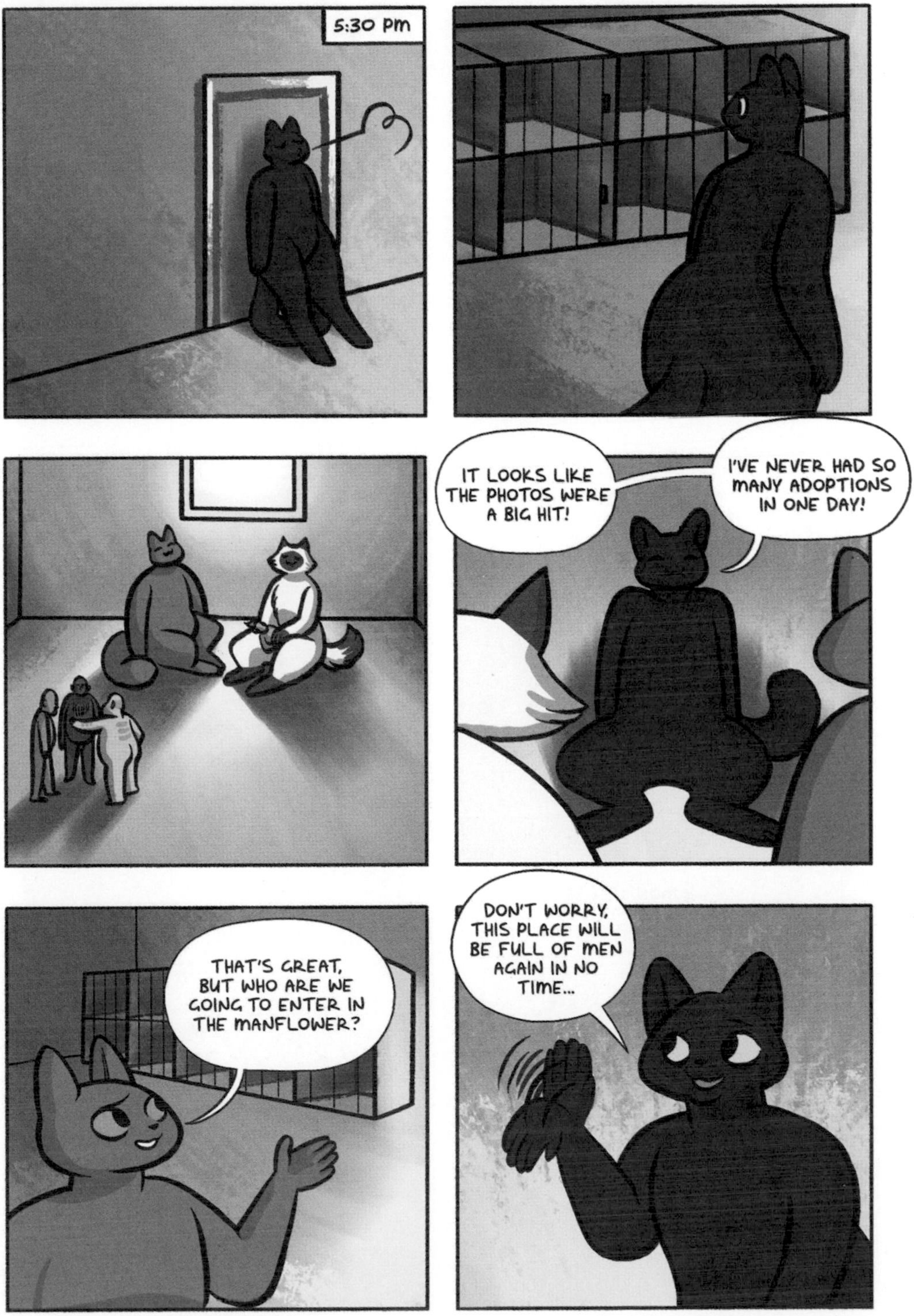
5:30 pm
IT LOOKS LIKE THE PHOTOS WERE A BIG HIT!
I'VE NEVER HAD SO MANY ADOPTIONS IN ONE DAY!
THAT'S GREAT, BUT WHO ARE WE GOING TO ENTER IN THE MANFLOWER?
DON'T WORRY, THIS PLACE WILL BE FULL OF MEN AGAIN IN NO TIME...

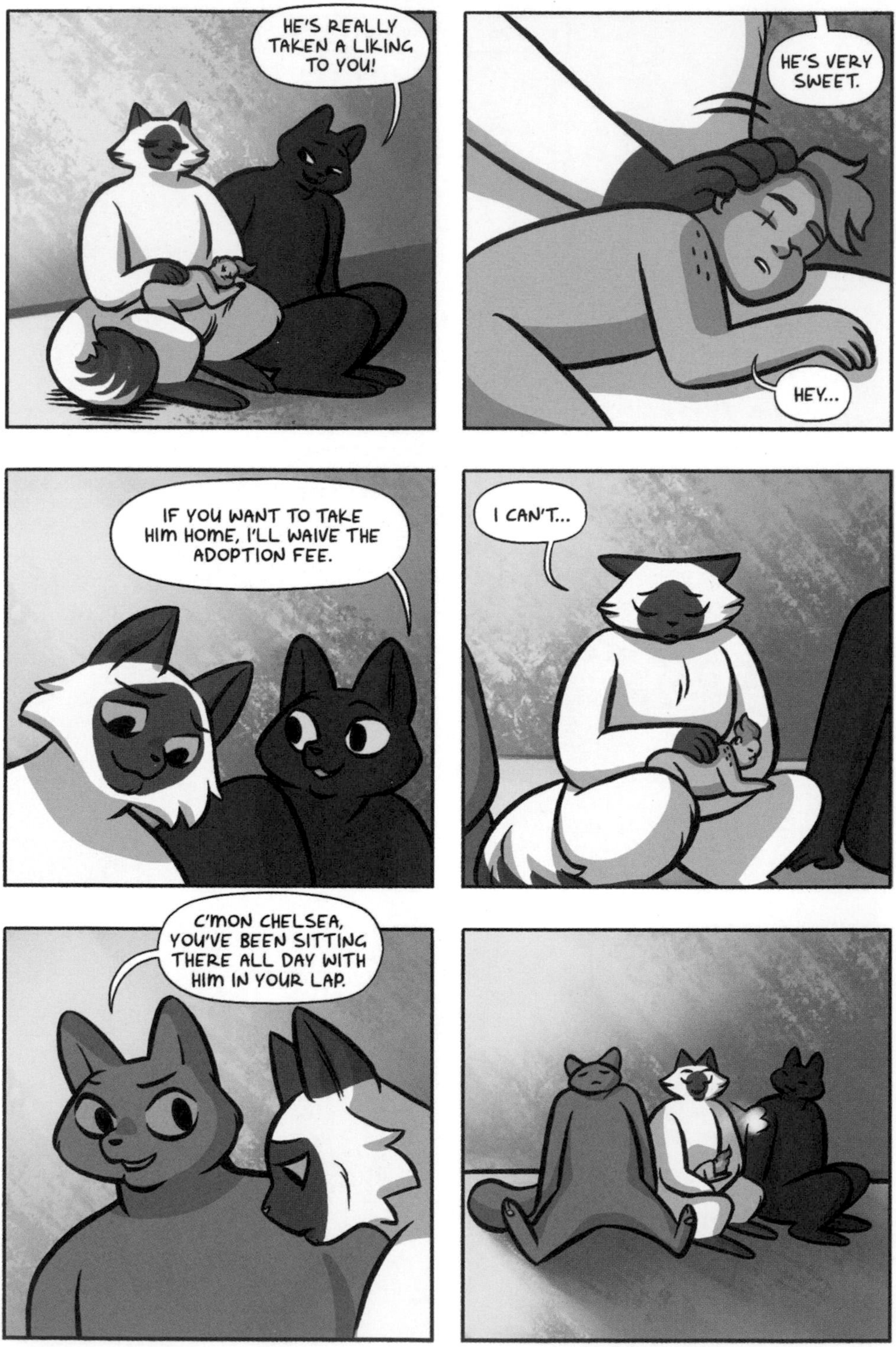
HE'S REALLY TAKEN A LIKING TO YOU!
HE'S VERY SWEET.
HEY...
IF YOU WANT TO TAKE HIM HOME, I'LL WAIVE THE ADOPTION FEE.
I CAN'T...
C'MON CHELSEA, YOU'VE BEEN SITTING THERE ALL DAY WITH HIM IN YOUR LAP.

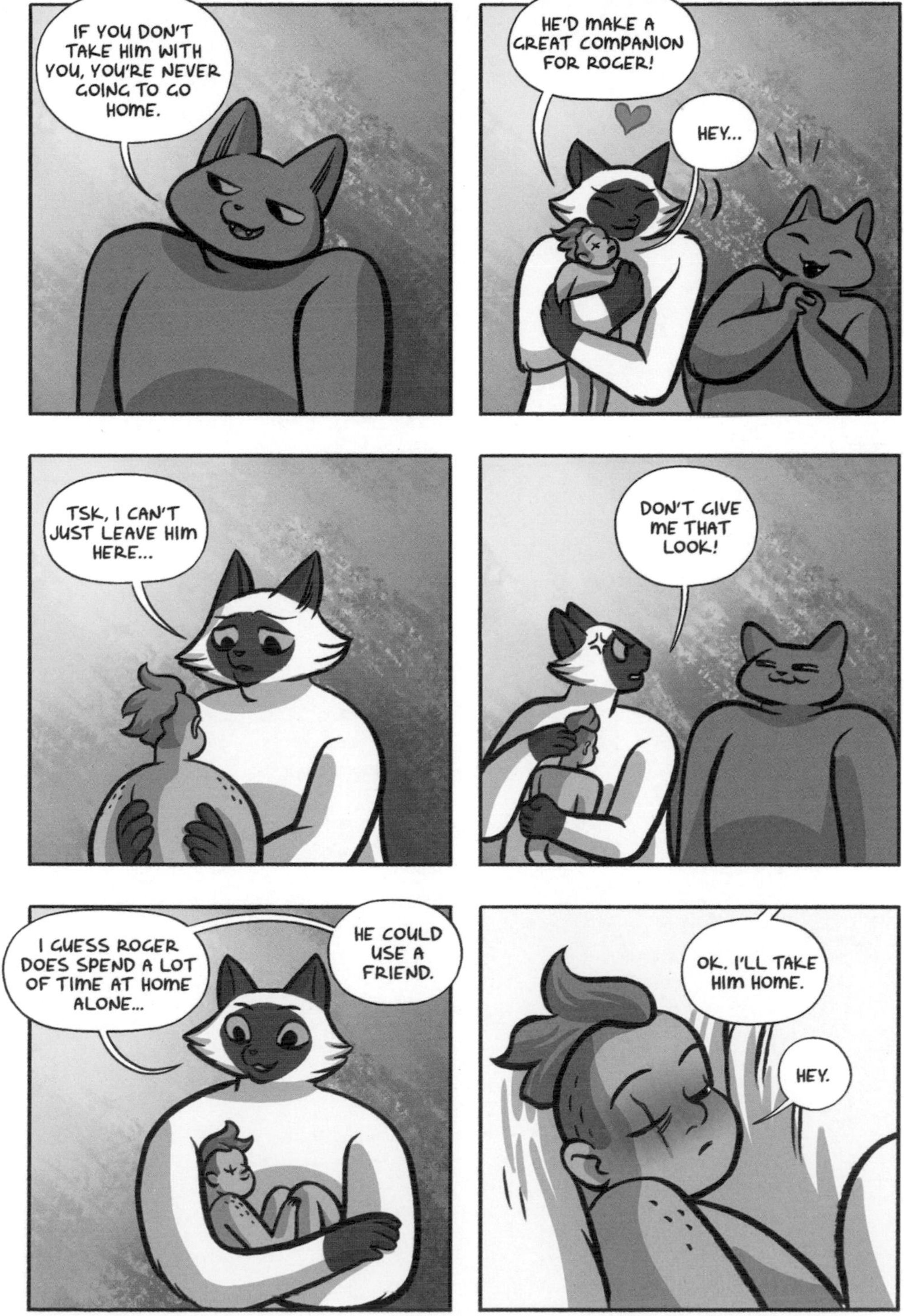
IF YOU DON'T TAKE HIM WITH YOU, YOU'RE NEVER GOING TO GO HOME.
HE'D MAKE A GREAT COMPANION FOR ROGER!
HEY...
TSK, I CAN'T JUST LEAVE HIM HERE...
DON'T GIVE ME THAT LOOK!
I GUESS ROGER DOES SPEND A LOT OF TIME AT HOME ALONE...
HE COULD USE A FRIEND.
OK. I'LL TAKE HIM HOME.
HEY.

PART THREE

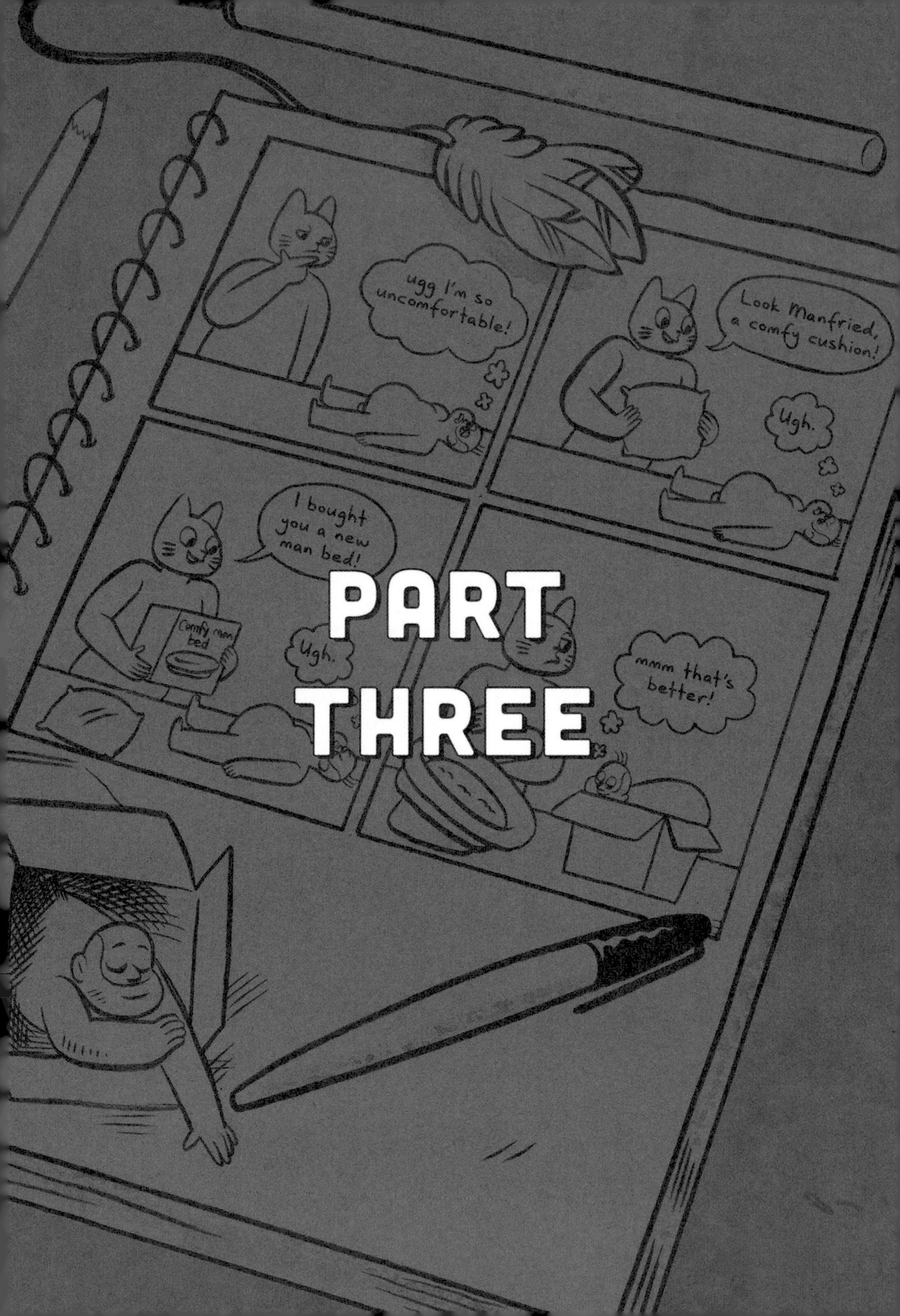

ugg I'm so uncomfortable!
Look Manfried, a comfy cushion!
Ugh.
I bought you a new man bed!
Comfy man bed
Ugh.
mmm that's better!

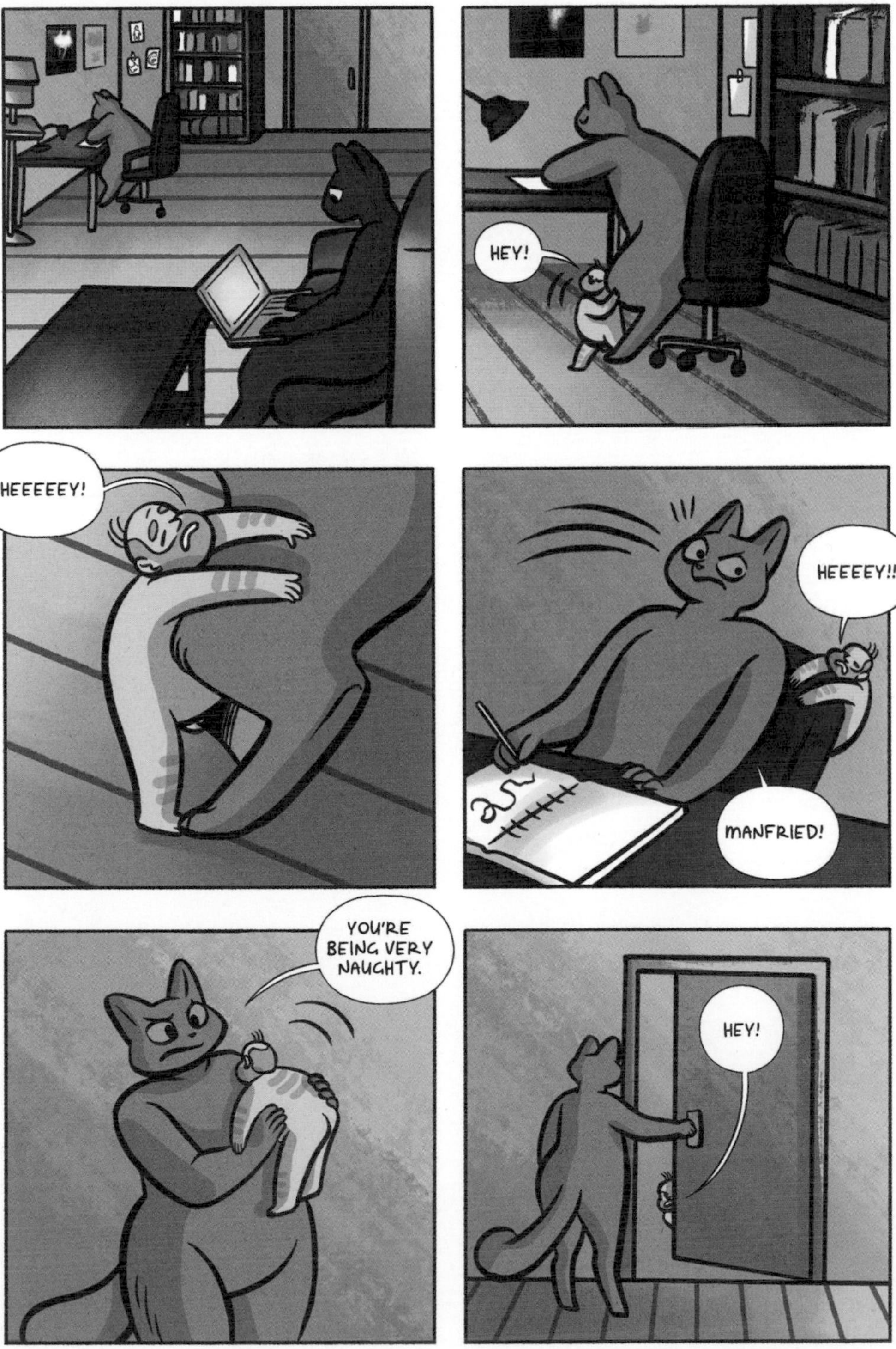
HEY!
HEEEEEY!
HEEEEY!!
MANFRIED!
YOU'RE BEING VERY NAUGHTY.
HEY!

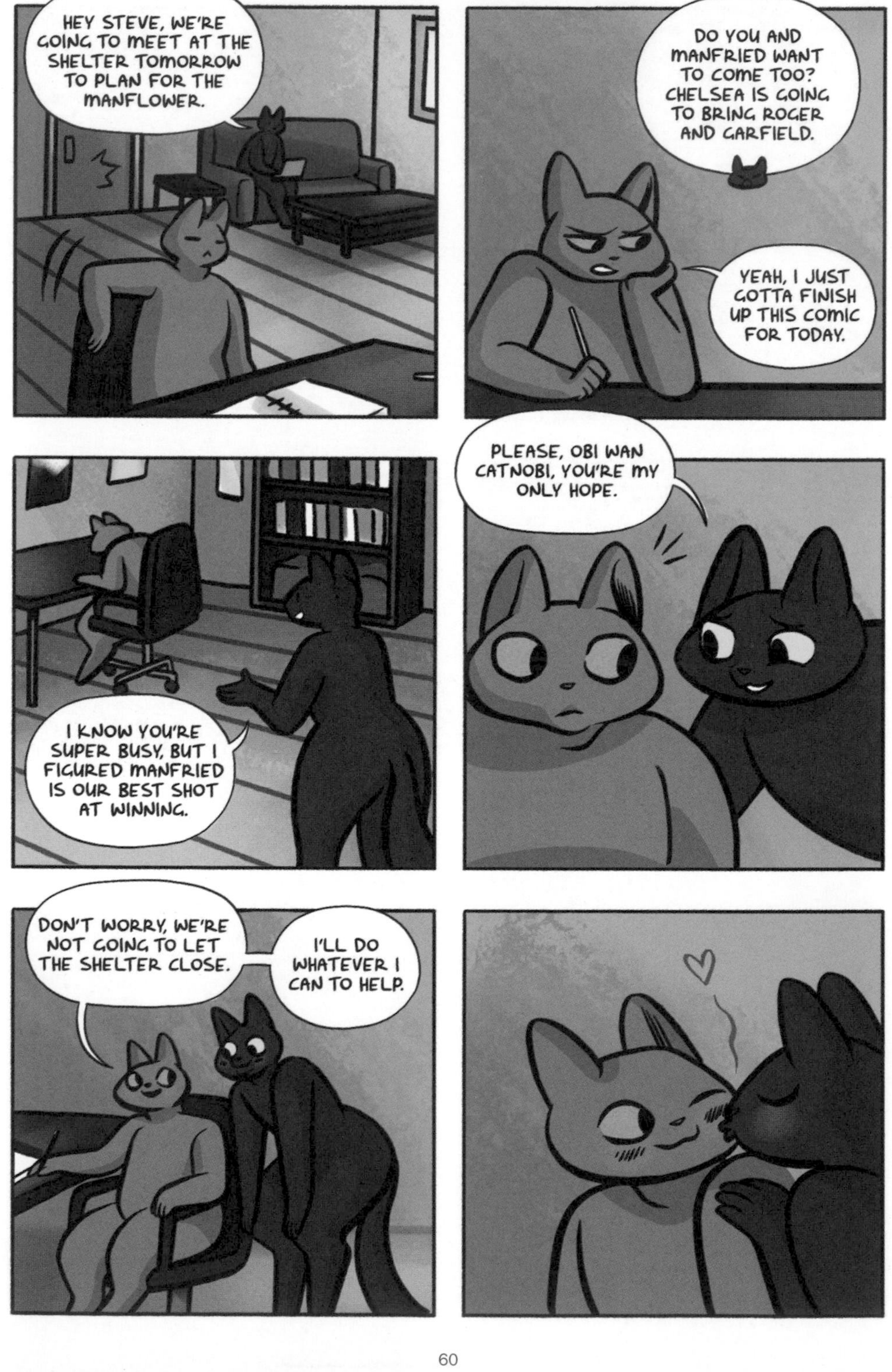
HEY STEVE, WE'RE GOING TO MEET AT THE SHELTER TOMORROW TO PLAN FOR THE MANFLOWER.
DO YOU AND MANFRIED WANT TO COME TOO? CHELSEA IS GOING TO BRING ROGER AND GARFIELD.
YEAH, I JUST GOTTA FINISH UP THIS COMIC FOR TODAY.
I KNOW YOU'RE SUPER BUSY, BUT I FIGURED MANFRIED IS OUR BEST SHOT AT WINNING.
PLEASE, OBI WAN CATNOBI, YOU'RE MY ONLY HOPE.
DON'T WORRY, WE'RE NOT GOING TO LET THE SHELTER CLOSE.
I'LL DO WHATEVER I CAN TO HELP.

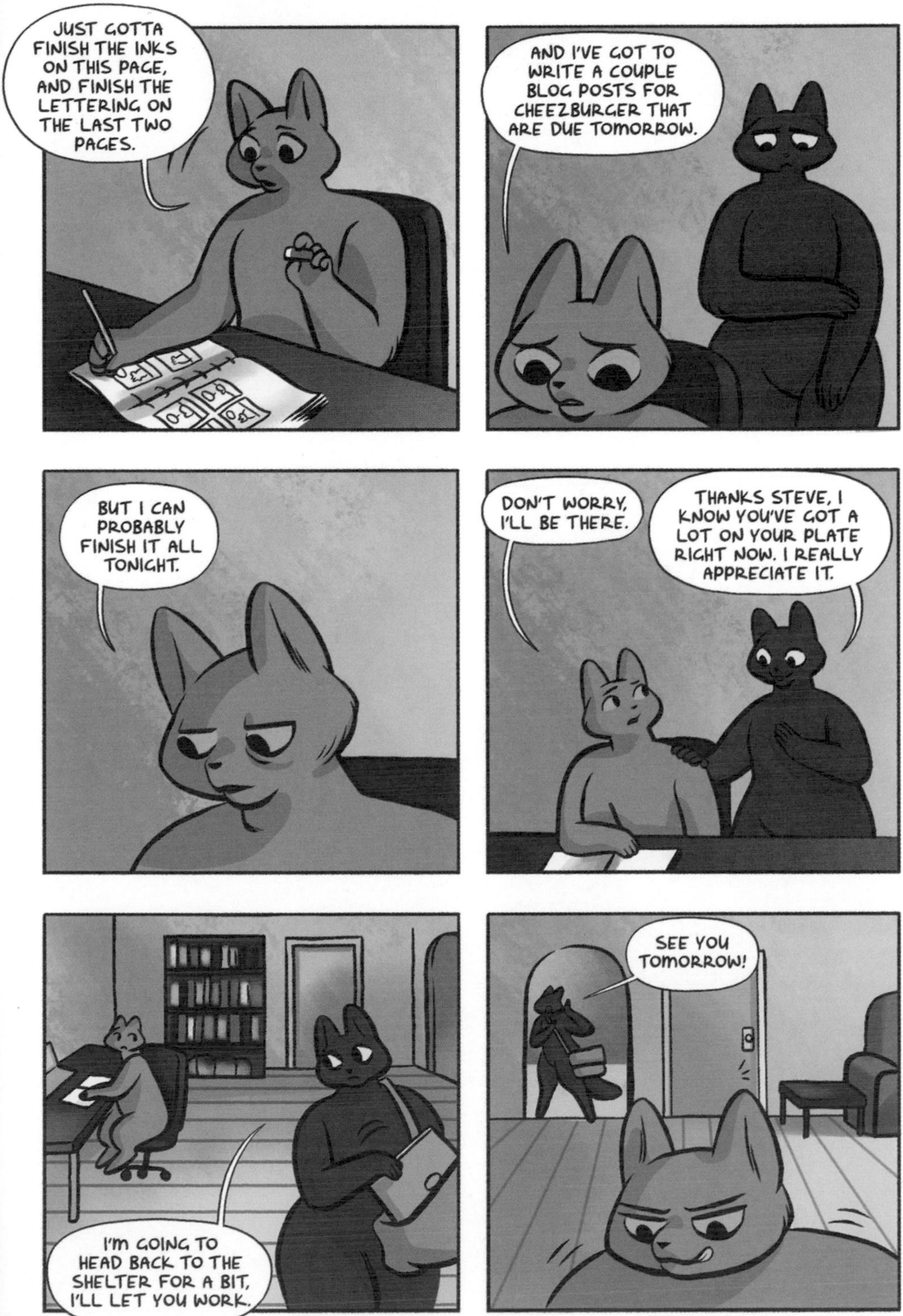
JUST GOTTA FINISH THE INKS ON THIS PAGE, AND FINISH THE LETTERING ON THE LAST TWO PAGES.
AND I'VE GOT TO WRITE A COUPLE BLOG POSTS FOR CHEEZBURGER THAT ARE DUE TOMORROW.
BUT I CAN PROBABLY FINISH IT ALL TONIGHT.
DON'T WORRY, I'LL BE THERE.
THANKS STEVE, I KNOW YOU'VE GOT A LOT ON YOUR PLATE RIGHT NOW. I REALLY APPRECIATE IT.
I'M GOING TO HEAD BACK TO THE SHELTER FOR A BIT, I'LL LET YOU WORK.
SEE YOU TOMORROW!

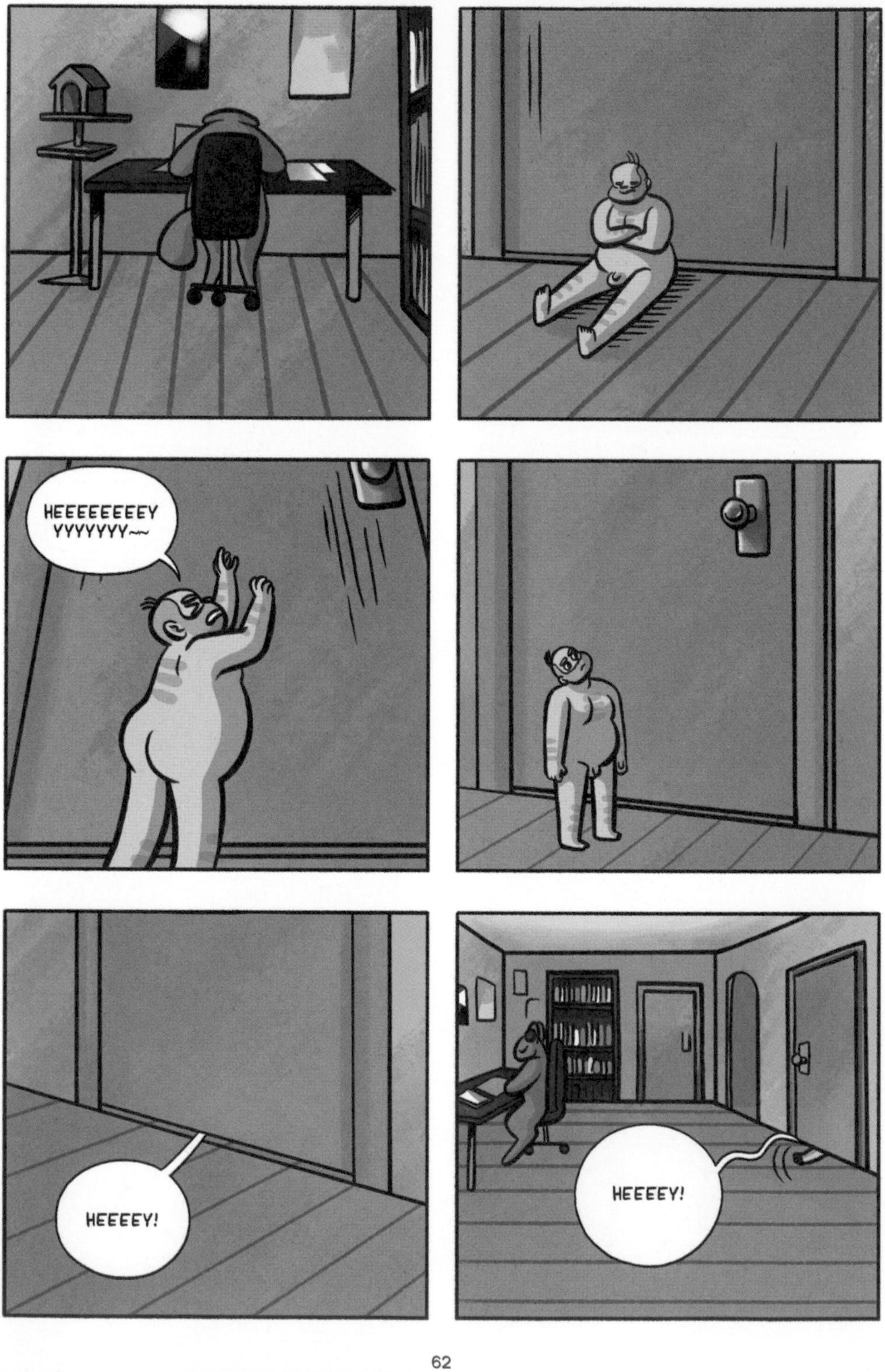
HEEEEEEEEY YYYYYYY~~
HEEEEY!
HEEEEY!

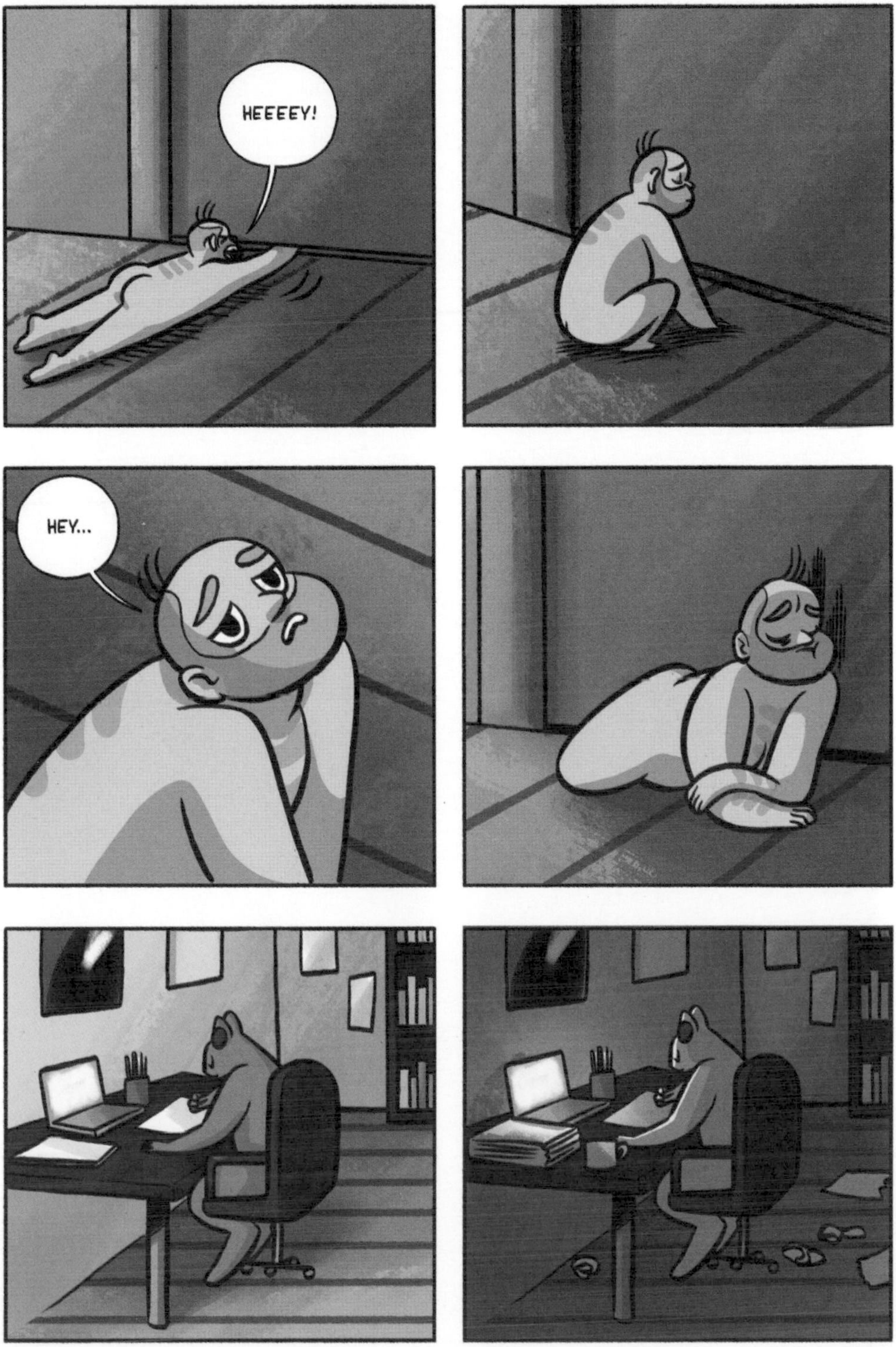
HEEEEY!
HEY...

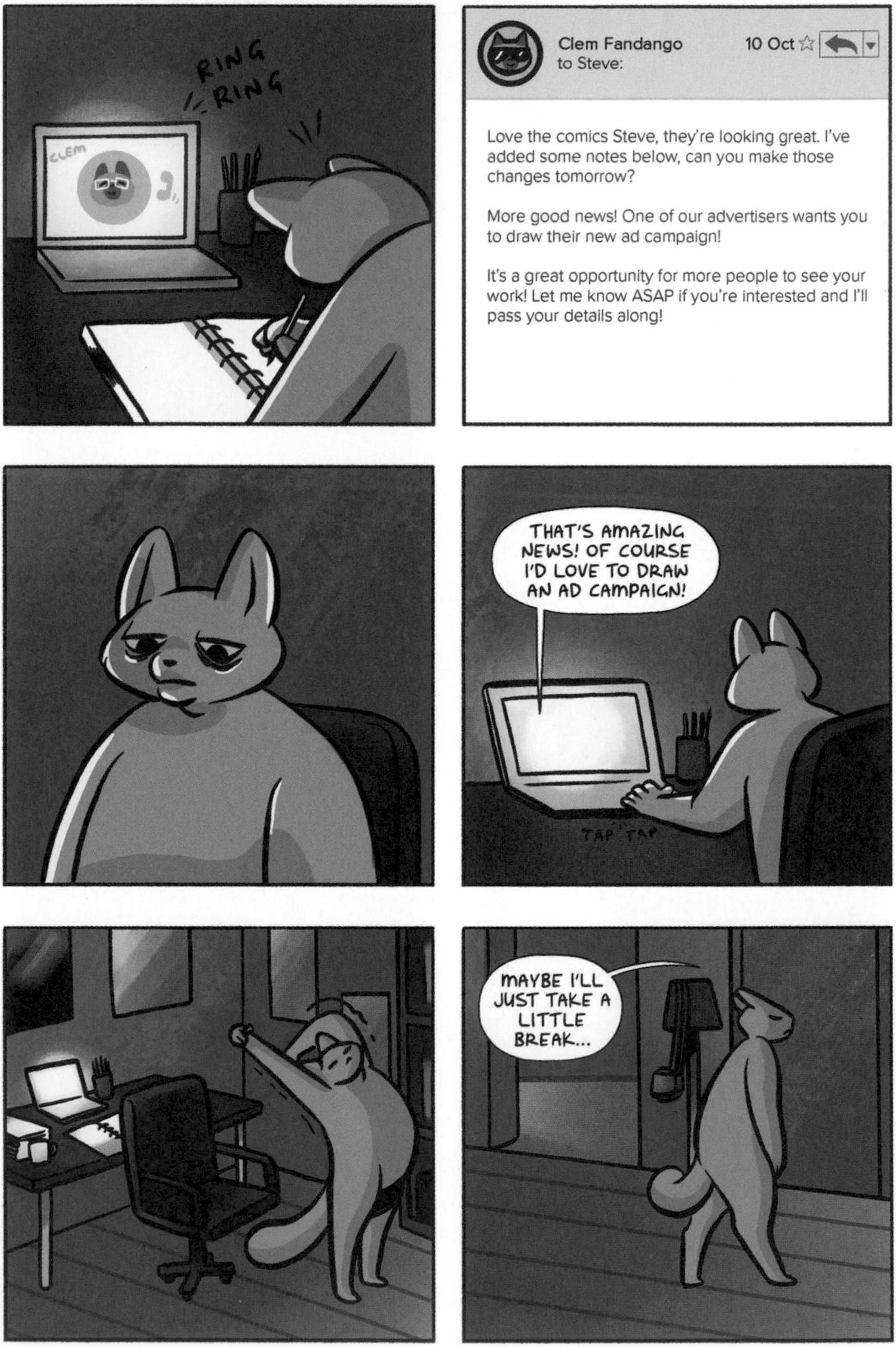
RING RING
CLEM
Clem Fandango
to Steve:
10 Oct
Love the comics Steve, they're looking great. I've added some notes below, can you make those changes tomorrow?
More good news! One of our advertisers wants you to draw their new ad campaign!
It's a great opportunity for more people to see your work! Let me know ASAP if you're interested and I'll pass your details along!
THAT'S AMAZING NEWS! OF COURSE I'D LOVE TO DRAW AN AD CAMPAIGN!
TAP TAP
MAYBE I'LL JUST TAKE A LITTLE BREAK...

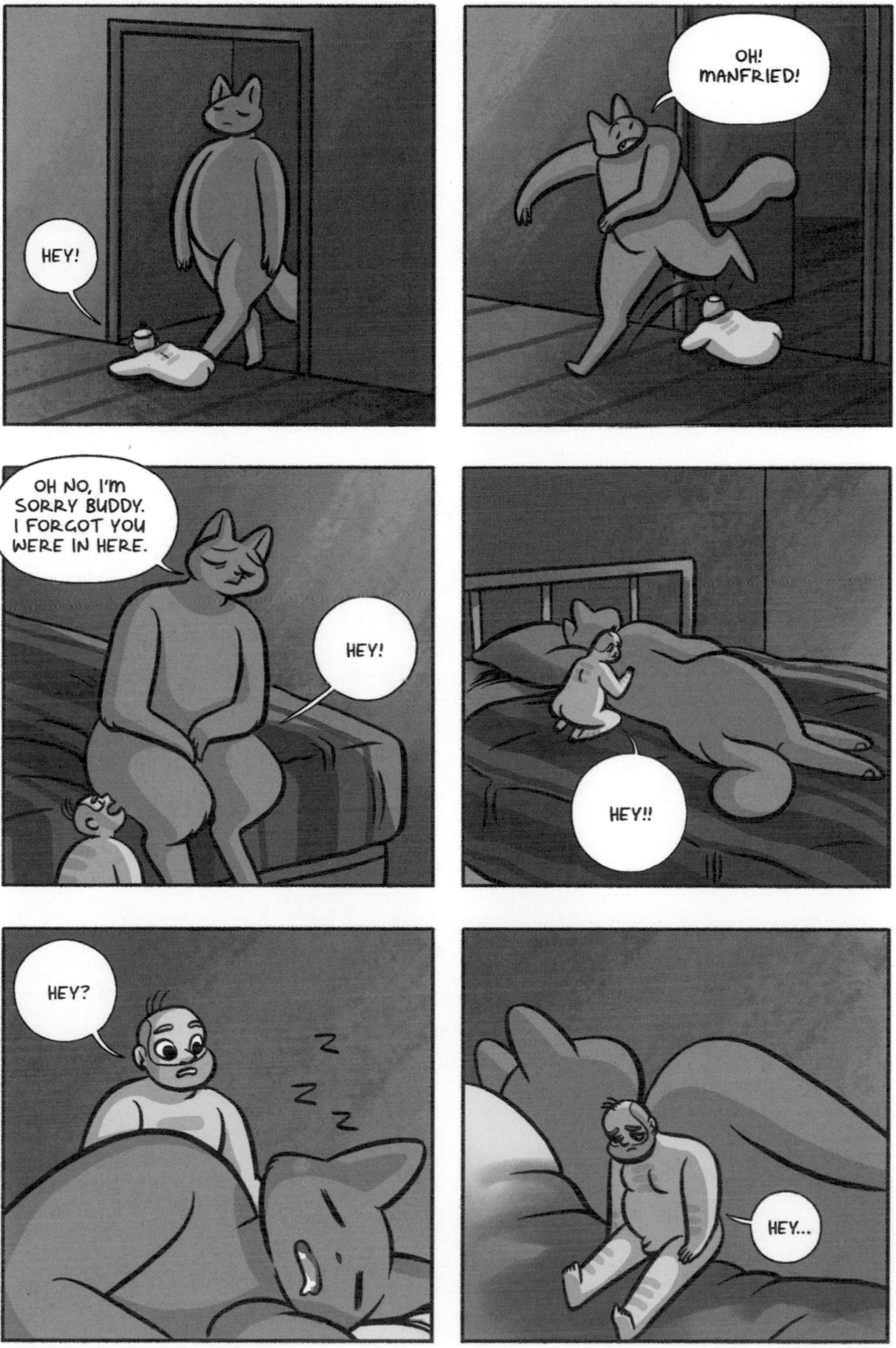
HEY!
OH! MANFRIED!
OH NO, I'M SORRY BUDDY. I FORGOT YOU WERE IN HERE.
HEY!
HEY!!
HEY?
Z Z Z
HEY...

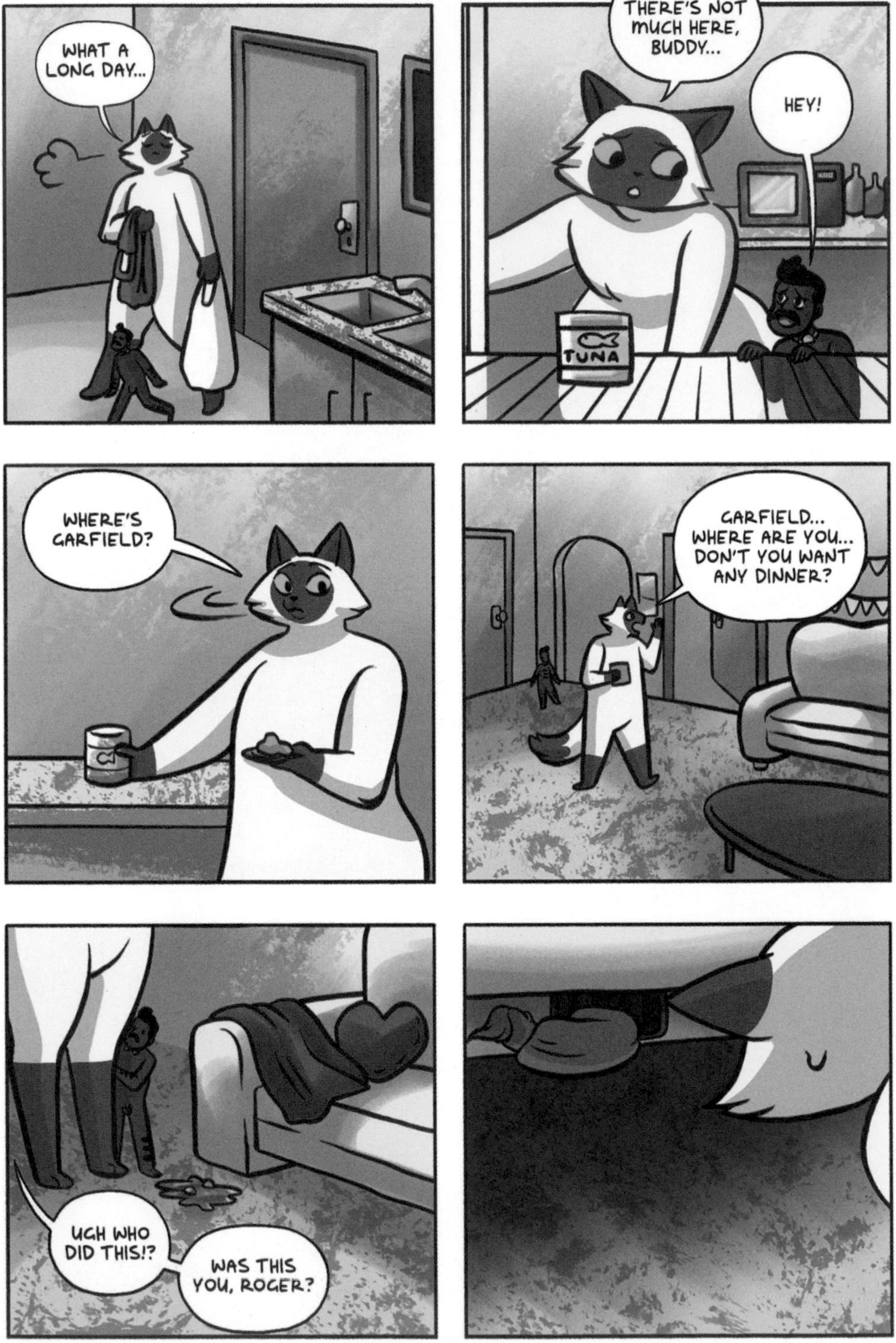
WHAT A LONG DAY...
THERE'S NOT MUCH HERE, BUDDY...
HEY!
WHERE'S GARFIELD?
GARFIELD... WHERE ARE YOU... DON'T YOU WANT ANY DINNER?
UGH WHO DID THIS!?
WAS THIS YOU, ROGER?

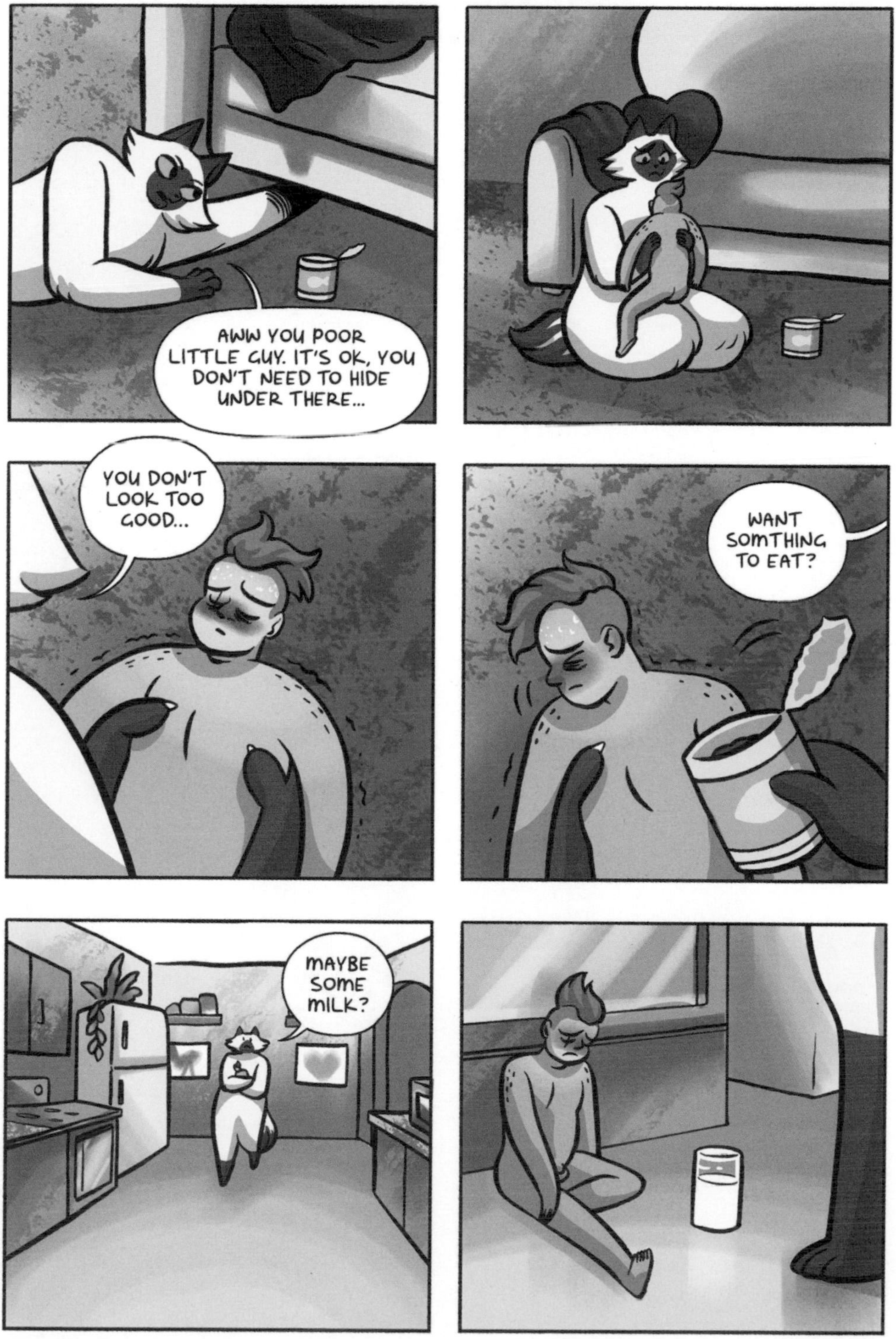
AWW YOU POOR LITTLE GUY. IT'S OK, YOU DON'T NEED TO HIDE UNDER THERE...
YOU DON'T LOOK TOO GOOD...
WANT SOMTHING TO EAT?
MAYBE SOME MILK?

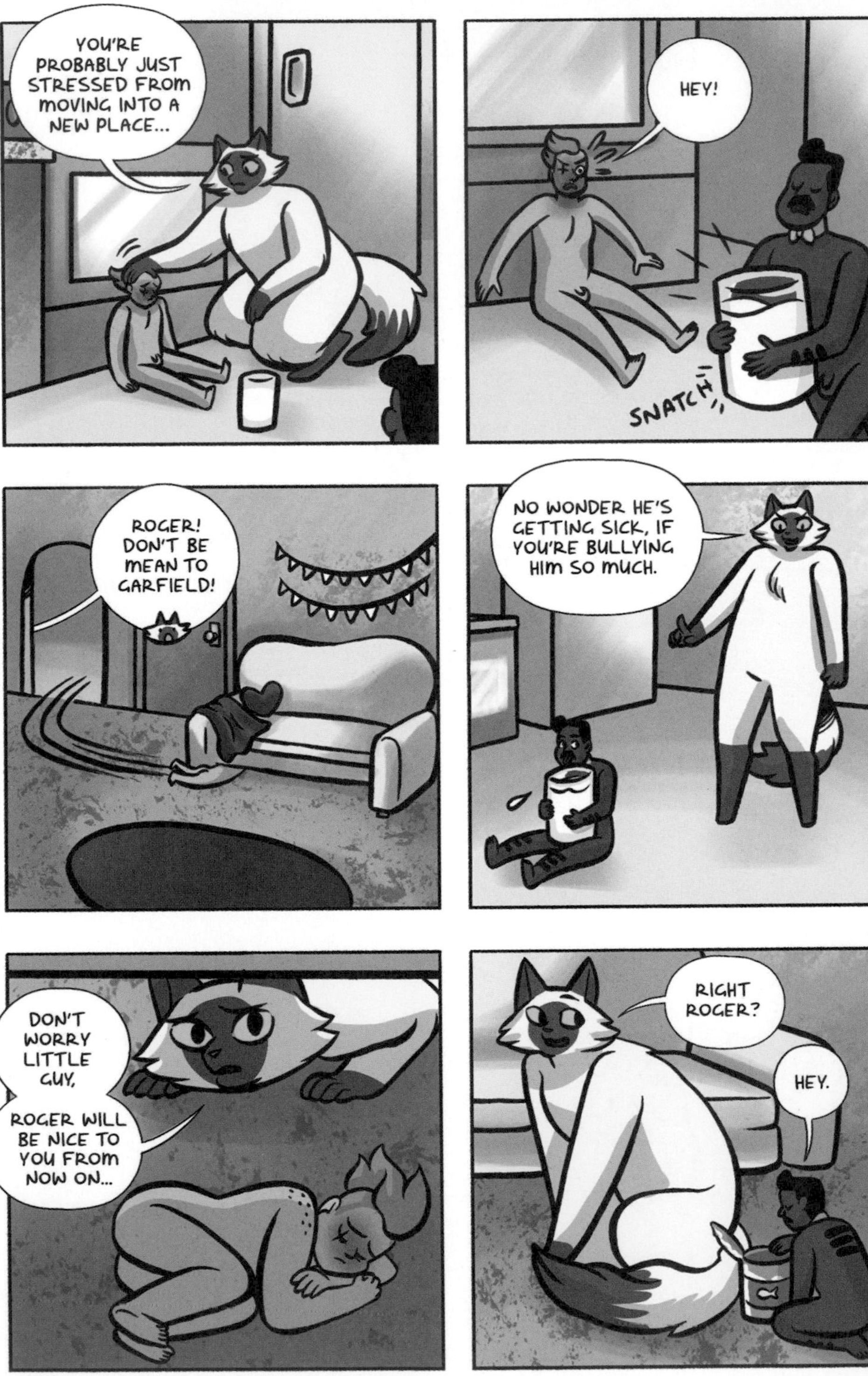
YOU'RE PROBABLY JUST STRESSED FROM MOVING INTO A NEW PLACE...
HEY!
SNATCH
ROGER! DON'T BE MEAN TO GARFIELD!
NO WONDER HE'S GETTING SICK, IF YOU'RE BULLYING HIM SO MUCH.
DON'T WORRY LITTLE GUY,
ROGER WILL BE NICE TO YOU FROM NOW ON...
RIGHT ROGER?
HEY.

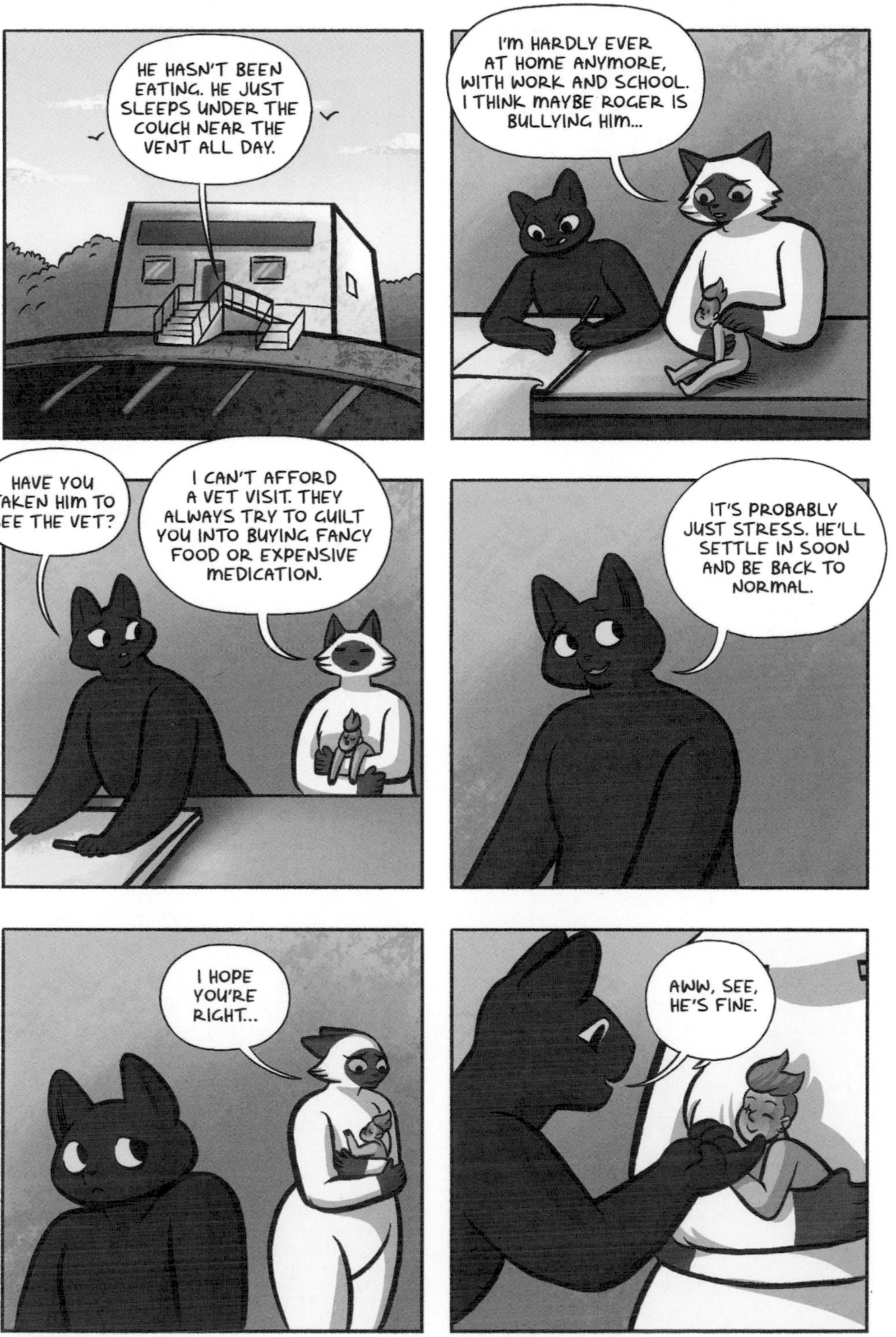
HE HASN'T BEEN EATING. HE JUST SLEEPS UNDER THE COUCH NEAR THE VENT ALL DAY.
I'M HARDLY EVER AT HOME ANYMORE, WITH WORK AND SCHOOL. I THINK MAYBE ROGER IS BULLYING HIM...
HAVE YOU TAKEN HIM TO SEE THE VET?
I CAN'T AFFORD A VET VISIT. THEY ALWAYS TRY TO GUILT YOU INTO BUYING FANCY FOOD OR EXPENSIVE MEDICATION.
IT'S PROBABLY JUST STRESS. HE'LL SETTLE IN SOON AND BE BACK TO NORMAL.
I HOPE YOU'RE RIGHT...
AWW, SEE, HE'S FINE.

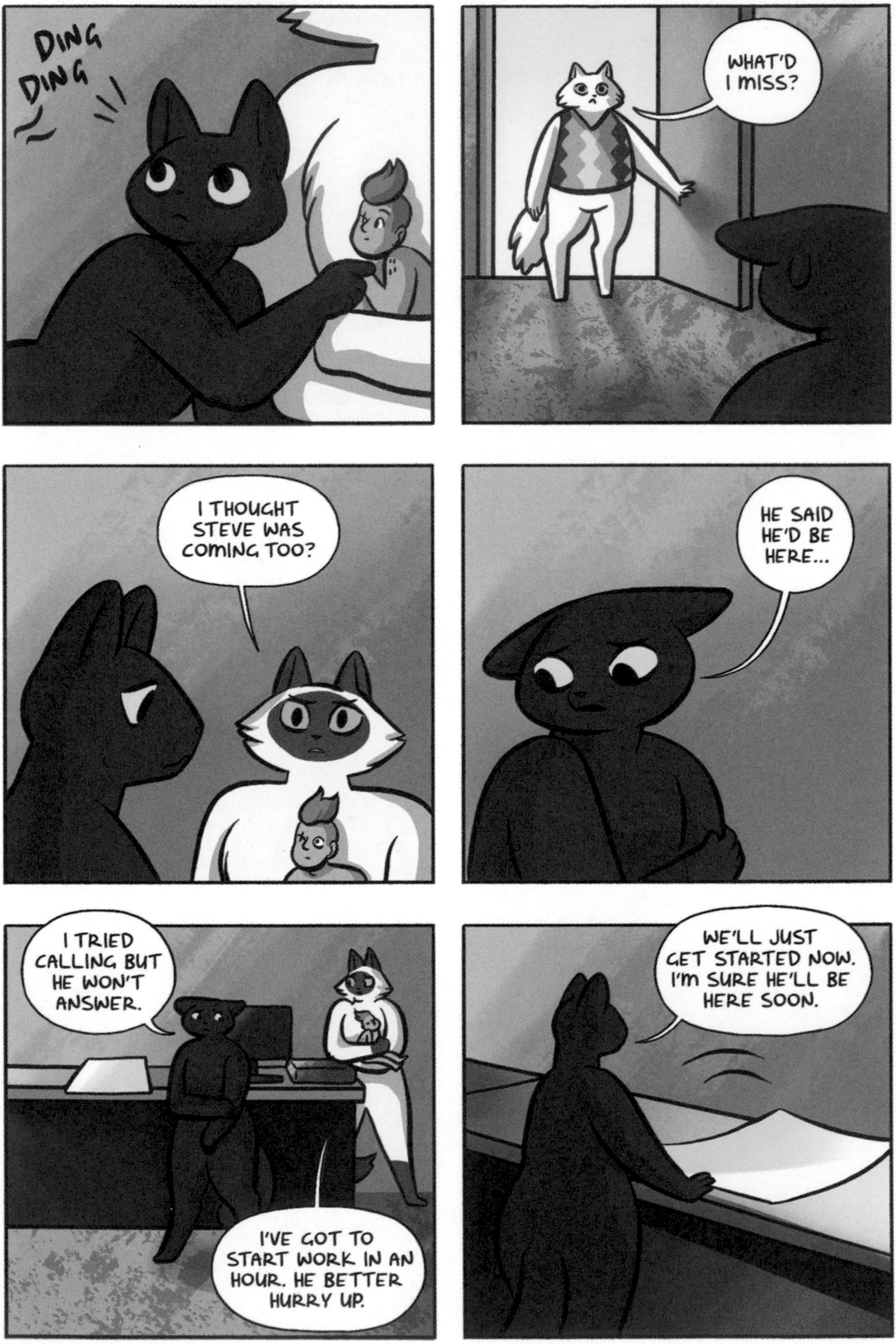
DING DING
WHAT'D I MISS?
I THOUGHT STEVE WAS COMING TOO?
HE SAID HE'D BE HERE...
I TRIED CALLING BUT HE WON'T ANSWER.
I'VE GOT TO START WORK IN AN HOUR. HE BETTER HURRY UP.
WE'LL JUST GET STARTED NOW. I'M SURE HE'LL BE HERE SOON.

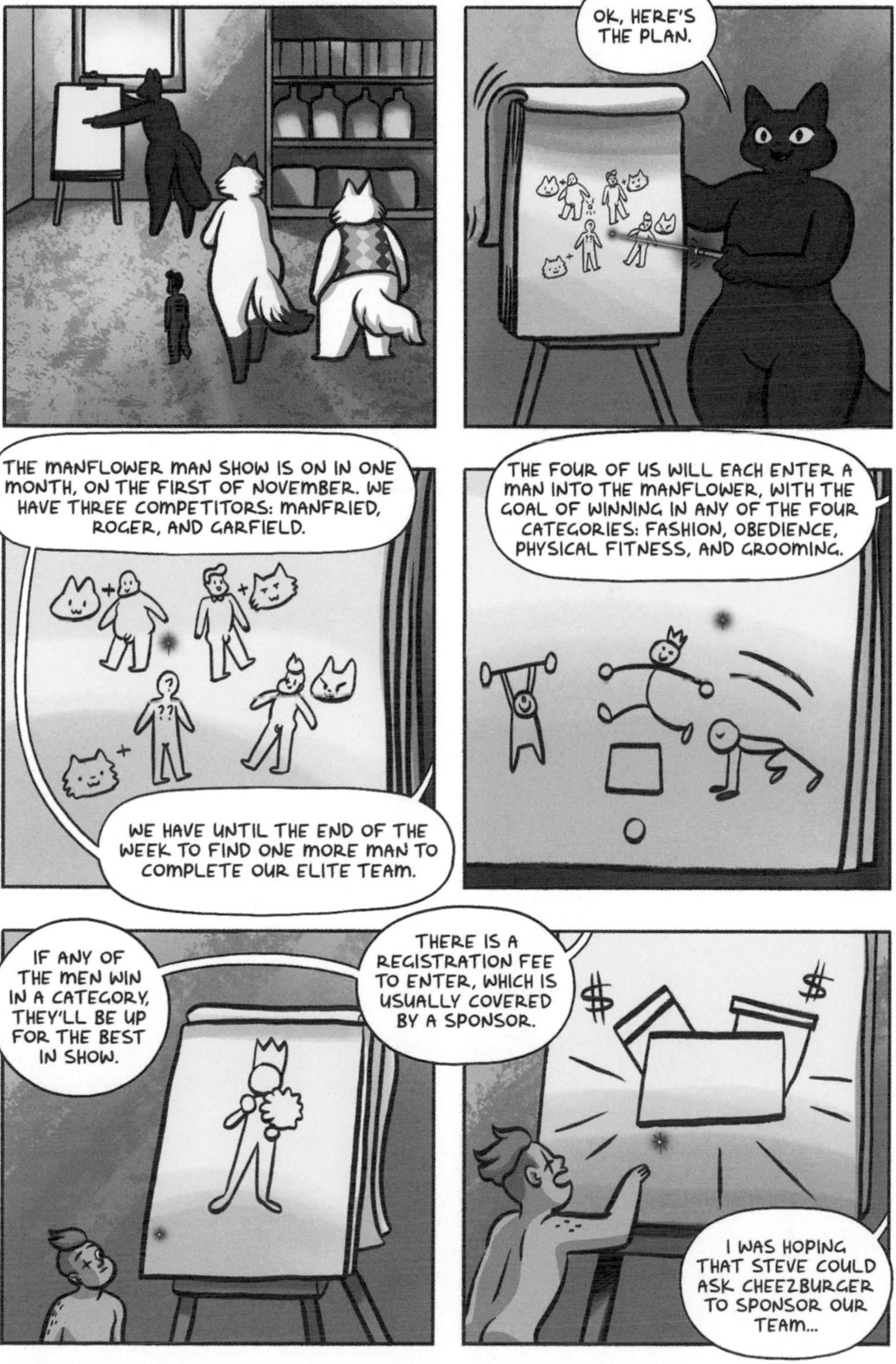
OK, HERE'S THE PLAN.
THE MANFLOWER MAN SHOW IS ON IN ONE MONTH, ON THE FIRST OF NOVEMBER. WE HAVE THREE COMPETITORS: MANFRIED, ROGER, AND GARFIELD.
WE HAVE UNTIL THE END OF THE WEEK TO FIND ONE MORE MAN TO COMPLETE OUR ELITE TEAM.
THE FOUR OF US WILL EACH ENTER A MAN INTO THE MANFLOWER, WITH THE GOAL OF WINNING IN ANY OF THE FOUR CATEGORIES: FASHION, OBEDIENCE, PHYSICAL FITNESS, AND GROOMING.
IF ANY OF THE MEN WIN IN A CATEGORY, THEY'LL BE UP FOR THE BEST IN SHOW.
THERE IS A REGISTRATION FEE TO ENTER, WHICH IS USUALLY COVERED BY A SPONSOR.
$
$
I WAS HOPING THAT STEVE COULD ASK CHEEZBURGER TO SPONSOR OUR TEAM...

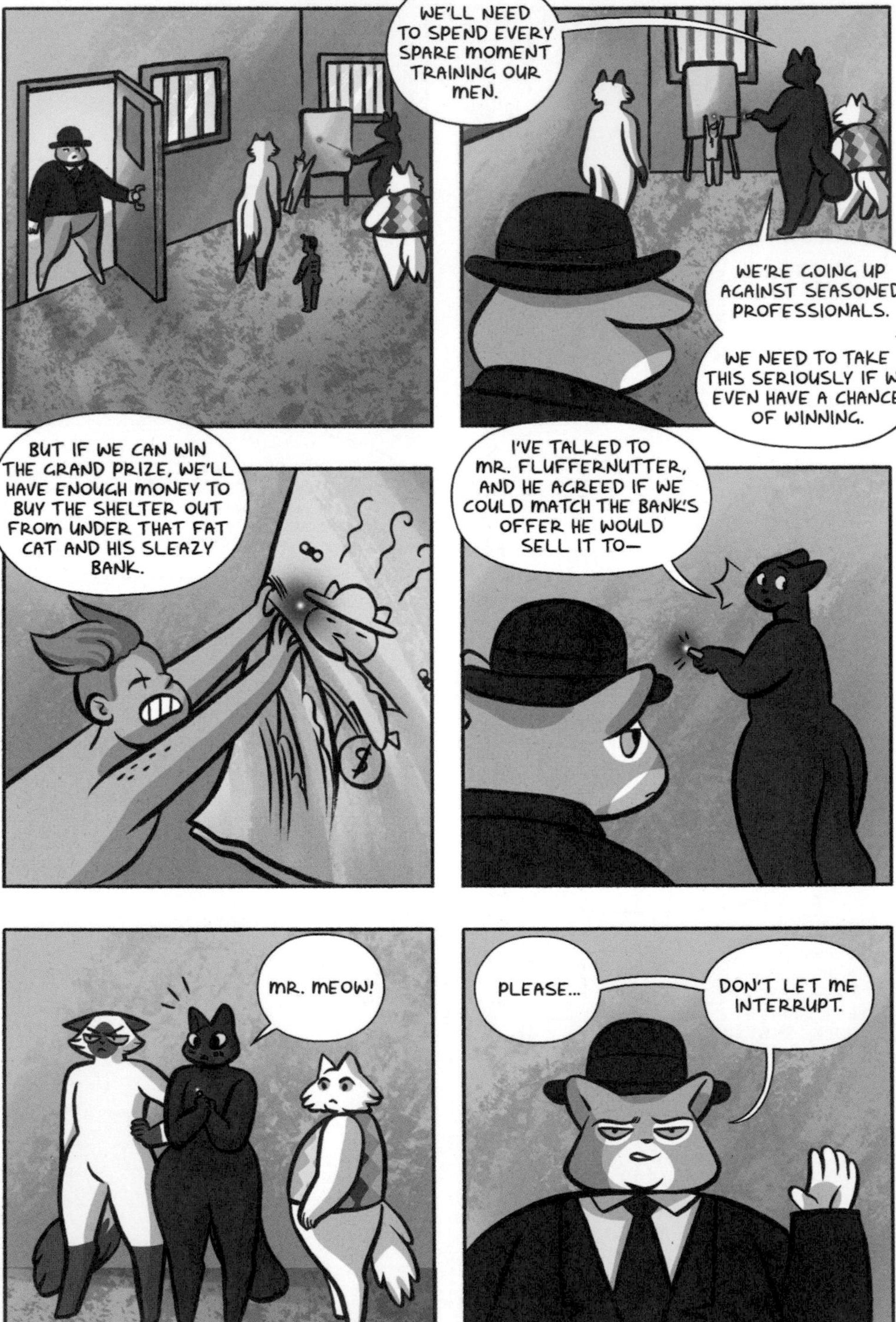

WE'LL NEED TO SPEND EVERY SPARE MOMENT TRAINING OUR MEN.
WE'RE GOING UP AGAINST SEASONED PROFESSIONALS.
WE NEED TO TAKE THIS SERIOUSLY IF WE EVEN HAVE A CHANCE OF WINNING.
BUT IF WE CAN WIN THE GRAND PRIZE, WE'LL HAVE ENOUGH MONEY TO BUY THE SHELTER OUT FROM UNDER THAT FAT CAT AND HIS SLEAZY BANK.
I'VE TALKED TO MR. FLUFFERNUTTER, AND HE AGREED IF WE COULD MATCH THE BANK'S OFFER HE WOULD SELL IT TO—
MR. MEOW!
PLEASE...
DON'T LET ME INTERRUPT.

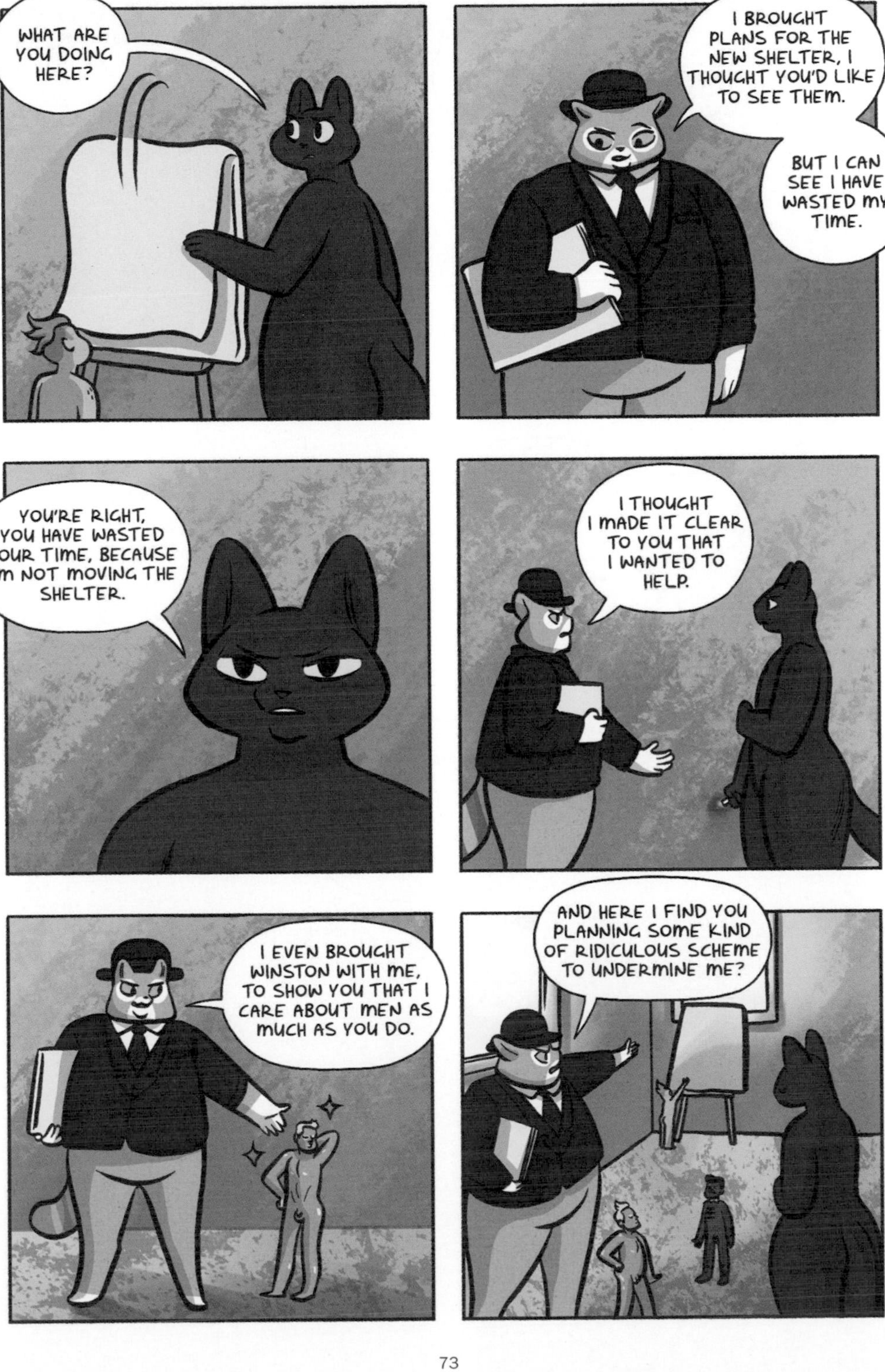
WHAT ARE YOU DOING HERE?
I BROUGHT PLANS FOR THE NEW SHELTER, I THOUGHT YOU'D LIKE TO SEE THEM.
BUT I CAN SEE I HAVE WASTED MY TIME.
YOU'RE RIGHT, YOU HAVE WASTED YOUR TIME, BECAUSE I'M NOT MOVING THE SHELTER.
I THOUGHT I MADE IT CLEAR TO YOU THAT I WANTED TO HELP.
I EVEN BROUGHT WINSTON WITH ME, TO SHOW YOU THAT I CARE ABOUT MEN AS MUCH AS YOU DO.
AND HERE I FIND YOU PLANNING SOME KIND OF RIDICULOUS SCHEME TO UNDERMINE ME?

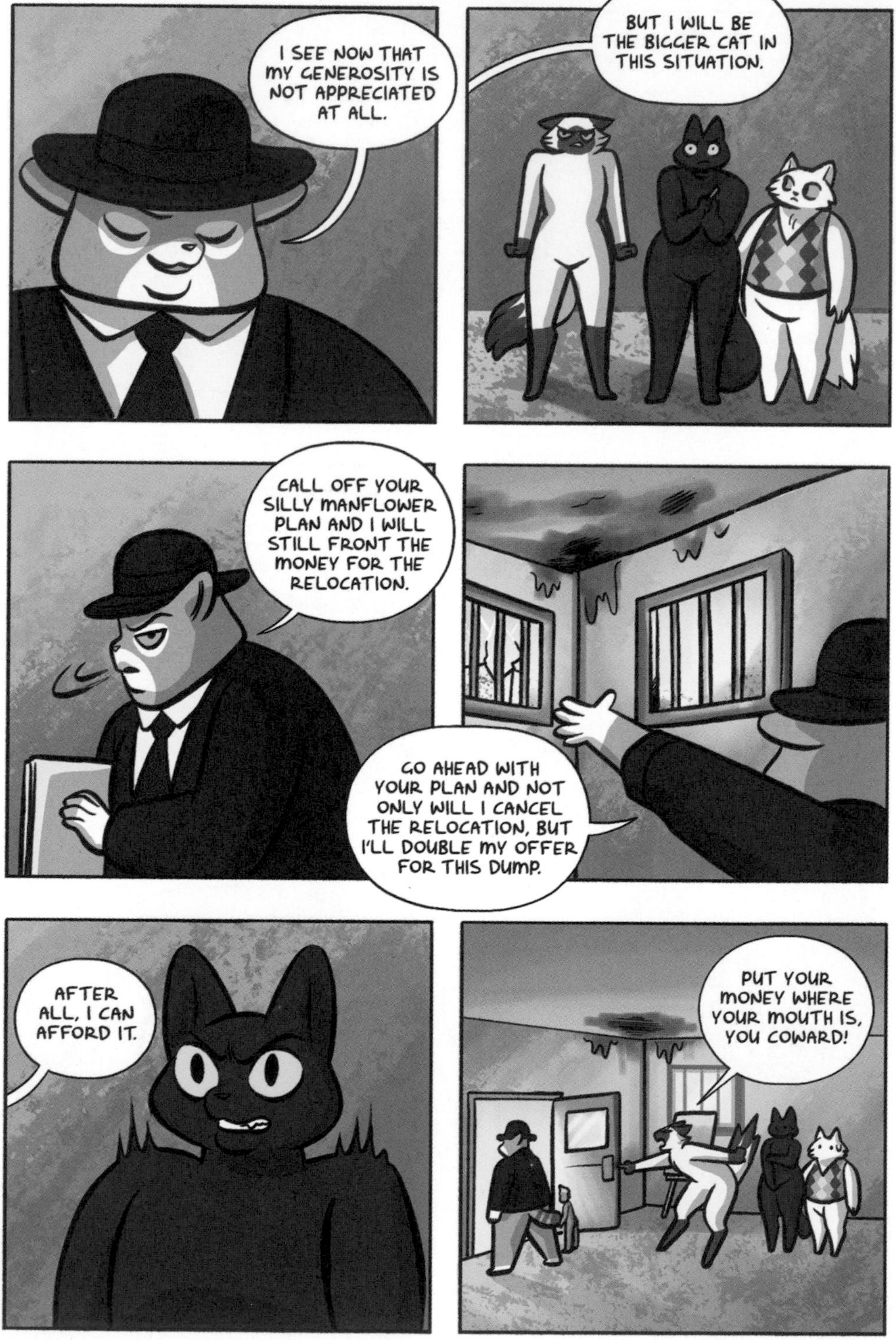
I SEE NOW THAT MY GENEROSITY IS NOT APPRECIATED AT ALL.
BUT I WILL BE THE BIGGER CAT IN THIS SITUATION.
CALL OFF YOUR SILLY MANFLOWER PLAN AND I WILL STILL FRONT THE MONEY FOR THE RELOCATION.
GO AHEAD WITH YOUR PLAN AND NOT ONLY WILL I CANCEL THE RELOCATION, BUT I'LL DOUBLE MY OFFER FOR THIS DUMP.
AFTER ALL, I CAN AFFORD IT.
PUT YOUR MONEY WHERE YOUR MOUTH IS, YOU COWARD!

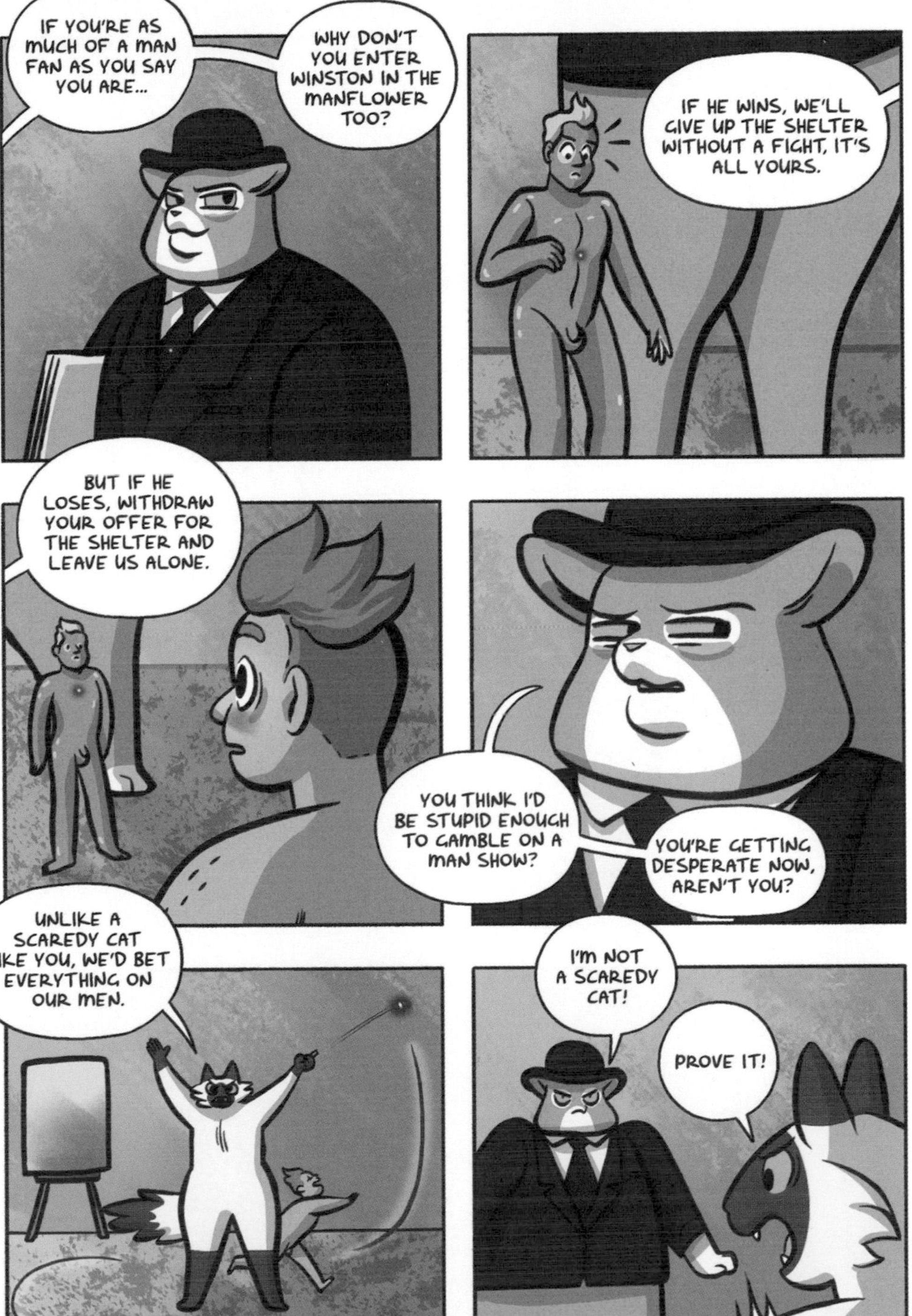
IF YOU'RE AS MUCH OF A MAN FAN AS YOU SAY YOU ARE...
WHY DON'T YOU ENTER WINSTON IN THE MANFLOWER TOO?
IF HE WINS, WE'LL GIVE UP THE SHELTER WITHOUT A FIGHT, IT'S ALL YOURS.
BUT IF HE LOSES, WITHDRAW YOUR OFFER FOR THE SHELTER AND LEAVE US ALONE.
YOU THINK I'D BE STUPID ENOUGH TO GAMBLE ON A MAN SHOW?
YOU'RE GETTING DESPERATE NOW, AREN'T YOU?
UNLIKE A SCAREDY CAT LIKE YOU, WE'D BET EVERYTHING ON OUR MEN.
I'M NOT A SCAREDY CAT!
PROVE IT!

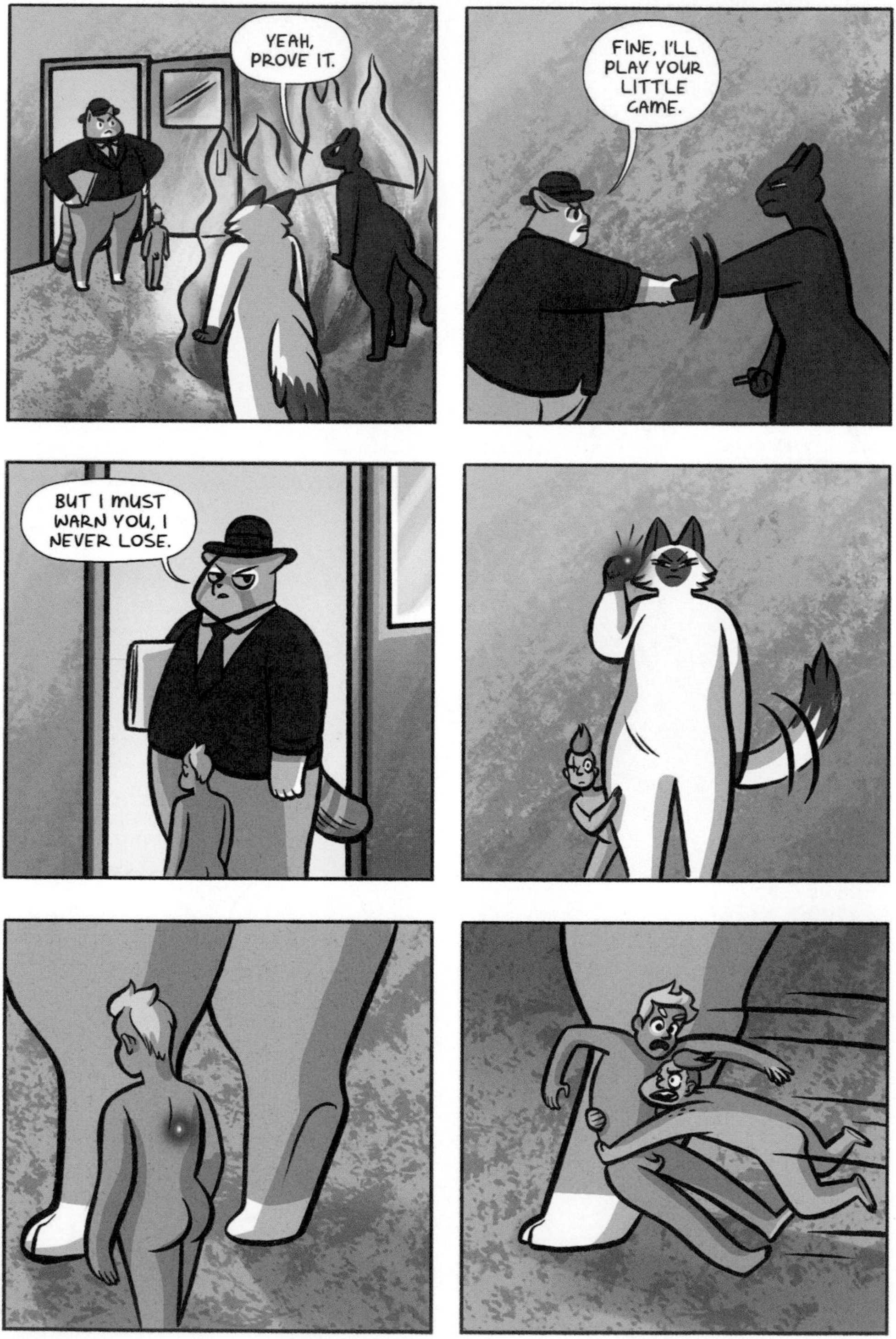
YEAH, PROVE IT.
FINE, I'LL PLAY YOUR LITTLE GAME.
BUT I MUST WARN YOU, I NEVER LOSE.

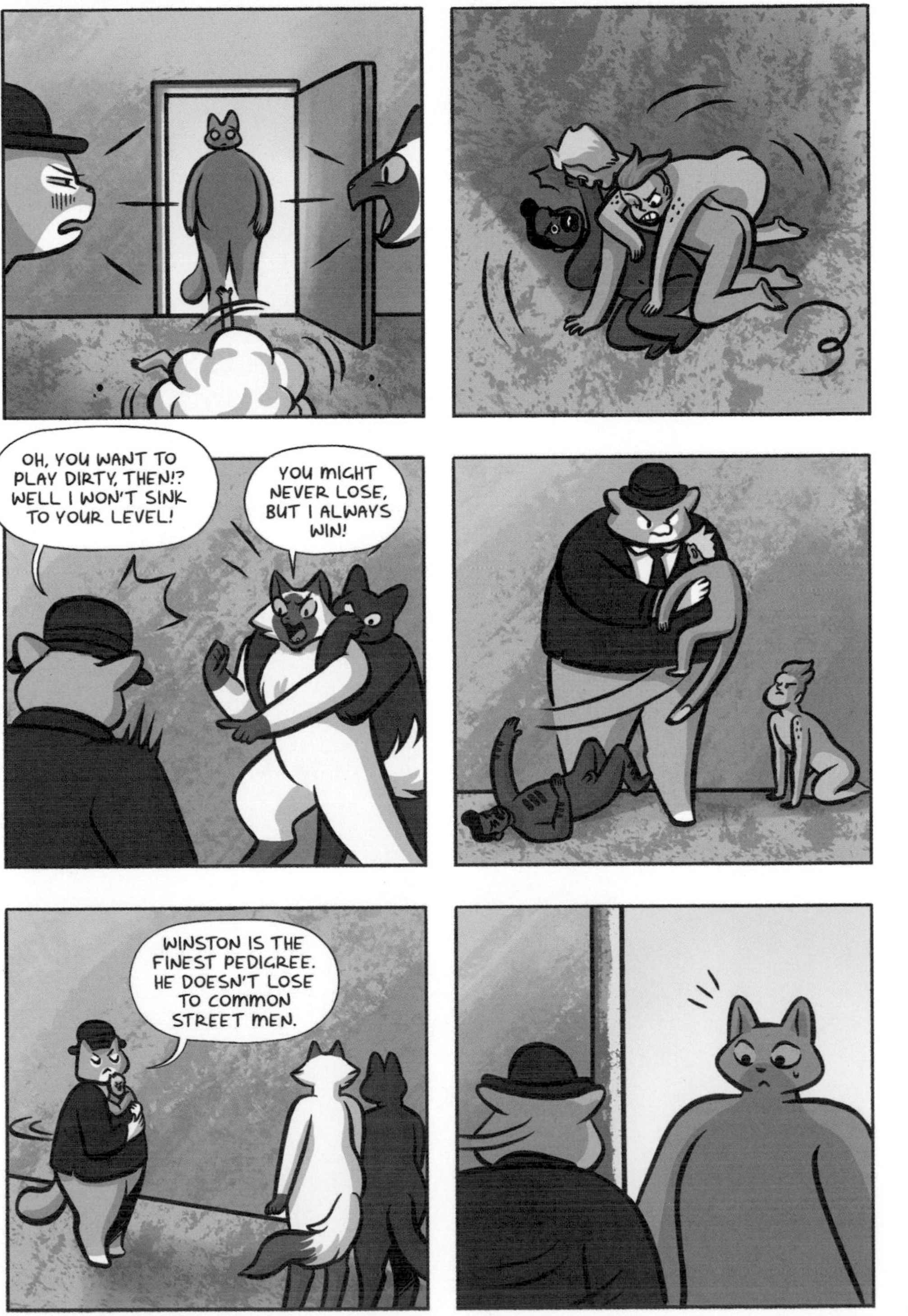
OH, YOU WANT TO PLAY DIRTY, THEN!? WELL I WON'T SINK TO YOUR LEVEL!
YOU MIGHT NEVER LOSE, BUT I ALWAYS WIN!
WINSTON IS THE FINEST PEDIGREE. HE DOESN'T LOSE TO COMMON STREET MEN.

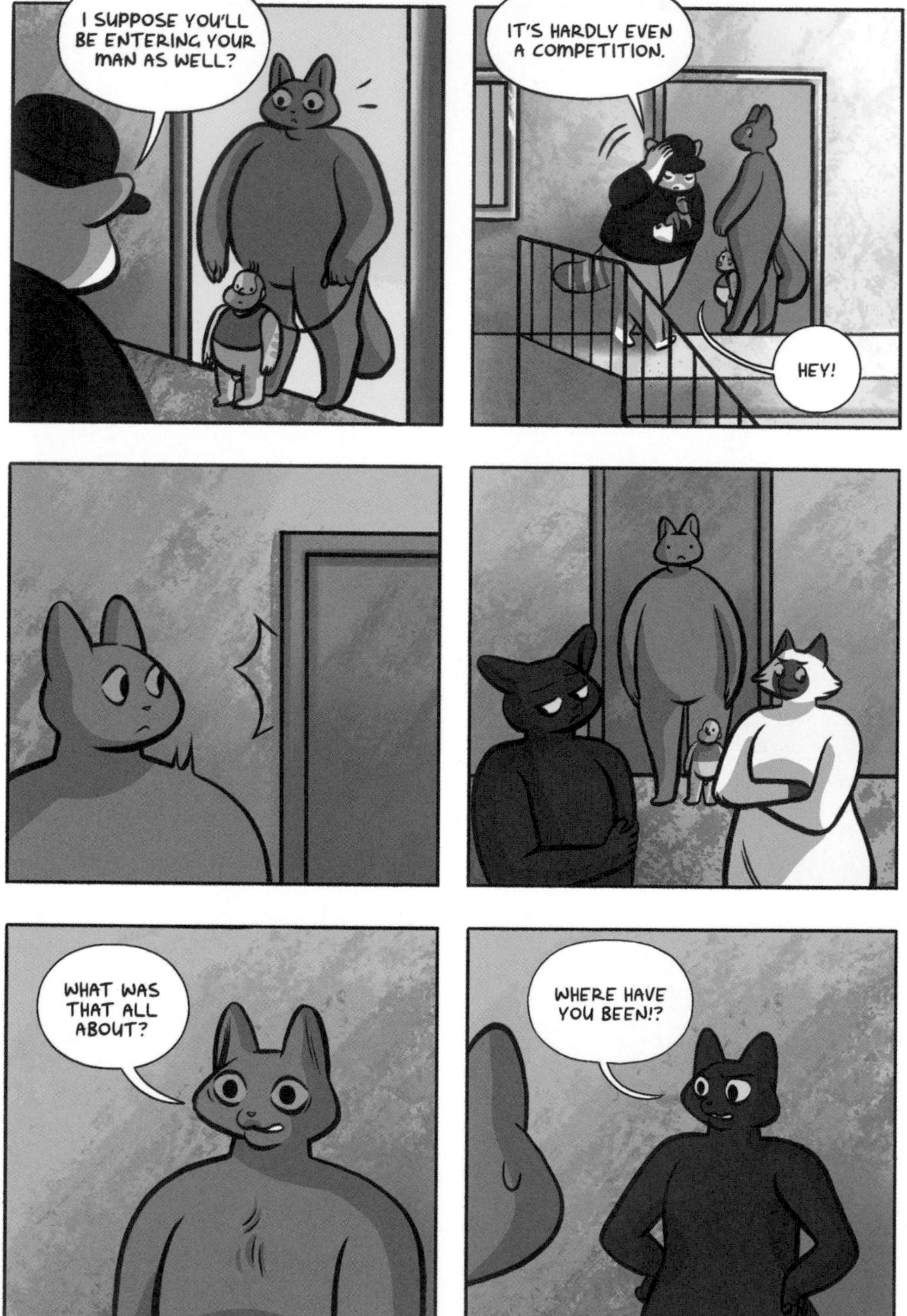
I SUPPOSE YOU'LL BE ENTERING YOUR MAN AS WELL?
IT'S HARDLY EVEN A COMPETITION.
HEY!
WHAT WAS THAT ALL ABOUT?
WHERE HAVE YOU BEEN!?

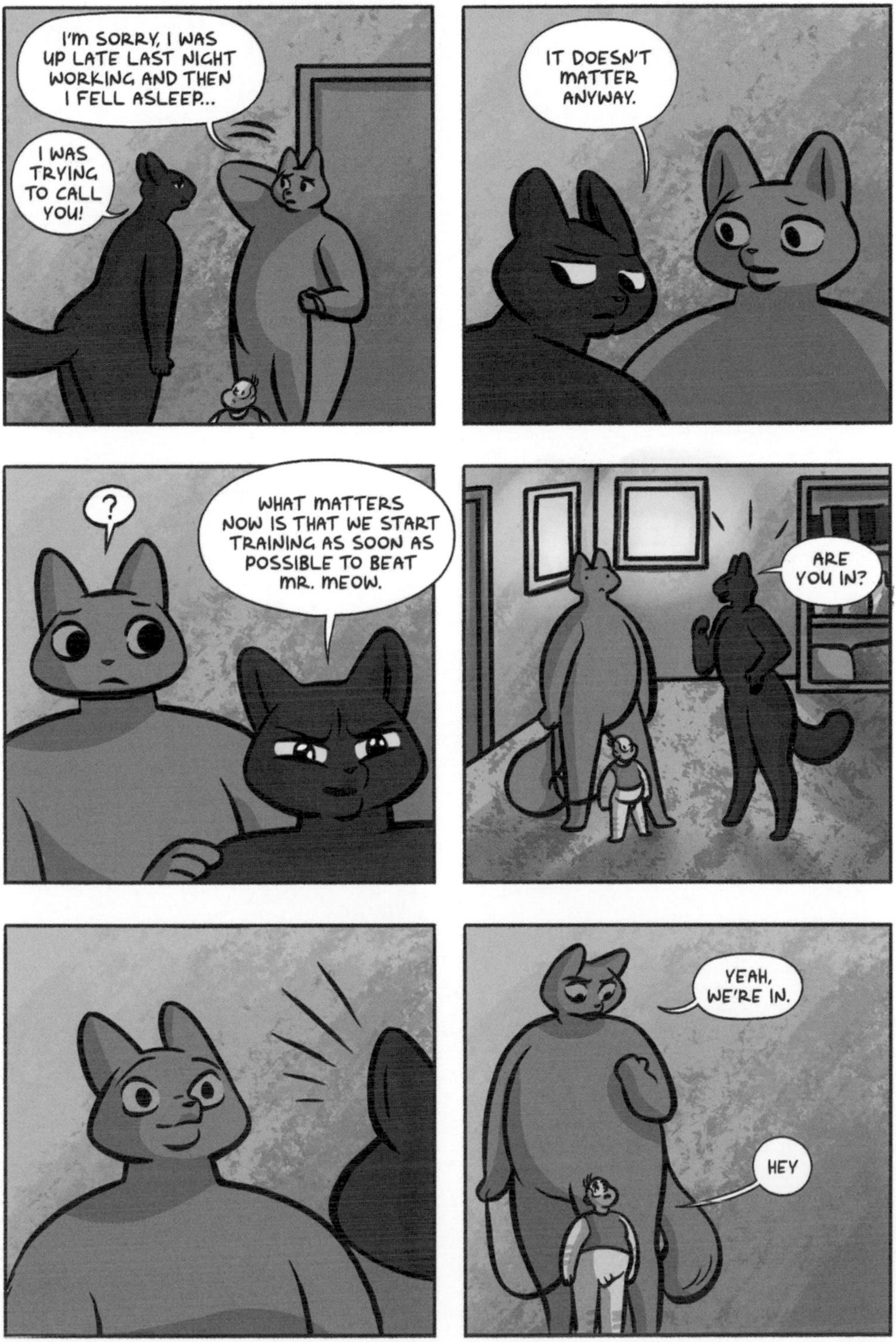

I'M SORRY, I WAS UP LATE LAST NIGHT WORKING AND THEN I FELL ASLEEP...
I WAS TRYING TO CALL YOU!
IT DOESN'T MATTER ANYWAY.
?
WHAT MATTERS NOW IS THAT WE START TRAINING AS SOON AS POSSIBLE TO BEAT MR. MEOW.
ARE YOU IN?
YEAH, WE'RE IN.
HEY

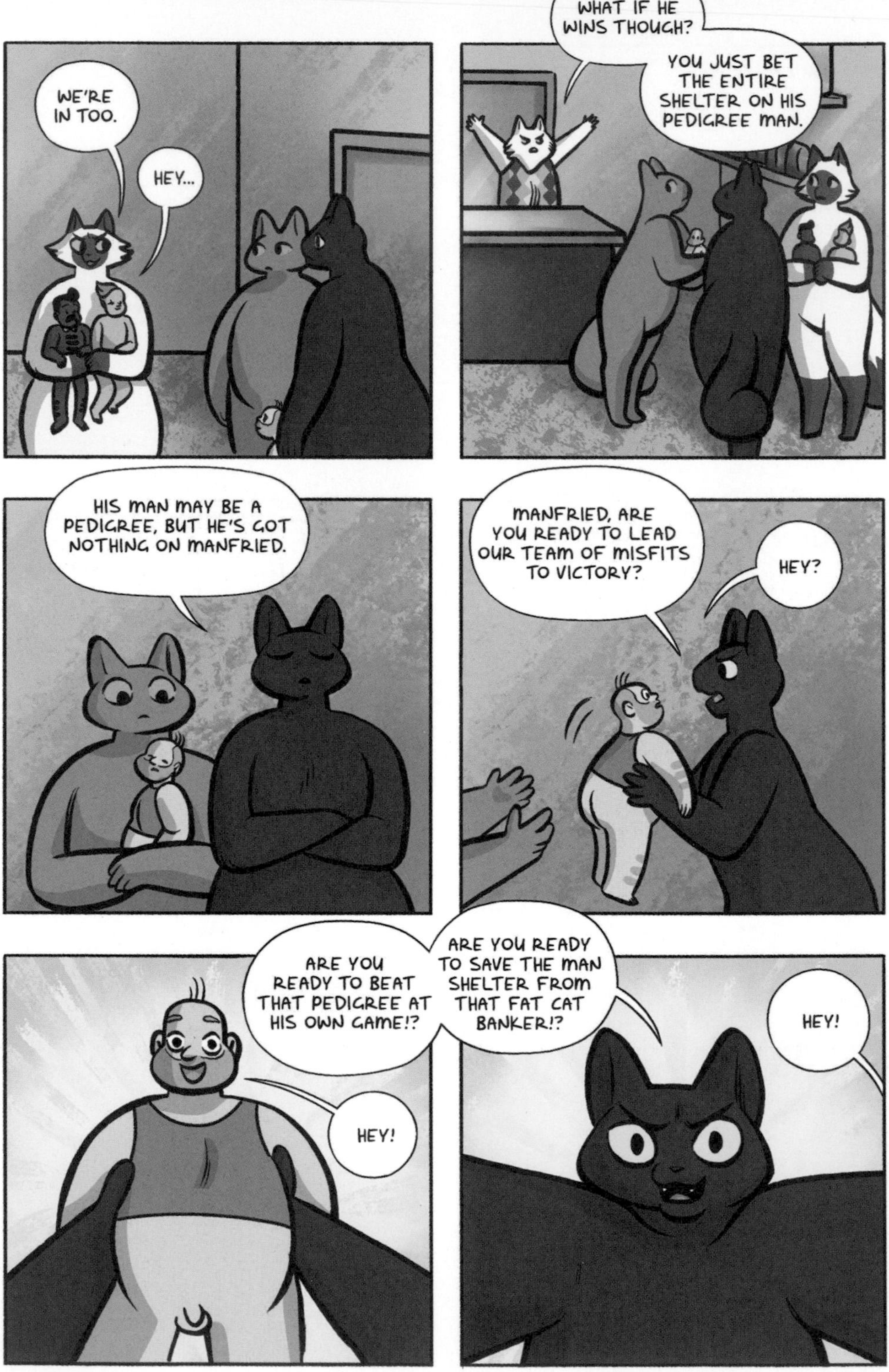
WE'RE IN TOO.
HEY...
WHAT IF HE WINS THOUGH?
YOU JUST BET THE ENTIRE SHELTER ON HIS PEDIGREE MAN.
HIS MAN MAY BE A PEDIGREE, BUT HE'S GOT NOTHING ON MANFRIED.
MANFRIED, ARE YOU READY TO LEAD OUR TEAM OF MISFITS TO VICTORY?
HEY?
ARE YOU READY TO BEAT THAT PEDIGREE AT HIS OWN GAME!?
HEY!
ARE YOU READY TO SAVE THE MAN SHELTER FROM THAT FAT CAT BANKER!?
HEY!

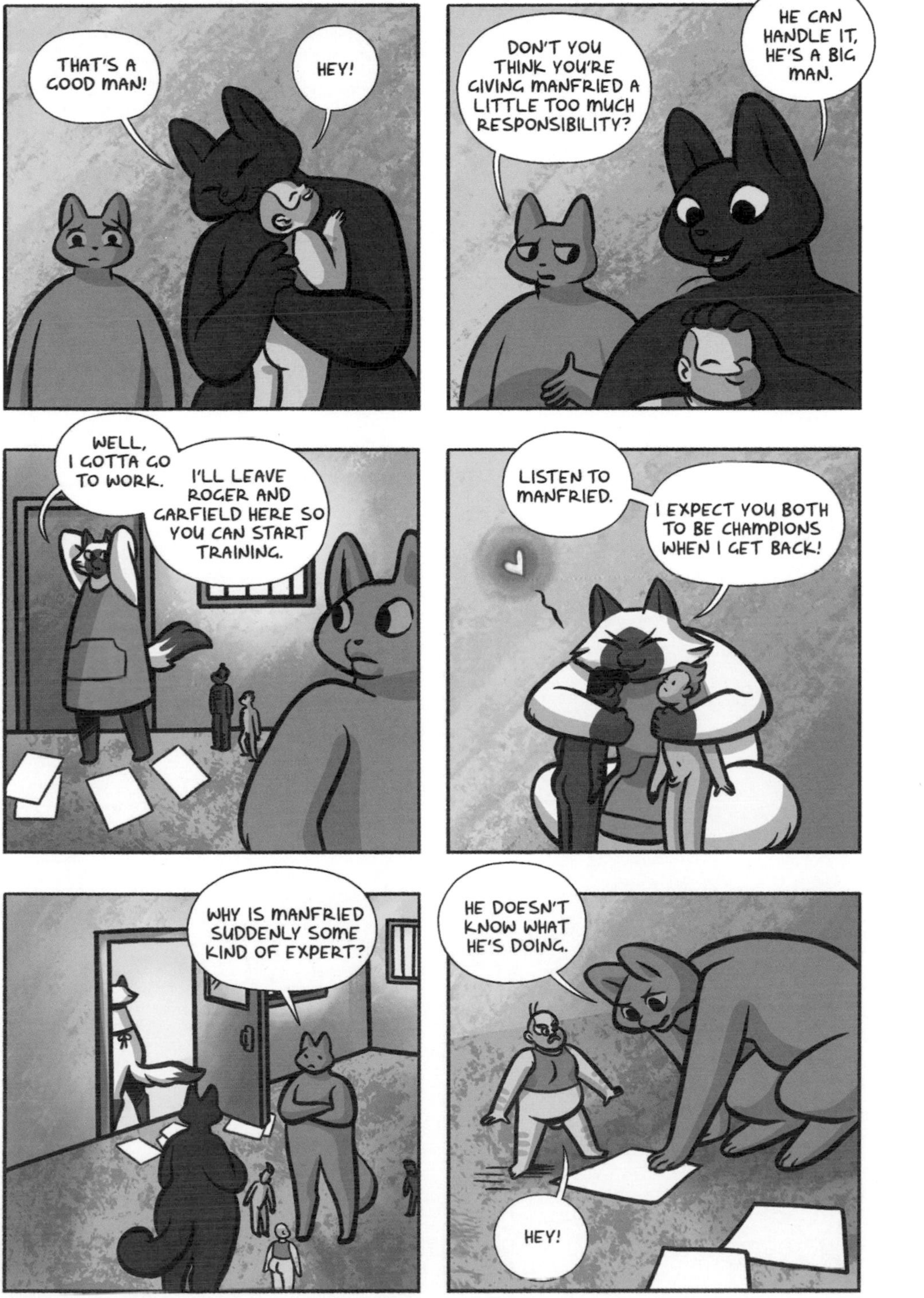
THAT'S A GOOD MAN!
HEY!
DON'T YOU THINK YOU'RE GIVING MANFRIED A LITTLE TOO MUCH RESPONSIBILITY?
HE CAN HANDLE IT, HE'S A BIG MAN.
WELL, I GOTTA GO TO WORK.
I'LL LEAVE ROGER AND GARFIELD HERE SO YOU CAN START TRAINING.
LISTEN TO MANFRIED.
I EXPECT YOU BOTH TO BE CHAMPIONS WHEN I GET BACK!
WHY IS MANFRIED SUDDENLY SOME KIND OF EXPERT?
HE DOESN'T KNOW WHAT HE'S DOING.
HEY!

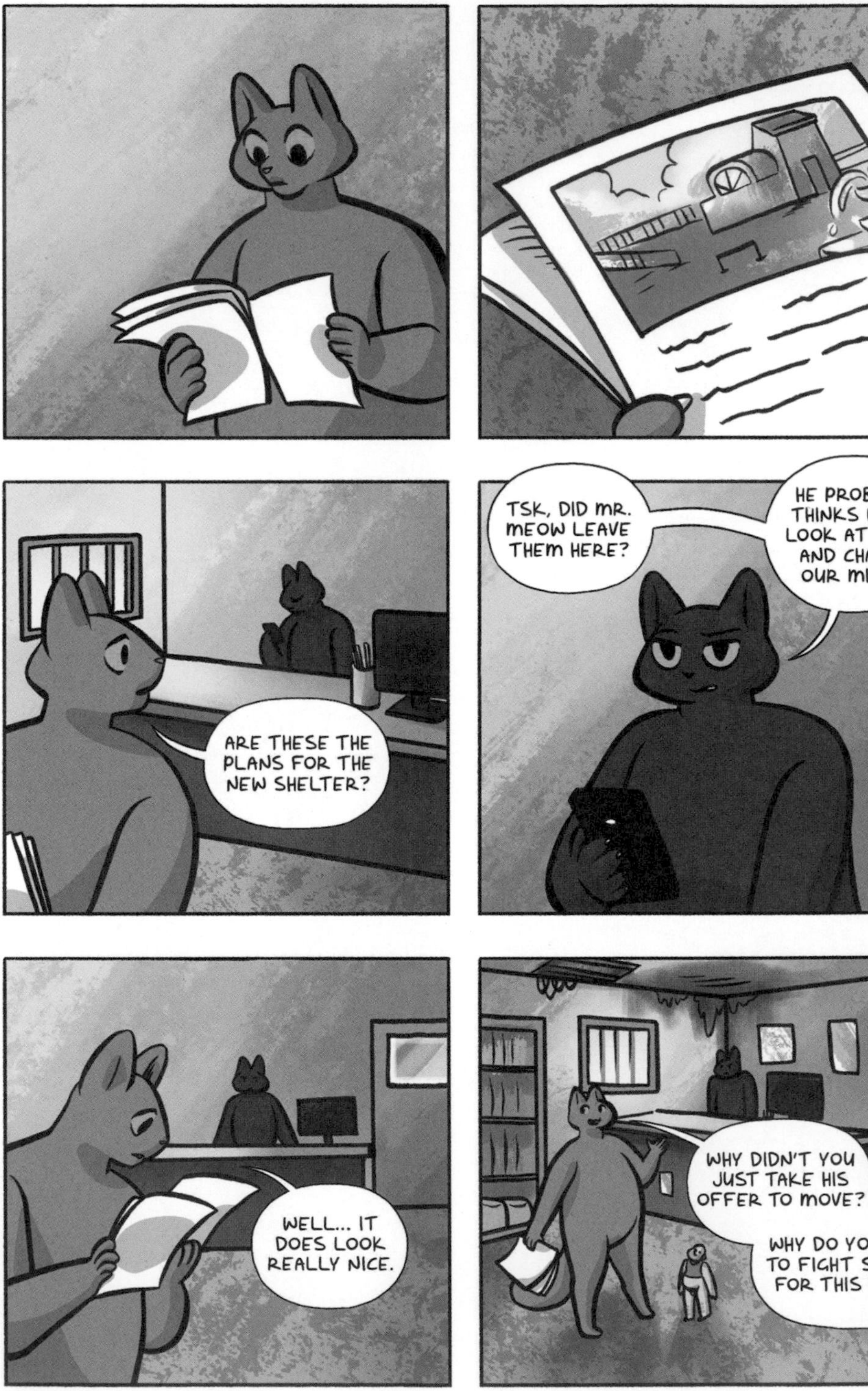
ARE THESE THE PLANS FOR THE NEW SHELTER?
TSK, DID MR. MEOW LEAVE THEM HERE?
HE PROBABLY THINKS WE'LL LOOK AT THEM AND CHANGE OUR MINDS.
WELL... IT DOES LOOK REALLY NICE.
WHY DIDN'T YOU JUST TAKE HIS OFFER TO MOVE?
WHY DO YOU NEED TO FIGHT SO HARD FOR THIS DUMP?

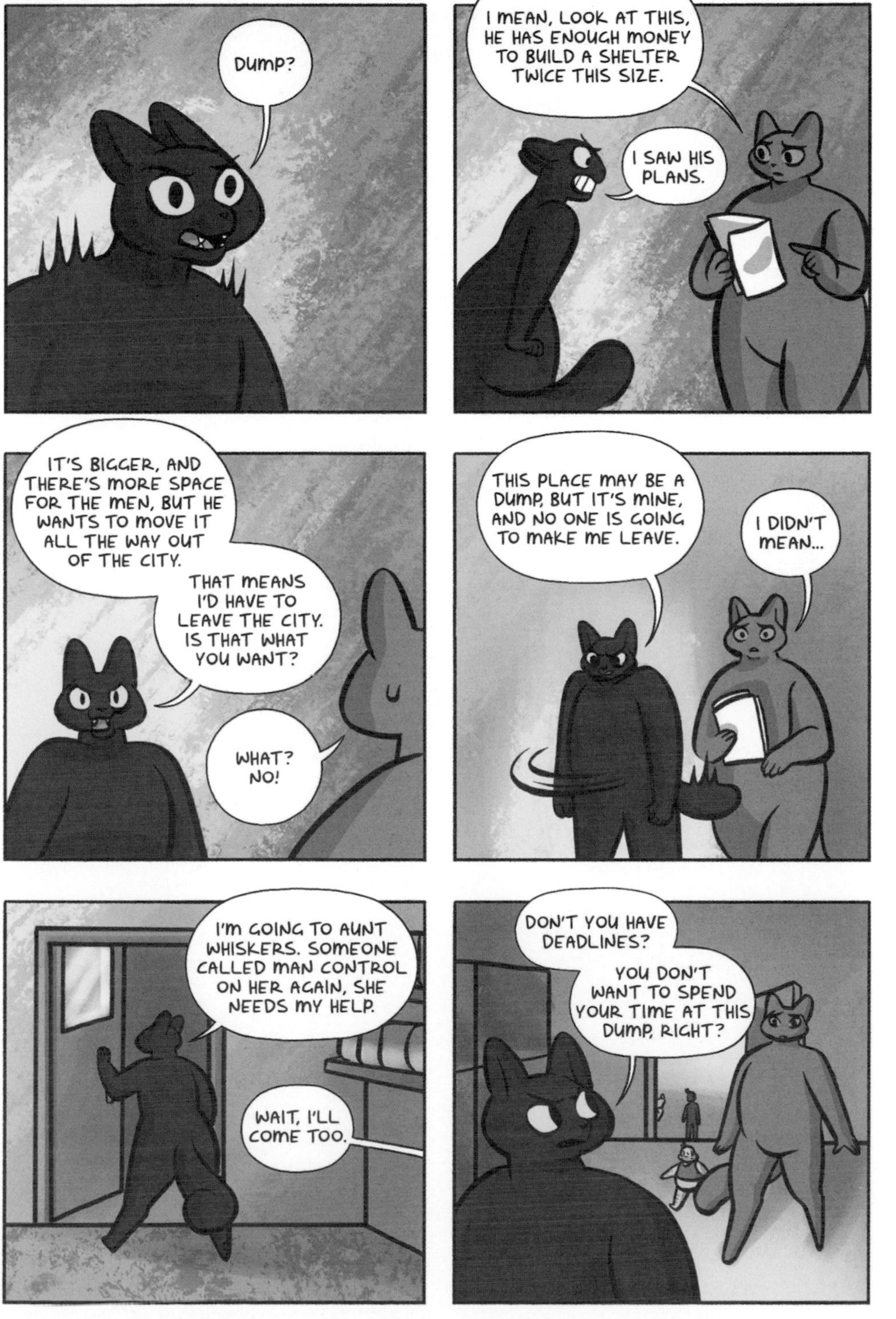
DUMP?
I MEAN, LOOK AT THIS, HE HAS ENOUGH MONEY TO BUILD A SHELTER TWICE THIS SIZE.
I SAW HIS PLANS.
IT'S BIGGER, AND THERE'S MORE SPACE FOR THE MEN, BUT HE WANTS TO MOVE IT ALL THE WAY OUT OF THE CITY.
THAT MEANS I'D HAVE TO LEAVE THE CITY. IS THAT WHAT YOU WANT?
WHAT? NO!
THIS PLACE MAY BE A DUMP, BUT IT'S MINE, AND NO ONE IS GOING TO MAKE ME LEAVE.
I DIDN'T MEAN...
I'M GOING TO AUNT WHISKERS. SOMEONE CALLED MAN CONTROL ON HER AGAIN, SHE NEEDS MY HELP.
WAIT, I'LL COME TOO.
DON'T YOU HAVE DEADLINES?
YOU DON'T WANT TO SPEND YOUR TIME AT THIS DUMP, RIGHT?

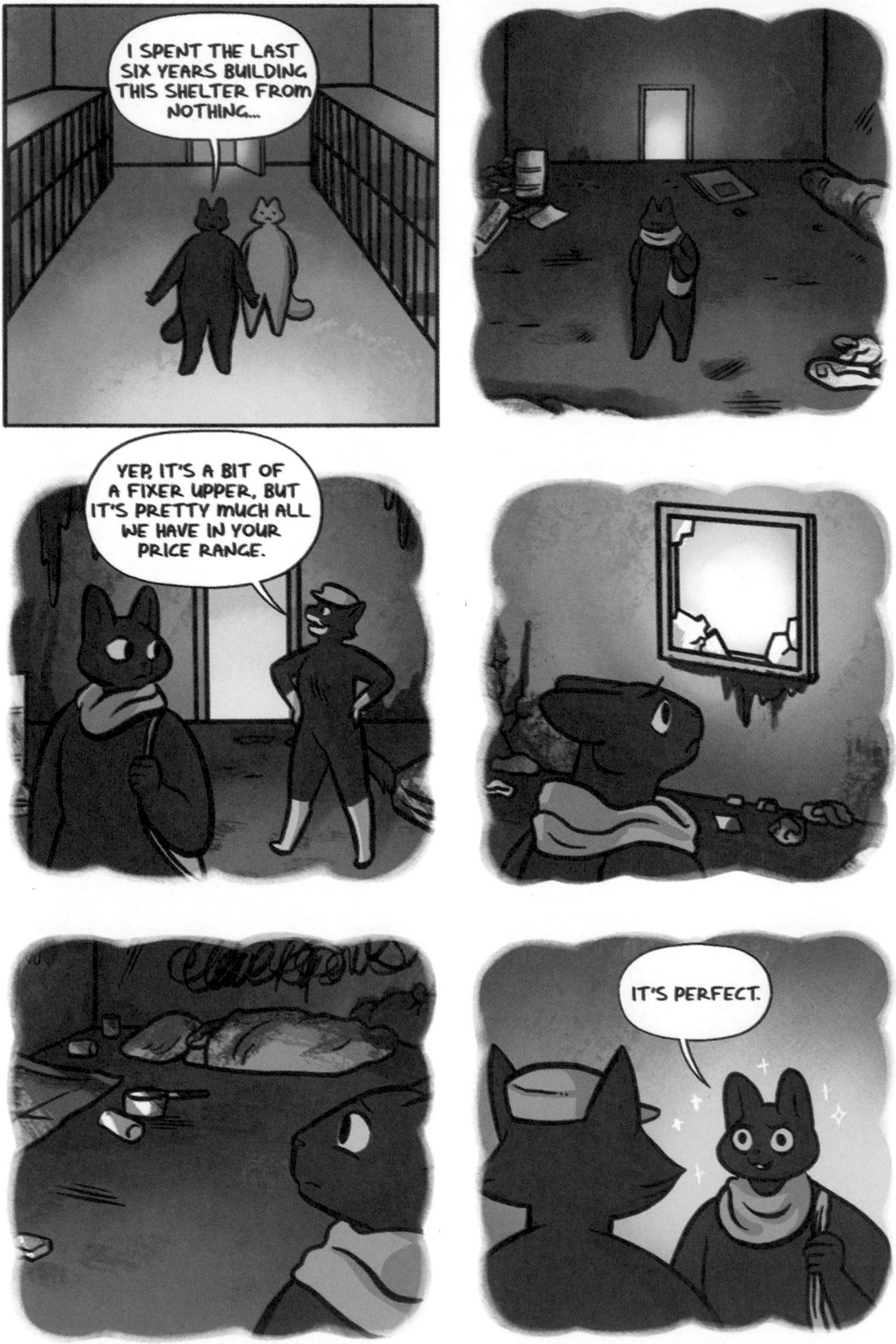
I SPENT THE LAST SIX YEARS BUILDING THIS SHELTER FROM NOTHING...
YEP, IT'S A BIT OF A FIXER UPPER, BUT IT'S PRETTY MUCH ALL WE HAVE IN YOUR PRICE RANGE.
IT'S PERFECT.

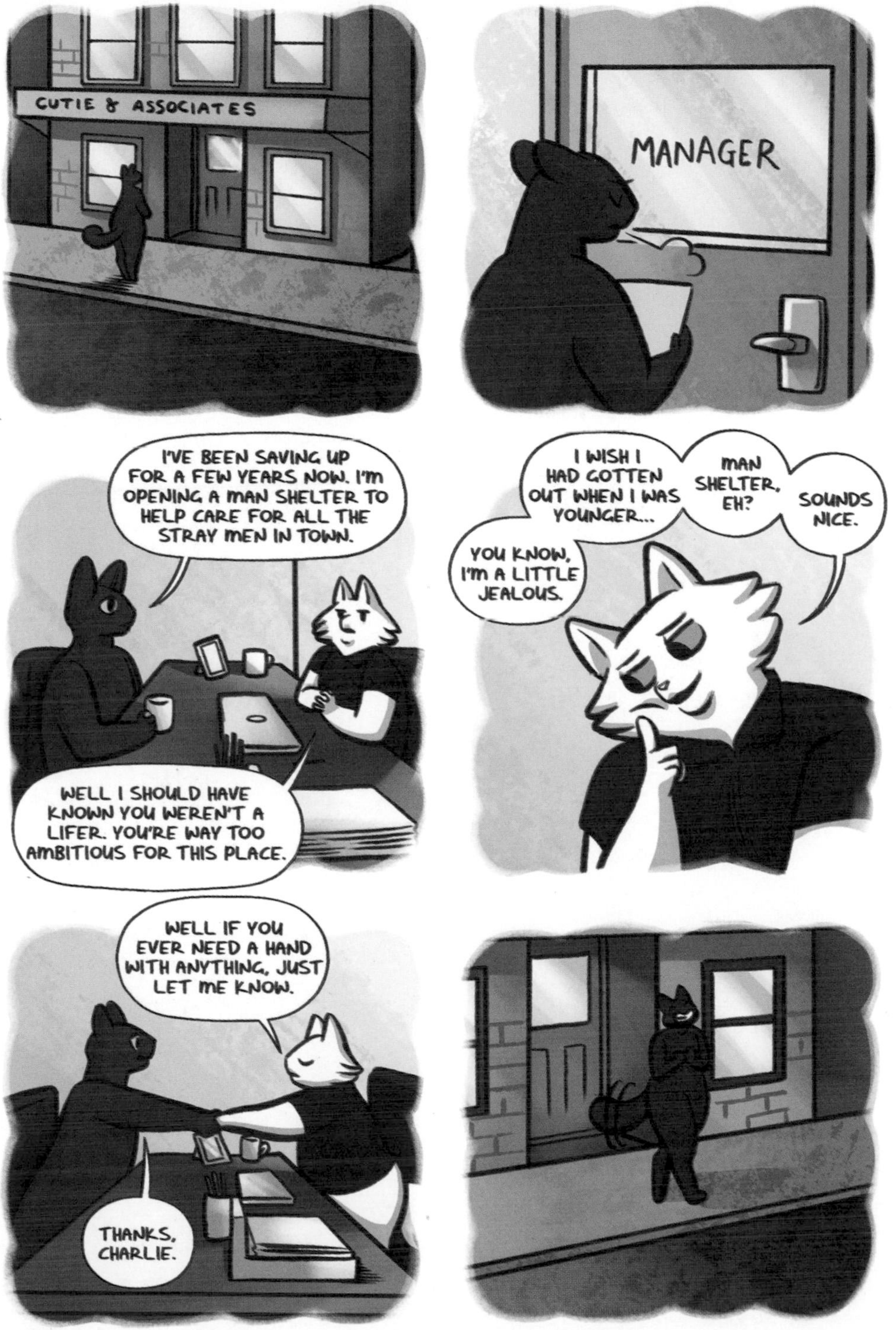
CUTIE & ASSOCIATES
MANAGER
I'VE BEEN SAVING UP FOR A FEW YEARS NOW. I'M OPENING A MAN SHELTER TO HELP CARE FOR ALL THE STRAY MEN IN TOWN.
WELL I SHOULD HAVE KNOWN YOU WEREN'T A LIFER. YOU'RE WAY TOO AMBITIOUS FOR THIS PLACE.
MAN SHELTER, EH?
SOUNDS NICE.
YOU KNOW, I'M A LITTLE JEALOUS.
I WISH I HAD GOTTEN OUT WHEN I WAS YOUNGER...
WELL IF YOU EVER NEED A HAND WITH ANYTHING, JUST LET ME KNOW.
THANKS, CHARLIE.

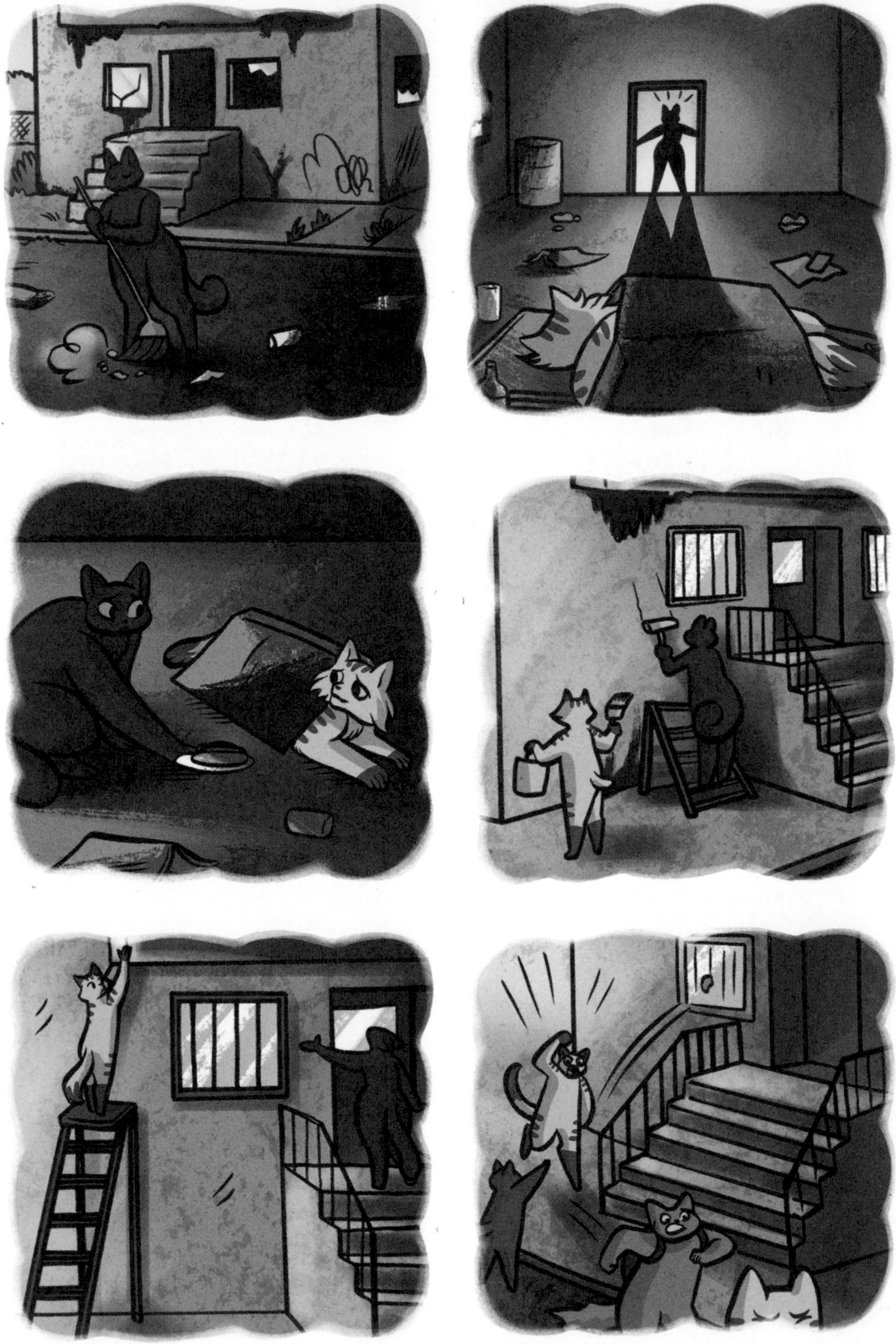

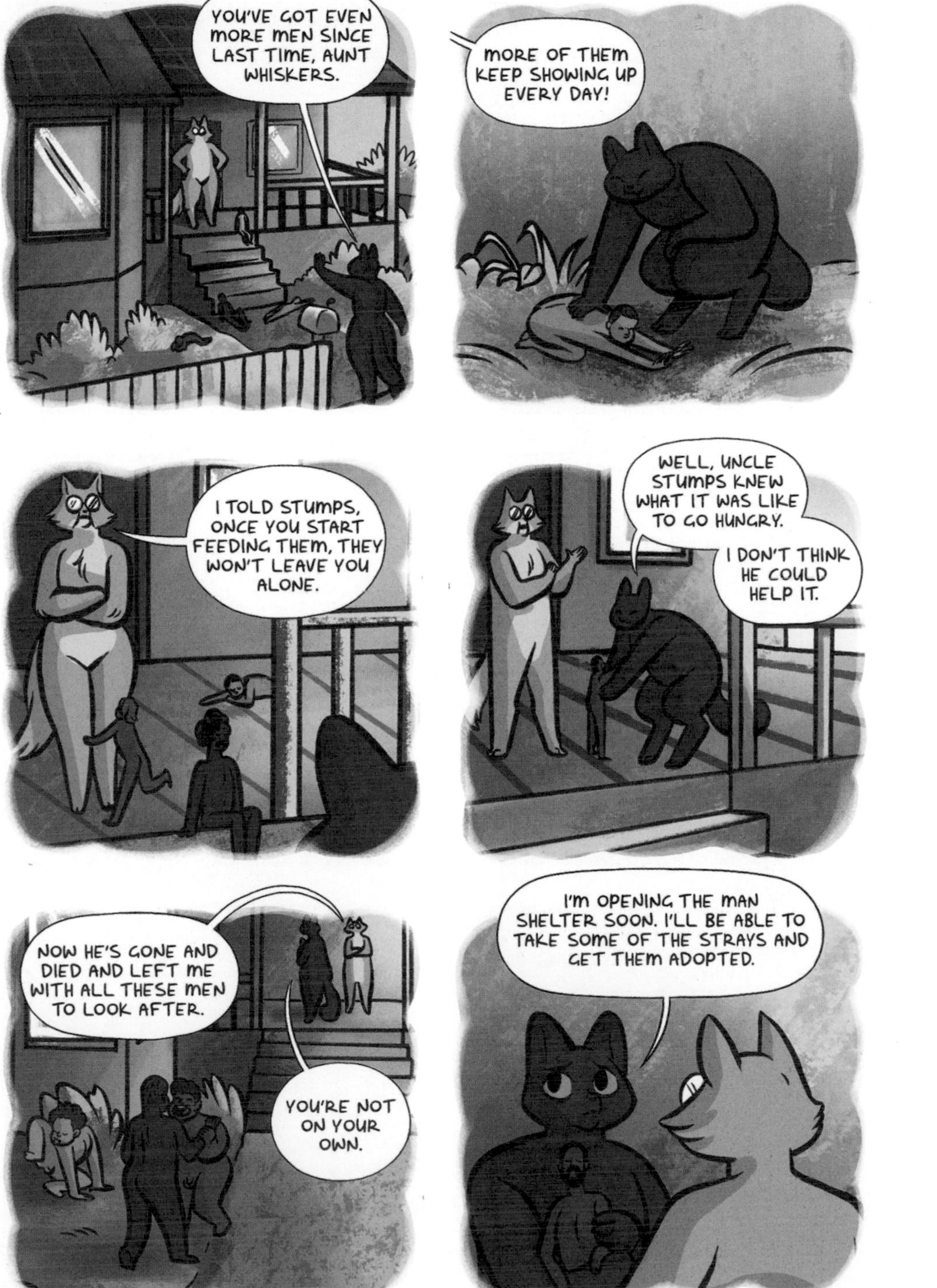
YOU'VE GOT EVEN MORE MEN SINCE LAST TIME, AUNT WHISKERS.
MORE OF THEM KEEP SHOWING UP EVERY DAY!
I TOLD STUMPS, ONCE YOU START FEEDING THEM, THEY WON'T LEAVE YOU ALONE.
WELL, UNCLE STUMPS KNEW WHAT IT WAS LIKE TO GO HUNGRY.
I DON'T THINK HE COULD HELP IT.
NOW HE'S GONE AND DIED AND LEFT ME WITH ALL THESE MEN TO LOOK AFTER.
YOU'RE NOT ON YOUR OWN.
I'M OPENING THE MAN SHELTER SOON. I'LL BE ABLE TO TAKE SOME OF THE STRAYS AND GET THEM ADOPTED.

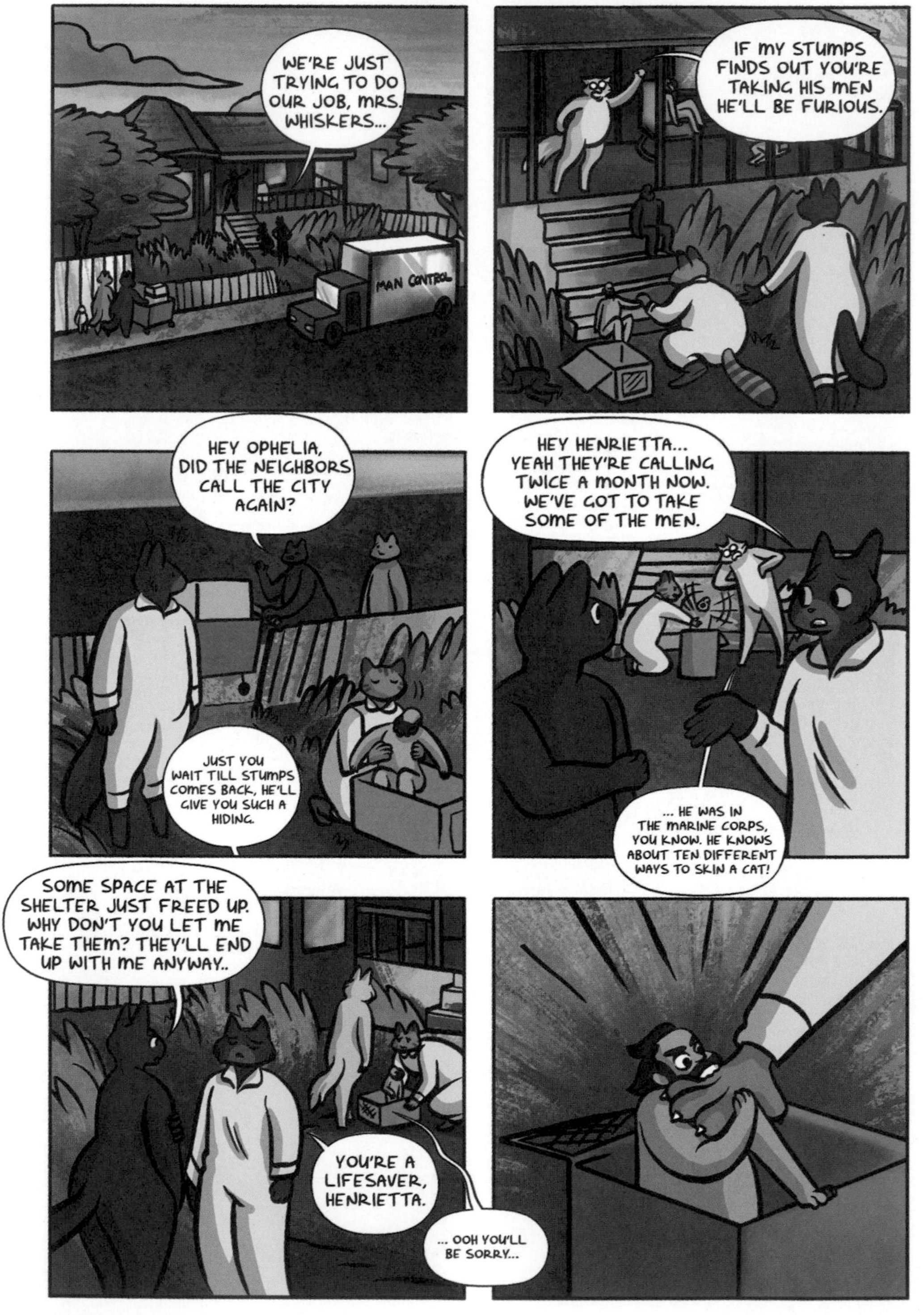

WE'RE JUST TRYING TO DO OUR JOB, MRS. WHISKERS...
MAN CONTROL
IF MY STUMPS FINDS OUT YOU'RE TAKING HIS MEN HE'LL BE FURIOUS.
HEY OPHELIA, DID THE NEIGHBORS CALL THE CITY AGAIN?
JUST YOU WAIT TILL STUMPS COMES BACK, HE'LL GIVE YOU SUCH A HIDING.
HEY HENRIETTA... YEAH THEY'RE CALLING TWICE A MONTH NOW. WE'VE GOT TO TAKE SOME OF THE MEN.
... HE WAS IN THE MARINE CORPS, YOU KNOW. HE KNOWS ABOUT TEN DIFFERENT WAYS TO SKIN A CAT!
SOME SPACE AT THE SHELTER JUST FREED UP. WHY DON'T YOU LET ME TAKE THEM? THEY'LL END UP WITH ME ANYWAY..
YOU'RE A LIFESAVER, HENRIETTA.
... OOH YOU'LL BE SORRY...

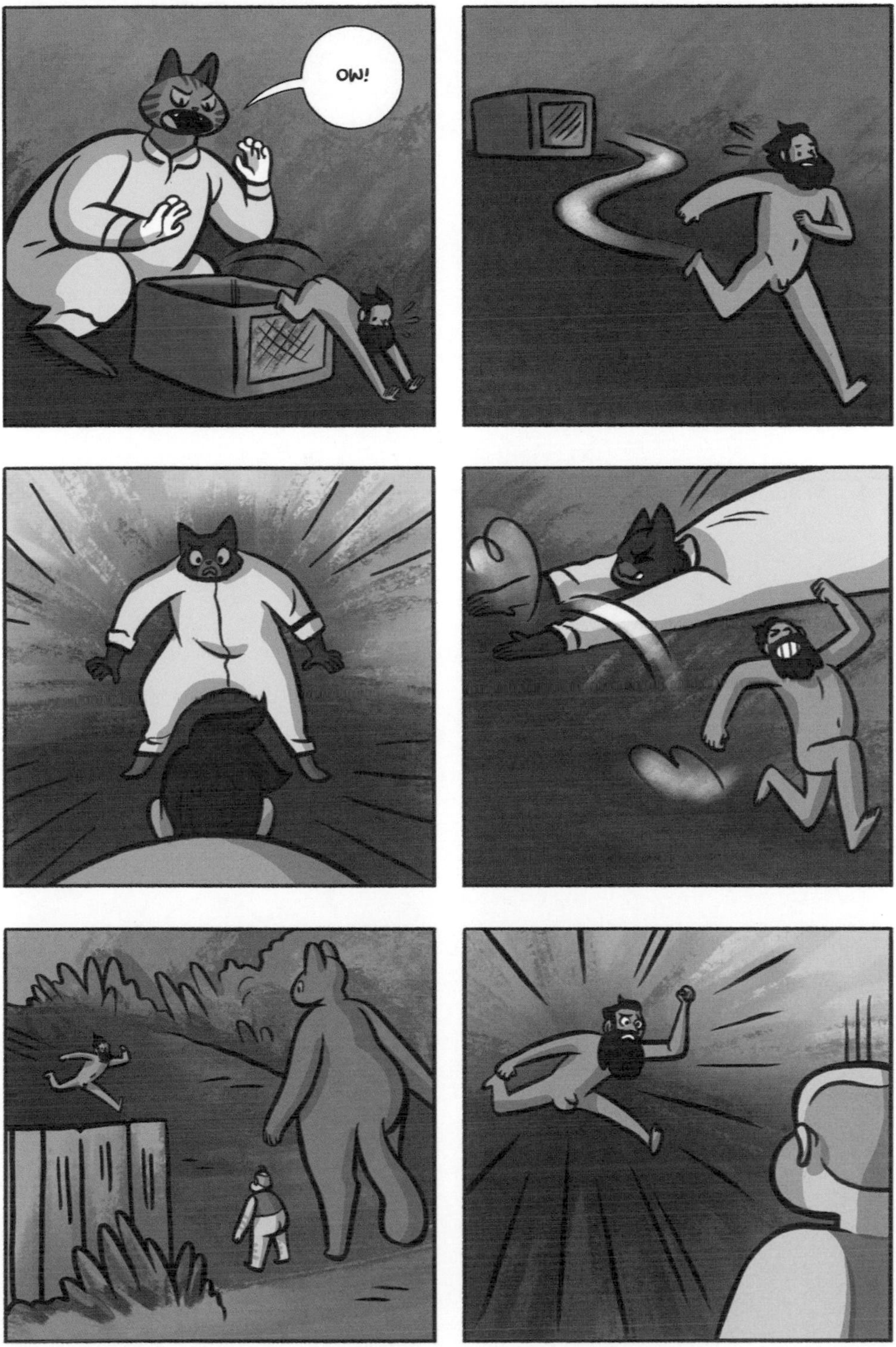
OW!

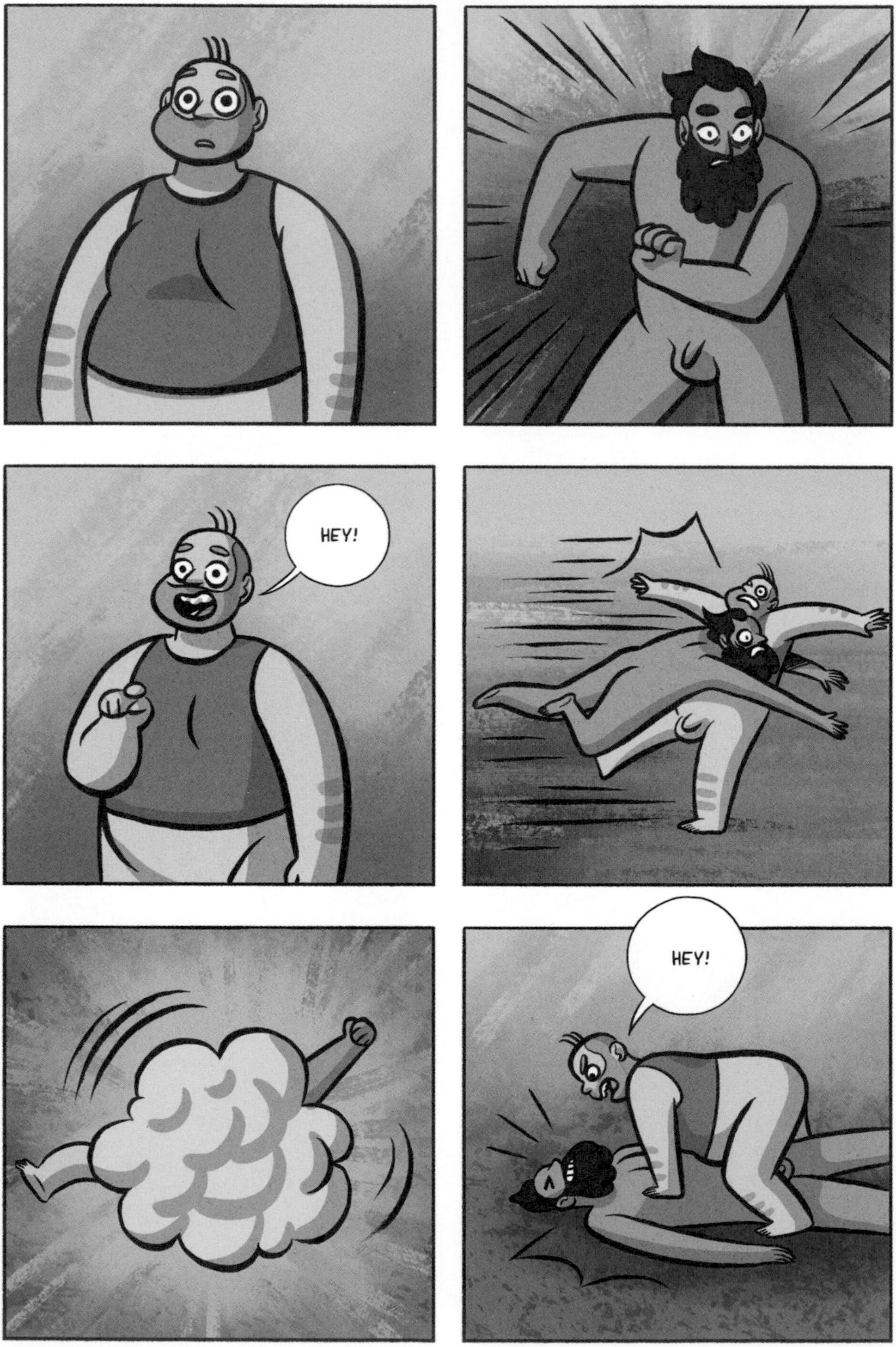
HEY!
HEY!

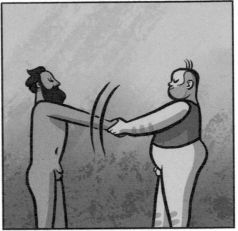

WHO'S THIS LITTLE GUY THEN? A FRIEND OF YOURS?

HEY.

AREN'T YOU A GOOD MAN?

HEY.

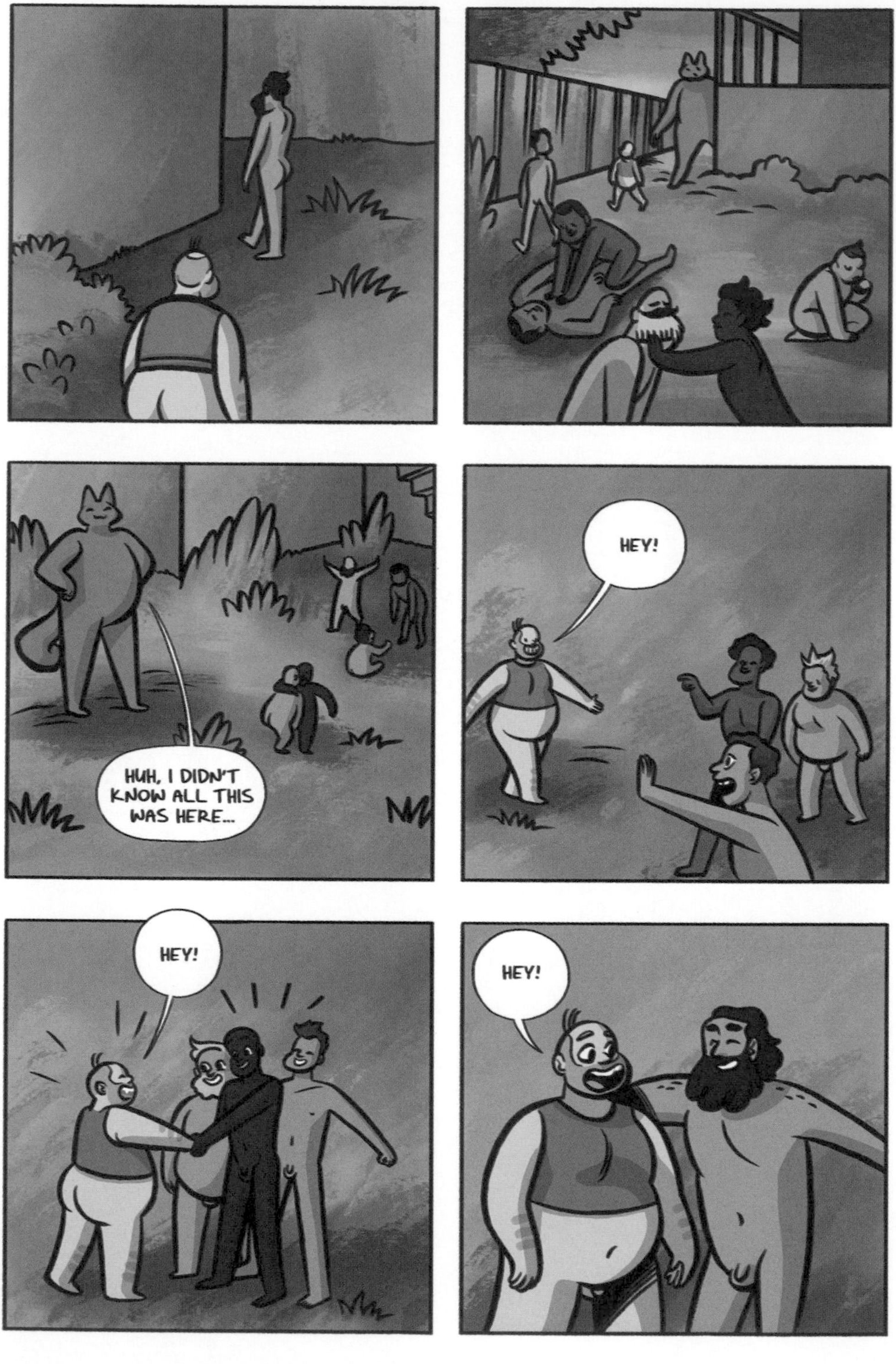
HUH, I DIDN'T KNOW ALL THIS WAS HERE...
HEY!
HEY!
HEY!

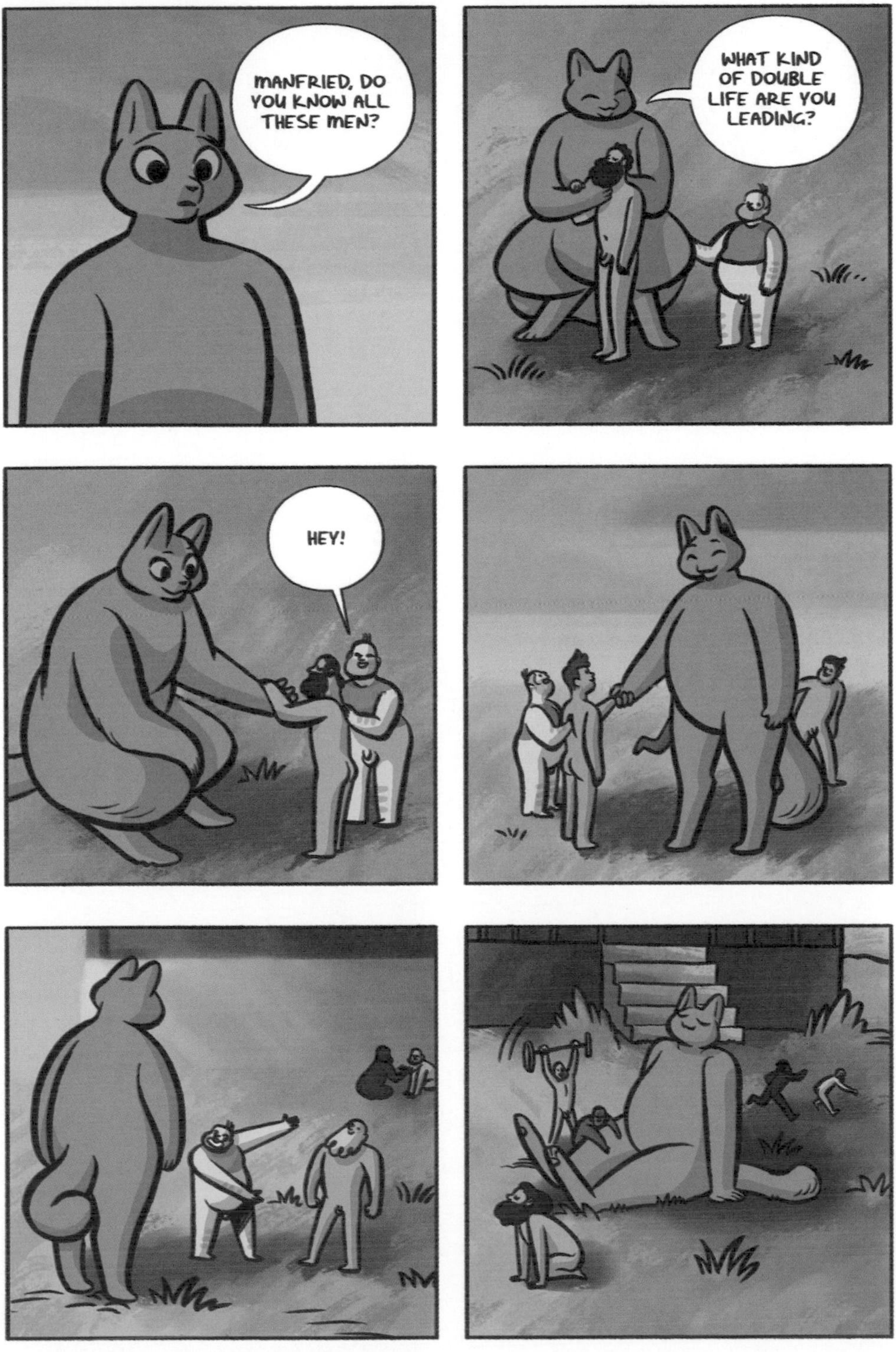
MANFRIED, DO YOU KNOW ALL THESE MEN?
WHAT KIND OF DOUBLE LIFE ARE YOU LEADING?
HEY!

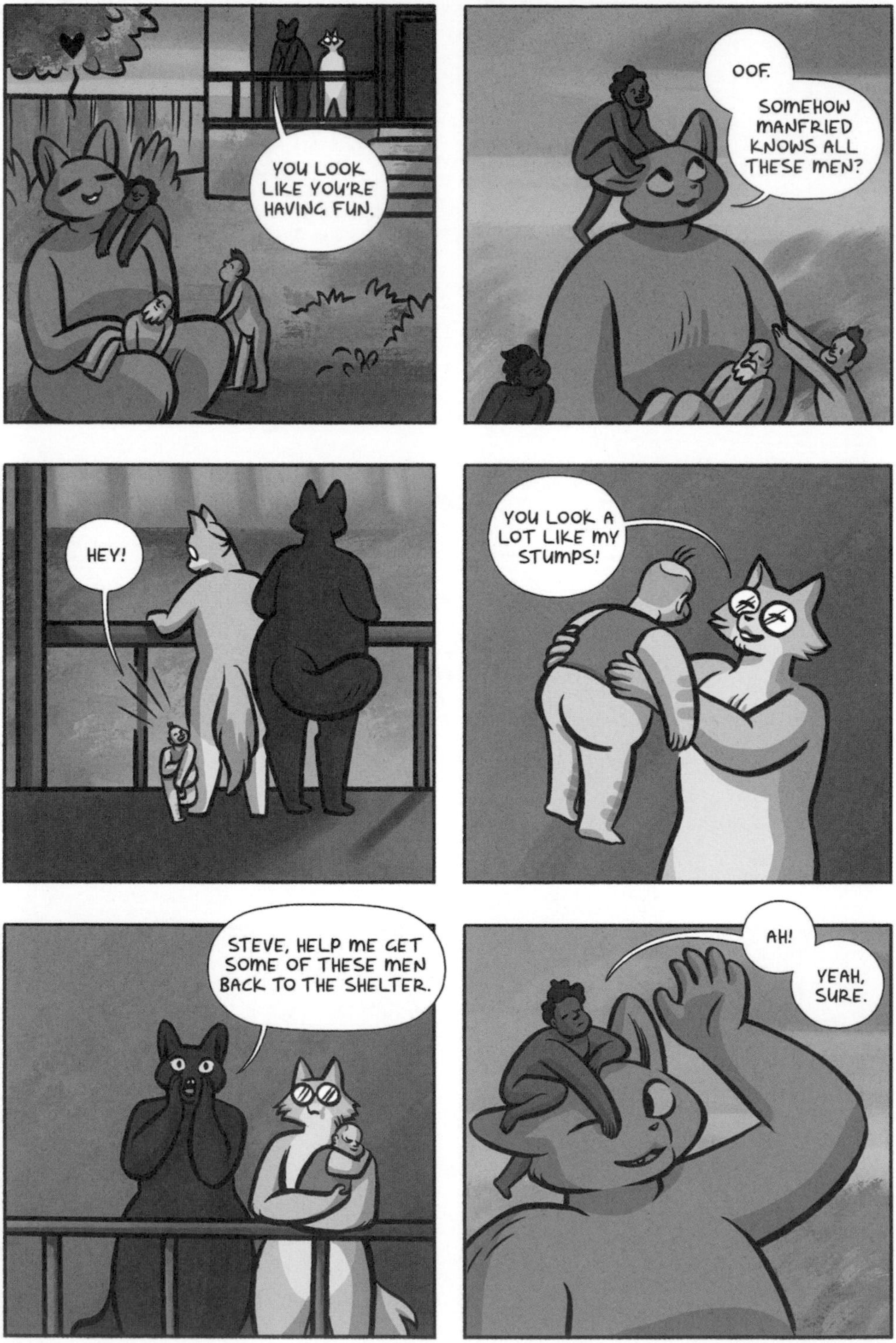
YOU LOOK LIKE YOU'RE HAVING FUN.
OOF.
SOMEHOW MANFRIED KNOWS ALL THESE MEN?
HEY!
YOU LOOK A LOT LIKE MY STUMPS!
STEVE, HELP ME GET SOME OF THESE MEN BACK TO THE SHELTER.
AH!
YEAH, SURE.

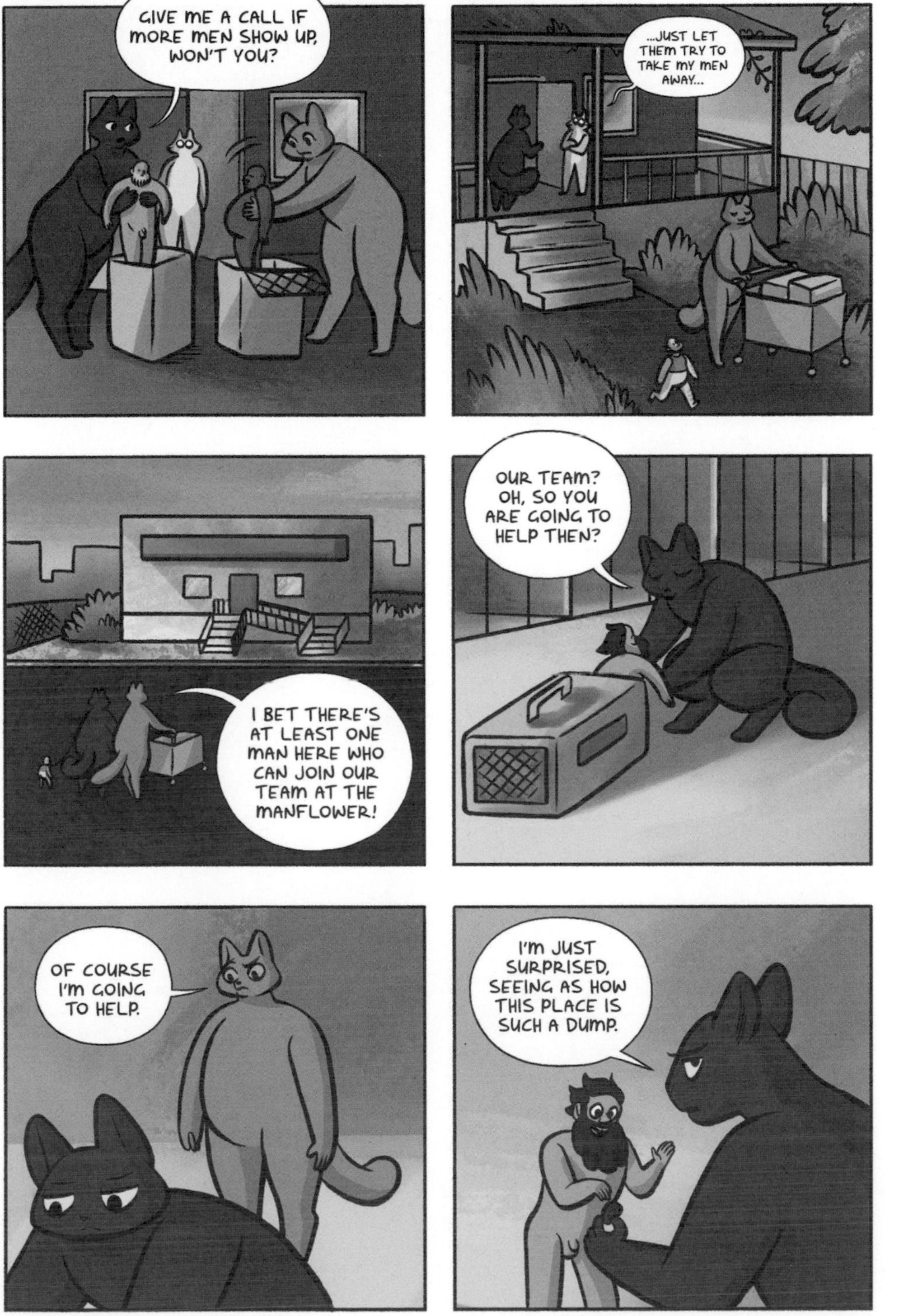
GIVE ME A CALL IF MORE MEN SHOW UP, WON'T YOU?
...JUST LET THEM TRY TO TAKE MY MEN AWAY...
I BET THERE'S AT LEAST ONE MAN HERE WHO CAN JOIN OUR TEAM AT THE MANFLOWER!
OUR TEAM? OH, SO YOU ARE GOING TO HELP THEN?
OF COURSE I'M GOING TO HELP.
I'M JUST SURPRISED, SEEING AS HOW THIS PLACE IS SUCH A DUMP.

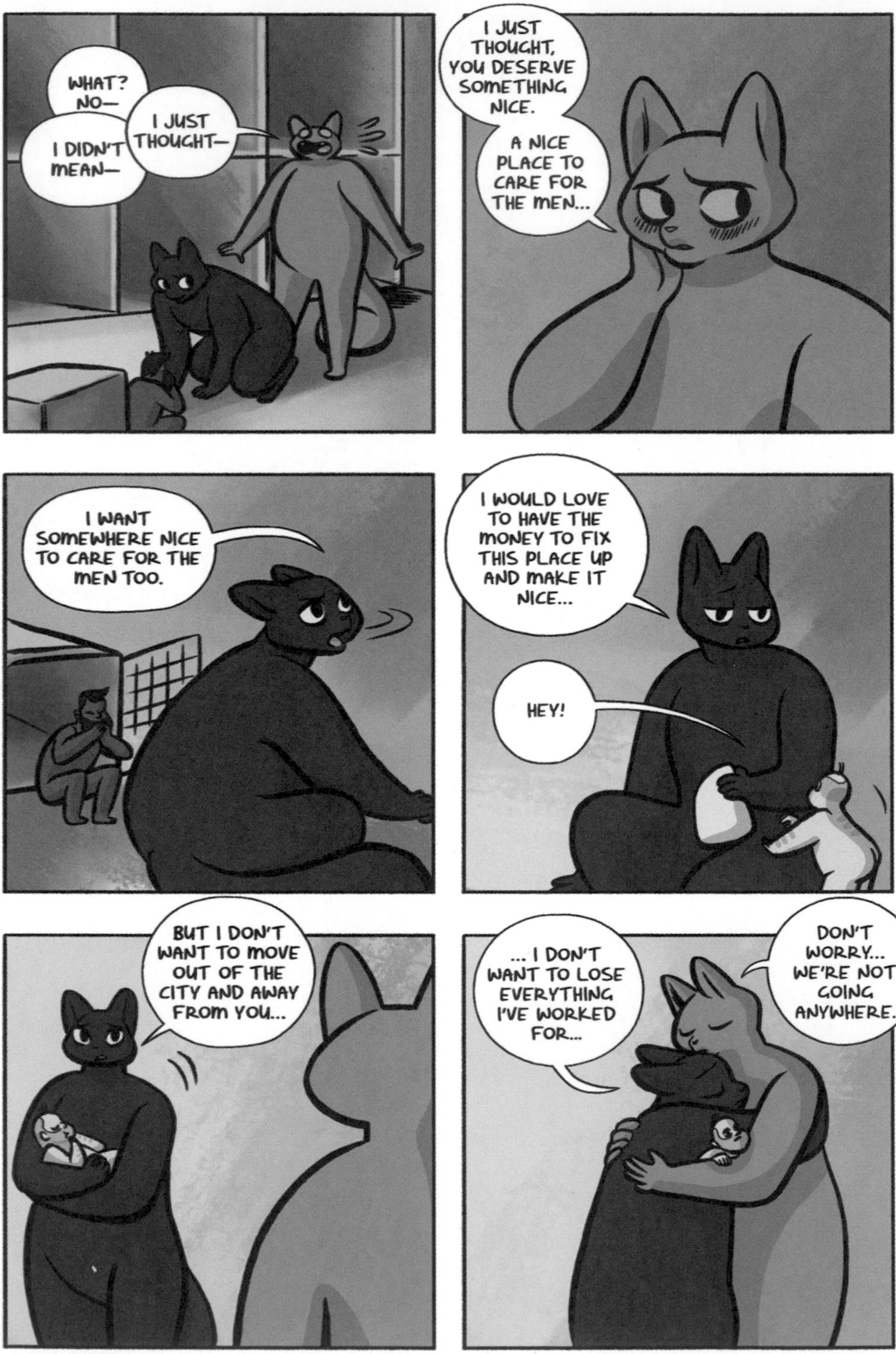
WHAT? NO—
I DIDN'T MEAN—
I JUST THOUGHT—
I JUST THOUGHT, YOU DESERVE SOMETHING NICE.
A NICE PLACE TO CARE FOR THE MEN...
I WANT SOMEWHERE NICE TO CARE FOR THE MEN TOO.
I WOULD LOVE TO HAVE THE MONEY TO FIX THIS PLACE UP AND MAKE IT NICE...
HEY!
BUT I DON'T WANT TO MOVE OUT OF THE CITY AND AWAY FROM YOU...
... I DON'T WANT TO LOSE EVERYTHING I'VE WORKED FOR...
DON'T WORRY... WE'RE NOT GOING ANYWHERE.

PART FOUR

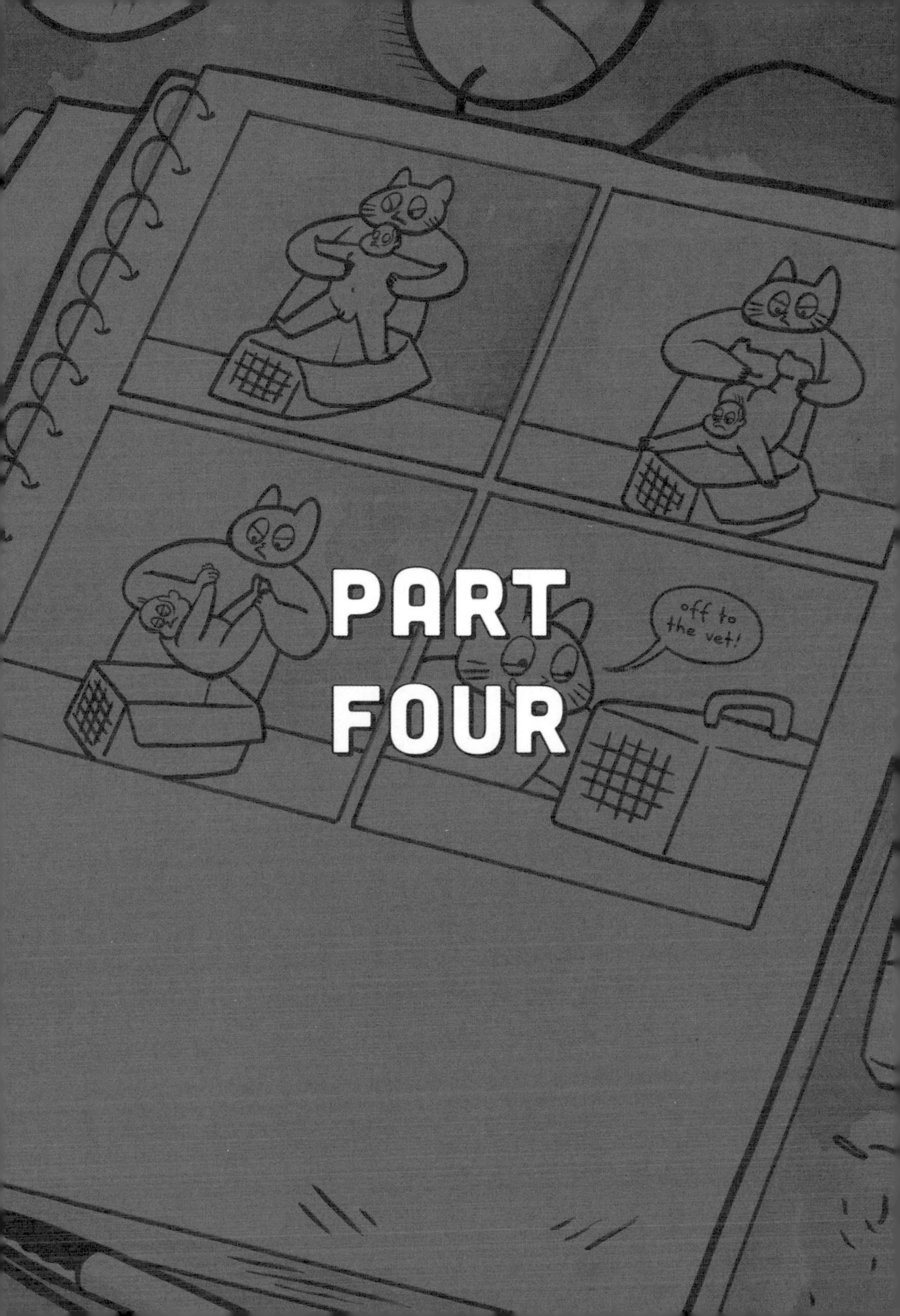
off to the vet!

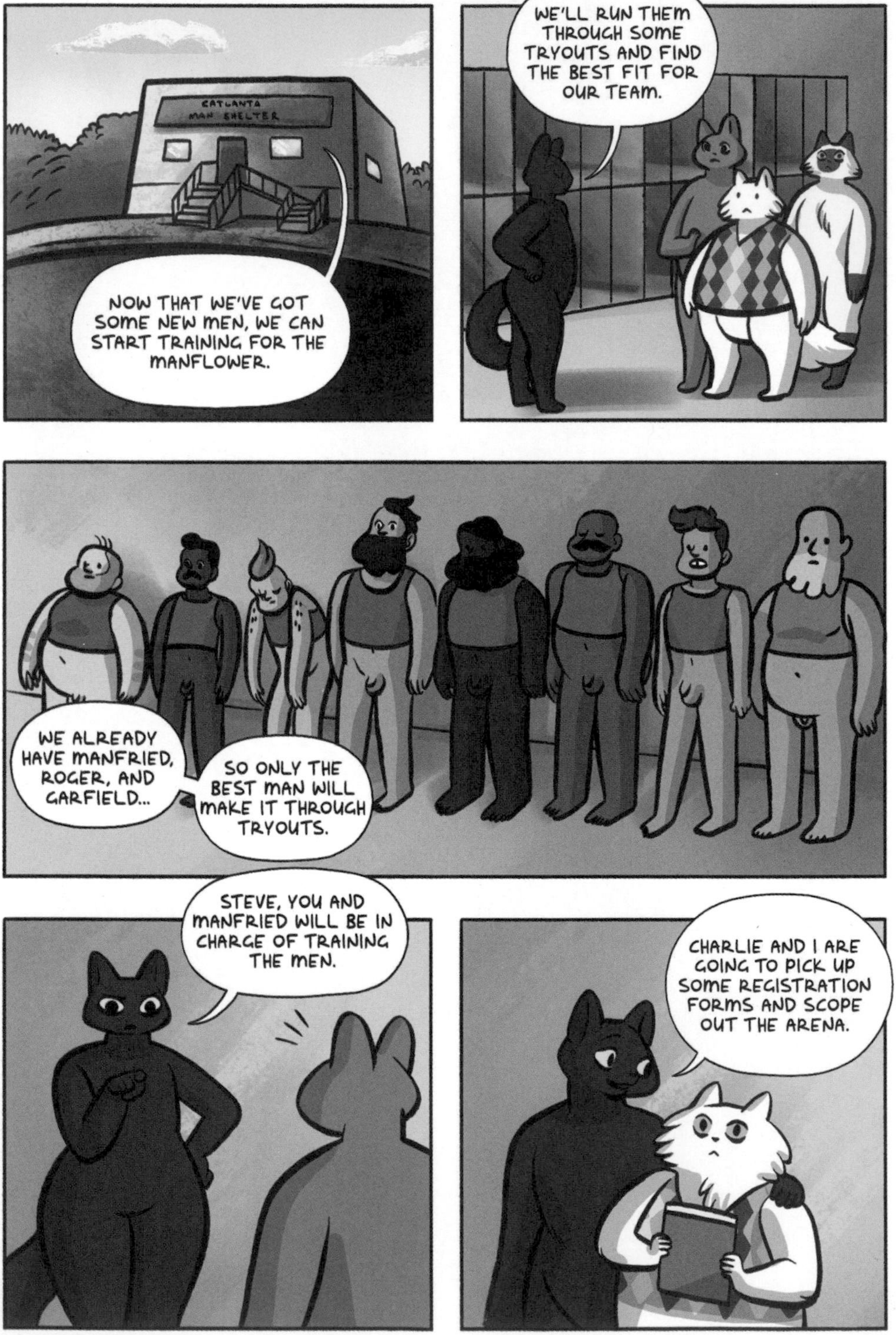
CATLANTA MAN SHELTER
NOW THAT WE'VE GOT SOME NEW MEN, WE CAN START TRAINING FOR THE MANFLOWER.
WE'LL RUN THEM THROUGH SOME TRYOUTS AND FIND THE BEST FIT FOR OUR TEAM.
WE ALREADY HAVE MANFRIED, ROGER, AND GARFIELD...
SO ONLY THE BEST MAN WILL MAKE IT THROUGH TRYOUTS.
STEVE, YOU AND MANFRIED WILL BE IN CHARGE OF TRAINING THE MEN.
CHARLIE AND I ARE GOING TO PICK UP SOME REGISTRATION FORMS AND SCOPE OUT THE ARENA.

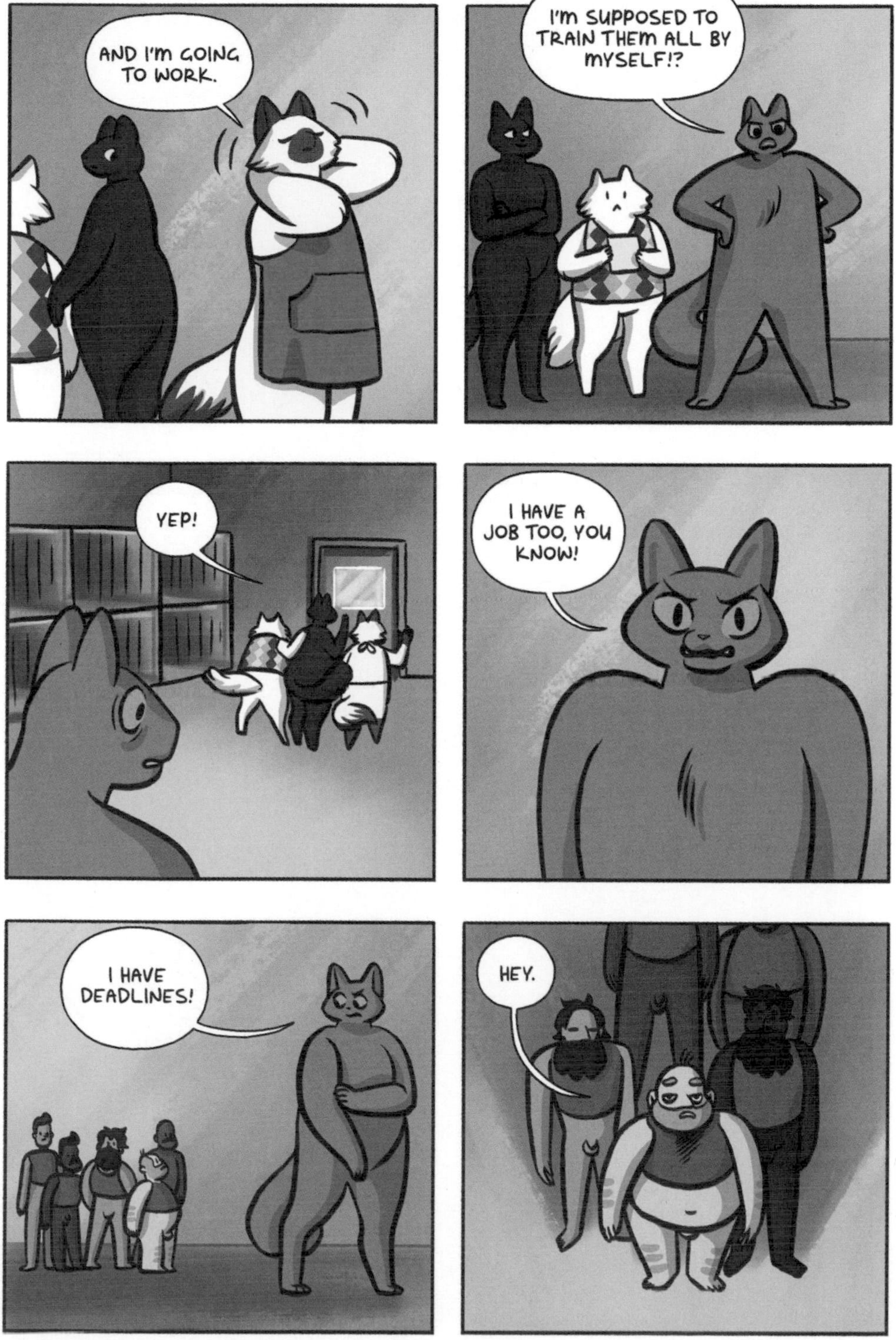
AND I'M GOING TO WORK.
I'M SUPPOSED TO TRAIN THEM ALL BY MYSELF!?
YEP!
I HAVE A JOB TOO, YOU KNOW!
I HAVE DEADLINES!
HEY.

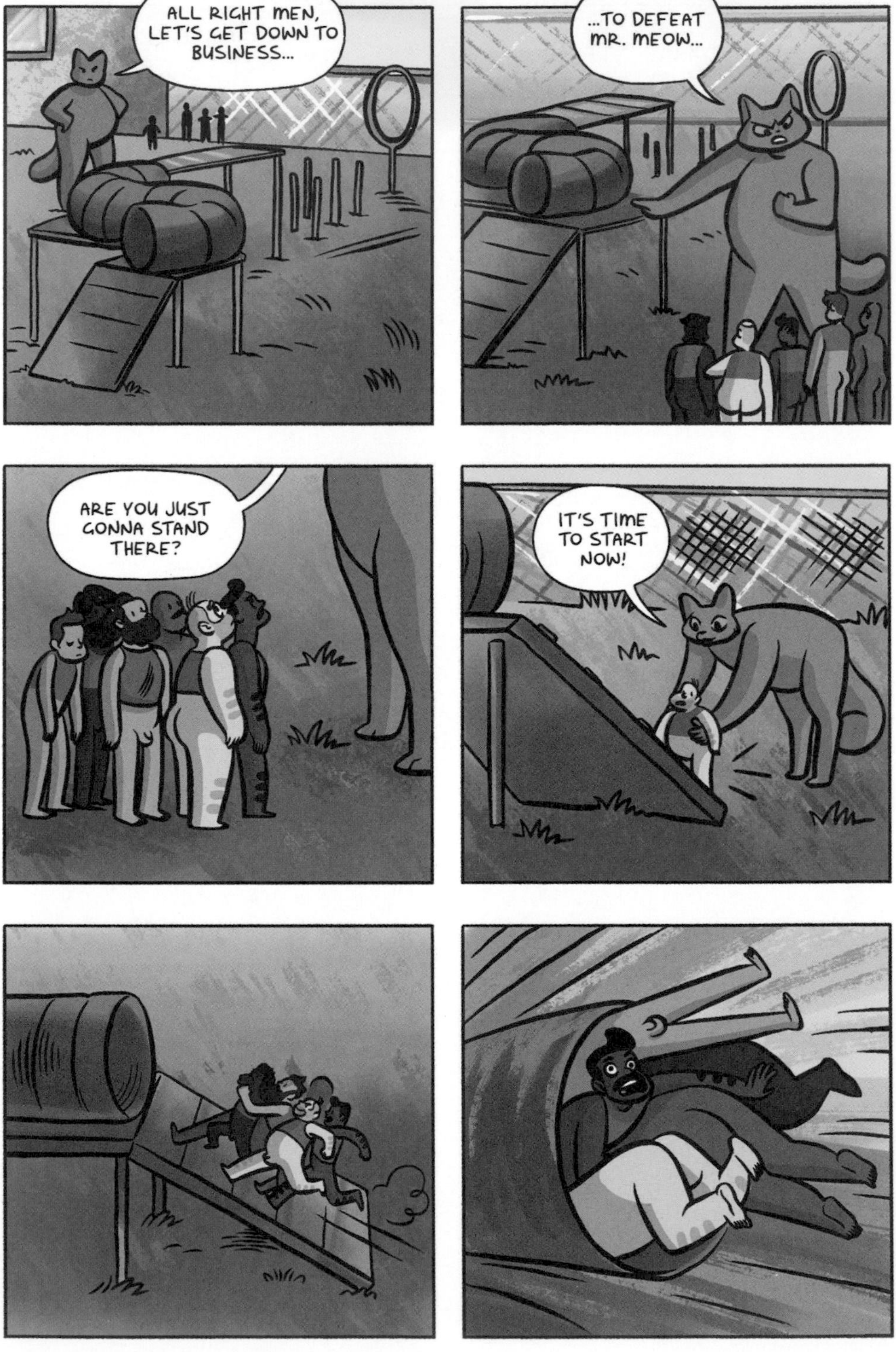
ALL RIGHT MEN, LET'S GET DOWN TO BUSINESS...
...TO DEFEAT MR. MEOW...
ARE YOU JUST GONNA STAND THERE?
IT'S TIME TO START NOW!

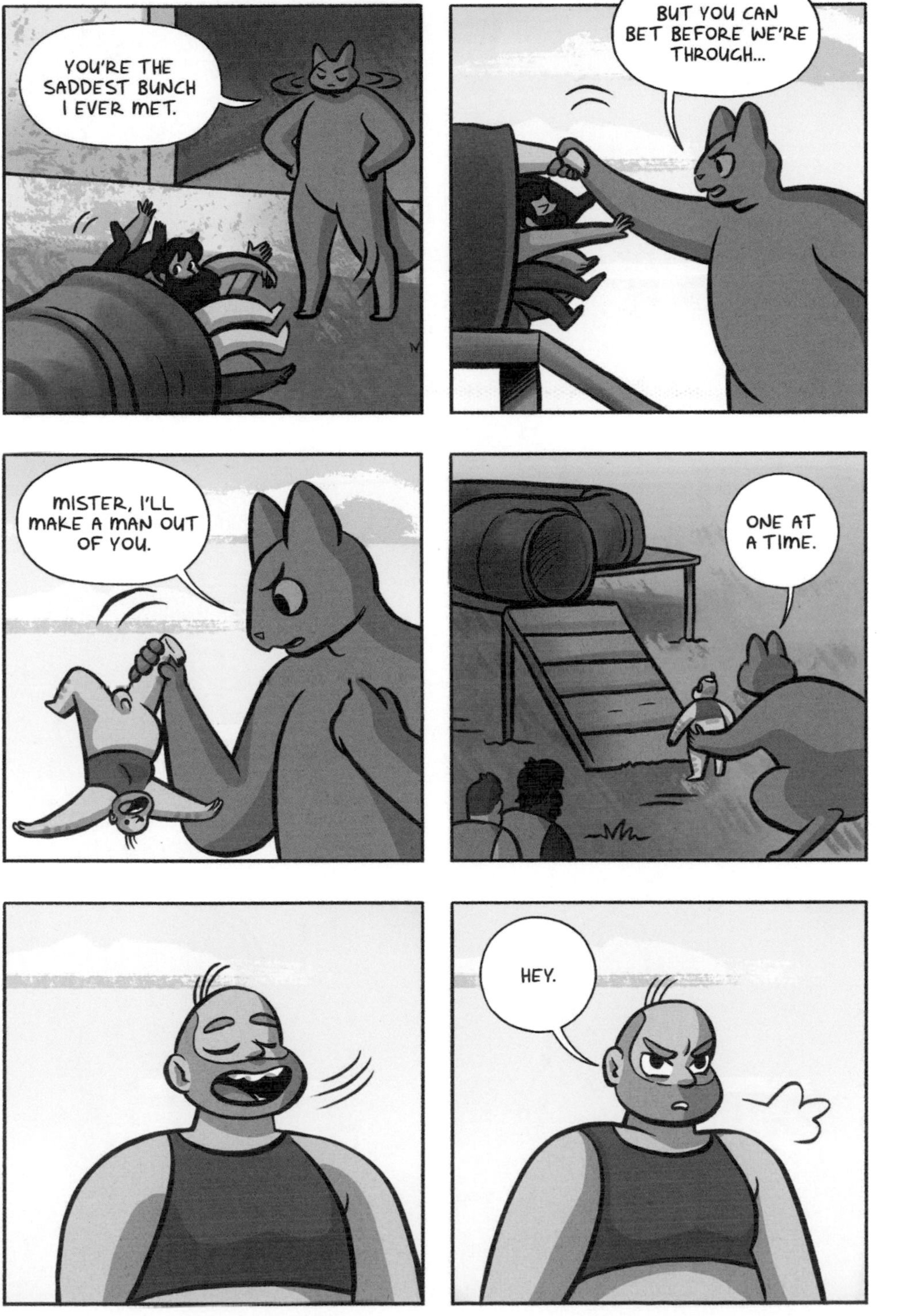
YOU'RE THE SADDEST BUNCH I EVER MET.
BUT YOU CAN BET BEFORE WE'RE THROUGH...
MISTER, I'LL MAKE A MAN OUT OF YOU.
ONE AT A TIME.
HEY.

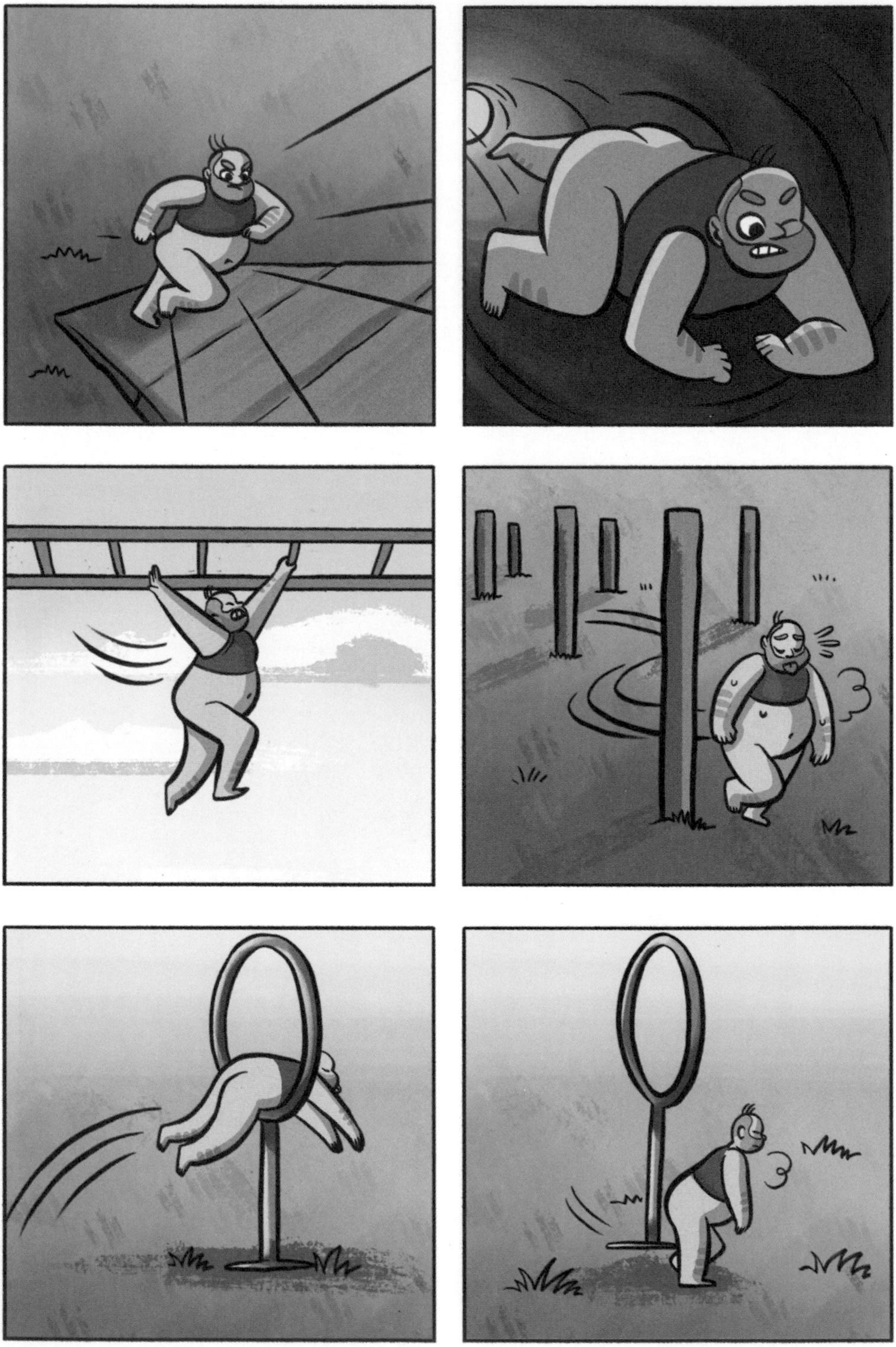

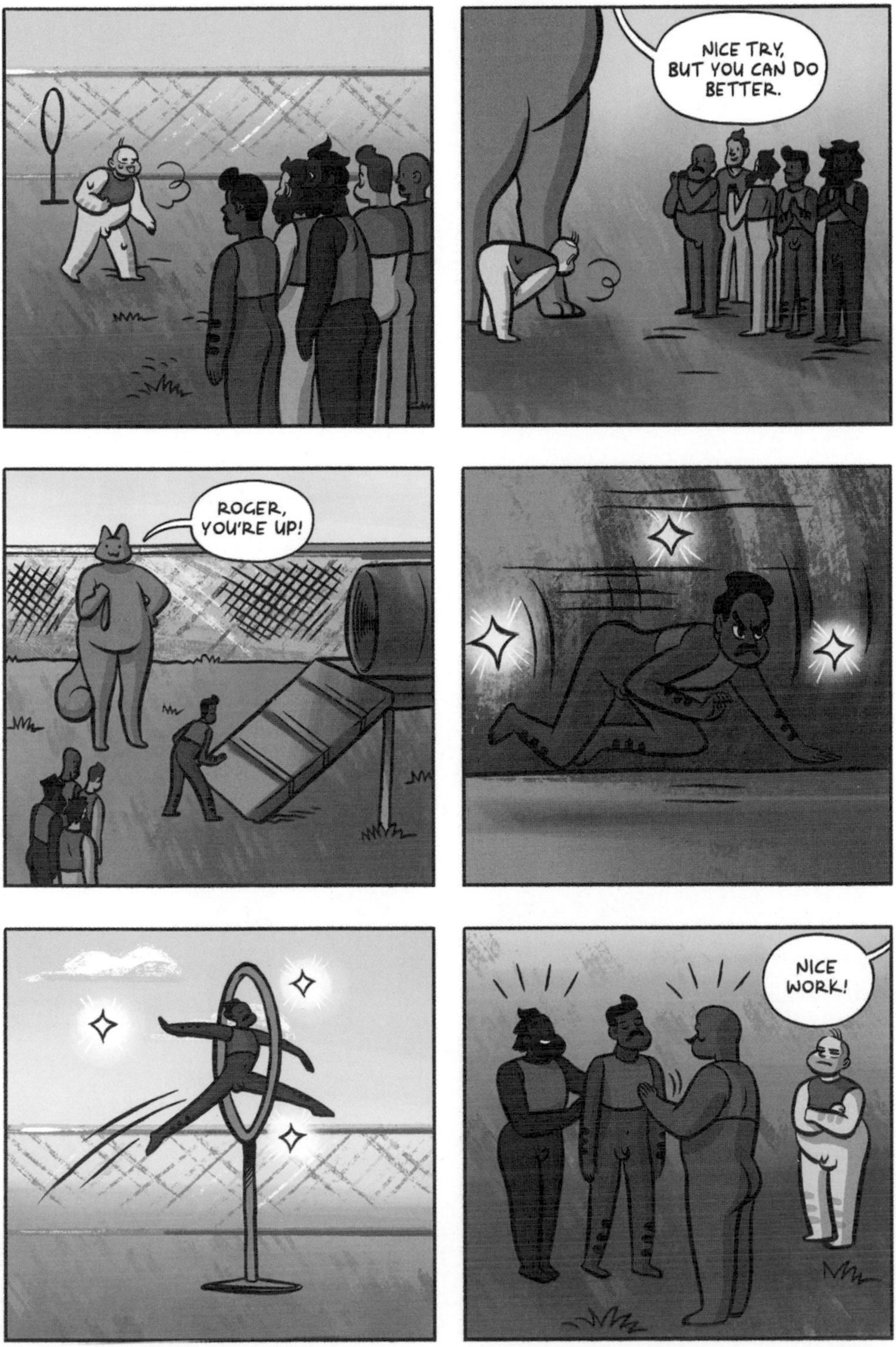
NICE TRY, BUT YOU CAN DO BETTER.
ROGER, YOU'RE UP!
NICE WORK!

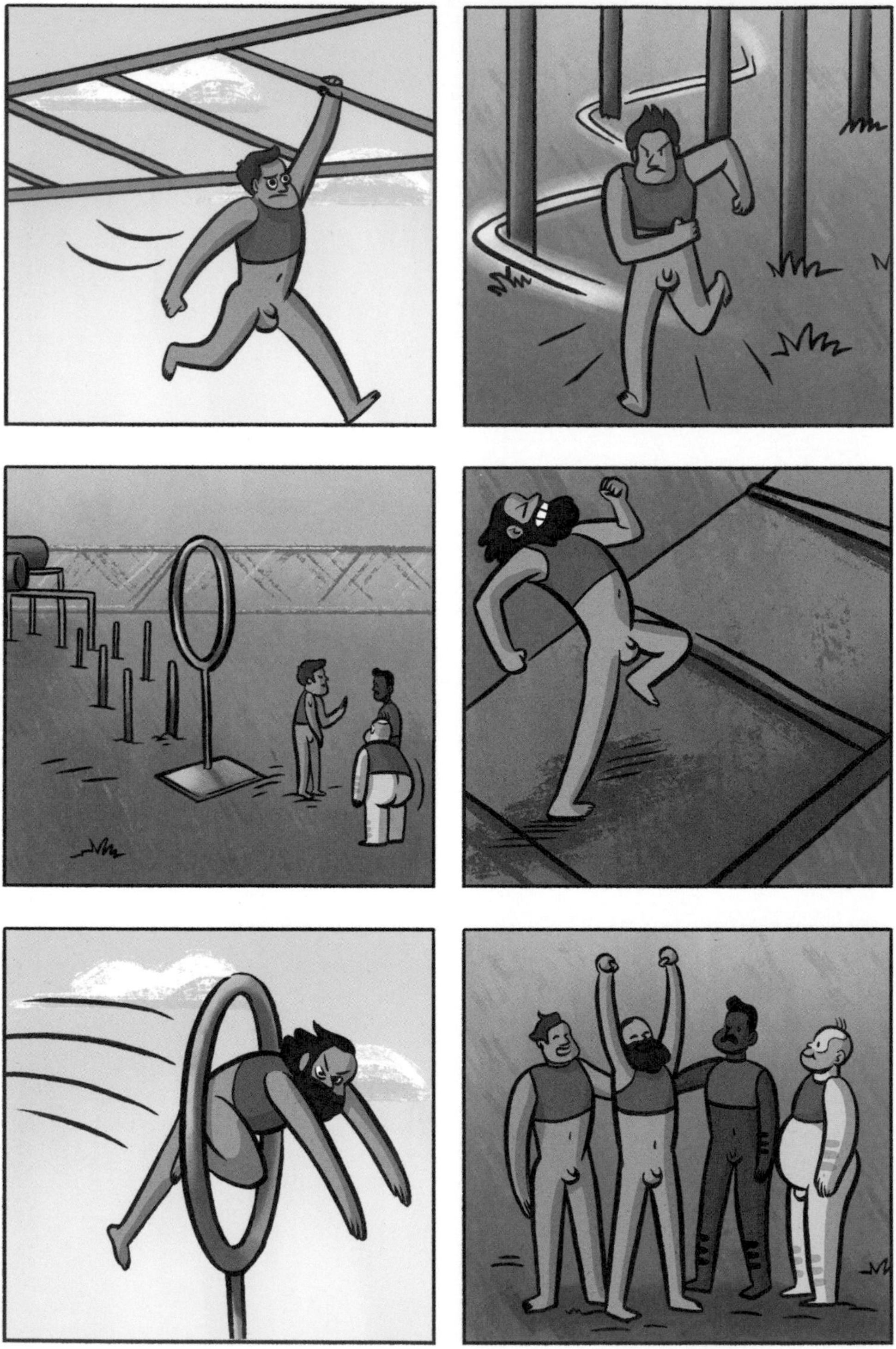

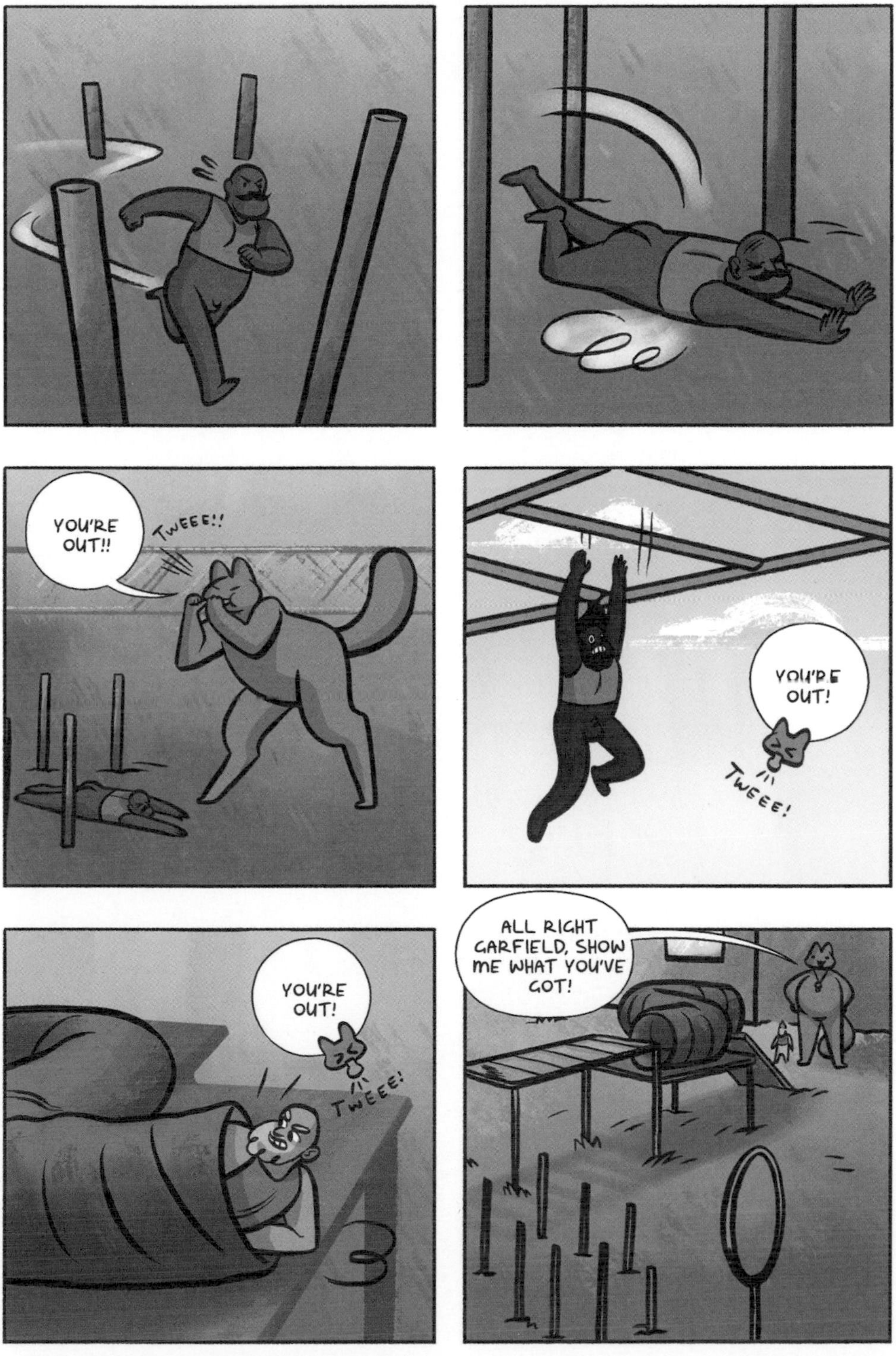
YOU'RE OUT!!
TWEEE!!
YOU'RE OUT!
TWEEE!
YOU'RE OUT!
TWEEE!
ALL RIGHT GARFIELD, SHOW ME WHAT YOU'VE GOT!

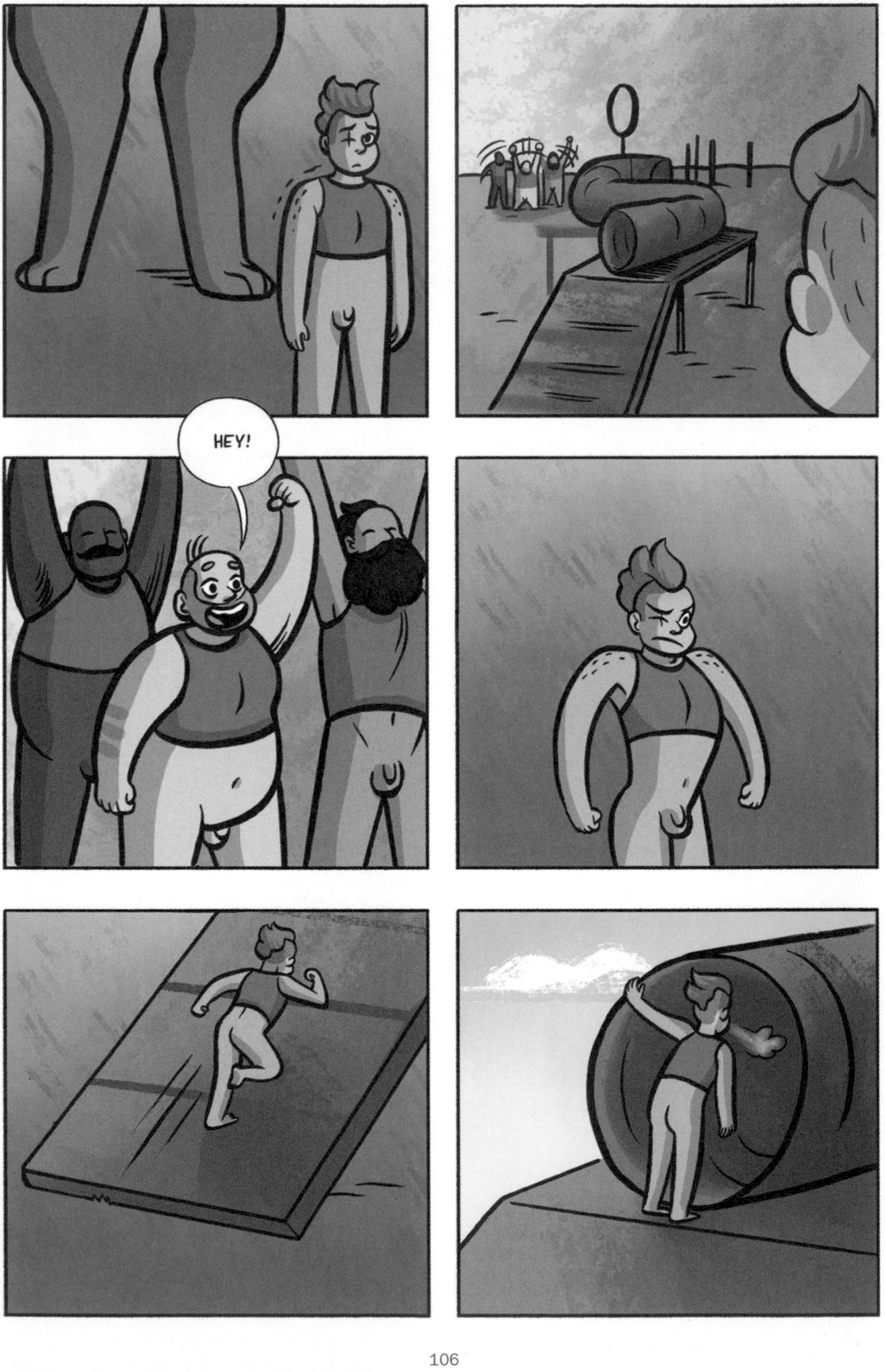
HEY!

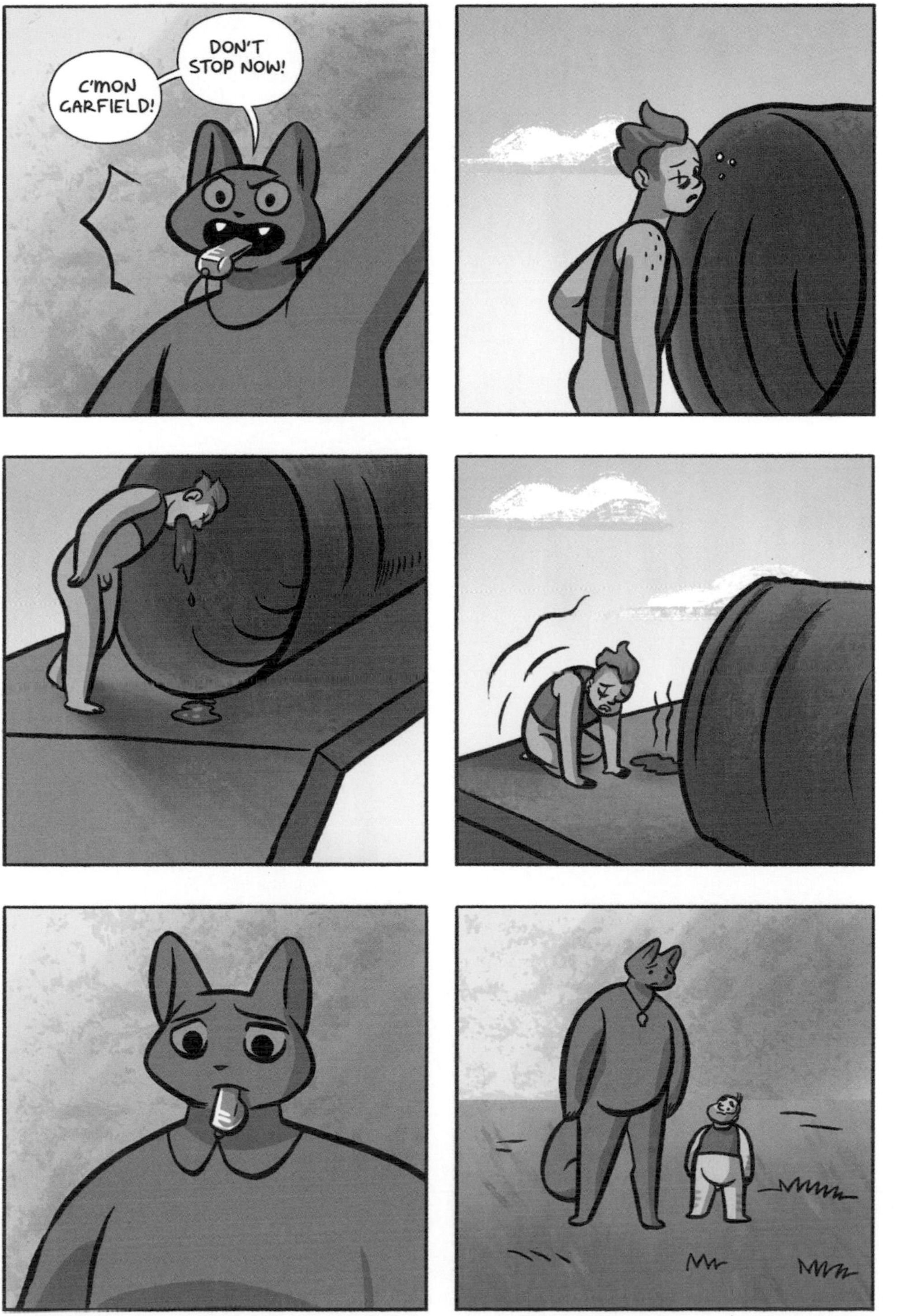
C'MON GARFIELD!
DON'T STOP NOW!

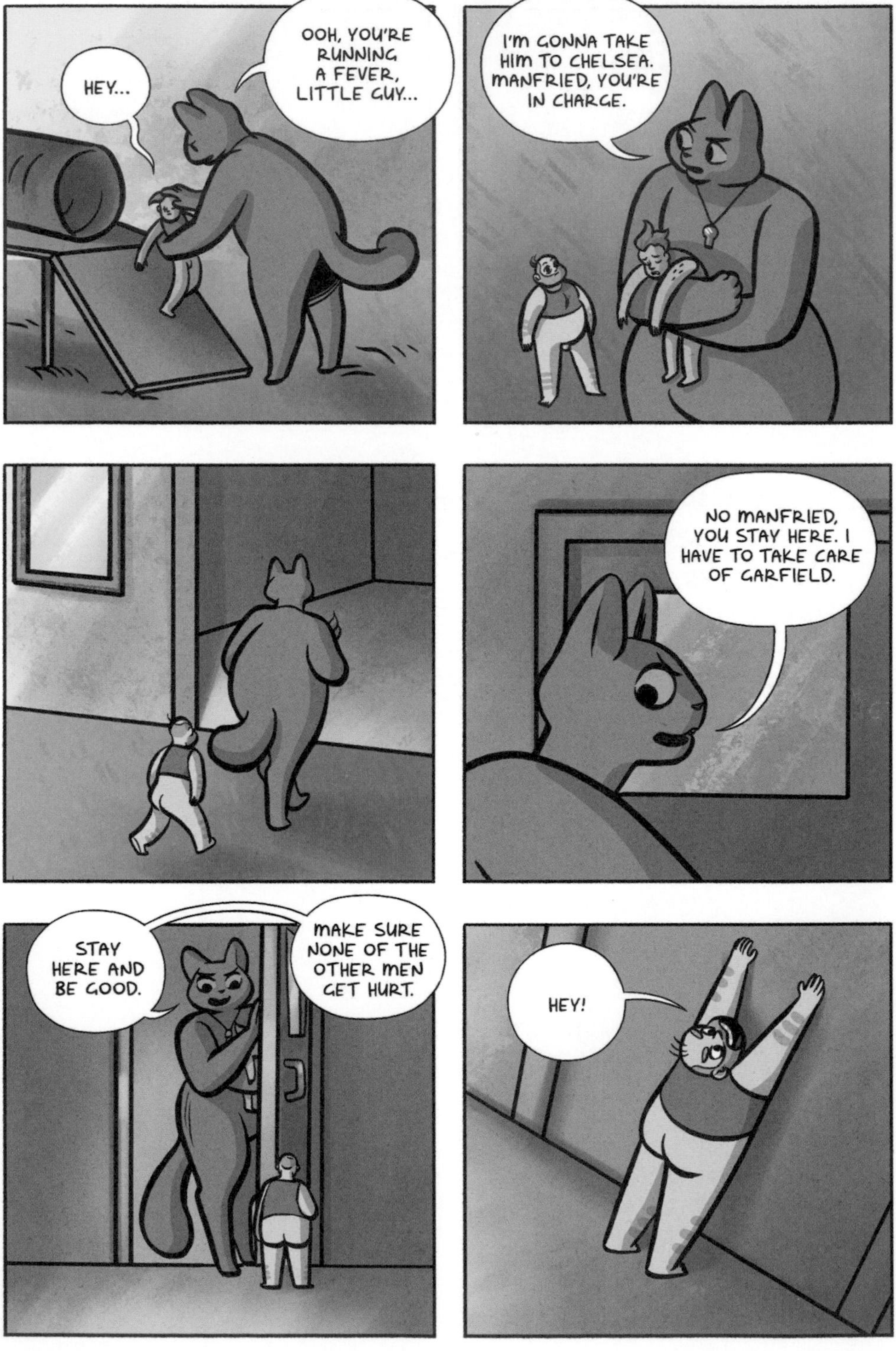
HEY...
OOH, YOU'RE RUNNING A FEVER, LITTLE GUY...
I'M GONNA TAKE HIM TO CHELSEA. MANFRIED, YOU'RE IN CHARGE.
NO MANFRIED, YOU STAY HERE. I HAVE TO TAKE CARE OF GARFIELD.
STAY HERE AND BE GOOD.
MAKE SURE NONE OF THE OTHER MEN GET HURT.
HEY!

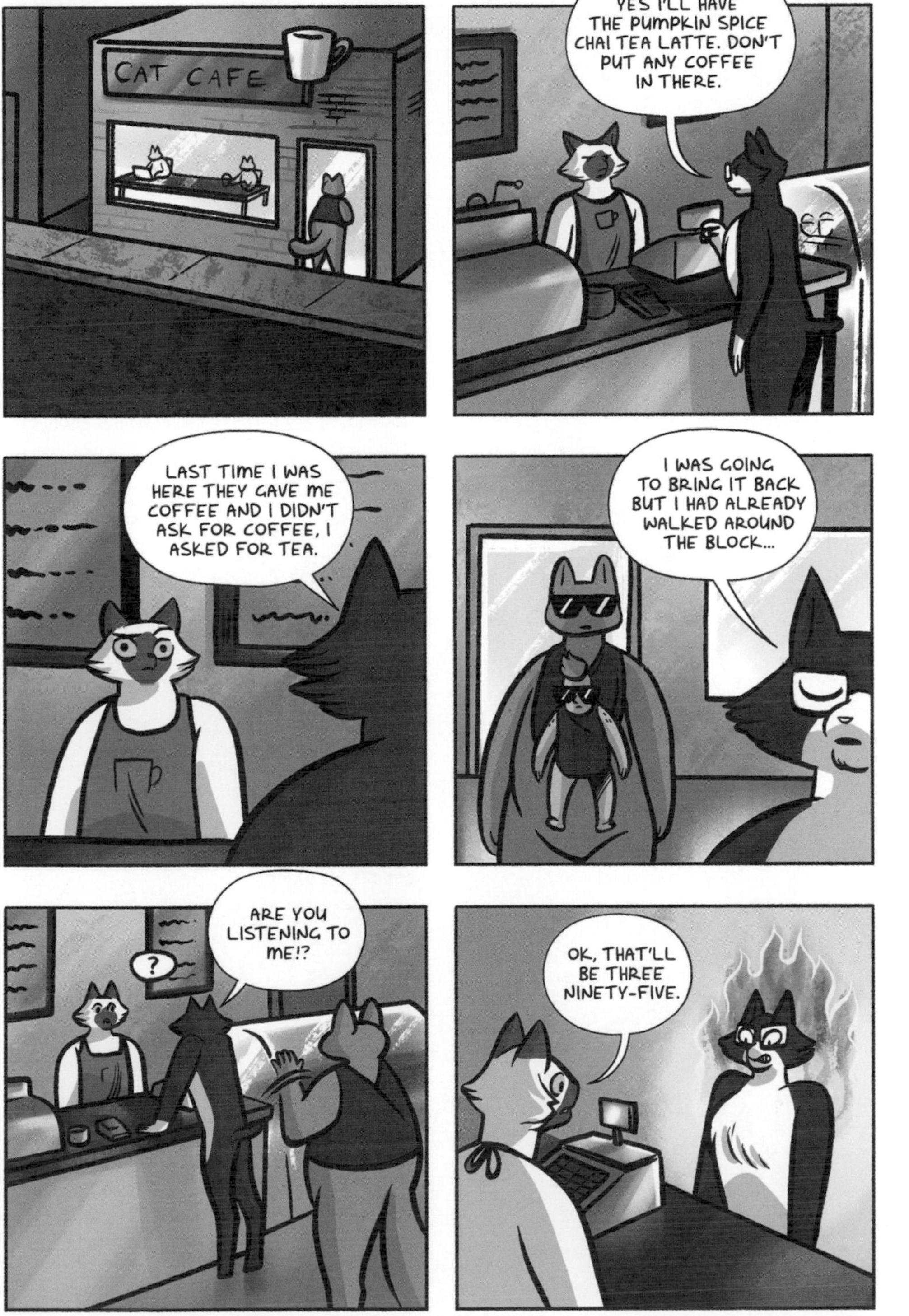
CAT CAFE
YES I'LL HAVE THE PUMPKIN SPICE CHAI TEA LATTE. DON'T PUT ANY COFFEE IN THERE.
LAST TIME I WAS HERE THEY GAVE ME COFFEE AND I DIDN'T ASK FOR COFFEE, I ASKED FOR TEA.
I WAS GOING TO BRING IT BACK BUT I HAD ALREADY WALKED AROUND THE BLOCK...
?
ARE YOU LISTENING TO ME!?
OK, THAT'LL BE THREE NINETY-FIVE.

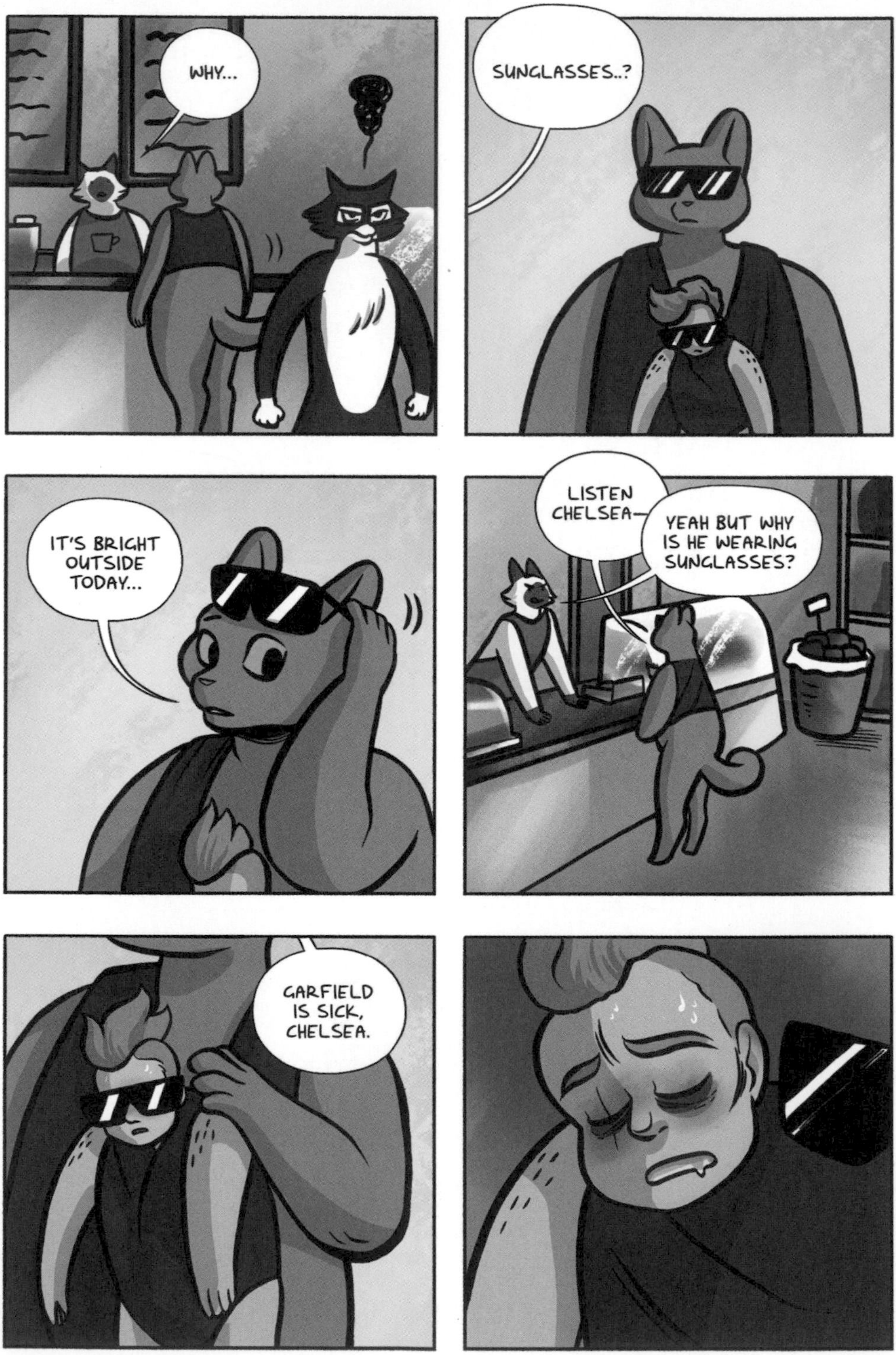
WHY...
SUNGLASSES..?
IT'S BRIGHT OUTSIDE TODAY...
LISTEN CHELSEA—
YEAH BUT WHY IS HE WEARING SUNGLASSES?
GARFIELD IS SICK, CHELSEA.

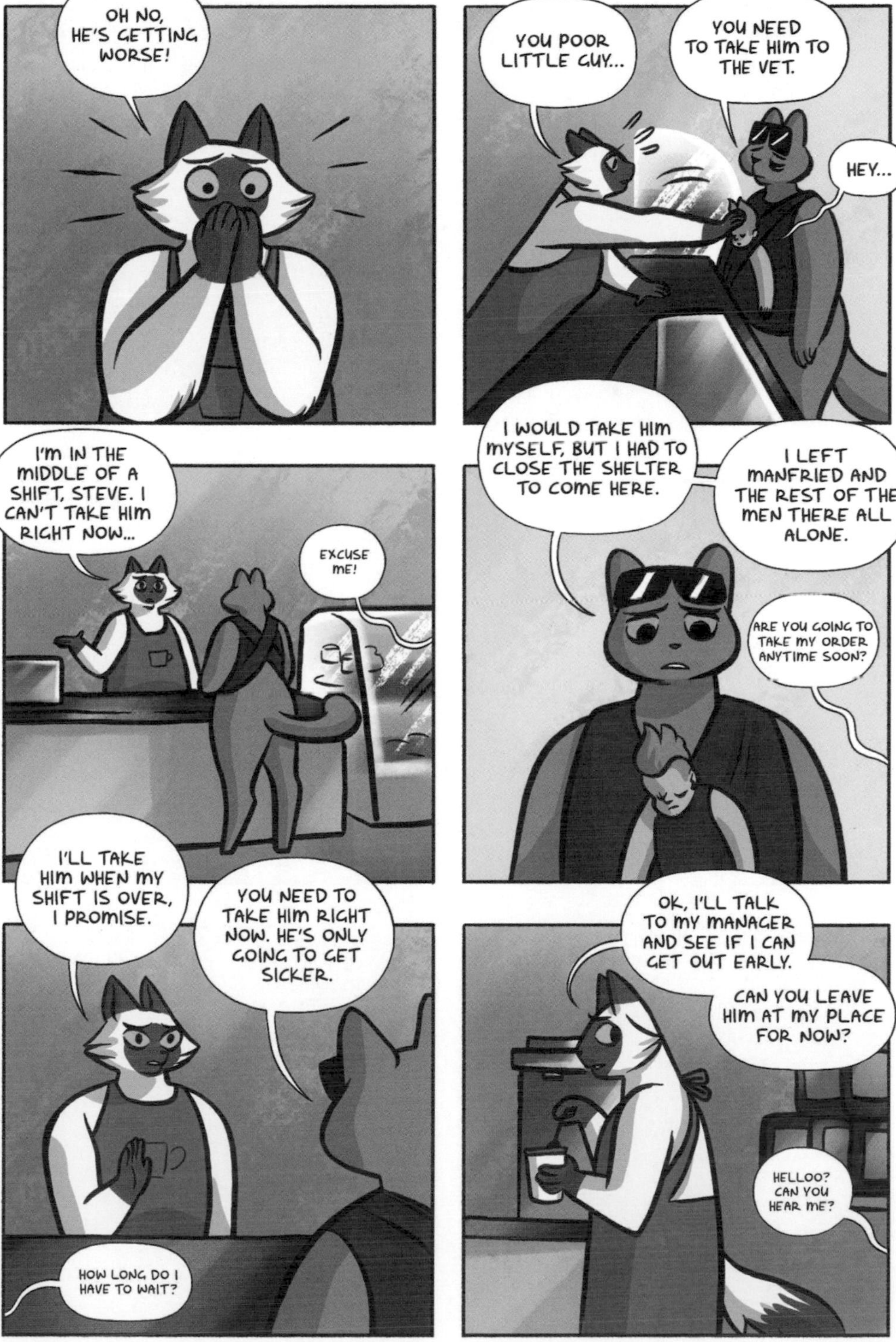
OH NO, HE'S GETTING WORSE!
YOU POOR LITTLE GUY...
YOU NEED TO TAKE HIM TO THE VET.
HEY...
I'M IN THE MIDDLE OF A SHIFT, STEVE. I CAN'T TAKE HIM RIGHT NOW...
EXCUSE ME!
I WOULD TAKE HIM MYSELF, BUT I HAD TO CLOSE THE SHELTER TO COME HERE.
I LEFT MANFRIED AND THE REST OF THE MEN THERE ALL ALONE.
ARE YOU GOING TO TAKE MY ORDER ANYTIME SOON?
I'LL TAKE HIM WHEN MY SHIFT IS OVER, I PROMISE.
YOU NEED TO TAKE HIM RIGHT NOW. HE'S ONLY GOING TO GET SICKER.
HOW LONG DO I HAVE TO WAIT?
OK, I'LL TALK TO MY MANAGER AND SEE IF I CAN GET OUT EARLY.
CAN YOU LEAVE HIM AT MY PLACE FOR NOW?
HELLOO? CAN YOU HEAR ME?

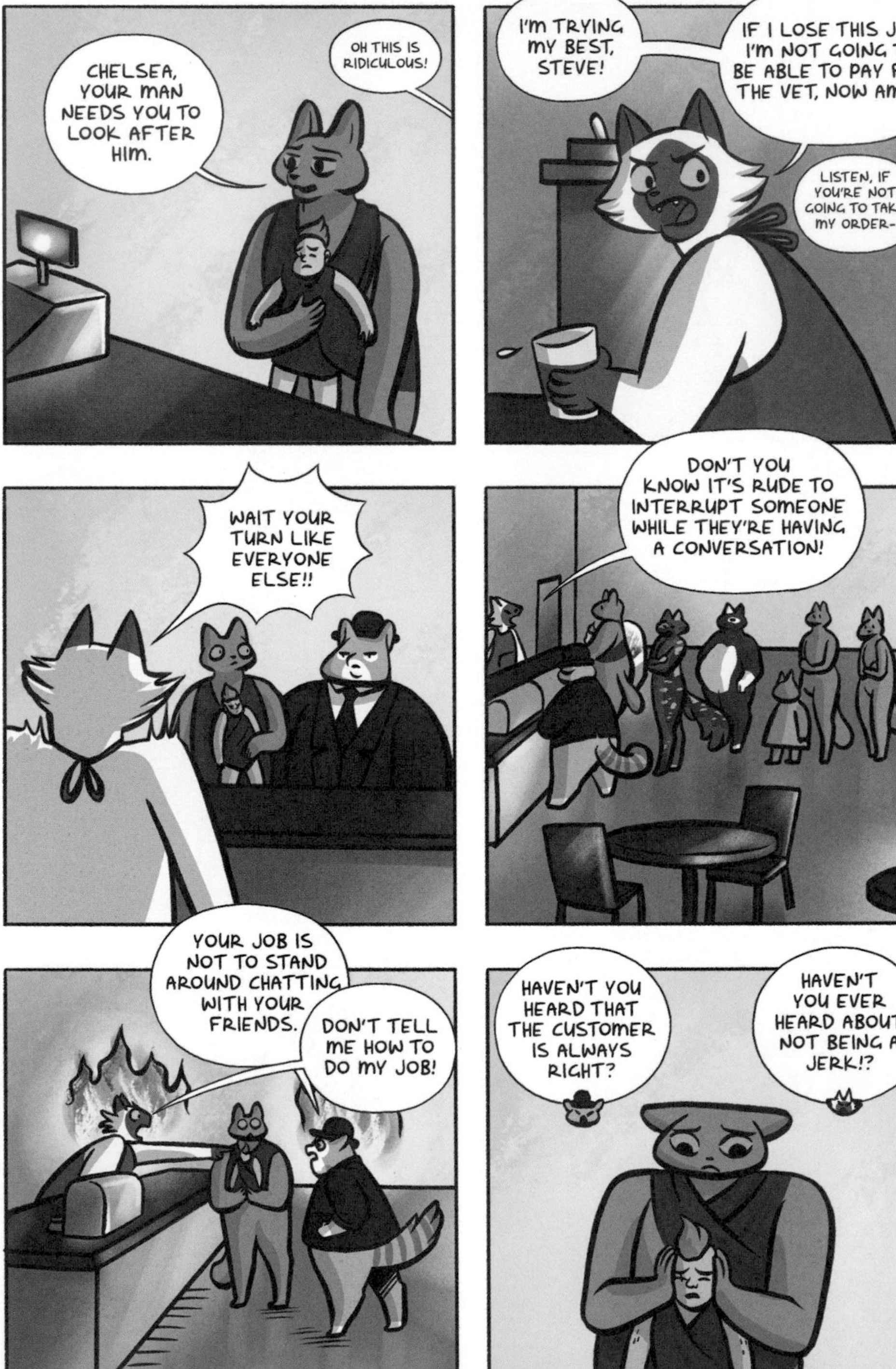
CHELSEA, YOUR MAN NEEDS YOU TO LOOK AFTER HIM.
OH THIS IS RIDICULOUS!
I'M TRYING MY BEST, STEVE!
IF I LOSE THIS JOB I'M NOT GOING TO BE ABLE TO PAY FOR THE VET, NOW AM I?
LISTEN, IF YOU'RE NOT GOING TO TAKE MY ORDER-
WAIT YOUR TURN LIKE EVERYONE ELSE!!
DON'T YOU KNOW IT'S RUDE TO INTERRUPT SOMEONE WHILE THEY'RE HAVING A CONVERSATION!
YOUR JOB IS NOT TO STAND AROUND CHATTING WITH YOUR FRIENDS.
DON'T TELL ME HOW TO DO MY JOB!
HAVEN'T YOU HEARD THAT THE CUSTOMER IS ALWAYS RIGHT?
HAVEN'T YOU EVER HEARD ABOUT NOT BEING A JERK!?

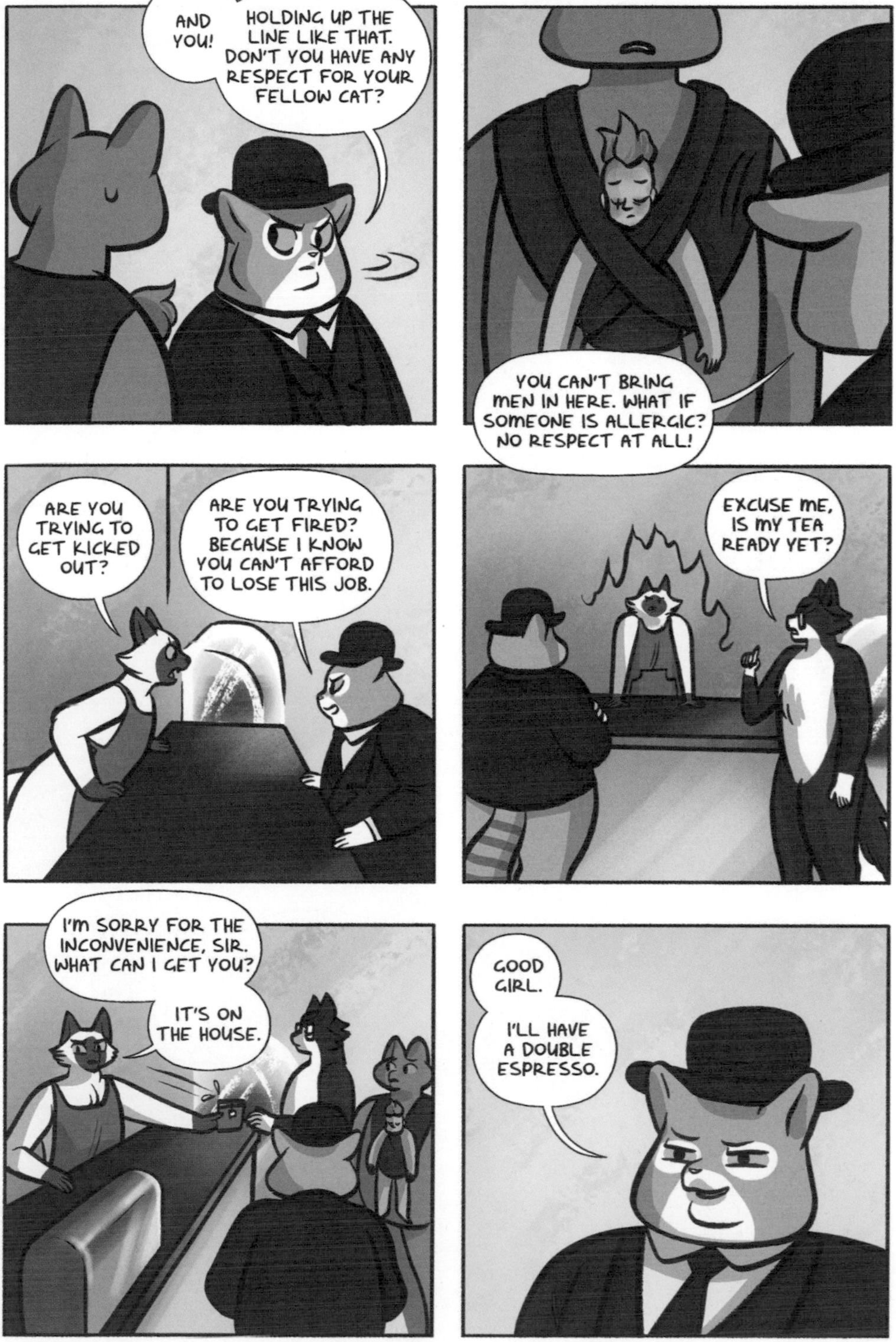
AND YOU!
HOLDING UP THE LINE LIKE THAT. DON'T YOU HAVE ANY RESPECT FOR YOUR FELLOW CAT?
YOU CAN'T BRING MEN IN HERE. WHAT IF SOMEONE IS ALLERGIC? NO RESPECT AT ALL!
ARE YOU TRYING TO GET KICKED OUT?
ARE YOU TRYING TO GET FIRED? BECAUSE I KNOW YOU CAN'T AFFORD TO LOSE THIS JOB.
EXCUSE ME, IS MY TEA READY YET?
I'M SORRY FOR THE INCONVENIENCE, SIR. WHAT CAN I GET YOU?
IT'S ON THE HOUSE.
GOOD GIRL.
I'LL HAVE A DOUBLE ESPRESSO.

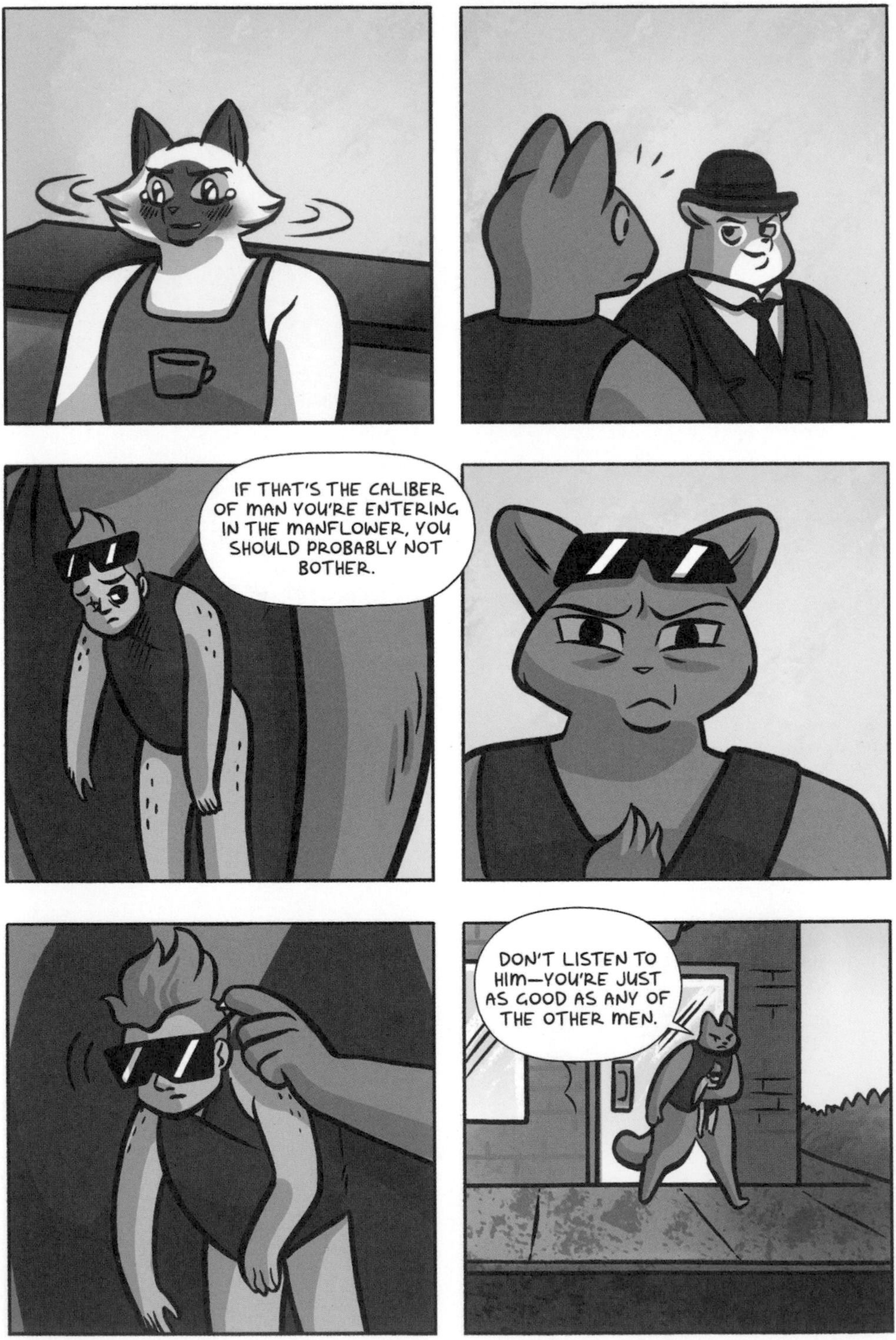
IF THAT'S THE CALIBER OF MAN YOU'RE ENTERING IN THE MANFLOWER, YOU SHOULD PROBABLY NOT BOTHER.
DON'T LISTEN TO HIM—YOU'RE JUST AS GOOD AS ANY OF THE OTHER MEN.

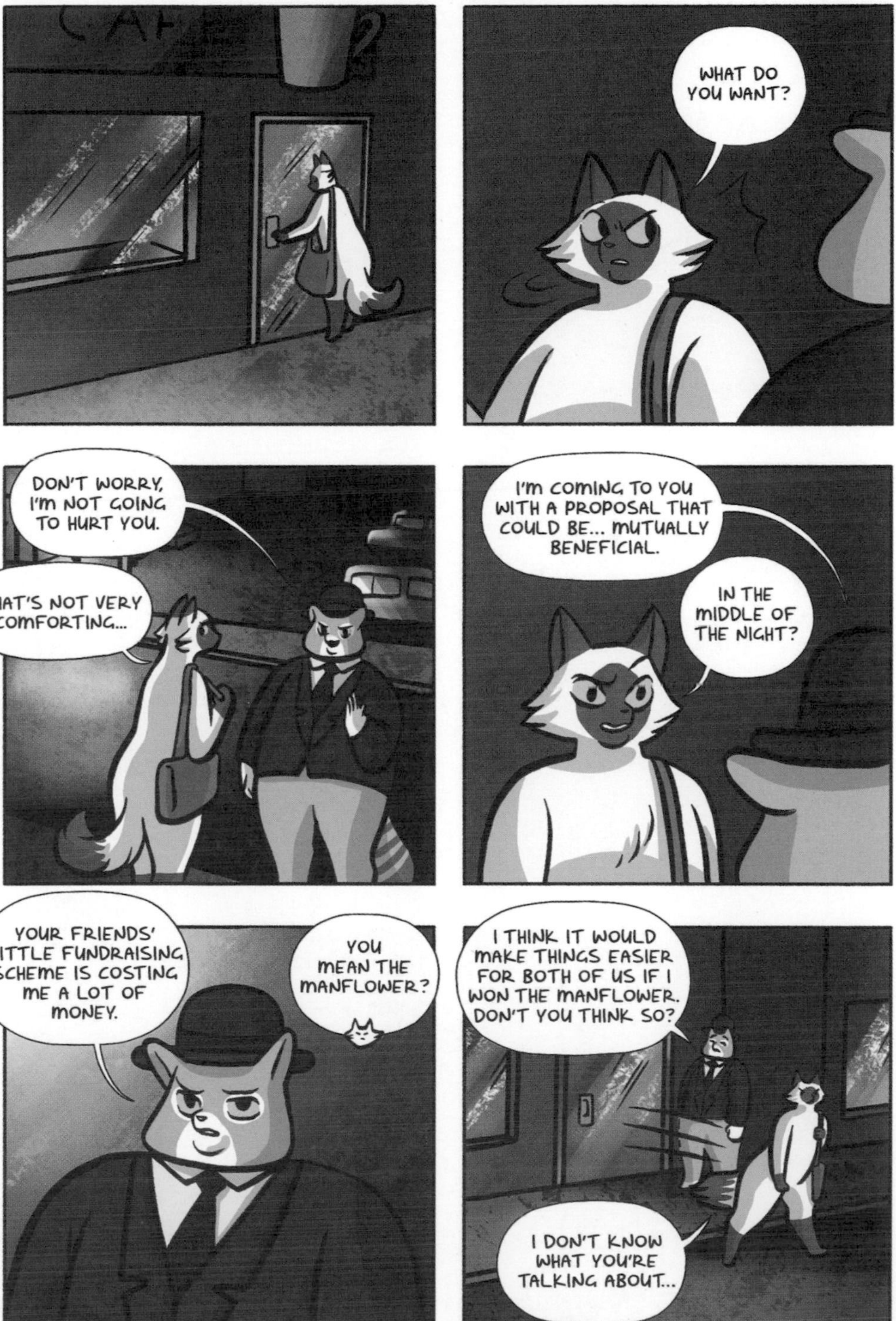
WHAT DO YOU WANT?
DON'T WORRY, I'M NOT GOING TO HURT YOU.
THAT'S NOT VERY COMFORTING...
I'M COMING TO YOU WITH A PROPOSAL THAT COULD BE... MUTUALLY BENEFICIAL.
IN THE MIDDLE OF THE NIGHT?
YOUR FRIENDS' LITTLE FUNDRAISING SCHEME IS COSTING ME A LOT OF MONEY.
YOU MEAN THE MANFLOWER?
I THINK IT WOULD MAKE THINGS EASIER FOR BOTH OF US IF I WON THE MANFLOWER. DON'T YOU THINK SO?
I DON'T KNOW WHAT YOU'RE TALKING ABOUT...

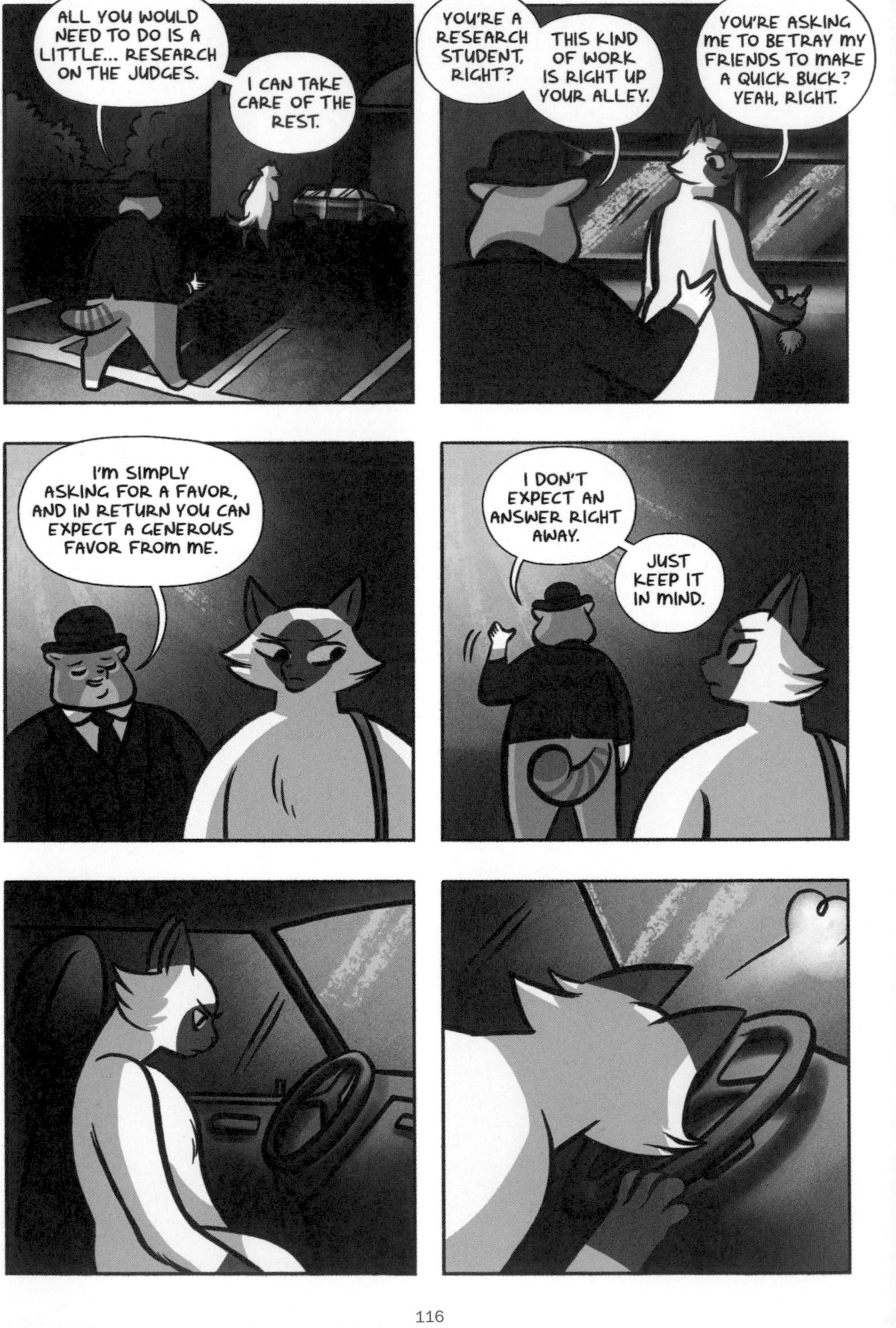
ALL YOU WOULD NEED TO DO IS A LITTLE... RESEARCH ON THE JUDGES.
I CAN TAKE CARE OF THE REST.
YOU'RE A RESEARCH STUDENT, RIGHT?
THIS KIND OF WORK IS RIGHT UP YOUR ALLEY.
YOU'RE ASKING ME TO BETRAY MY FRIENDS TO MAKE A QUICK BUCK? YEAH, RIGHT.
I'M SIMPLY ASKING FOR A FAVOR, AND IN RETURN YOU CAN EXPECT A GENEROUS FAVOR FROM ME.
I DON'T EXPECT AN ANSWER RIGHT AWAY.
JUST KEEP IT IN MIND.

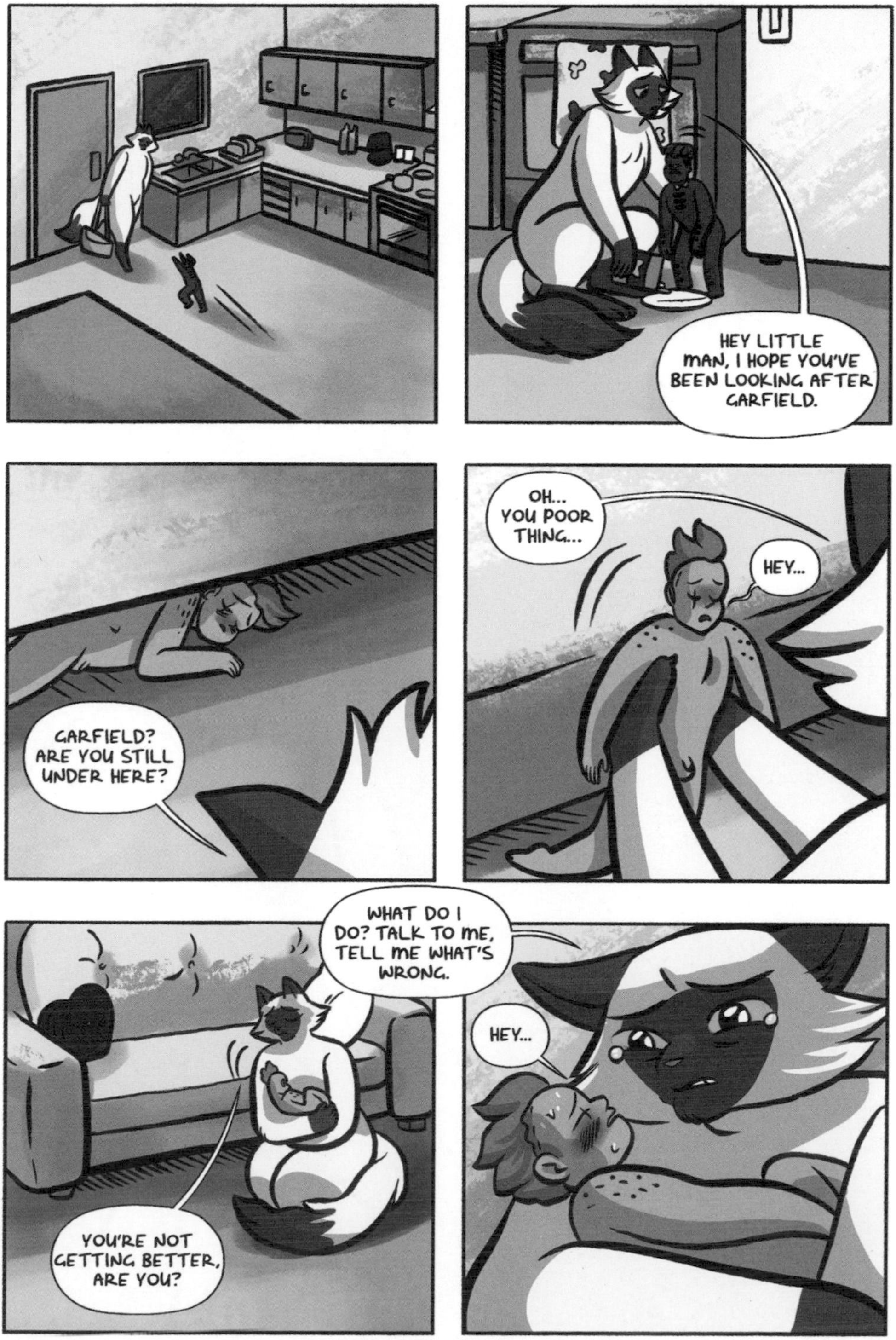

HEY LITTLE MAN, I HOPE YOU'VE BEEN LOOKING AFTER GARFIELD.
GARFIELD? ARE YOU STILL UNDER HERE?
OH... YOU POOR THING...
HEY...
WHAT DO I DO? TALK TO ME, TELL ME WHAT'S WRONG.
YOU'RE NOT GETTING BETTER, ARE YOU?
HEY...

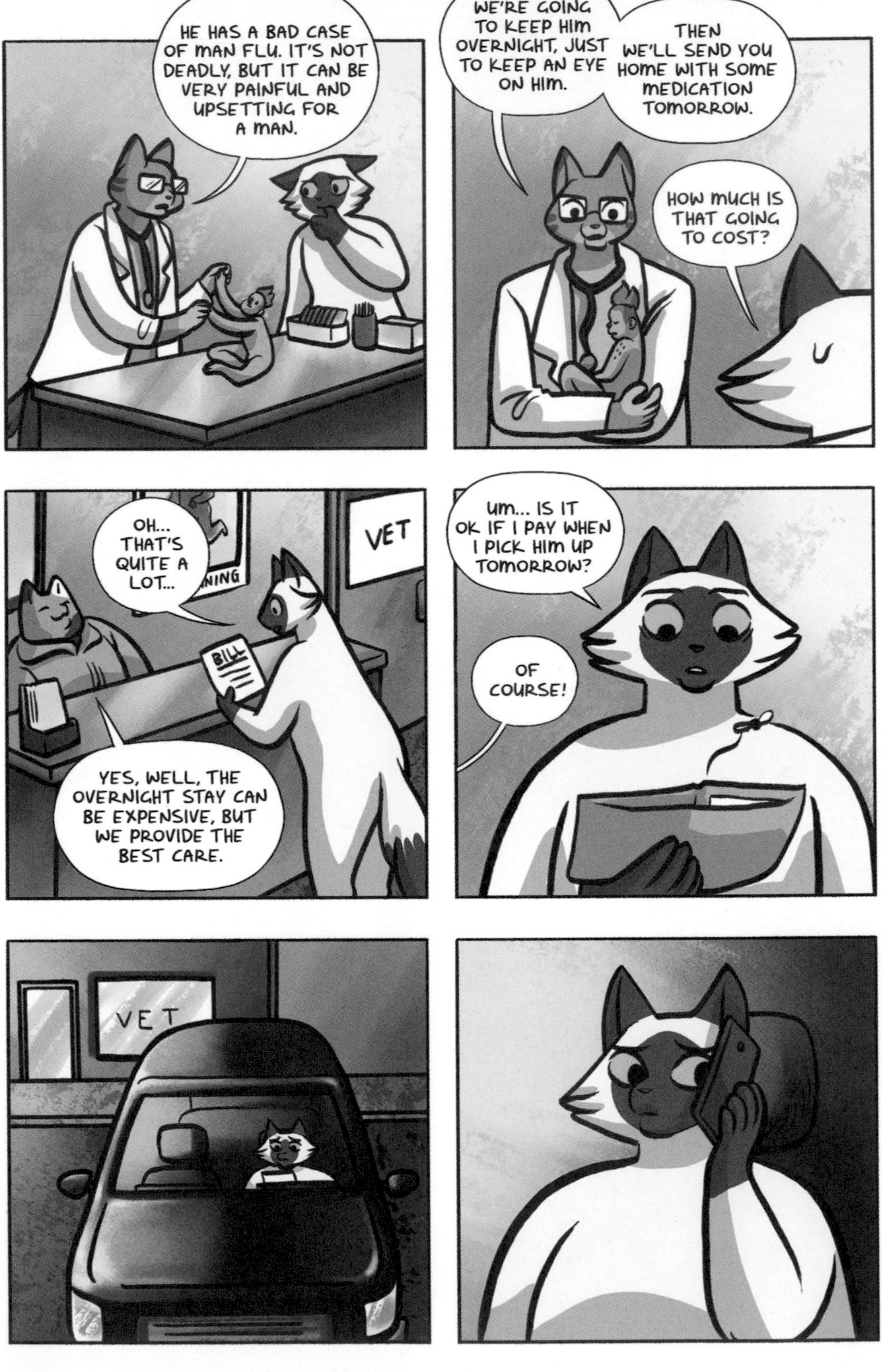
HE HAS A BAD CASE OF MAN FLU. IT'S NOT DEADLY, BUT IT CAN BE VERY PAINFUL AND UPSETTING FOR A MAN.
WE'RE GOING TO KEEP HIM OVERNIGHT, JUST TO KEEP AN EYE ON HIM.
THEN WE'LL SEND YOU HOME WITH SOME MEDICATION TOMORROW.
HOW MUCH IS THAT GOING TO COST?
VET
OH... THAT'S QUITE A LOT...
BILL
YES, WELL, THE OVERNIGHT STAY CAN BE EXPENSIVE, BUT WE PROVIDE THE BEST CARE.
UM... IS IT OK IF I PAY WHEN I PICK HIM UP TOMORROW?
OF COURSE!
VET

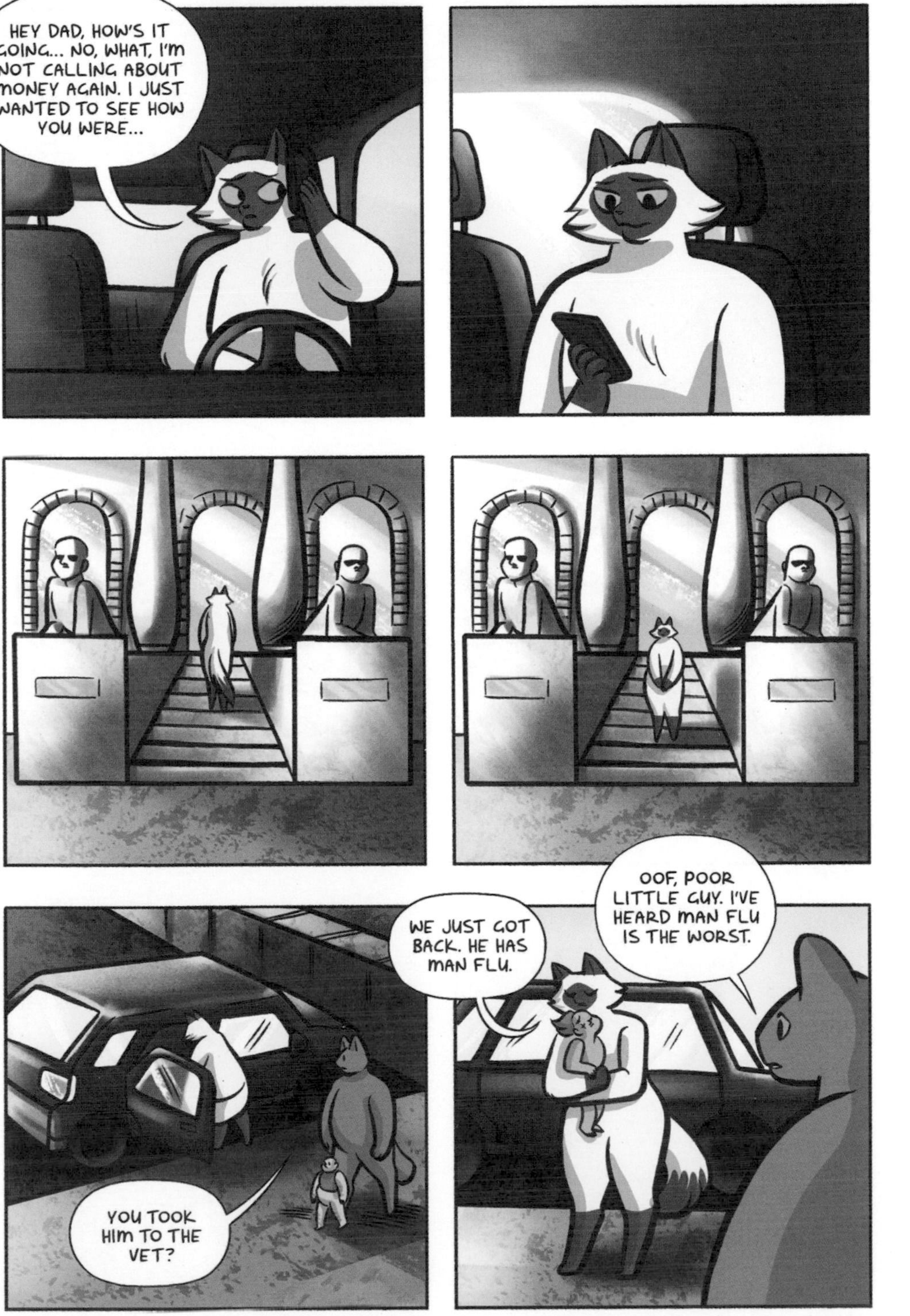
HEY DAD, HOW'S IT GOING... NO, WHAT, I'M NOT CALLING ABOUT MONEY AGAIN. I JUST WANTED TO SEE HOW YOU WERE...
WE JUST GOT BACK. HE HAS MAN FLU.
OOF, POOR LITTLE GUY. I'VE HEARD MAN FLU IS THE WORST.
YOU TOOK HIM TO THE VET?

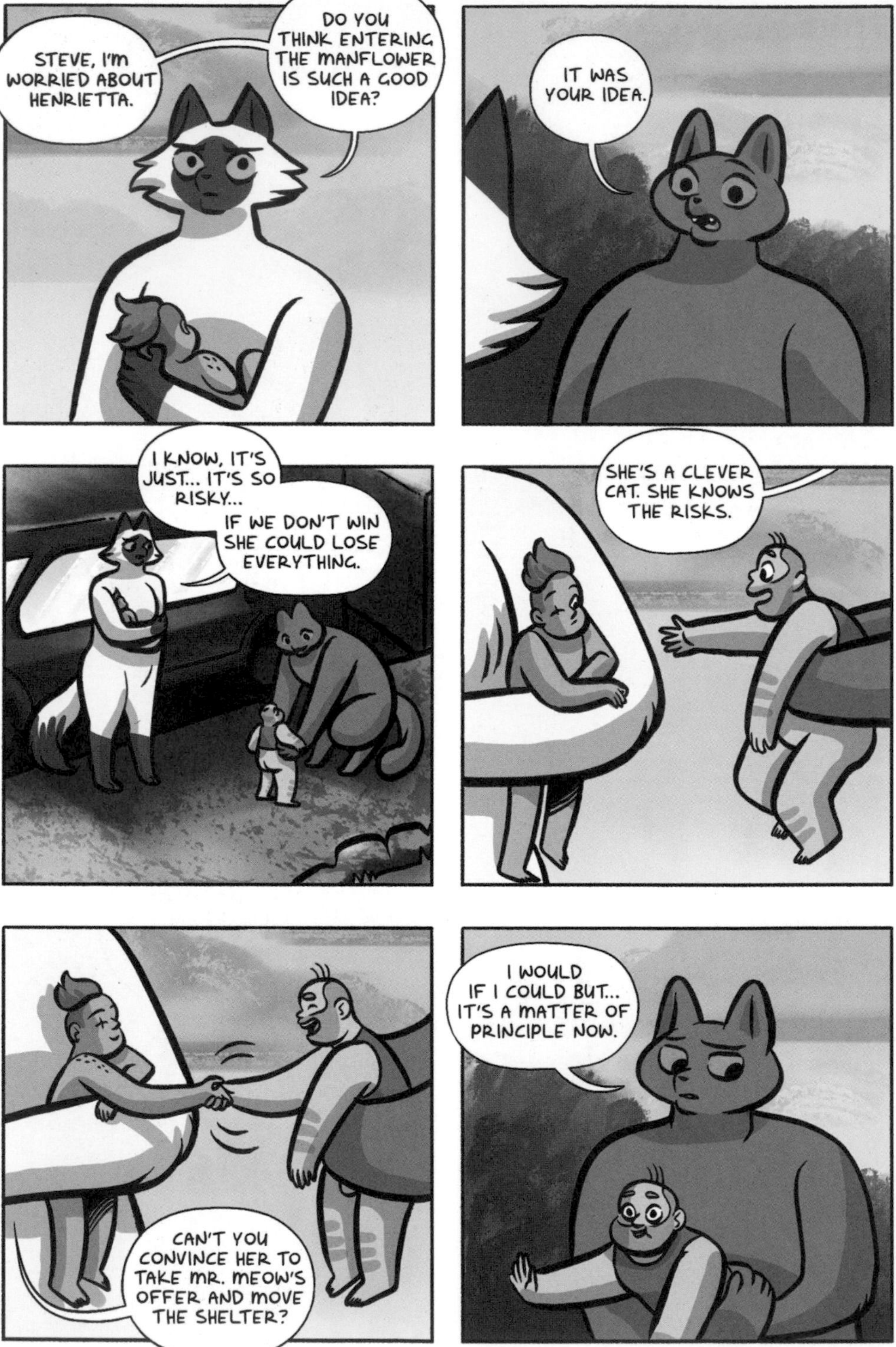
STEVE, I'M WORRIED ABOUT HENRIETTA.
DO YOU THINK ENTERING THE MANFLOWER IS SUCH A GOOD IDEA?
IT WAS YOUR IDEA.
I KNOW, IT'S JUST... IT'S SO RISKY...
IF WE DON'T WIN SHE COULD LOSE EVERYTHING.
SHE'S A CLEVER CAT. SHE KNOWS THE RISKS.
CAN'T YOU CONVINCE HER TO TAKE MR. MEOW'S OFFER AND MOVE THE SHELTER?
I WOULD IF I COULD BUT... IT'S A MATTER OF PRINCIPLE NOW.

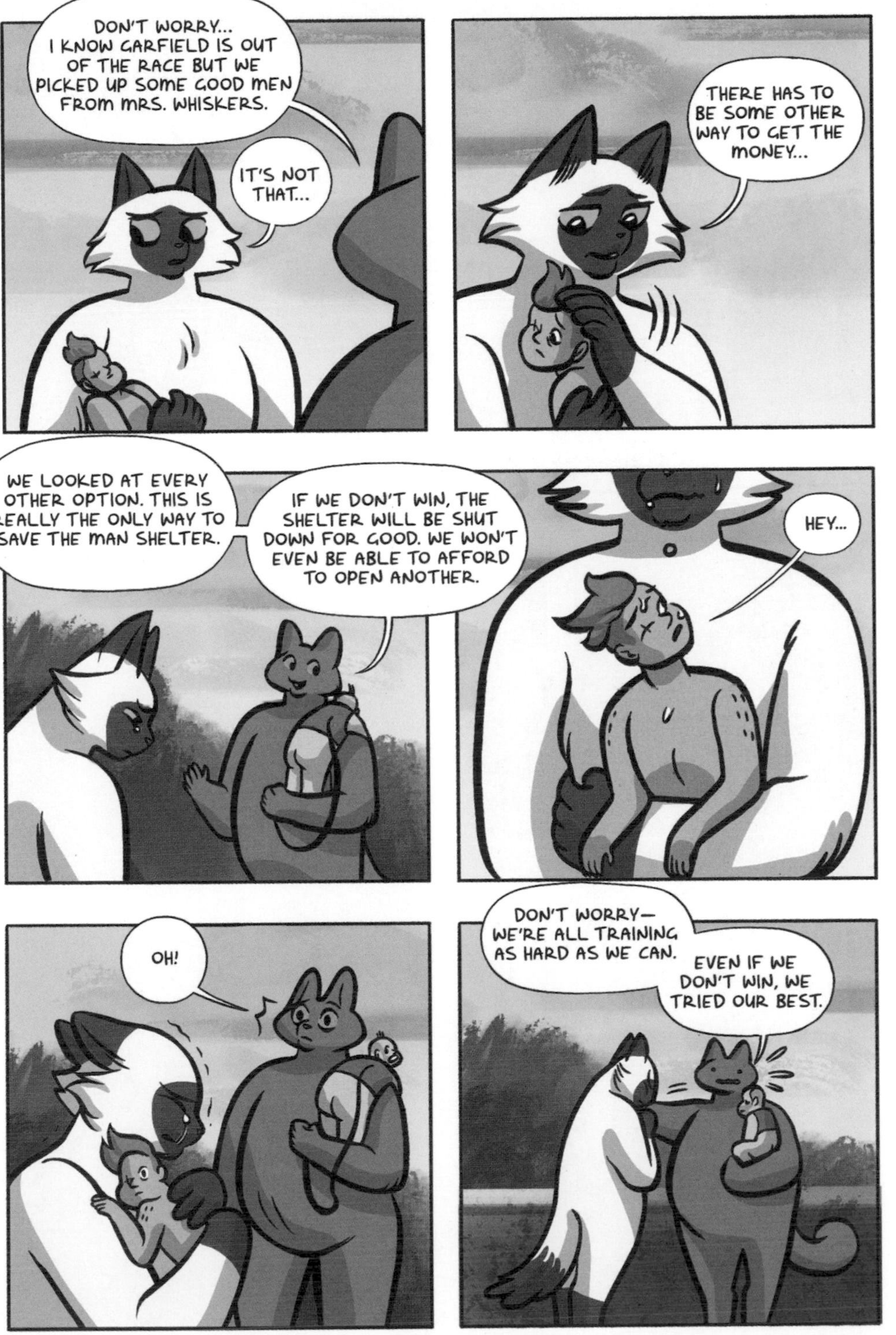
DON'T WORRY... I KNOW GARFIELD IS OUT OF THE RACE BUT WE PICKED UP SOME GOOD MEN FROM MRS. WHISKERS.
IT'S NOT THAT...
THERE HAS TO BE SOME OTHER WAY TO GET THE MONEY...
WE LOOKED AT EVERY OTHER OPTION. THIS IS REALLY THE ONLY WAY TO SAVE THE MAN SHELTER.
IF WE DON'T WIN, THE SHELTER WILL BE SHUT DOWN FOR GOOD. WE WON'T EVEN BE ABLE TO AFFORD TO OPEN ANOTHER.
HEY...
OH!
DON'T WORRY— WE'RE ALL TRAINING AS HARD AS WE CAN.
EVEN IF WE DON'T WIN, WE TRIED OUR BEST.

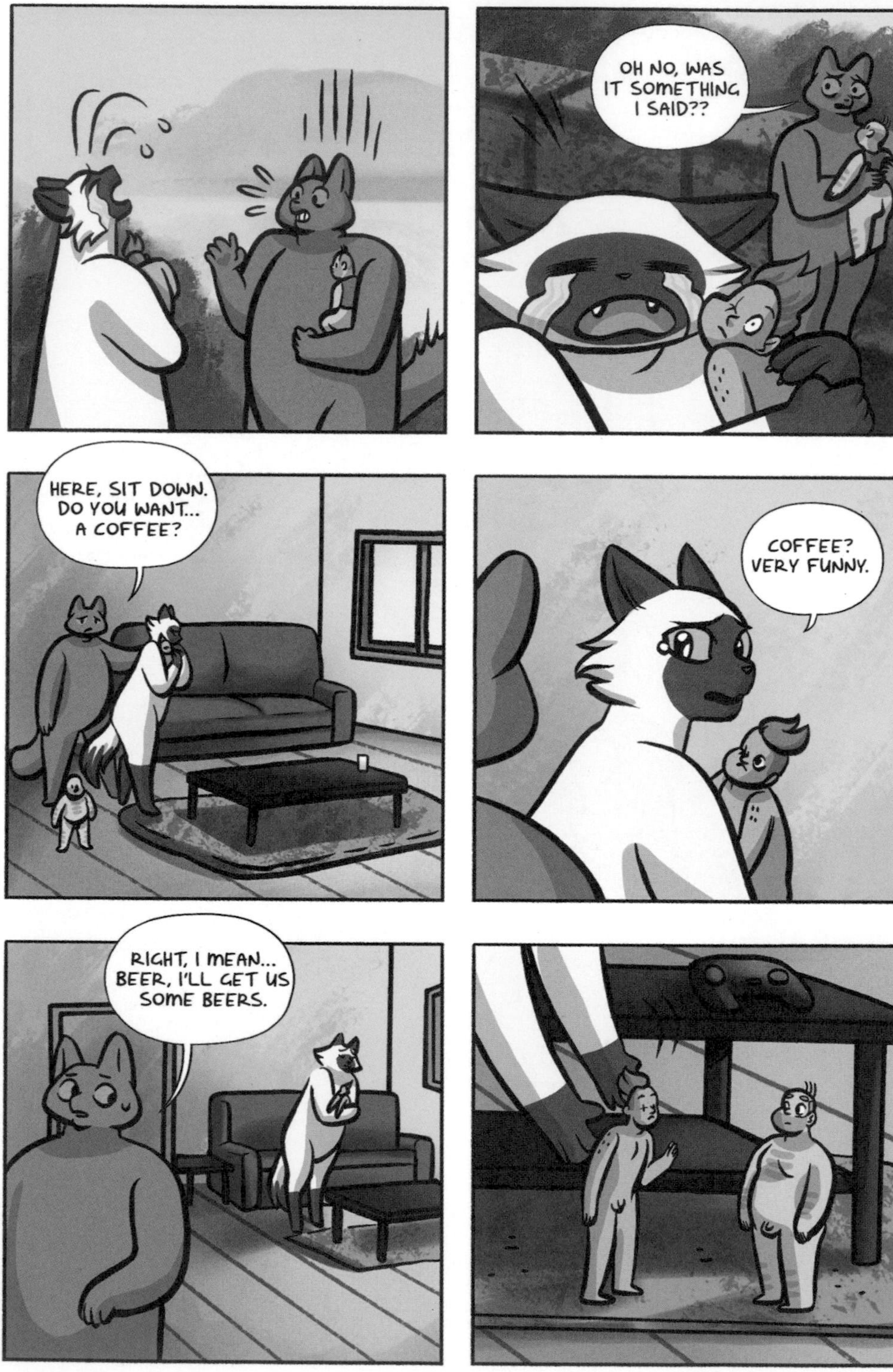
OH NO, WAS IT SOMETHING I SAID??
HERE, SIT DOWN. DO YOU WANT... A COFFEE?
COFFEE? VERY FUNNY.
RIGHT, I MEAN... BEER, I'LL GET US SOME BEERS.

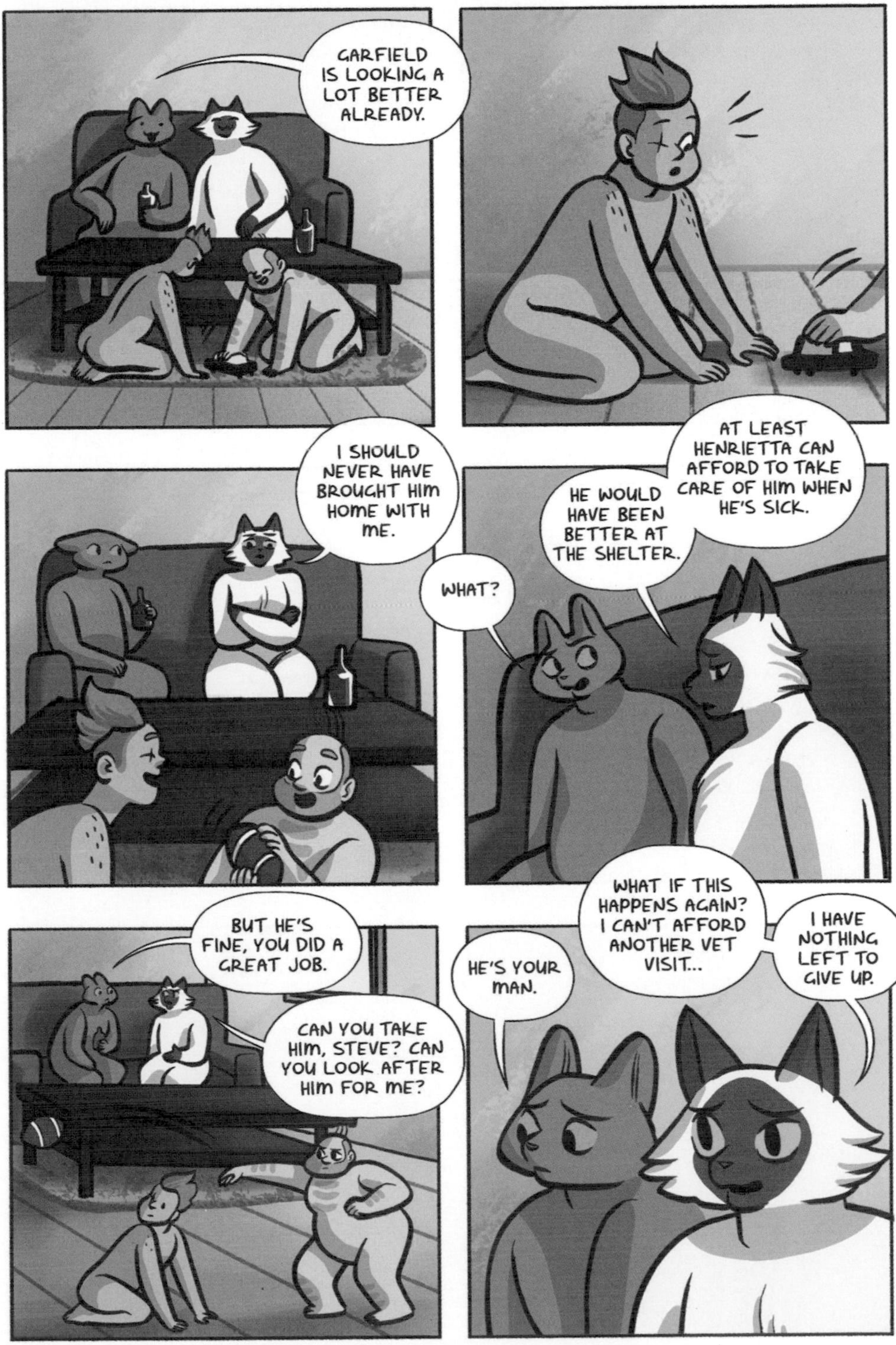
GARFIELD IS LOOKING A LOT BETTER ALREADY.
I SHOULD NEVER HAVE BROUGHT HIM HOME WITH ME.
WHAT?
HE WOULD HAVE BEEN BETTER AT THE SHELTER.
AT LEAST HENRIETTA CAN AFFORD TO TAKE CARE OF HIM WHEN HE'S SICK.
BUT HE'S FINE, YOU DID A GREAT JOB.
CAN YOU TAKE HIM, STEVE? CAN YOU LOOK AFTER HIM FOR ME?
HE'S YOUR MAN.
WHAT IF THIS HAPPENS AGAIN? I CAN'T AFFORD ANOTHER VET VISIT...
I HAVE NOTHING LEFT TO GIVE UP.

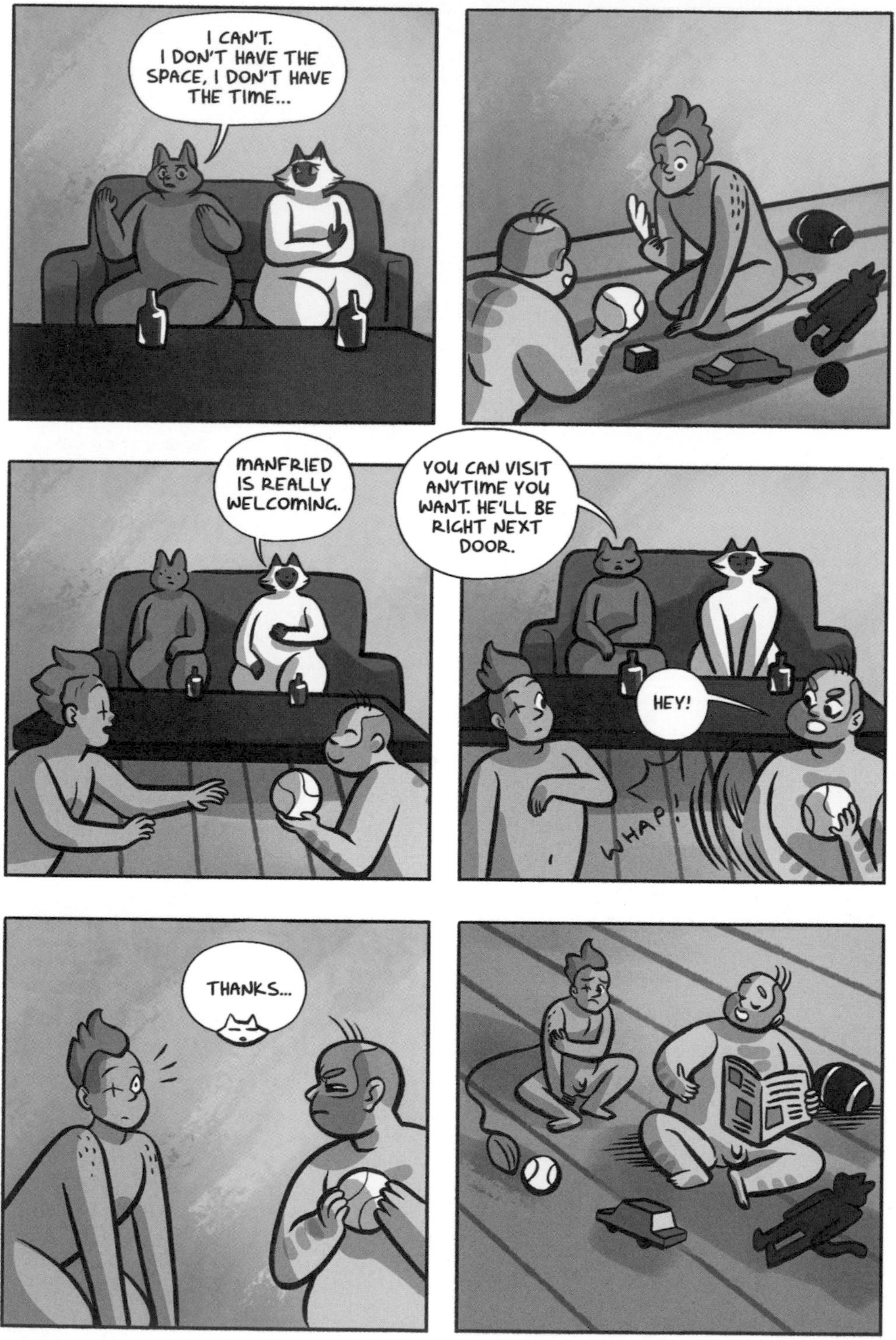
I CAN'T. I DON'T HAVE THE SPACE, I DON'T HAVE THE TIME...
MANFRIED IS REALLY WELCOMING.
YOU CAN VISIT ANYTIME YOU WANT. HE'LL BE RIGHT NEXT DOOR.
HEY!
WHAP!
THANKS...

PART FIVE

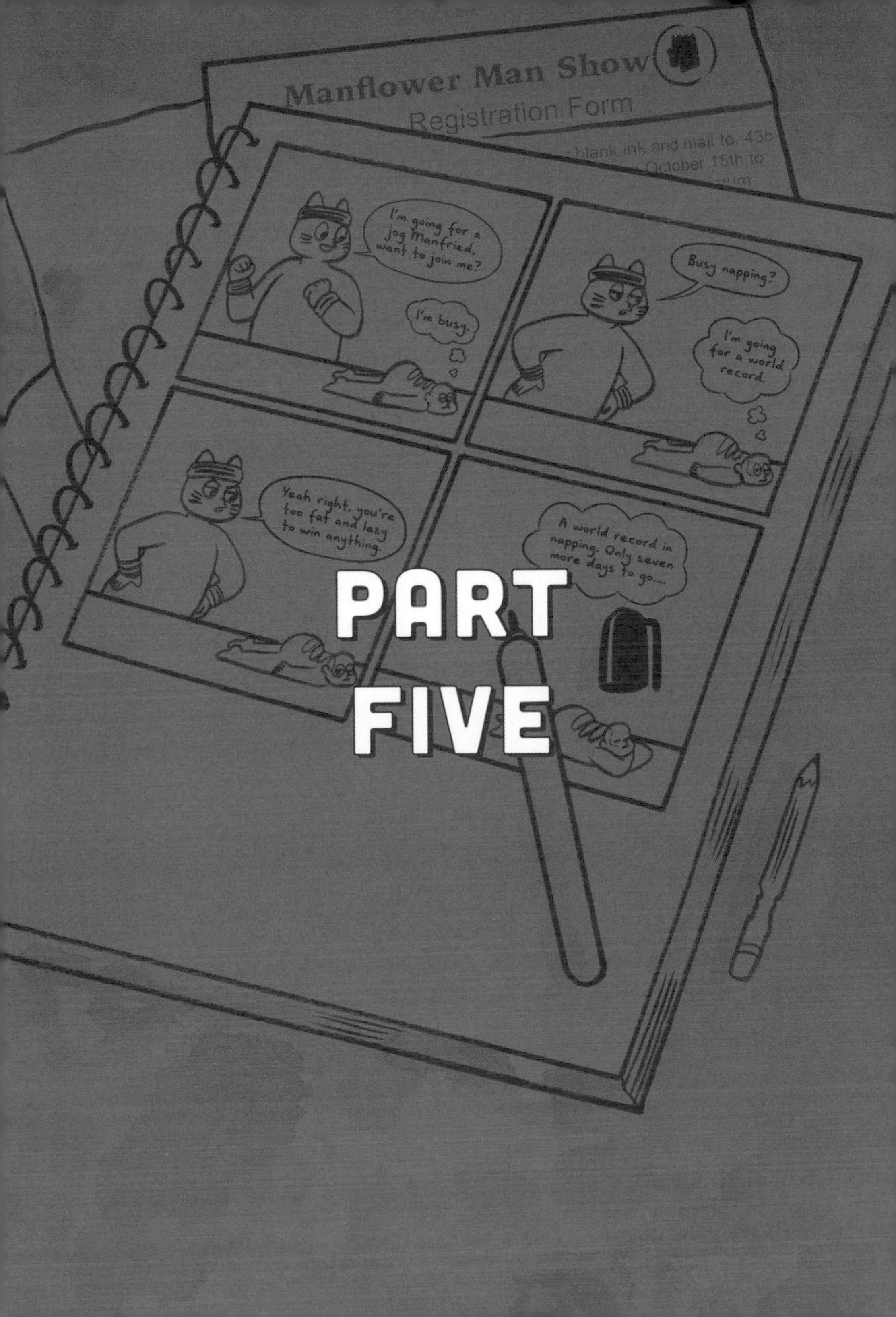
Manflower Man Show
Registration Form
I'm going for a jog Manfried, want to join me?
I'm busy.
Busy napping?
I'm going for a world record.
Yeah right, you're too fat and lazy to win anything.
A world record in napping. Only seven more days to go....

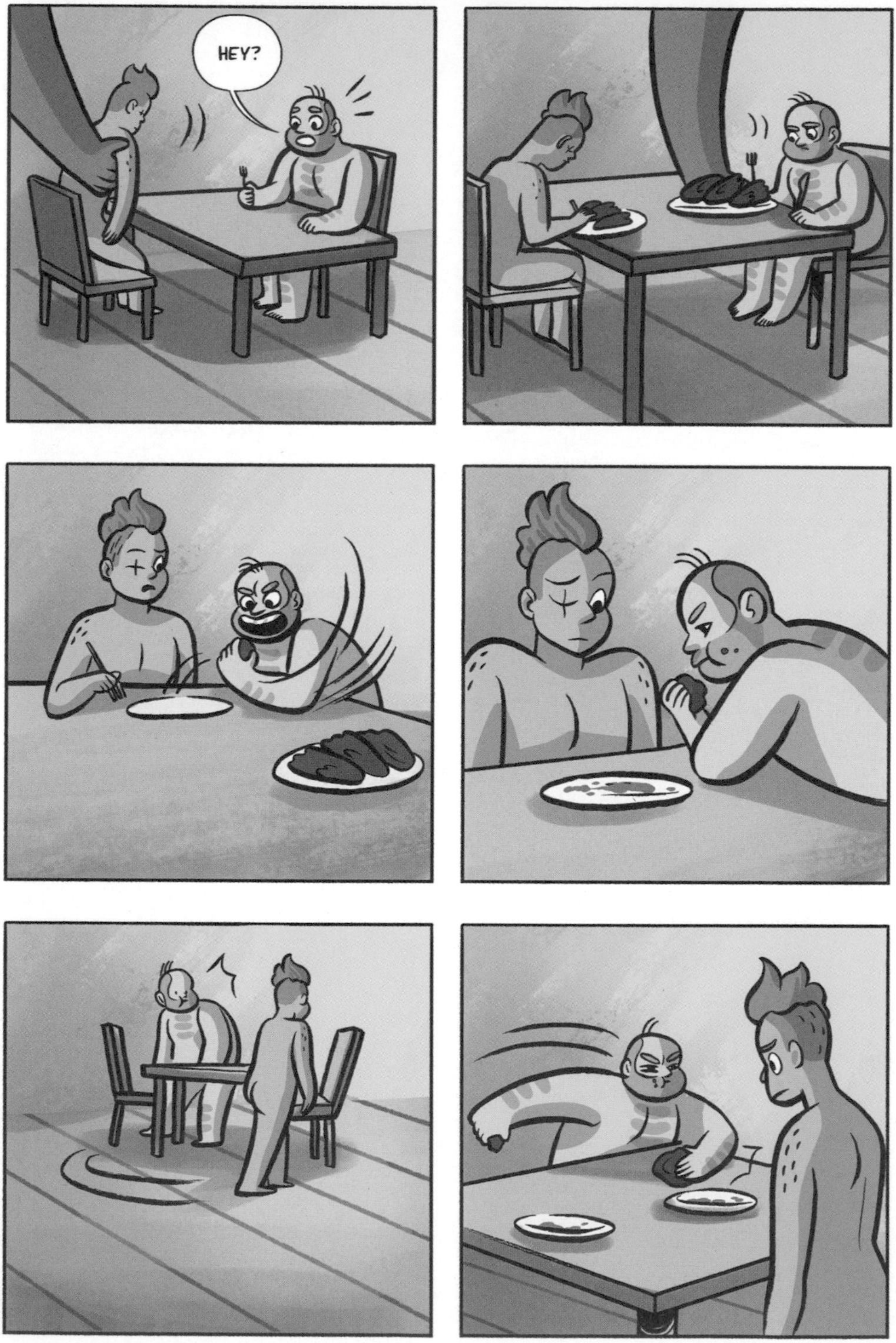
HEY?

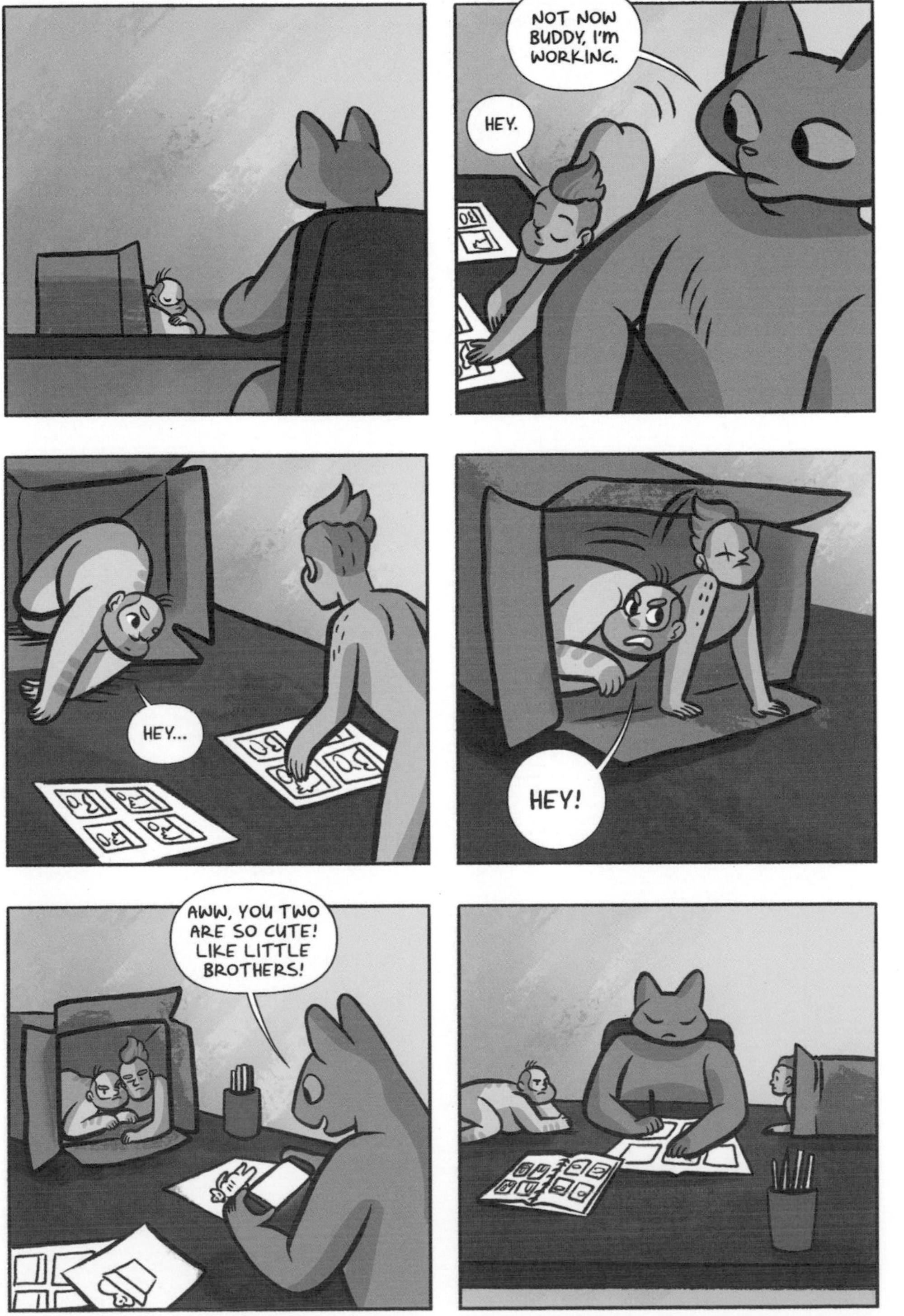
NOT NOW BUDDY, I'm WORKING.
HEY.
HEY...
HEY!
AWW, YOU TWO ARE SO CUTE! LIKE LITTLE BROTHERS!

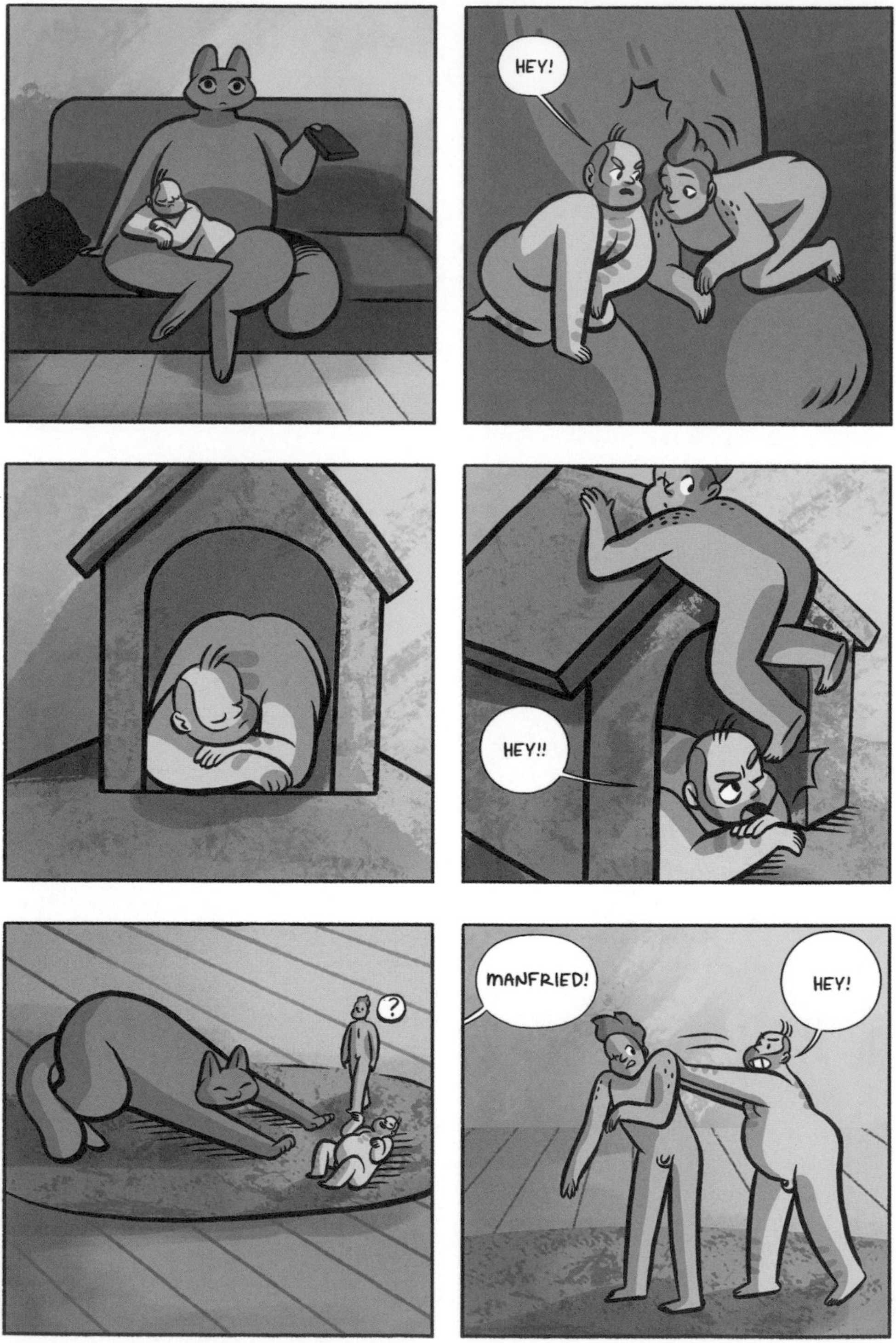
HEY!
HEY!!
?
MANFRIED!
HEY!

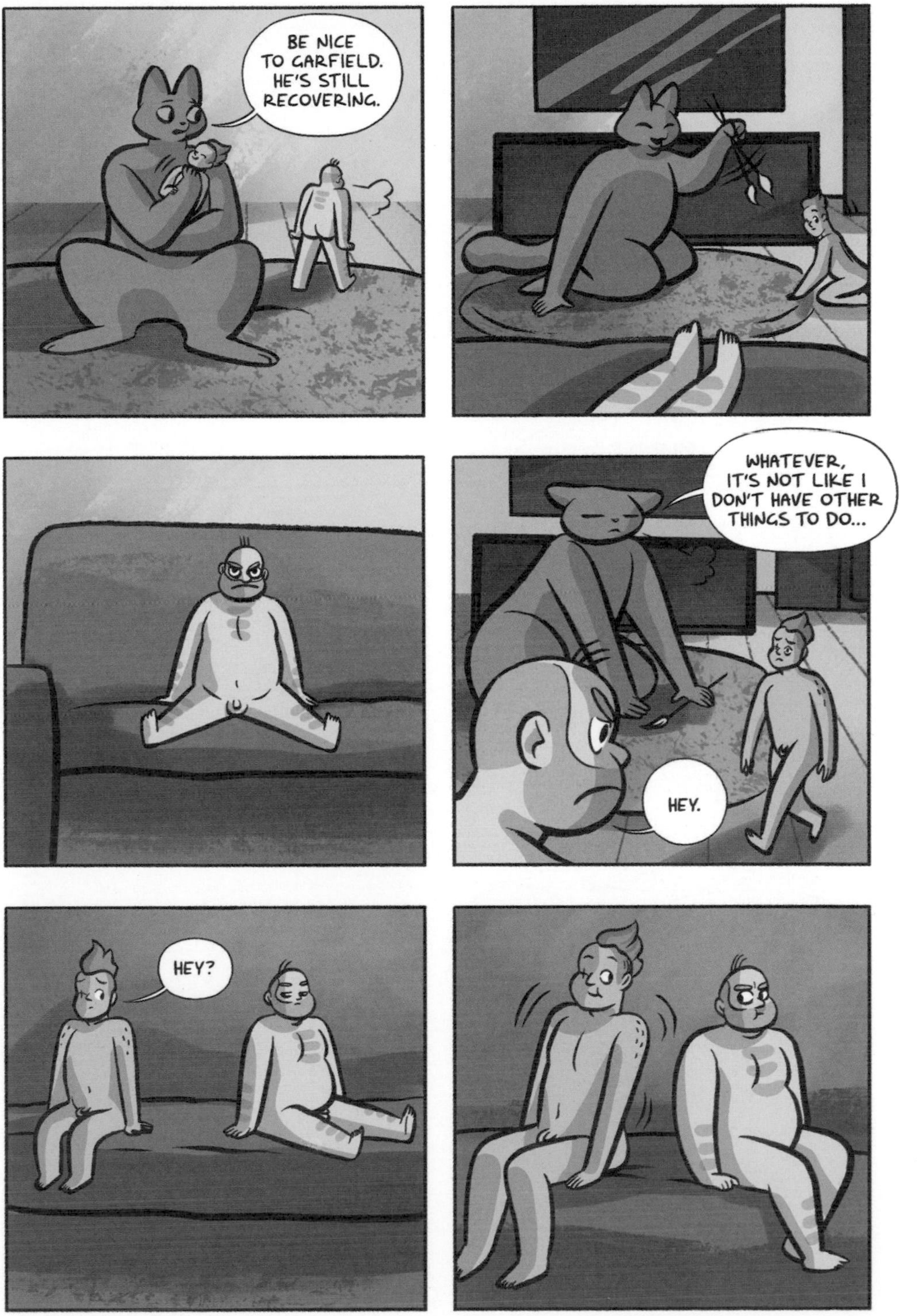
BE NICE TO GARFIELD. HE'S STILL RECOVERING.
WHATEVER, IT'S NOT LIKE I DON'T HAVE OTHER THINGS TO DO...
HEY.
HEY?

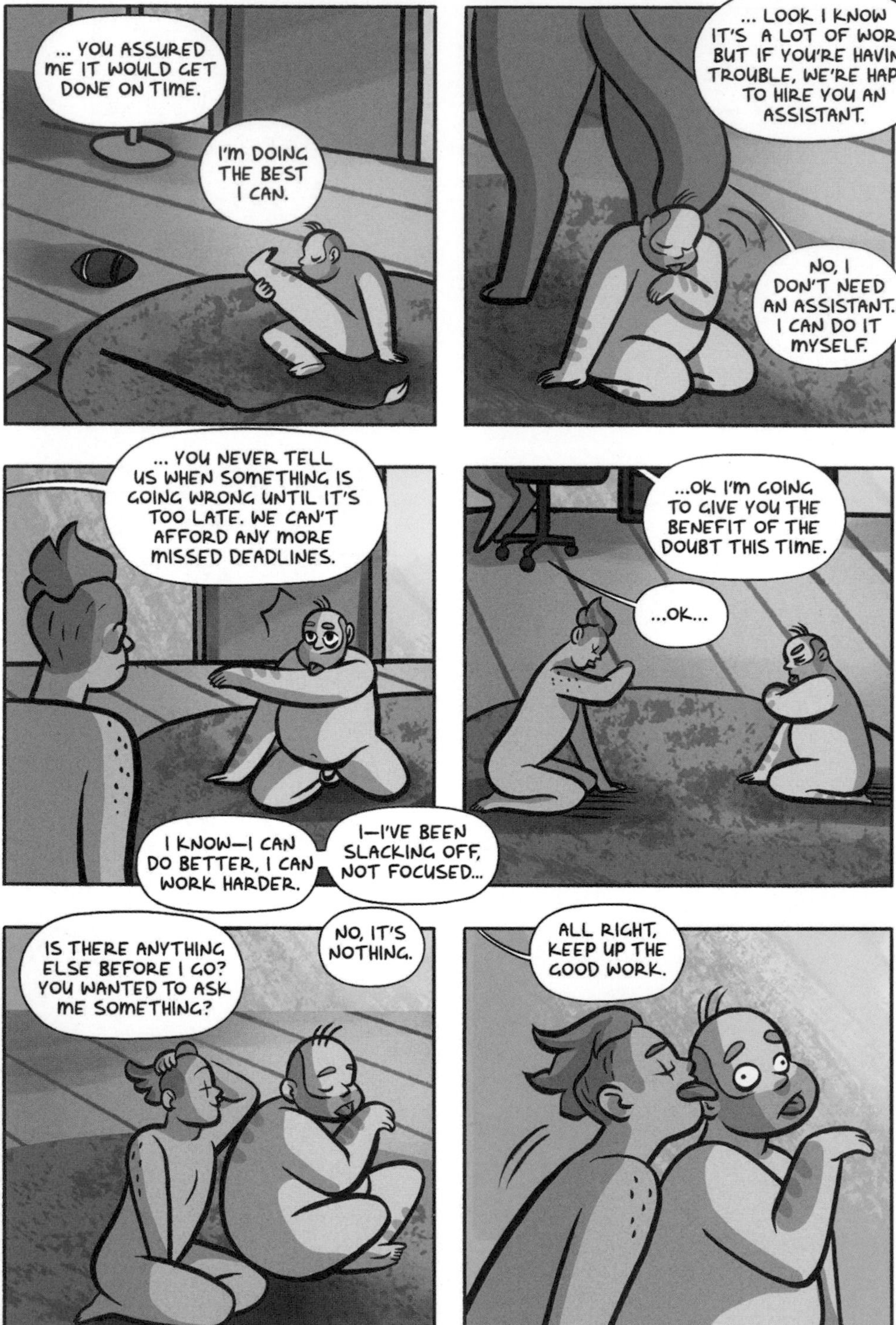
... YOU ASSURED ME IT WOULD GET DONE ON TIME.
I'M DOING THE BEST I CAN.
... LOOK I KNOW IT'S A LOT OF WORK, BUT IF YOU'RE HAVING TROUBLE, WE'RE HAPPY TO HIRE YOU AN ASSISTANT.
NO, I DON'T NEED AN ASSISTANT. I CAN DO IT MYSELF.
... YOU NEVER TELL US WHEN SOMETHING IS GOING WRONG UNTIL IT'S TOO LATE. WE CAN'T AFFORD ANY MORE MISSED DEADLINES.
I KNOW—I CAN DO BETTER, I CAN WORK HARDER.
I—I'VE BEEN SLACKING OFF, NOT FOCUSED...
...OK I'M GOING TO GIVE YOU THE BENEFIT OF THE DOUBT THIS TIME.
...OK...
IS THERE ANYTHING ELSE BEFORE I GO? YOU WANTED TO ASK ME SOMETHING?
NO, IT'S NOTHING.
ALL RIGHT, KEEP UP THE GOOD WORK.

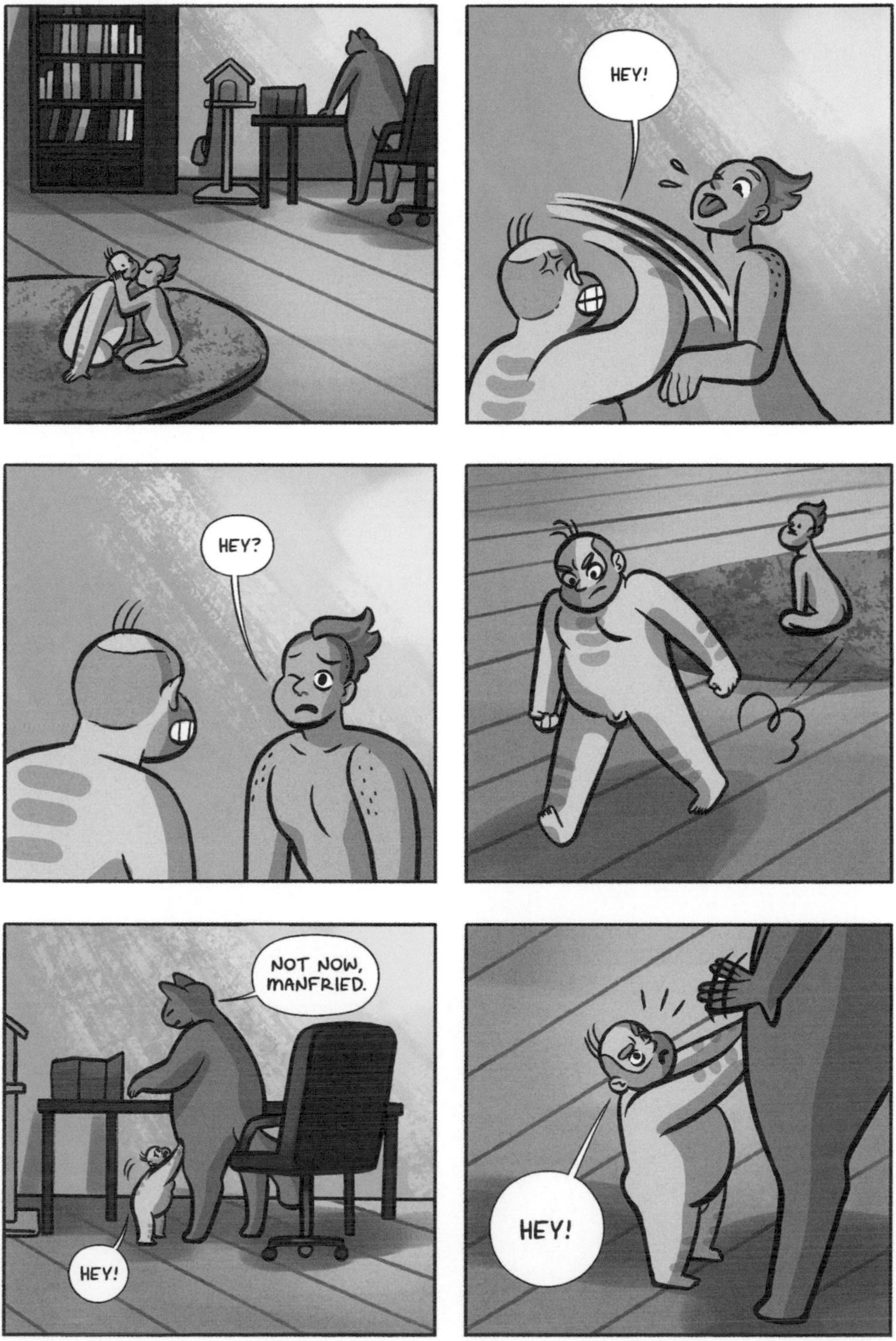
HEY!
HEY?
NOT NOW, MANFRIED.
HEY!
HEY!

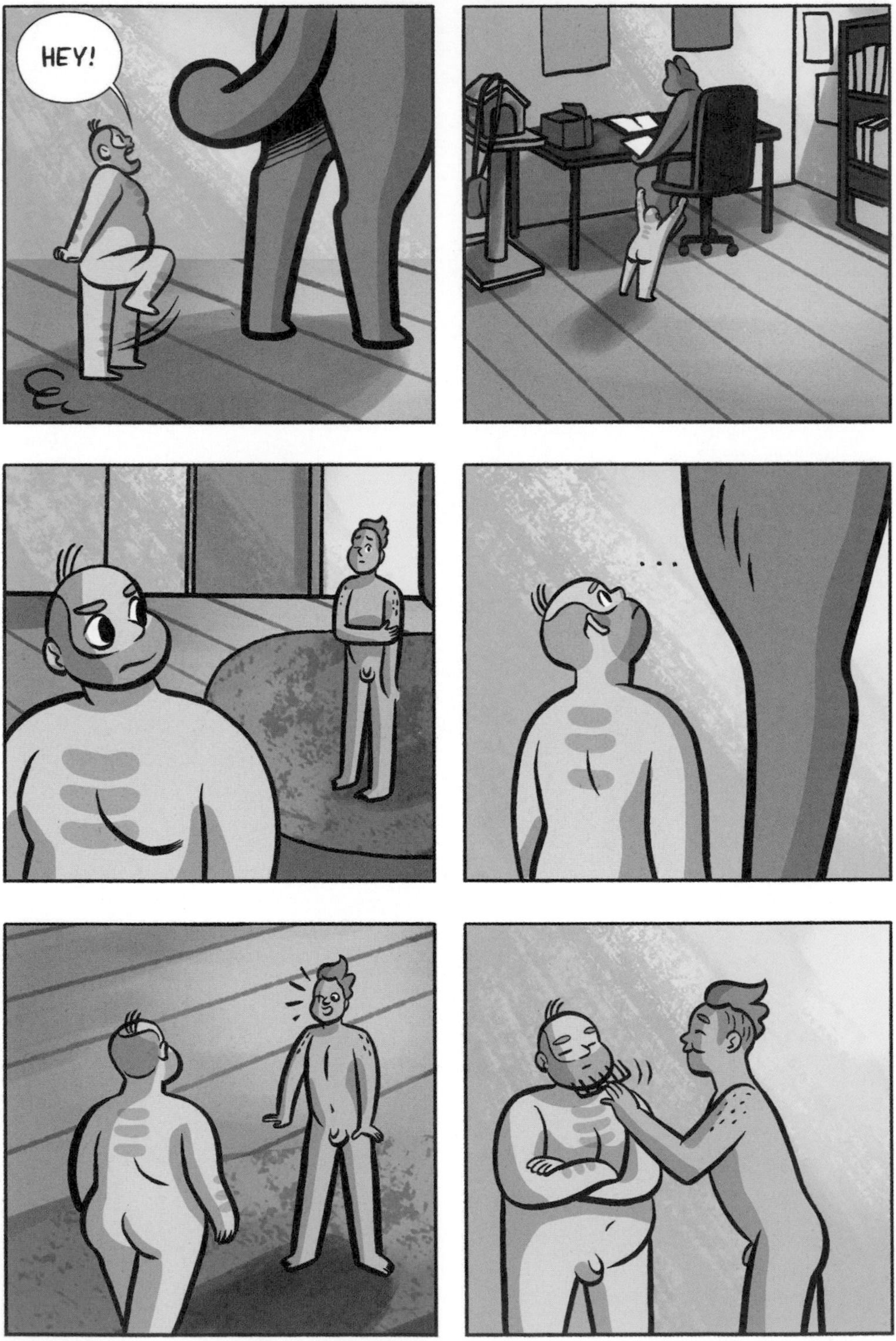
HEY!
...

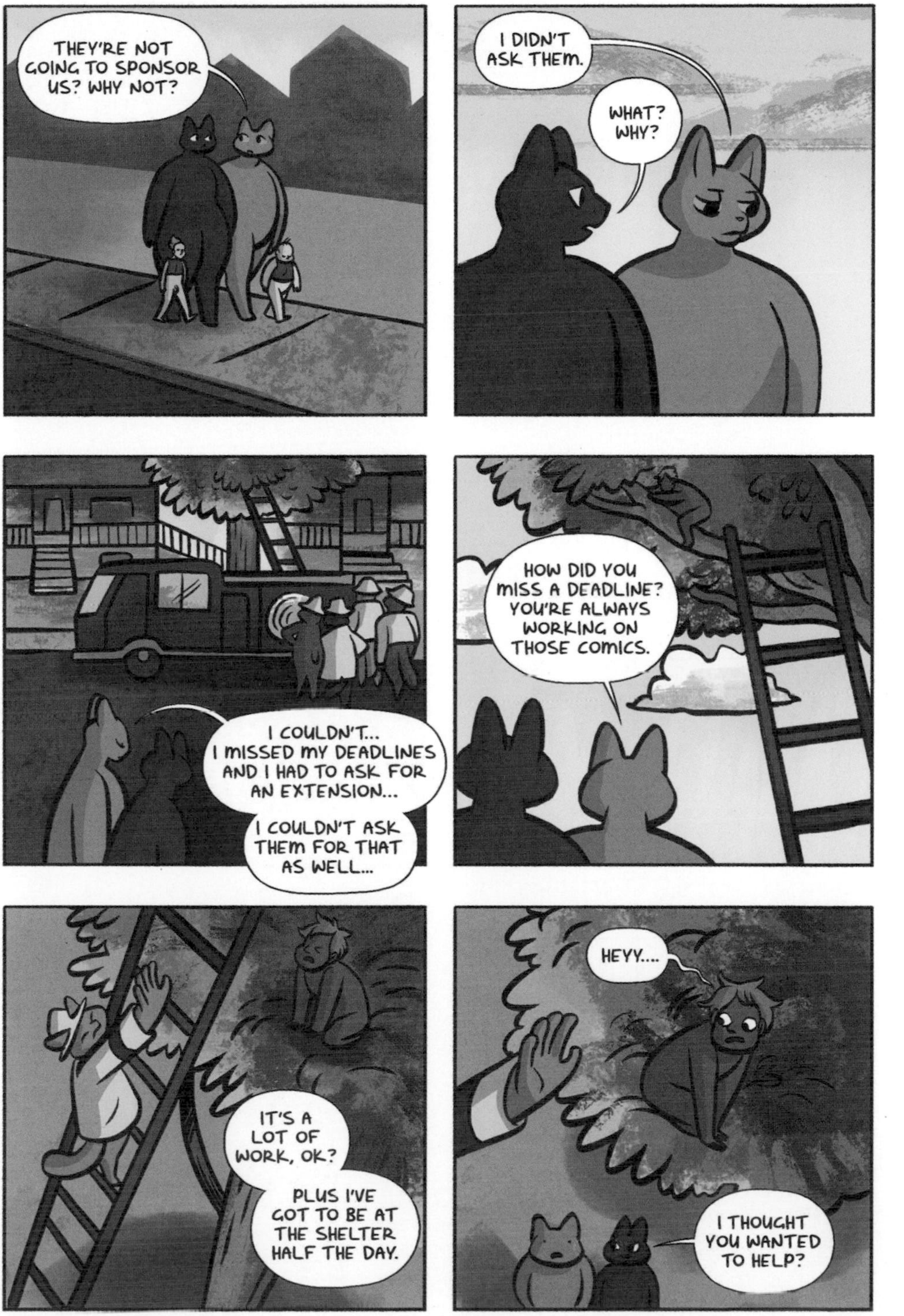
THEY'RE NOT GOING TO SPONSOR US? WHY NOT?
I DIDN'T ASK THEM.
WHAT? WHY?
I COULDN'T... I MISSED MY DEADLINES AND I HAD TO ASK FOR AN EXTENSION...
I COULDN'T ASK THEM FOR THAT AS WELL...
HOW DID YOU MISS A DEADLINE? YOU'RE ALWAYS WORKING ON THOSE COMICS.
IT'S A LOT OF WORK, OK?
PLUS I'VE GOT TO BE AT THE SHELTER HALF THE DAY.
HEYY....
I THOUGHT YOU WANTED TO HELP?

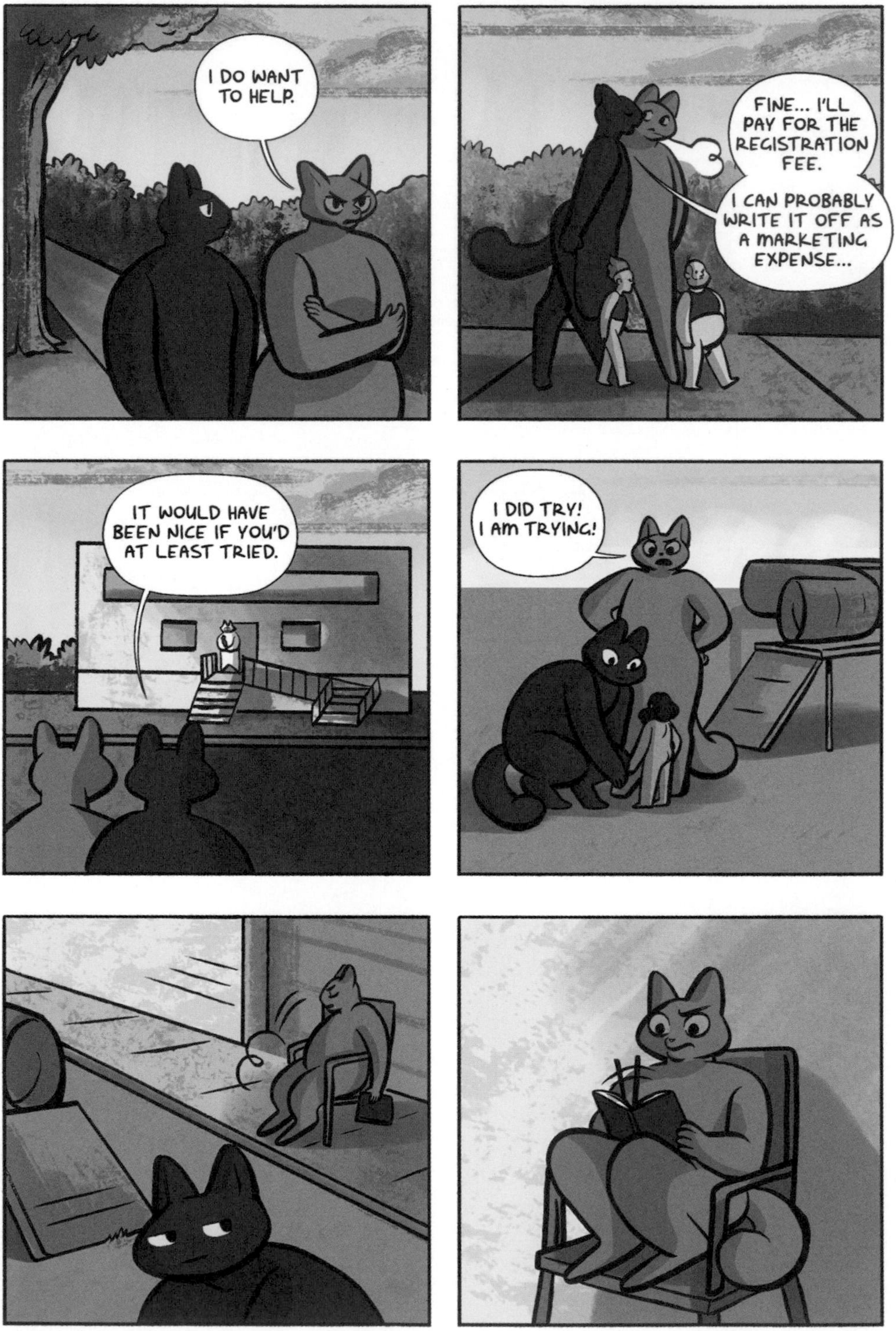
I DO WANT TO HELP.
FINE... I'LL PAY FOR THE REGISTRATION FEE.
I CAN PROBABLY WRITE IT OFF AS A MARKETING EXPENSE...
IT WOULD HAVE BEEN NICE IF YOU'D AT LEAST TRIED.
I DID TRY! I AM TRYING!

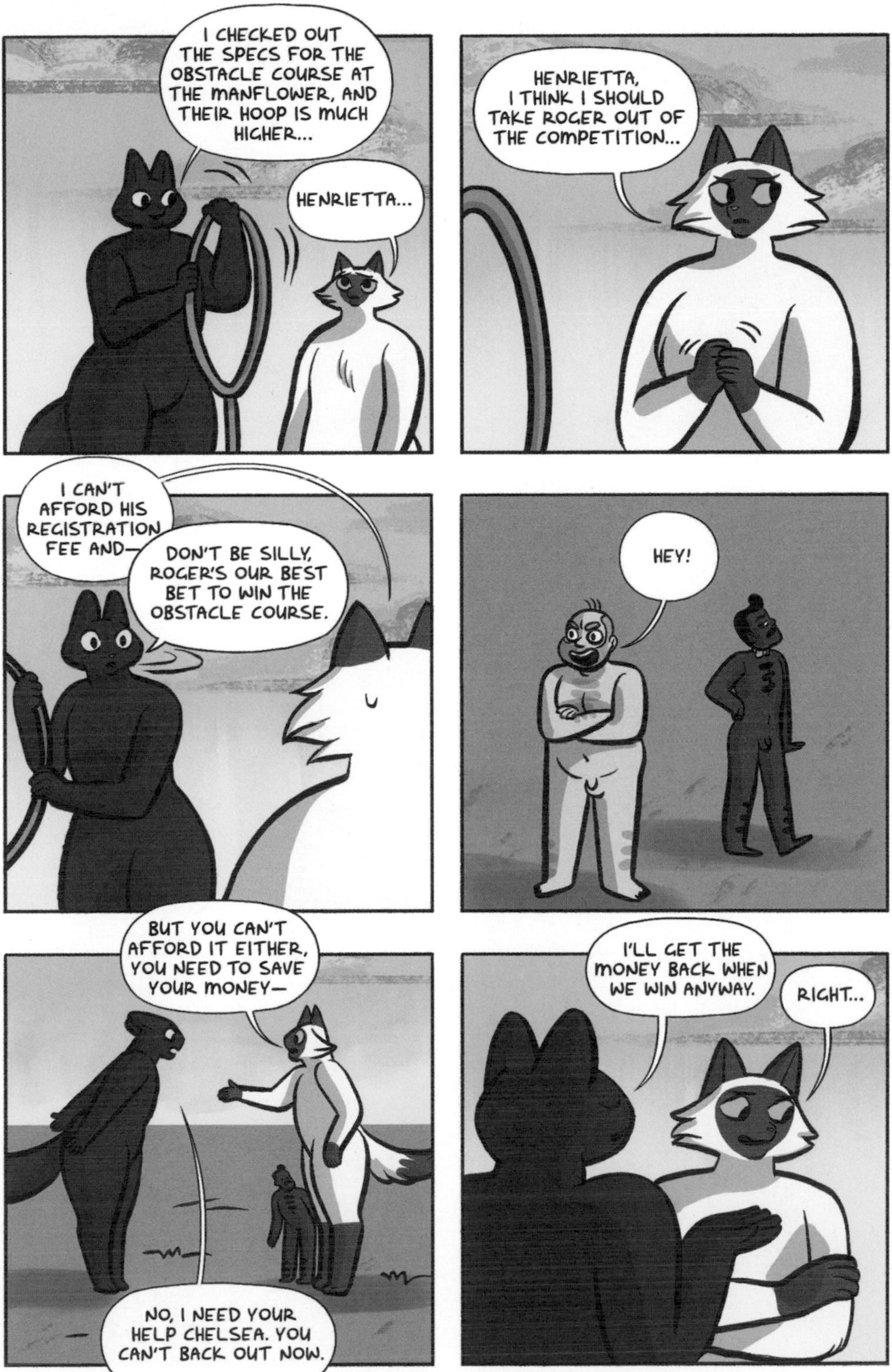
I CHECKED OUT THE SPECS FOR THE OBSTACLE COURSE AT THE MANFLOWER, AND THEIR HOOP IS MUCH HIGHER...
HENRIETTA...
HENRIETTA, I THINK I SHOULD TAKE ROGER OUT OF THE COMPETITION...
I CAN'T AFFORD HIS REGISTRATION FEE AND—
DON'T BE SILLY, ROGER'S OUR BEST BET TO WIN THE OBSTACLE COURSE.
HEY!
BUT YOU CAN'T AFFORD IT EITHER, YOU NEED TO SAVE YOUR MONEY—
NO, I NEED YOUR HELP CHELSEA. YOU CAN'T BACK OUT NOW.
I'LL GET THE MONEY BACK WHEN WE WIN ANYWAY.
RIGHT...

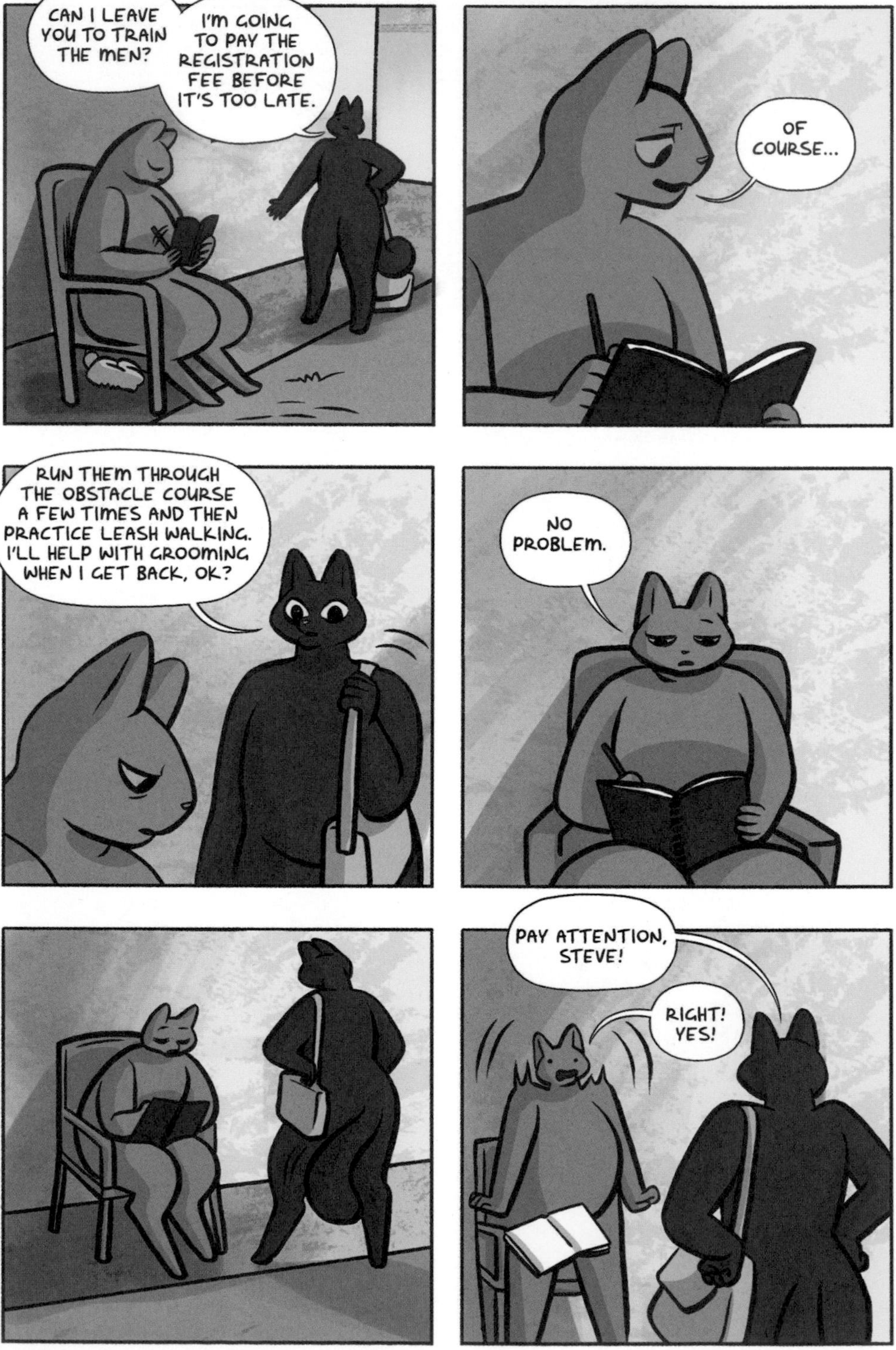
CAN I LEAVE YOU TO TRAIN THE MEN?
I'M GOING TO PAY THE REGISTRATION FEE BEFORE IT'S TOO LATE.
OF COURSE...
RUN THEM THROUGH THE OBSTACLE COURSE A FEW TIMES AND THEN PRACTICE LEASH WALKING. I'LL HELP WITH GROOMING WHEN I GET BACK, OK?
NO PROBLEM.
PAY ATTENTION, STEVE!
RIGHT! YES!

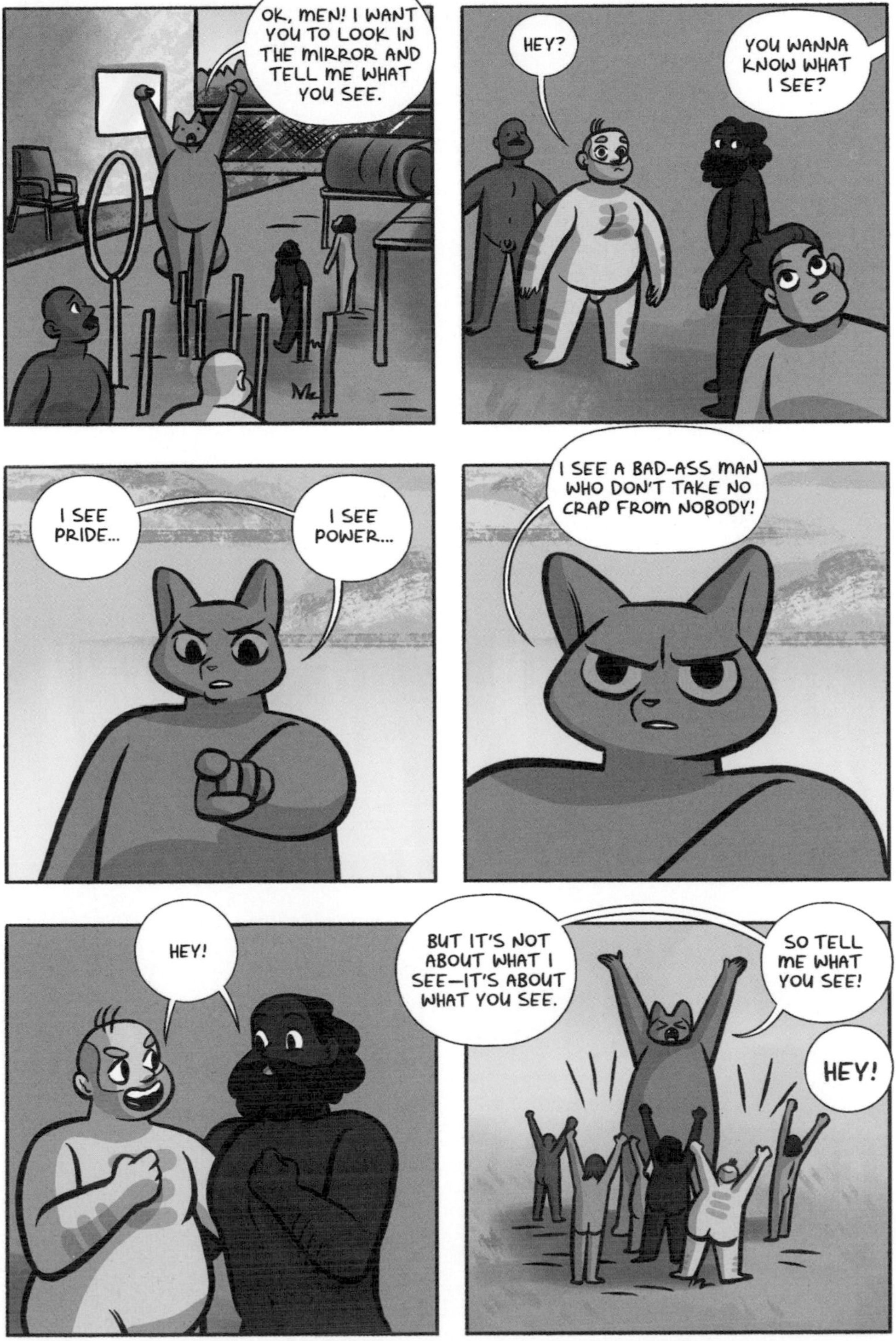
OK, MEN! I WANT YOU TO LOOK IN THE MIRROR AND TELL ME WHAT YOU SEE.
HEY?
YOU WANNA KNOW WHAT I SEE?
I SEE PRIDE...
I SEE POWER...
I SEE A BAD-ASS MAN WHO DON'T TAKE NO CRAP FROM NOBODY!
HEY!
BUT IT'S NOT ABOUT WHAT I SEE—IT'S ABOUT WHAT YOU SEE.
SO TELL ME WHAT YOU SEE!
HEY!

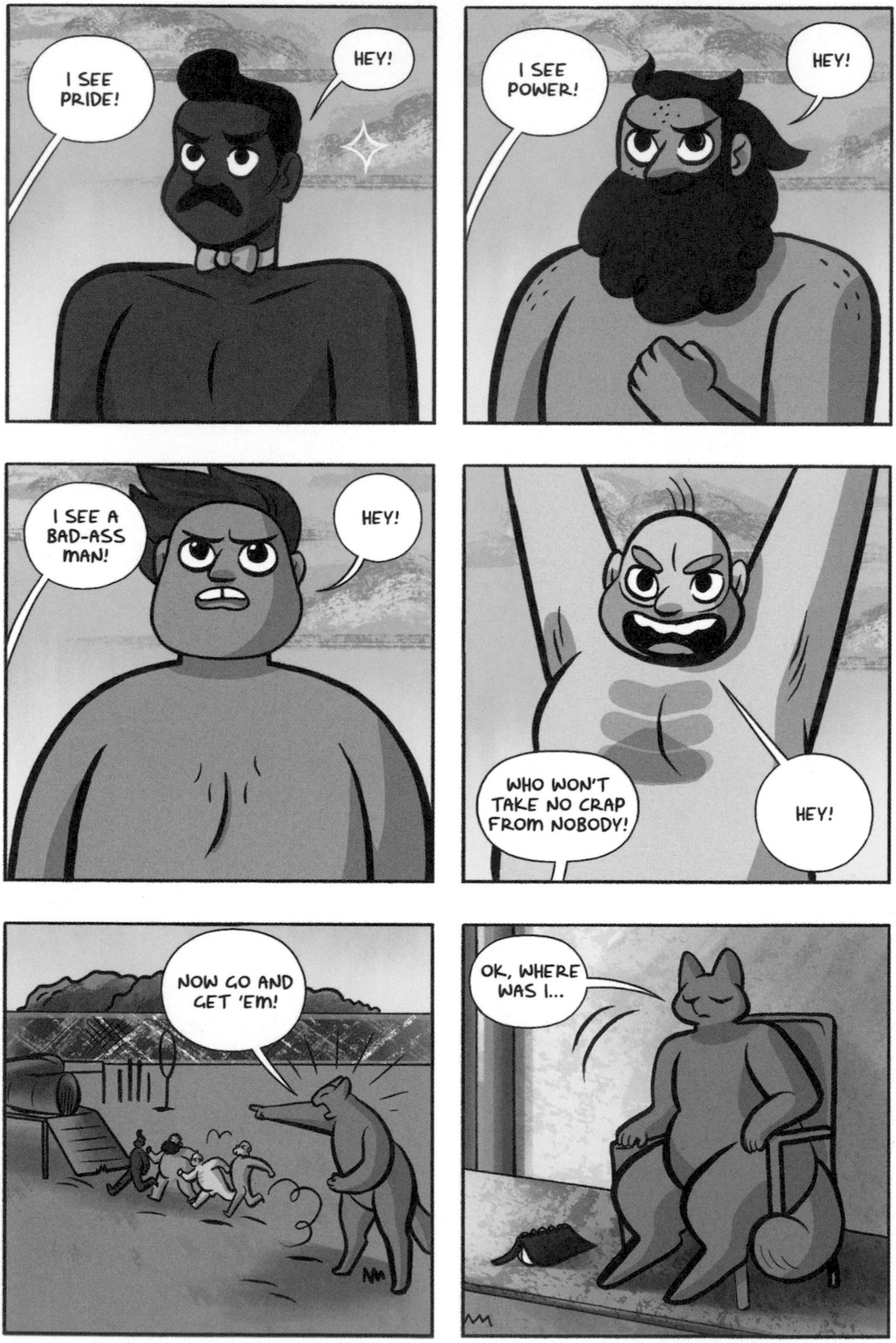
I SEE PRIDE!
HEY!
I SEE POWER!
HEY!
I SEE A BAD-ASS MAN!
HEY!
WHO WON'T TAKE NO CRAP FROM NOBODY!
HEY!
NOW GO AND GET 'EM!
OK, WHERE WAS I...

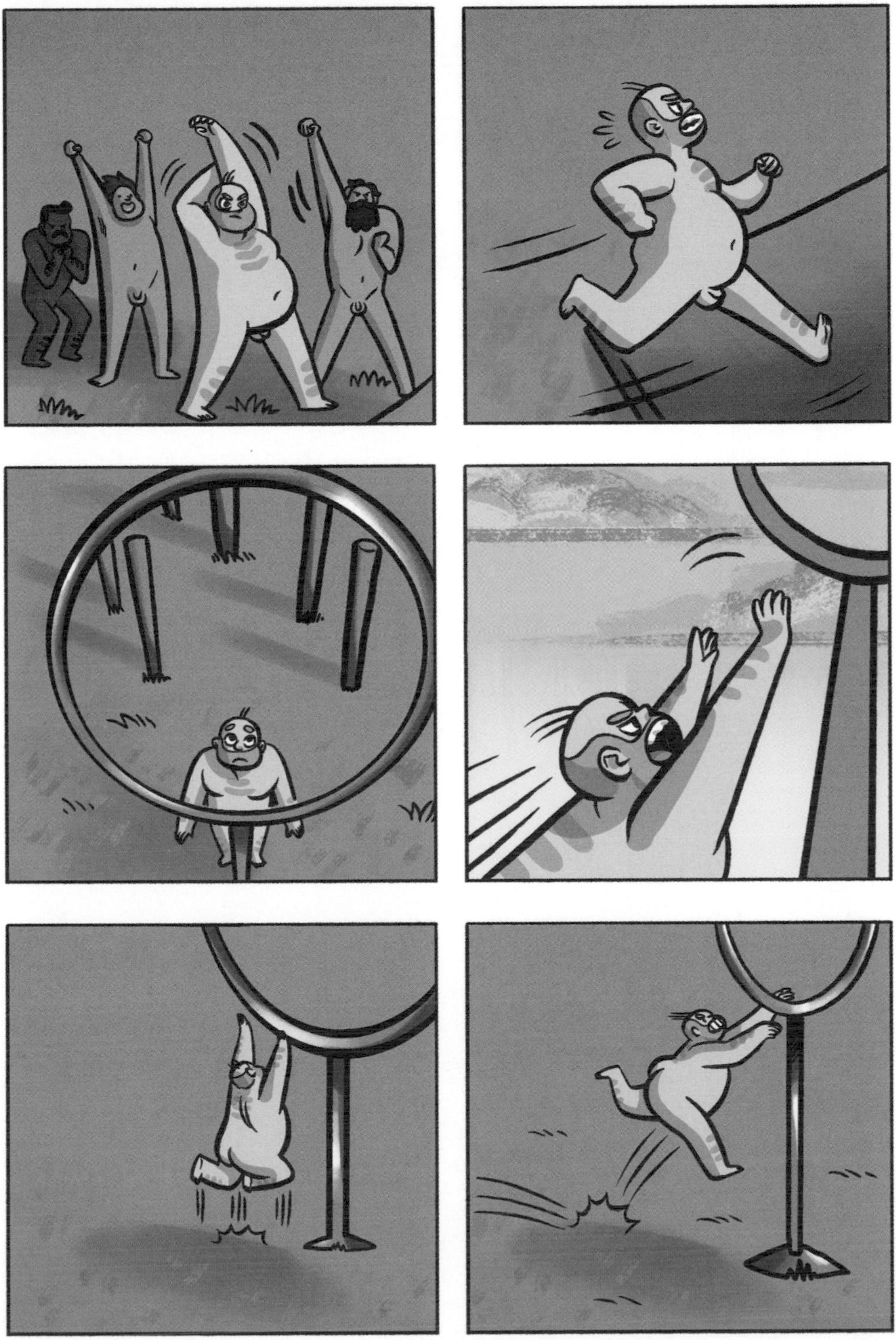

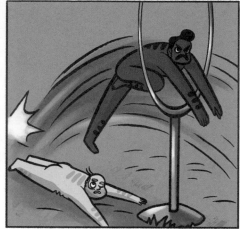

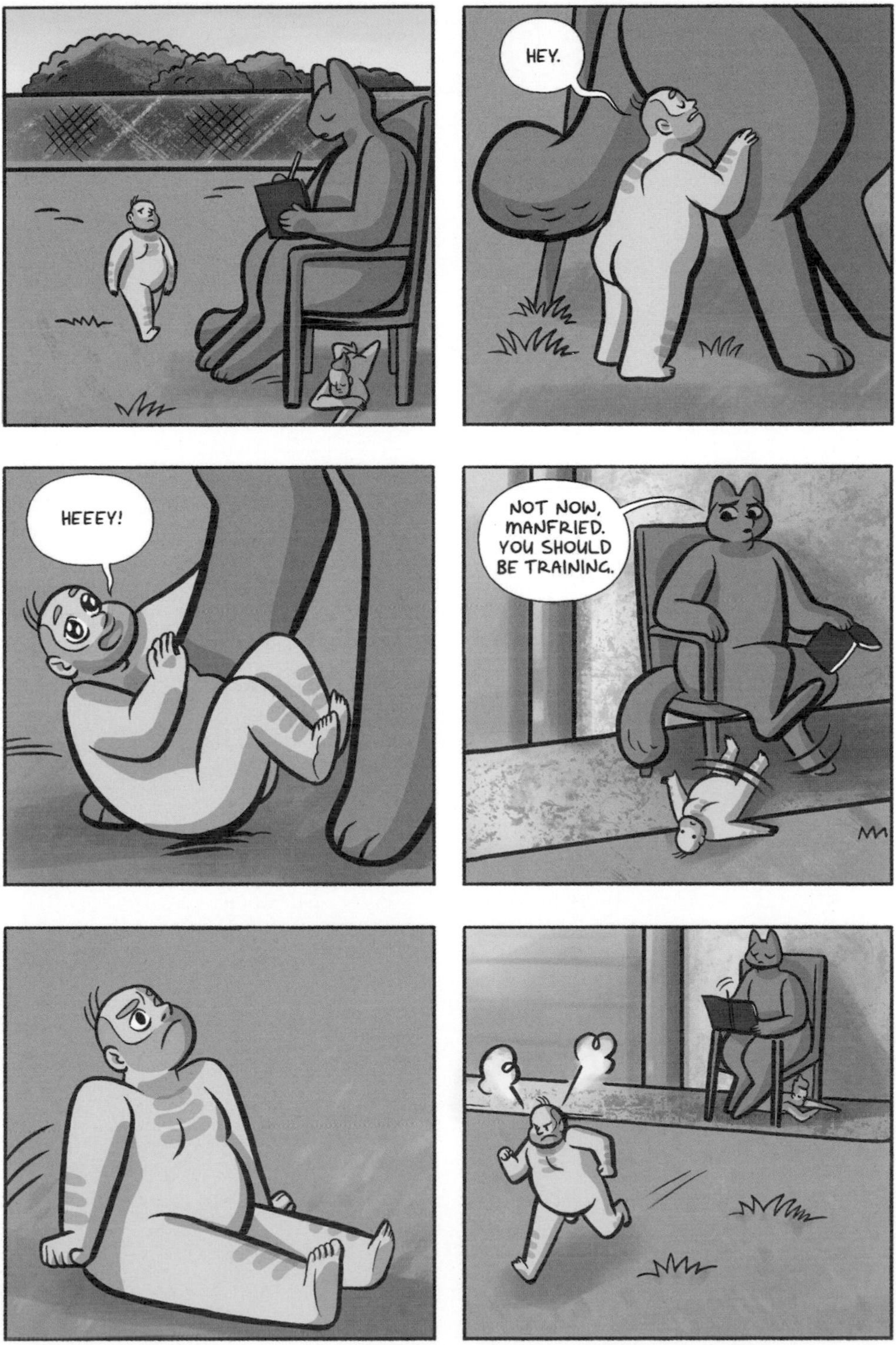
HEY.
HEEEY!
NOT NOW, MANFRIED. YOU SHOULD BE TRAINING.

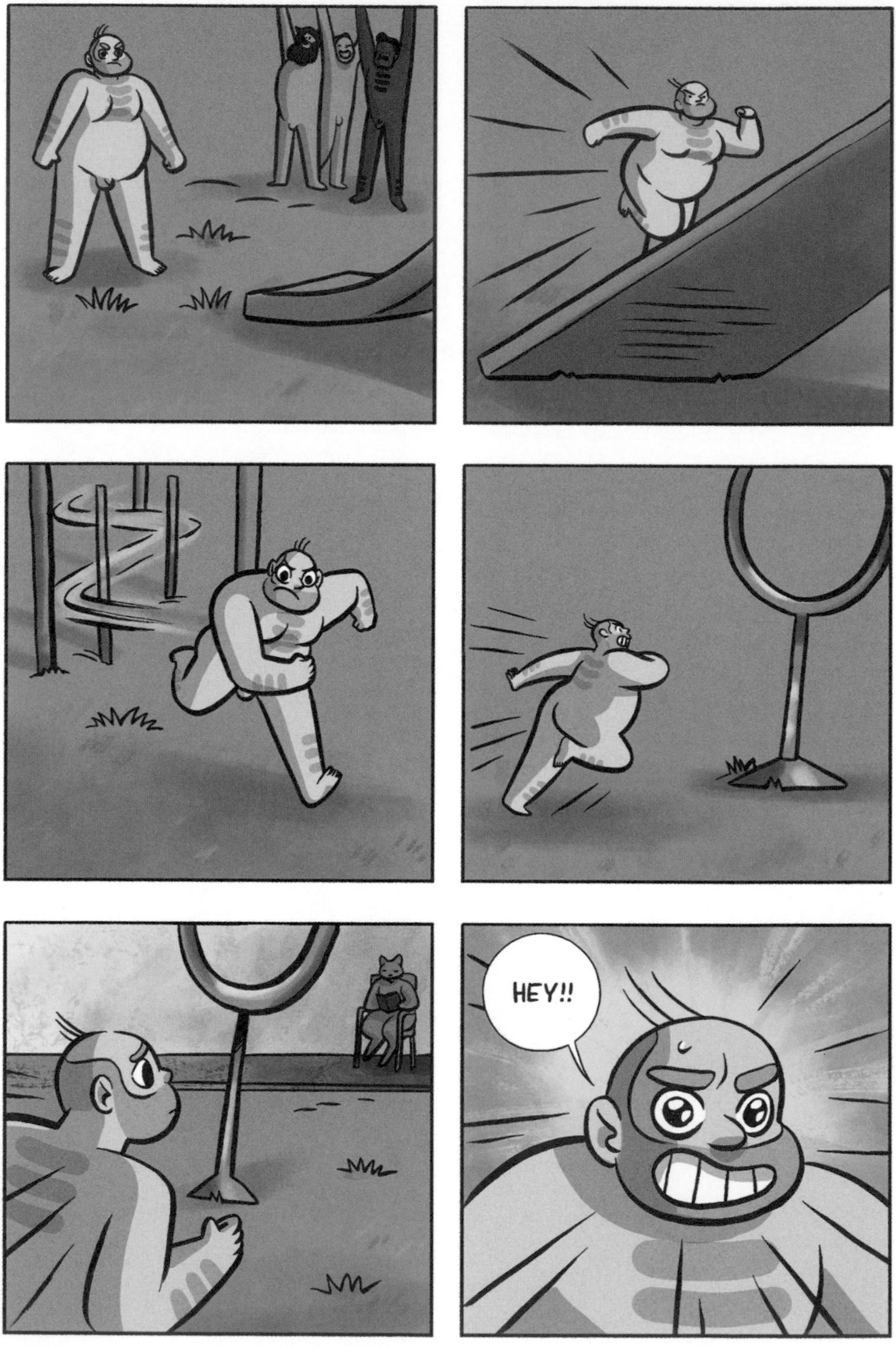
HEY!!

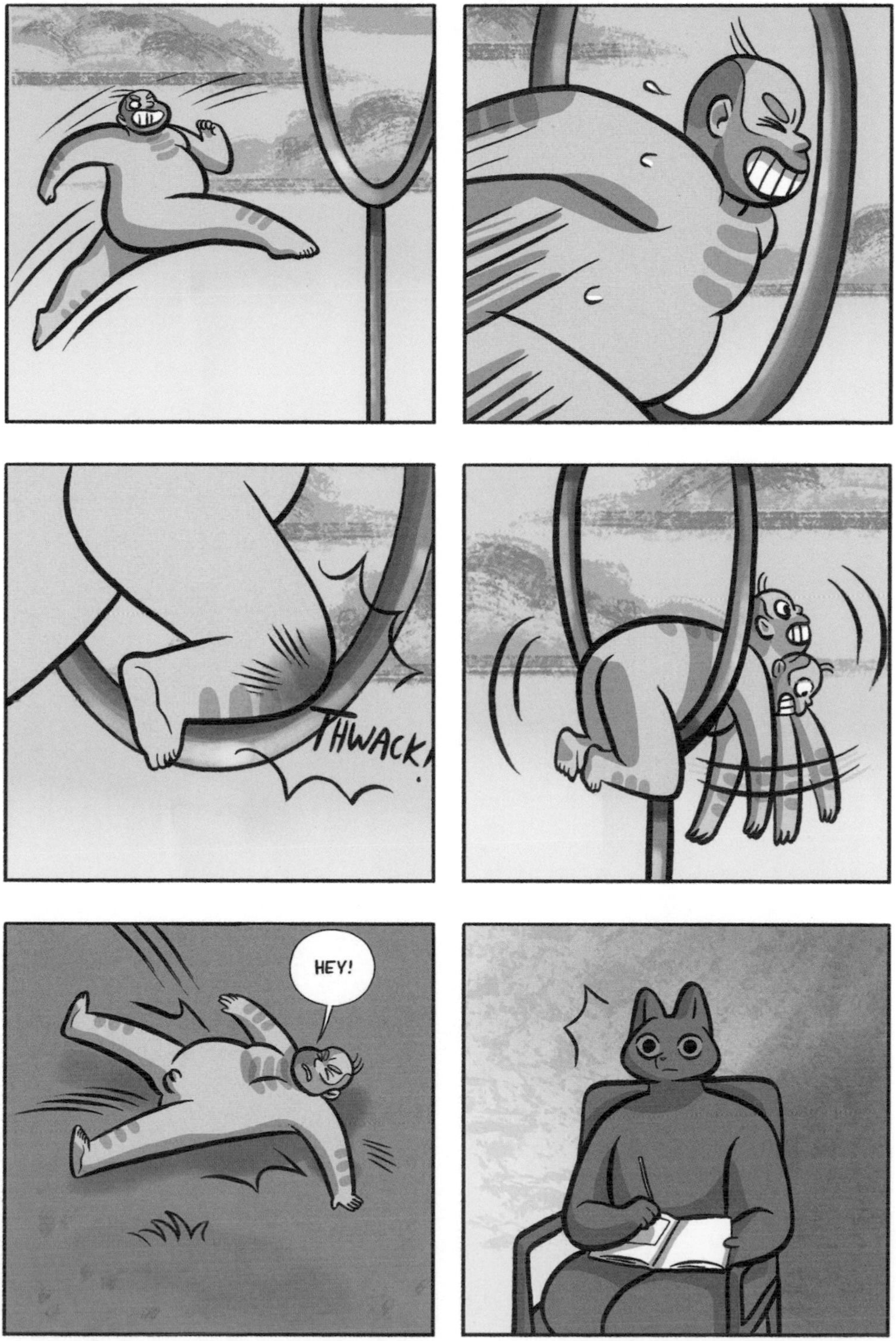
THWACK!
HEY!

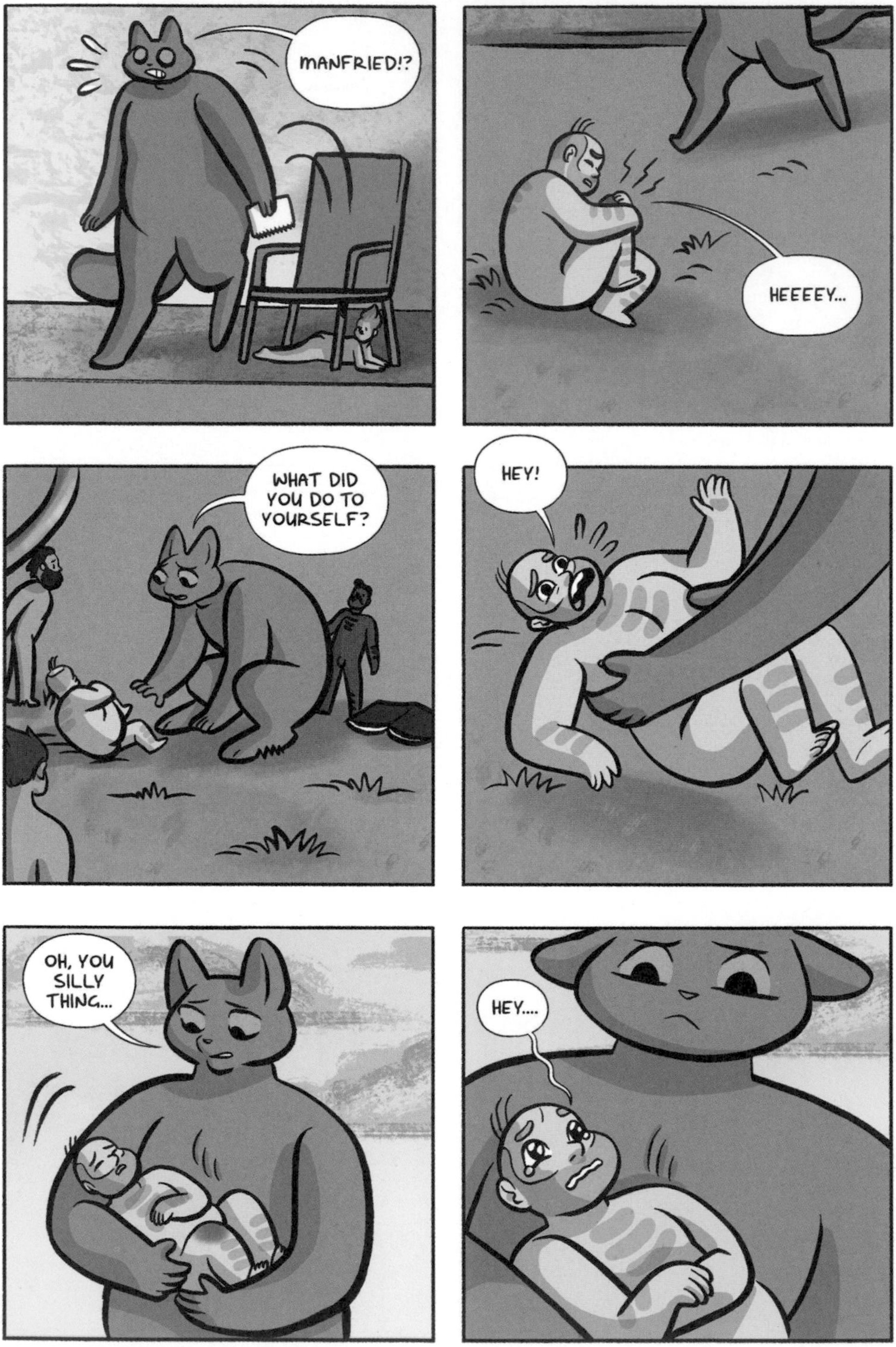
MANFRIED!?
HEEEEY...
WHAT DID YOU DO TO YOURSELF?
HEY!
OH, YOU SILLY THING...
HEY....

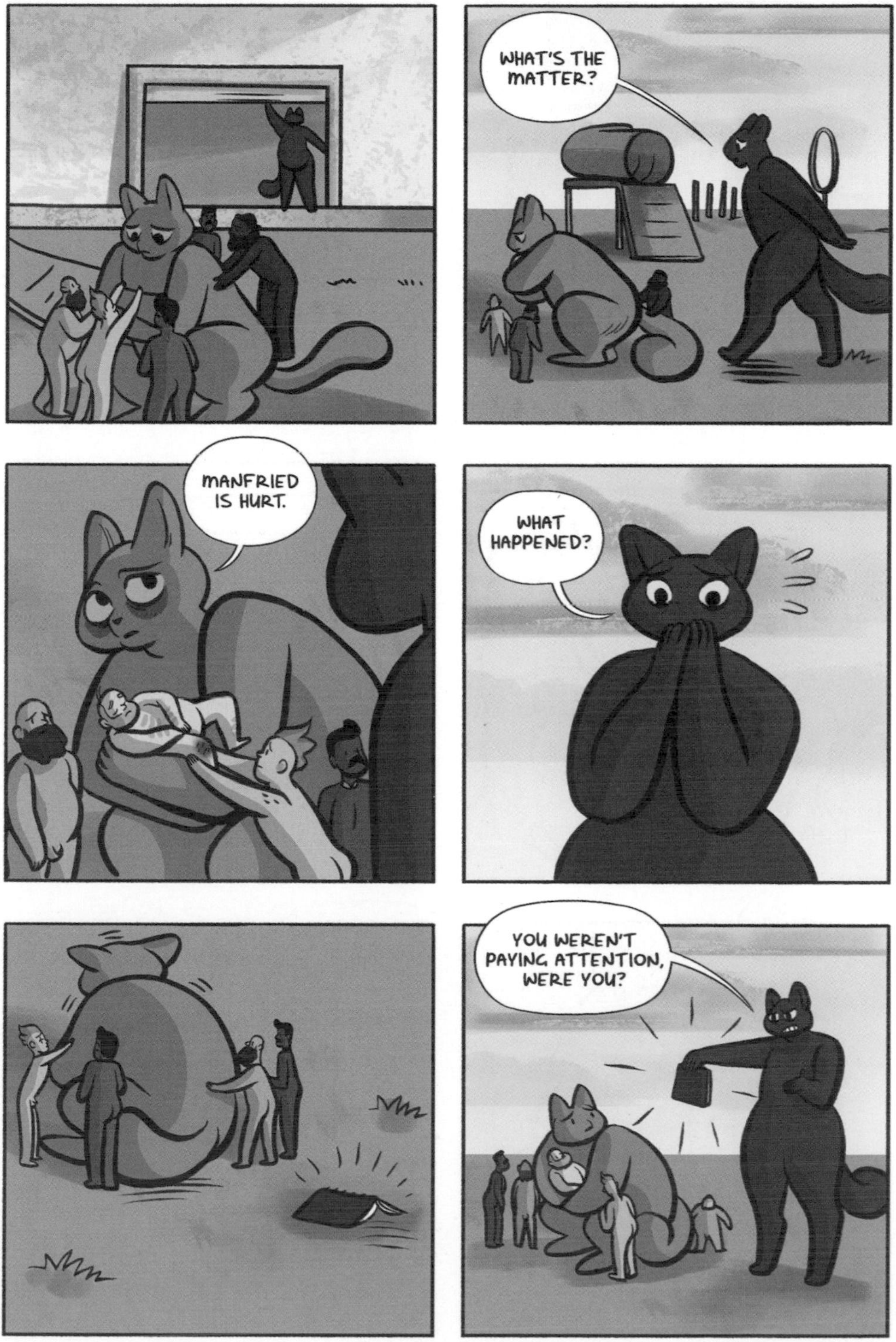
WHAT'S THE MATTER?
MANFRIED IS HURT.
WHAT HAPPENED?
YOU WEREN'T PAYING ATTENTION, WERE YOU?

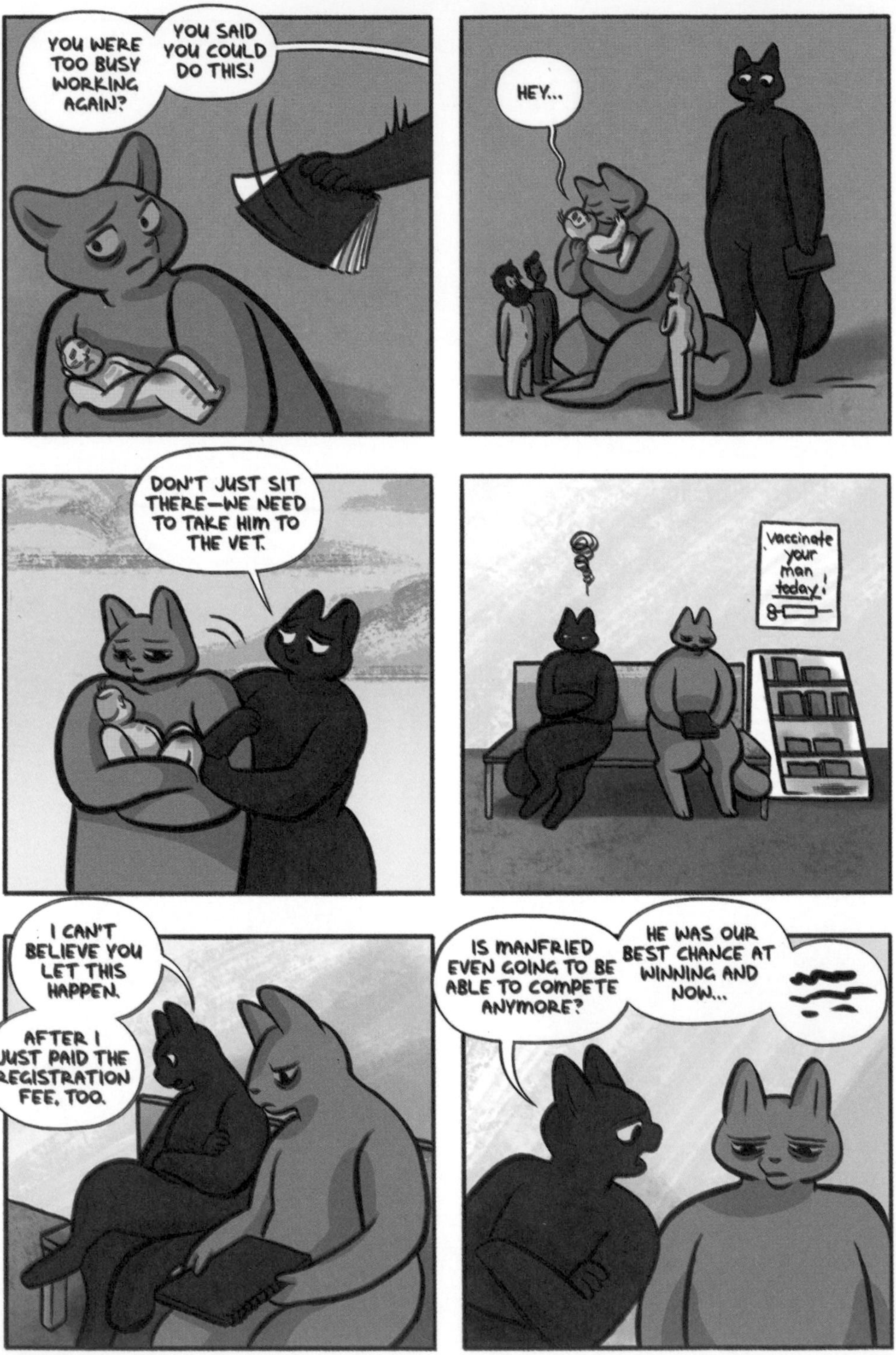

YOU WERE TOO BUSY WORKING AGAIN?
YOU SAID YOU COULD DO THIS!
HEY...
DON'T JUST SIT THERE—WE NEED TO TAKE HIM TO THE VET.
Vaccinate your man today!
I CAN'T BELIEVE YOU LET THIS HAPPEN.
AFTER I JUST PAID THE REGISTRATION FEE, TOO.
IS MANFRIED EVEN GOING TO BE ABLE TO COMPETE ANYMORE?
HE WAS OUR BEST CHANCE AT WINNING AND NOW...

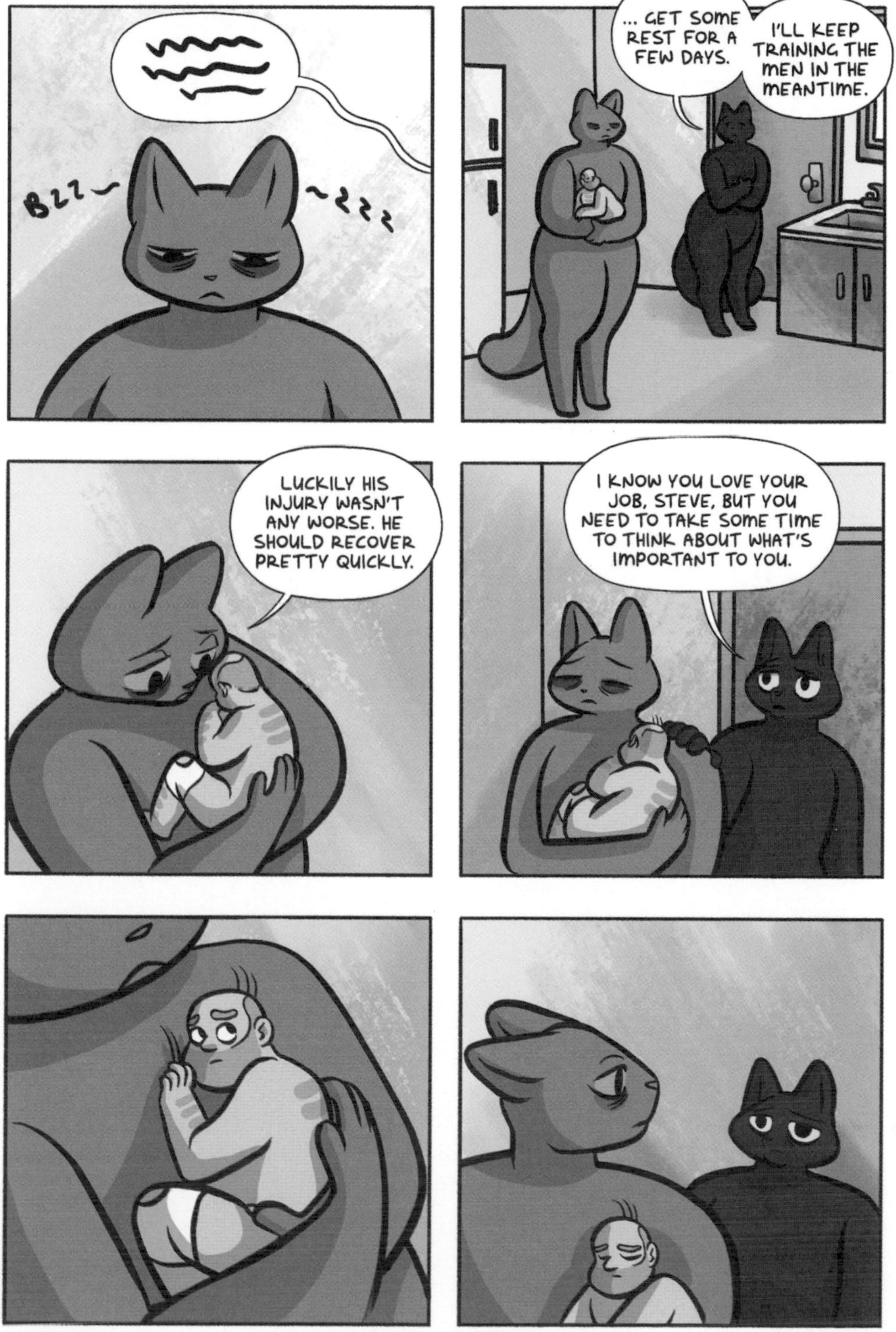
BZZ~ ~ZZZ
... GET SOME REST FOR A FEW DAYS.
I'LL KEEP TRAINING THE MEN IN THE MEANTIME.
LUCKILY HIS INJURY WASN'T ANY WORSE. HE SHOULD RECOVER PRETTY QUICKLY.
I KNOW YOU LOVE YOUR JOB, STEVE, BUT YOU NEED TO TAKE SOME TIME TO THINK ABOUT WHAT'S IMPORTANT TO YOU.

I'LL CHECK IN ON YOU AGAIN TOMORROW.

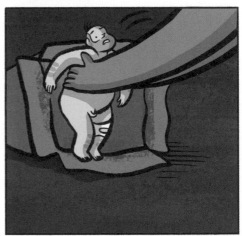

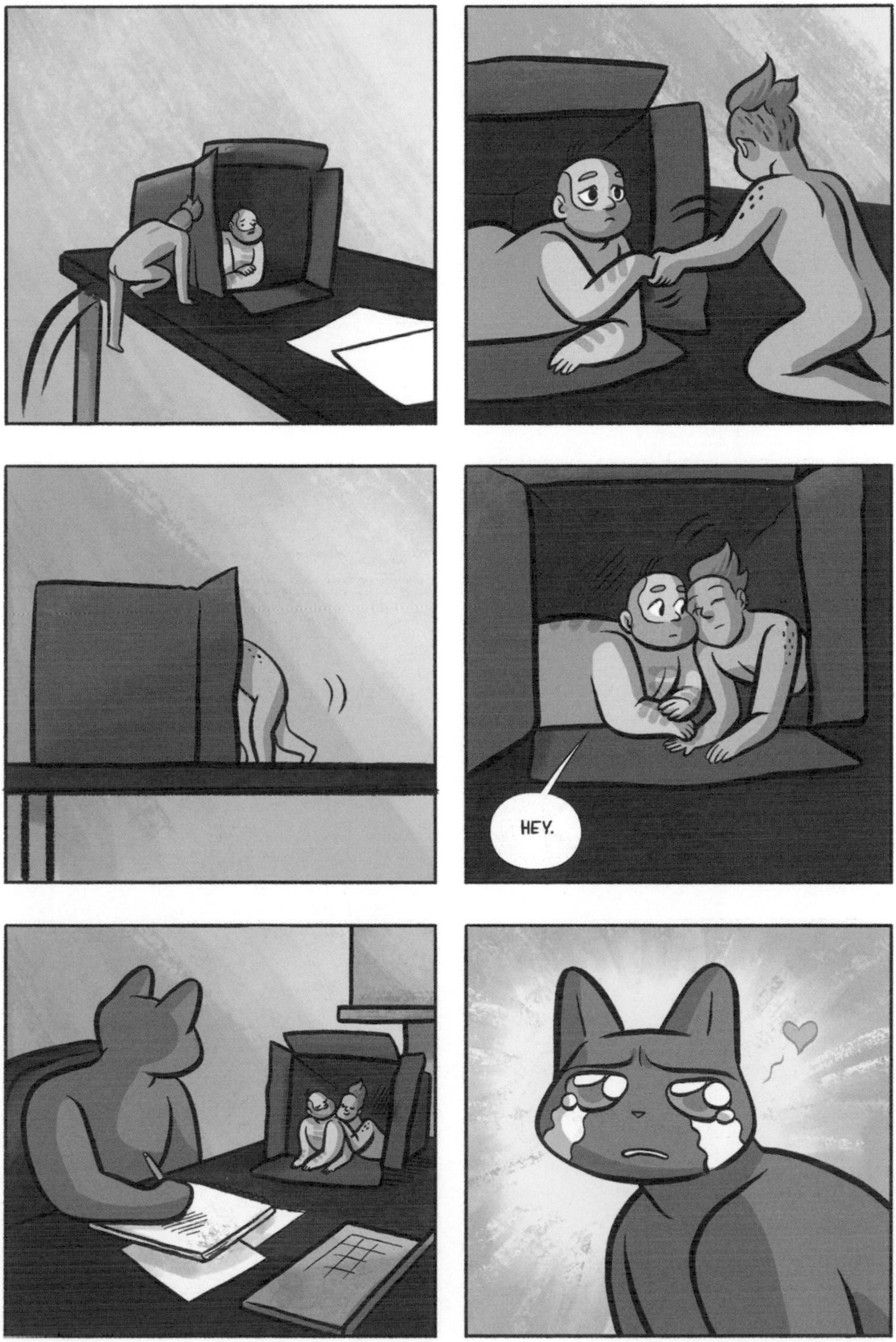
HEY.

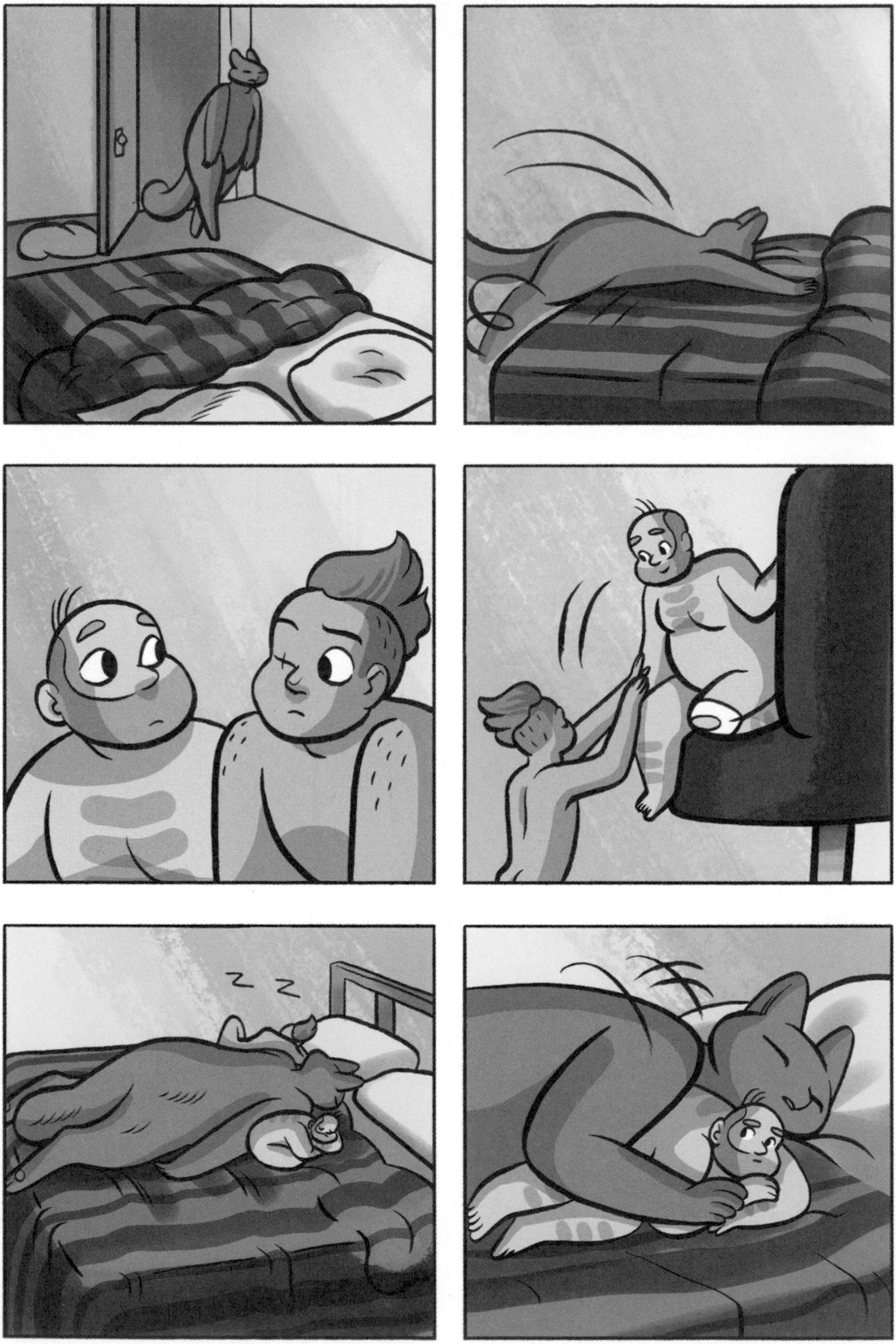
Z Z

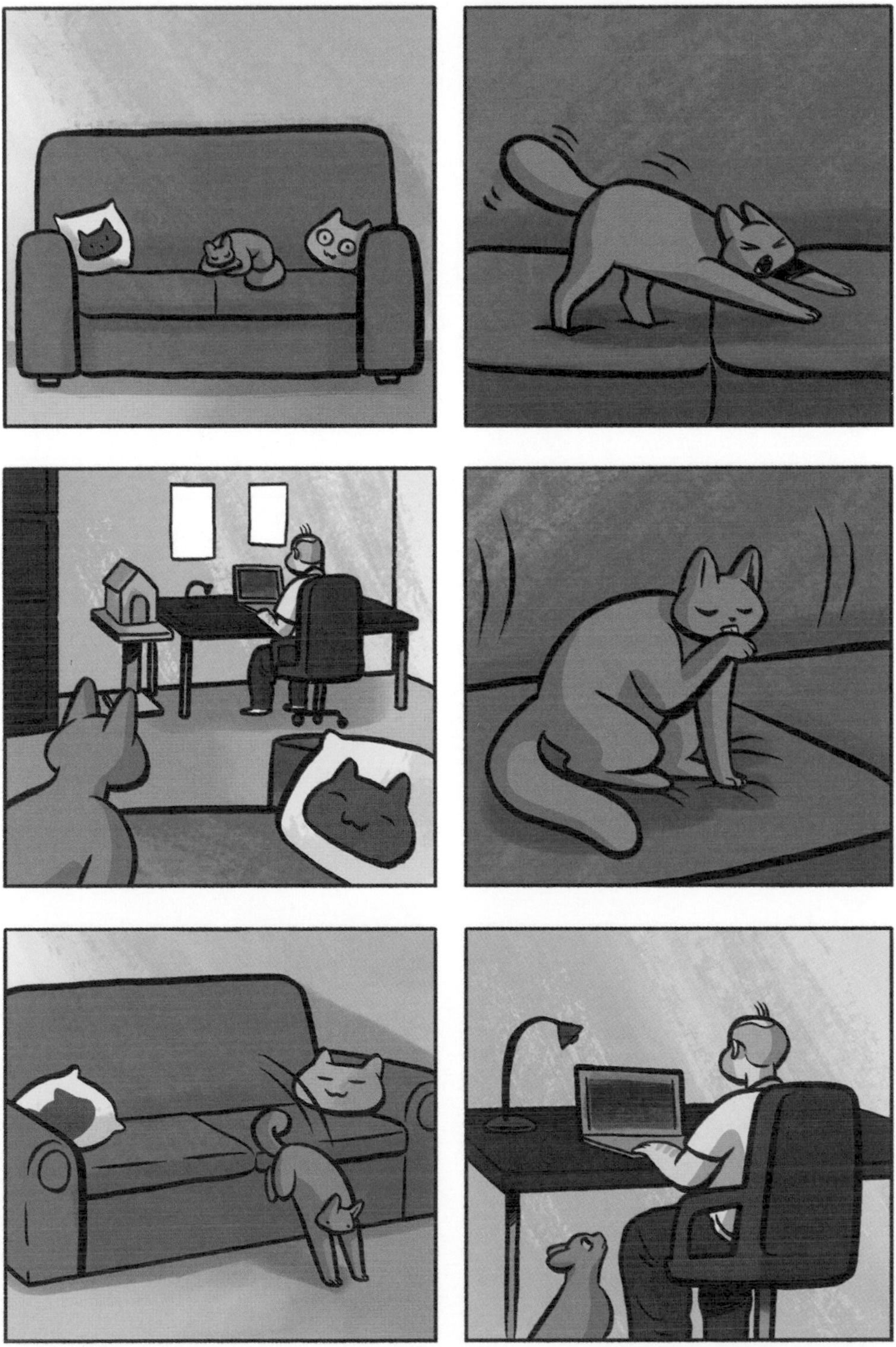

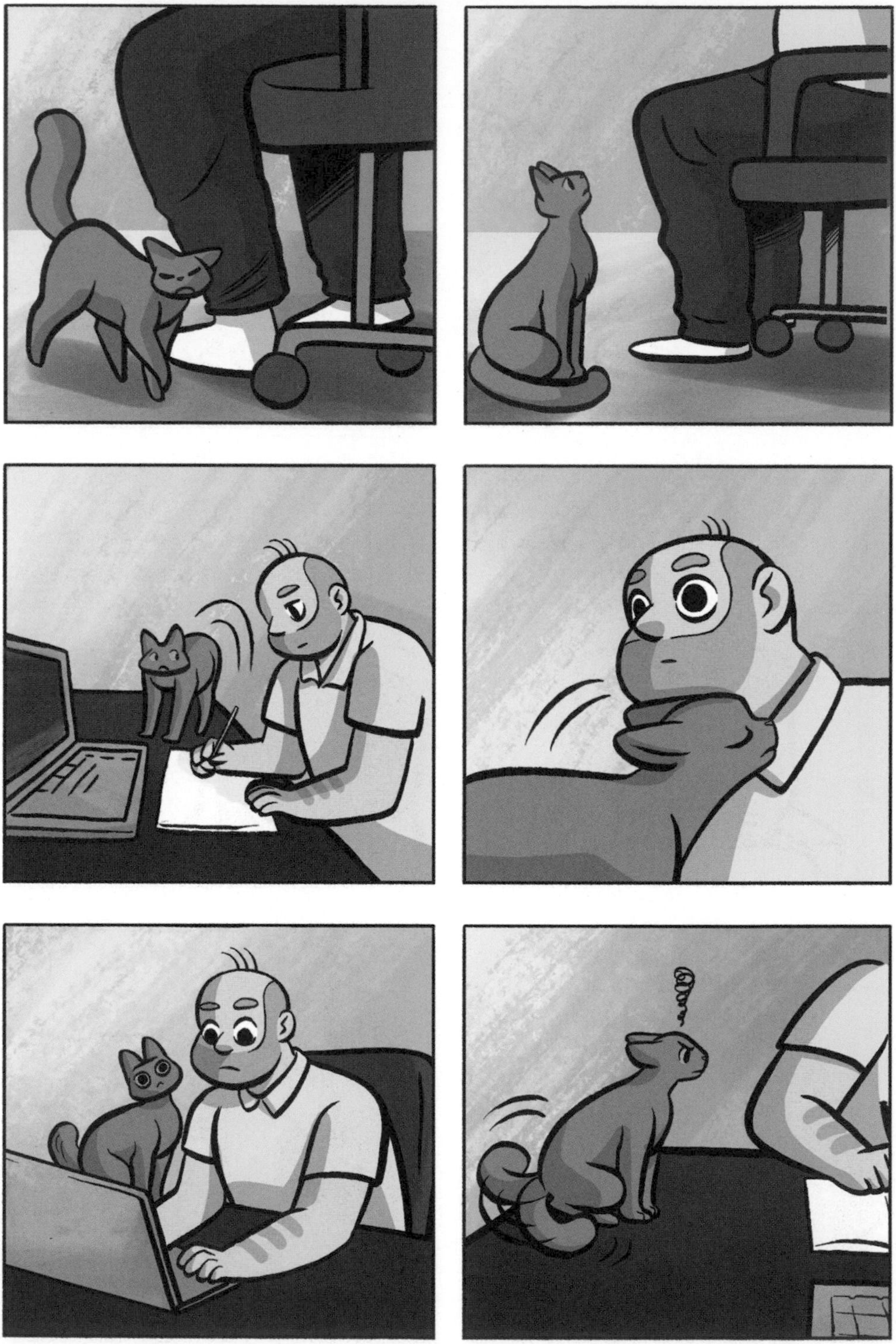

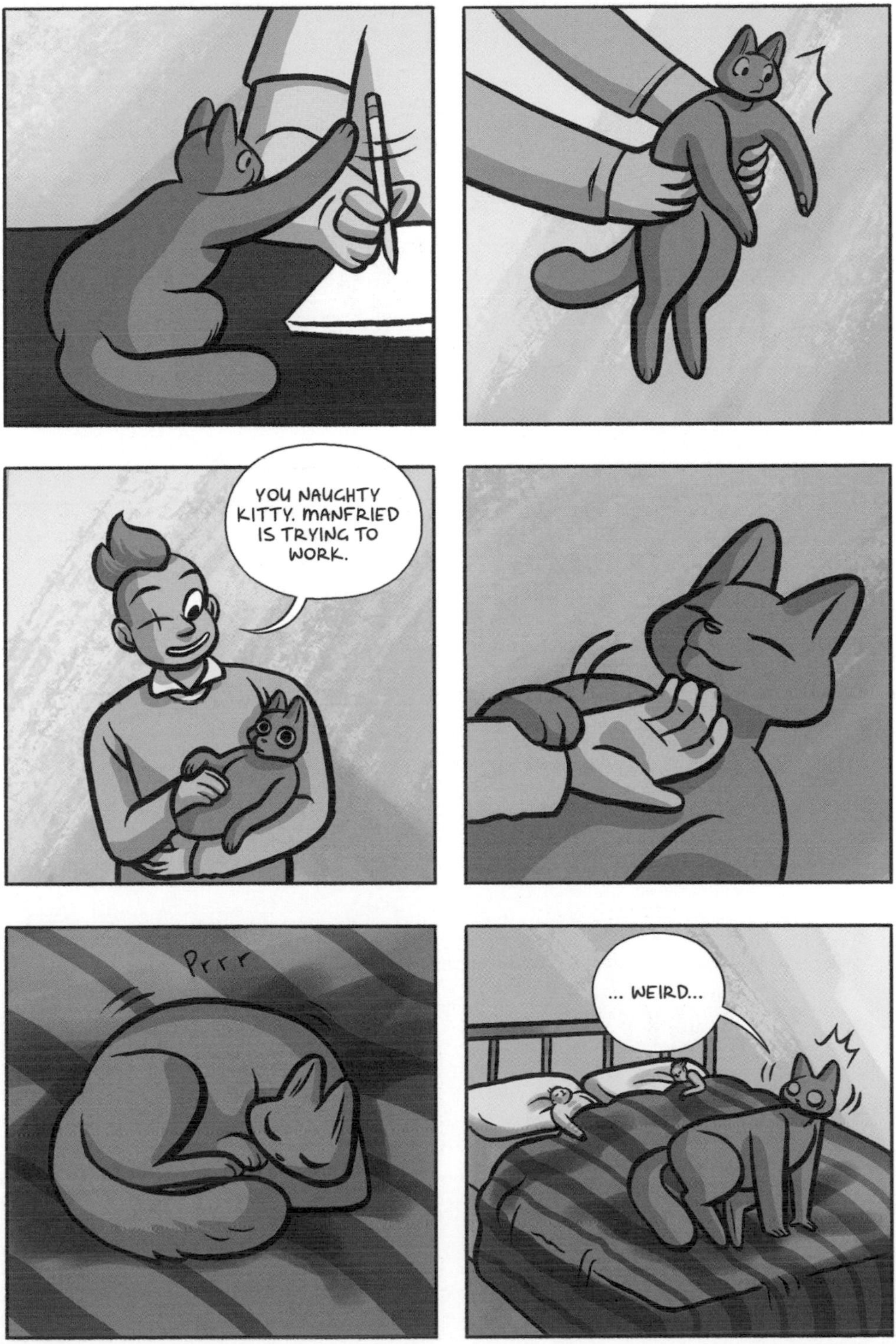
YOU NAUGHTY KITTY. MANFRIED IS TRYING TO WORK.
Prrr
... WEIRD...

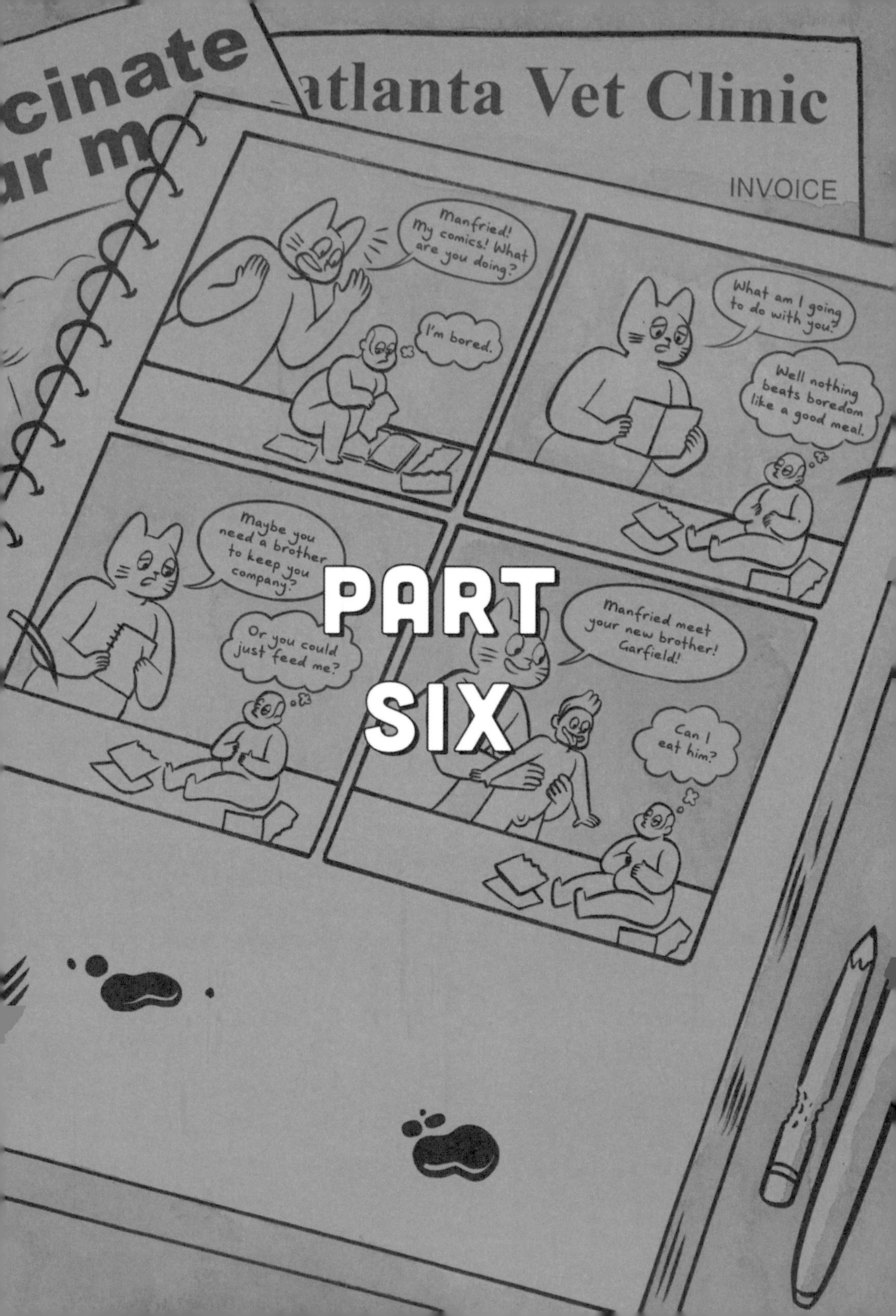

cinate
r m
atlanta Vet Clinic
INVOICE
Manfried! My comics! What are you doing?
I'm bored.
What am I going to do with you?
Well nothing beats boredom like a good meal.
Maybe you need a brother to keep you company?
Or you could just feed me?
Manfried meet your new brother! Garfield!
Can I eat him?

PART SIX

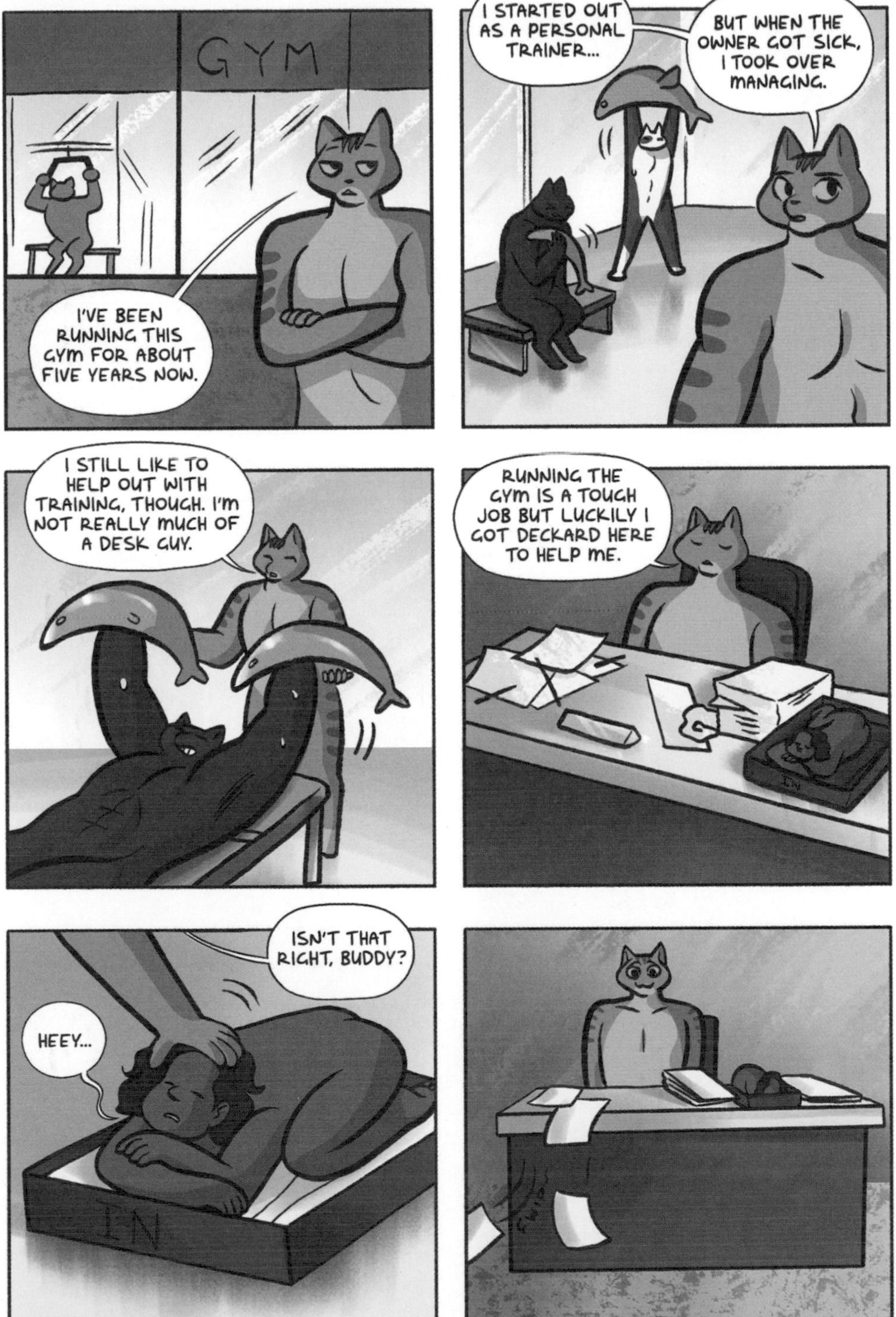
GYM
I'VE BEEN RUNNING THIS GYM FOR ABOUT FIVE YEARS NOW.
I STARTED OUT AS A PERSONAL TRAINER...
BUT WHEN THE OWNER GOT SICK, I TOOK OVER MANAGING.
I STILL LIKE TO HELP OUT WITH TRAINING, THOUGH. I'M NOT REALLY MUCH OF A DESK GUY.
RUNNING THE GYM IS A TOUGH JOB BUT LUCKILY I GOT DECKARD HERE TO HELP ME.
ISN'T THAT RIGHT, BUDDY?
HEEY...
IN

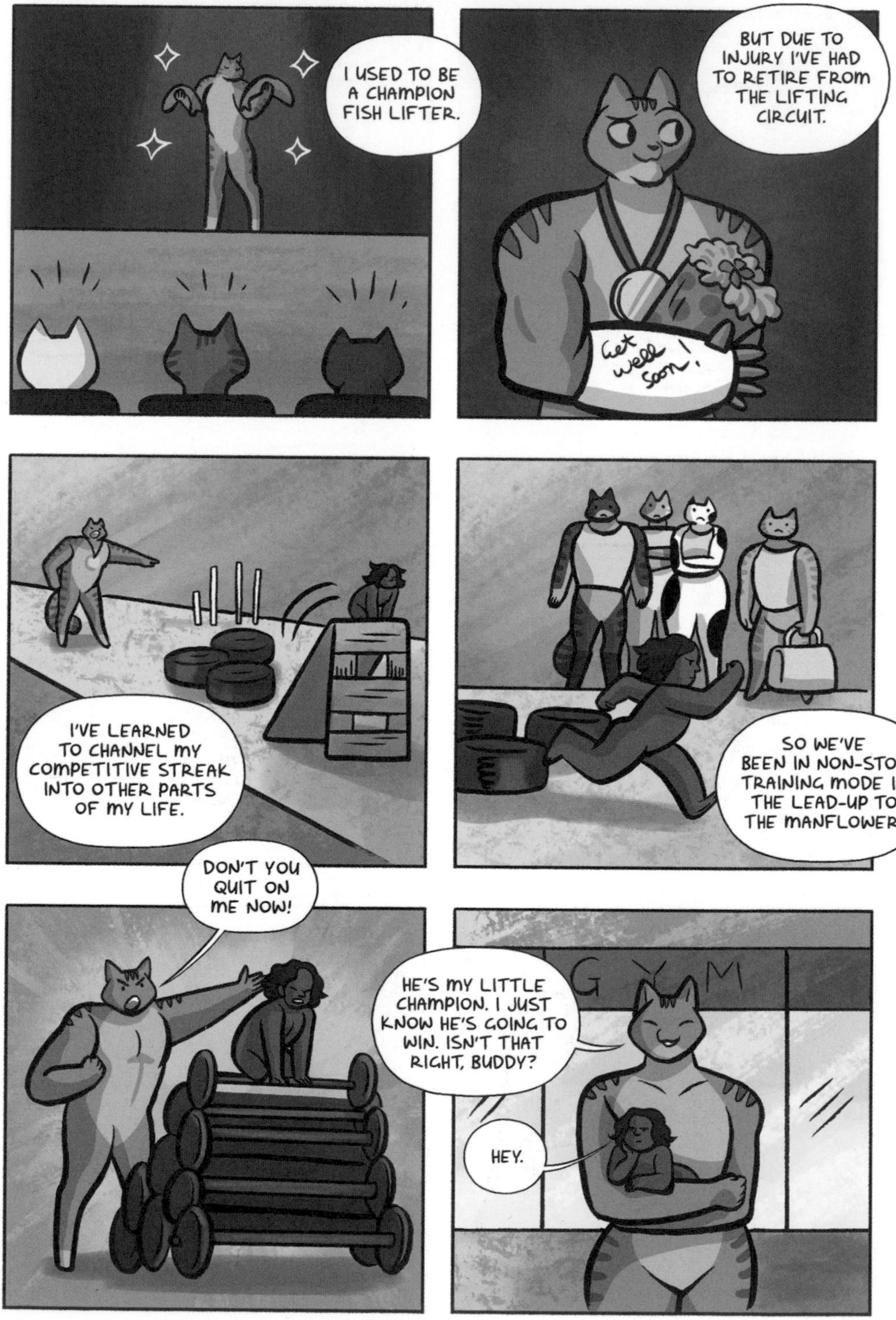
I USED TO BE A CHAMPION FISH LIFTER.
BUT DUE TO INJURY I'VE HAD TO RETIRE FROM THE LIFTING CIRCUIT.
Get well soon!
I'VE LEARNED TO CHANNEL MY COMPETITIVE STREAK INTO OTHER PARTS OF MY LIFE.
SO WE'VE BEEN IN NON-STOP TRAINING MODE IN THE LEAD-UP TO THE MANFLOWER.
DON'T YOU QUIT ON ME NOW!
GYM
HE'S MY LITTLE CHAMPION. I JUST KNOW HE'S GOING TO WIN. ISN'T THAT RIGHT, BUDDY?
HEY.

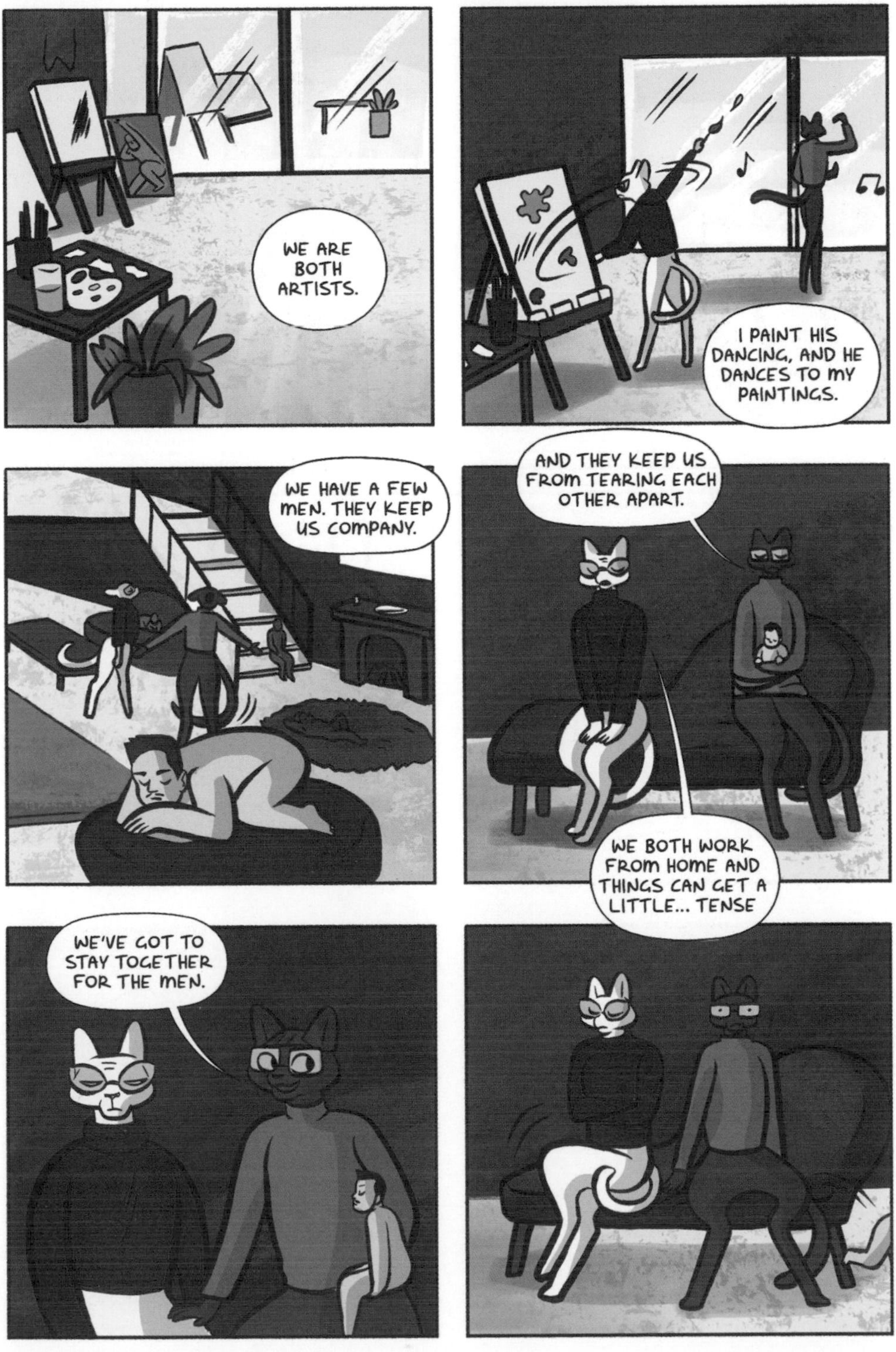
WE ARE BOTH ARTISTS.
I PAINT HIS DANCING, AND HE DANCES TO MY PAINTINGS.
WE HAVE A FEW MEN. THEY KEEP US COMPANY.
AND THEY KEEP US FROM TEARING EACH OTHER APART.
WE BOTH WORK FROM HOME AND THINGS CAN GET A LITTLE... TENSE
WE'VE GOT TO STAY TOGETHER FOR THE MEN.

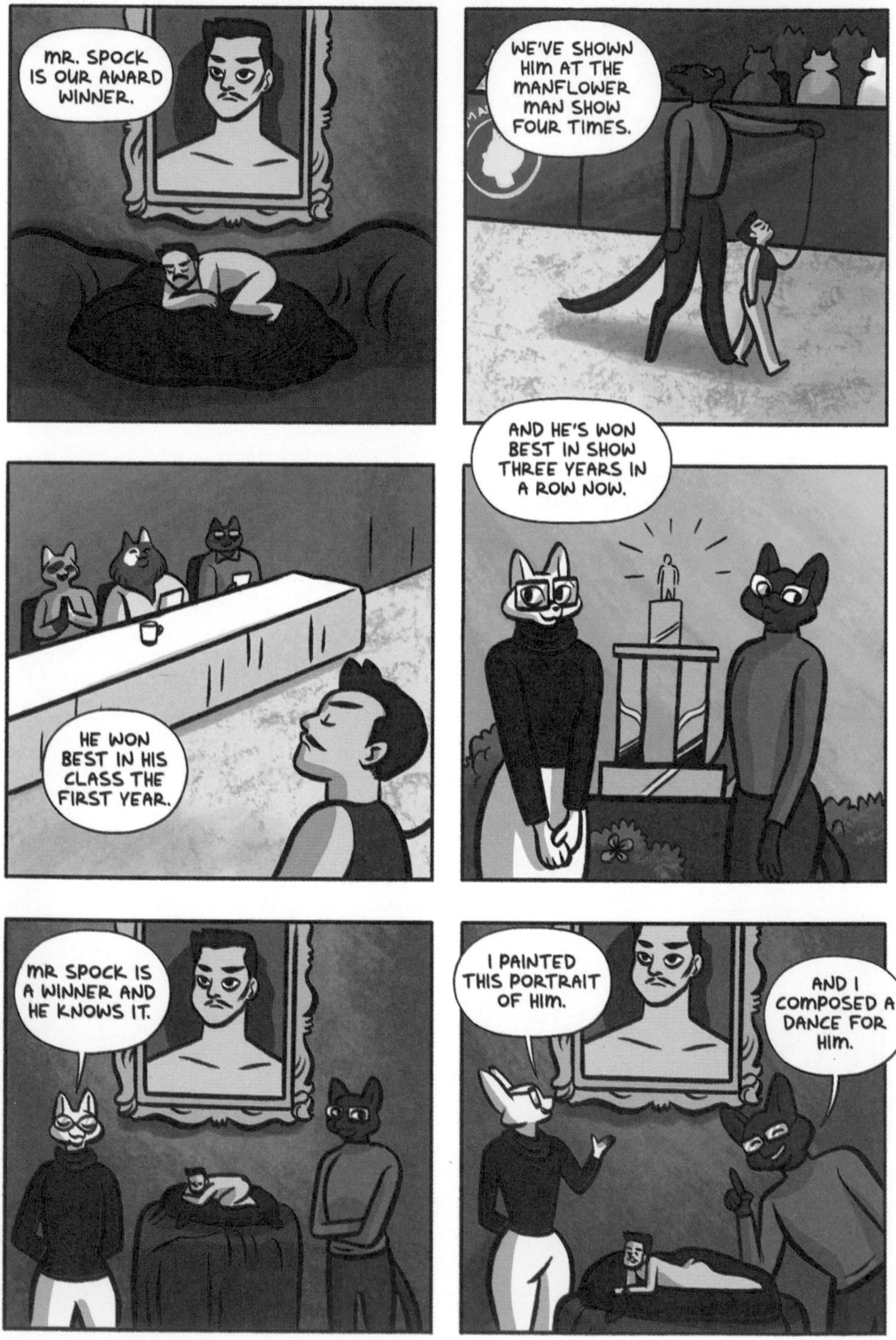
MR. SPOCK IS OUR AWARD WINNER.
WE'VE SHOWN HIM AT THE MANFLOWER MAN SHOW FOUR TIMES.
HE WON BEST IN HIS CLASS THE FIRST YEAR.
AND HE'S WON BEST IN SHOW THREE YEARS IN A ROW NOW.
MR SPOCK IS A WINNER AND HE KNOWS IT.
I PAINTED THIS PORTRAIT OF HIM.
AND I COMPOSED A DANCE FOR HIM.

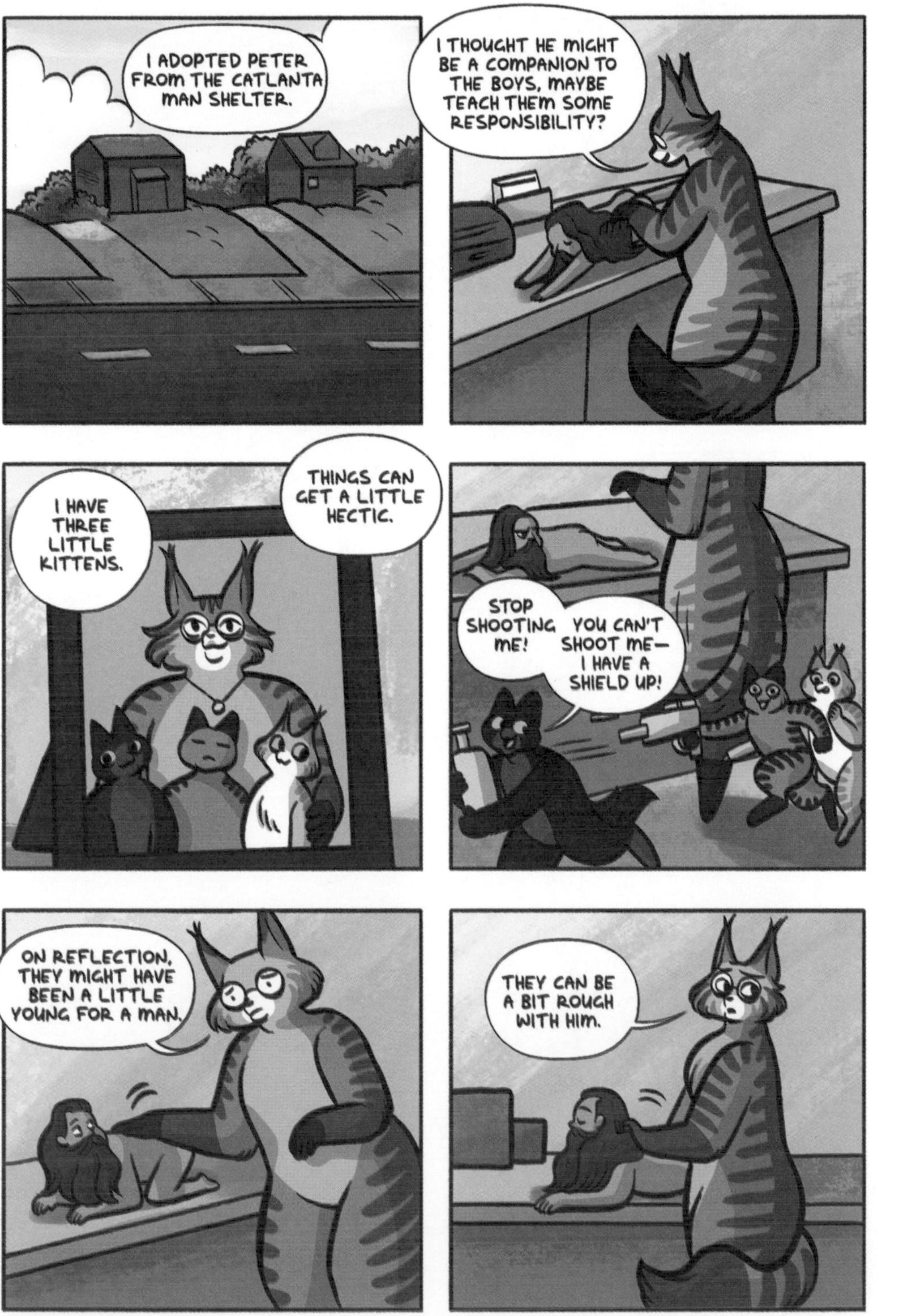
I ADOPTED PETER FROM THE CATLANTA MAN SHELTER.
I THOUGHT HE MIGHT BE A COMPANION TO THE BOYS, MAYBE TEACH THEM SOME RESPONSIBILITY?
I HAVE THREE LITTLE KITTENS.
THINGS CAN GET A LITTLE HECTIC.
STOP SHOOTING ME!
YOU CAN'T SHOOT ME— I HAVE A SHIELD UP!
ON REFLECTION, THEY MIGHT HAVE BEEN A LITTLE YOUNG FOR A MAN.
THEY CAN BE A BIT ROUGH WITH HIM.

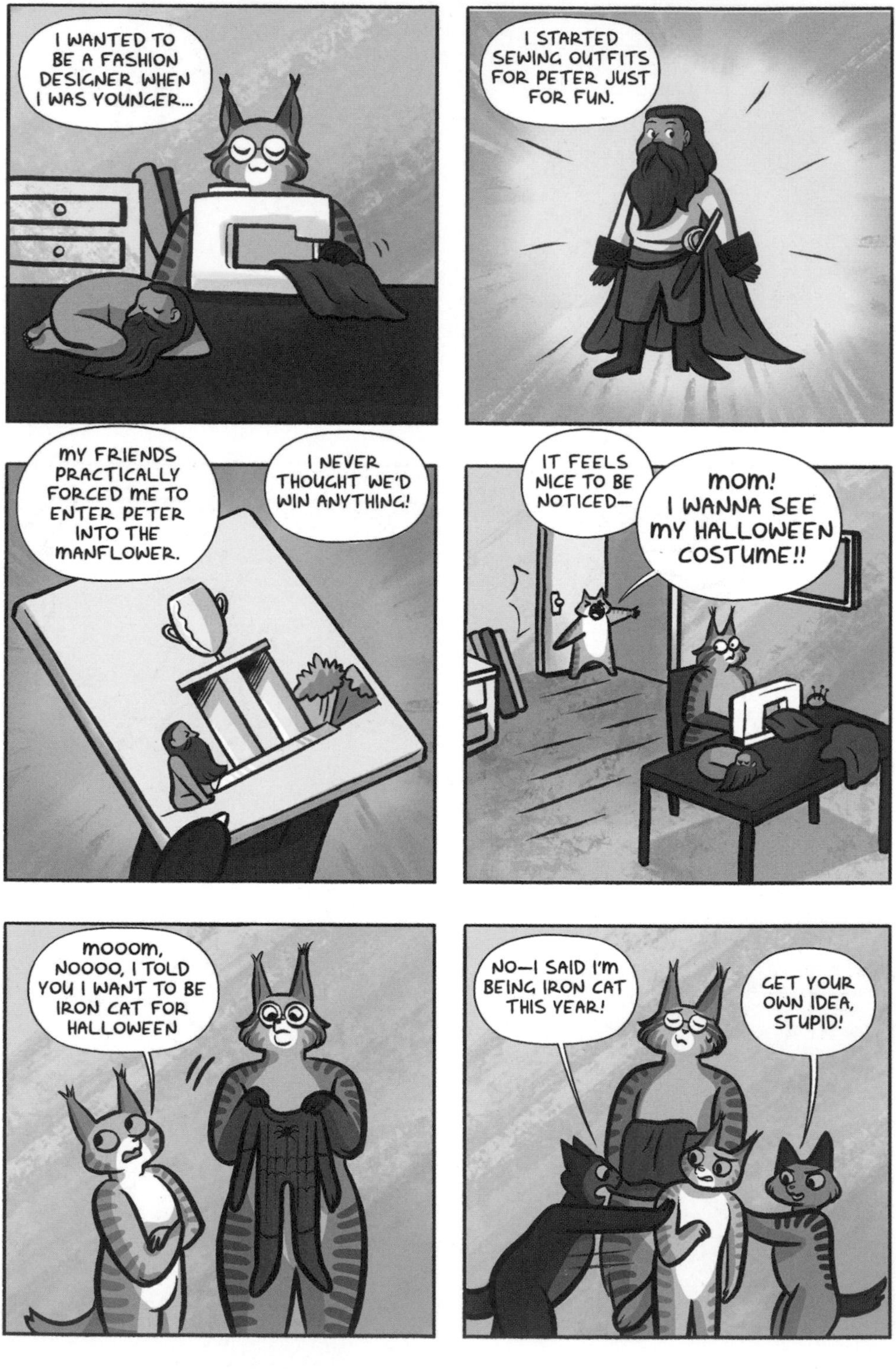
I WANTED TO BE A FASHION DESIGNER WHEN I WAS YOUNGER...
I STARTED SEWING OUTFITS FOR PETER JUST FOR FUN.
MY FRIENDS PRACTICALLY FORCED ME TO ENTER PETER INTO THE MANFLOWER.
I NEVER THOUGHT WE'D WIN ANYTHING!
IT FEELS NICE TO BE NOTICED—
MOM! I WANNA SEE MY HALLOWEEN COSTUME!!
MOOOM, NOOOO, I TOLD YOU I WANT TO BE IRON CAT FOR HALLOWEEN
NO—I SAID I'M BEING IRON CAT THIS YEAR!
GET YOUR OWN IDEA, STUPID!

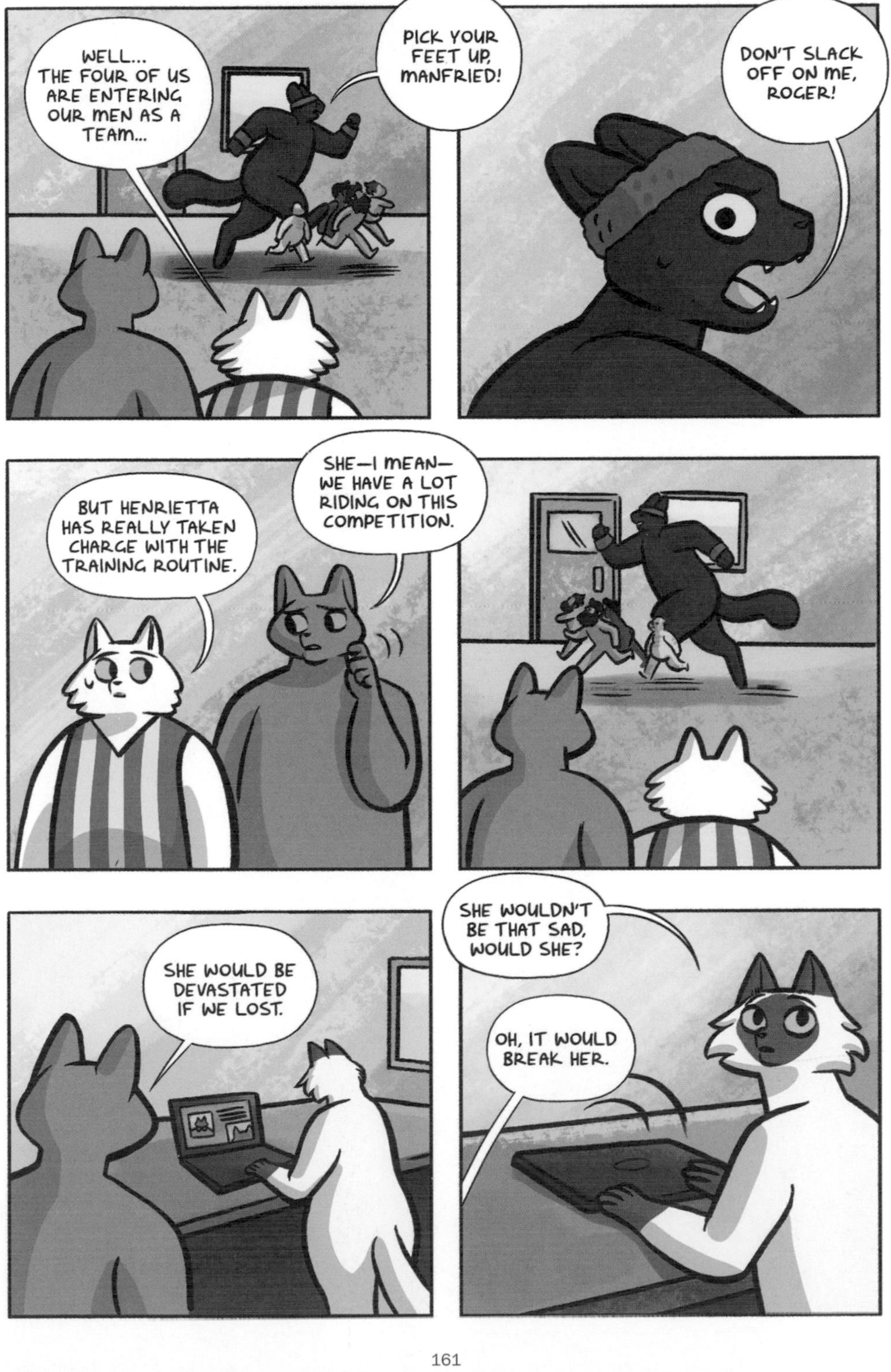
WELL... THE FOUR OF US ARE ENTERING OUR MEN AS A TEAM...
PICK YOUR FEET UP, MANFRIED!
DON'T SLACK OFF ON ME, ROGER!
BUT HENRIETTA HAS REALLY TAKEN CHARGE WITH THE TRAINING ROUTINE.
SHE—I MEAN—WE HAVE A LOT RIDING ON THIS COMPETITION.
SHE WOULD BE DEVASTATED IF WE LOST.
SHE WOULDN'T BE THAT SAD, WOULD SHE?
OH, IT WOULD BREAK HER.

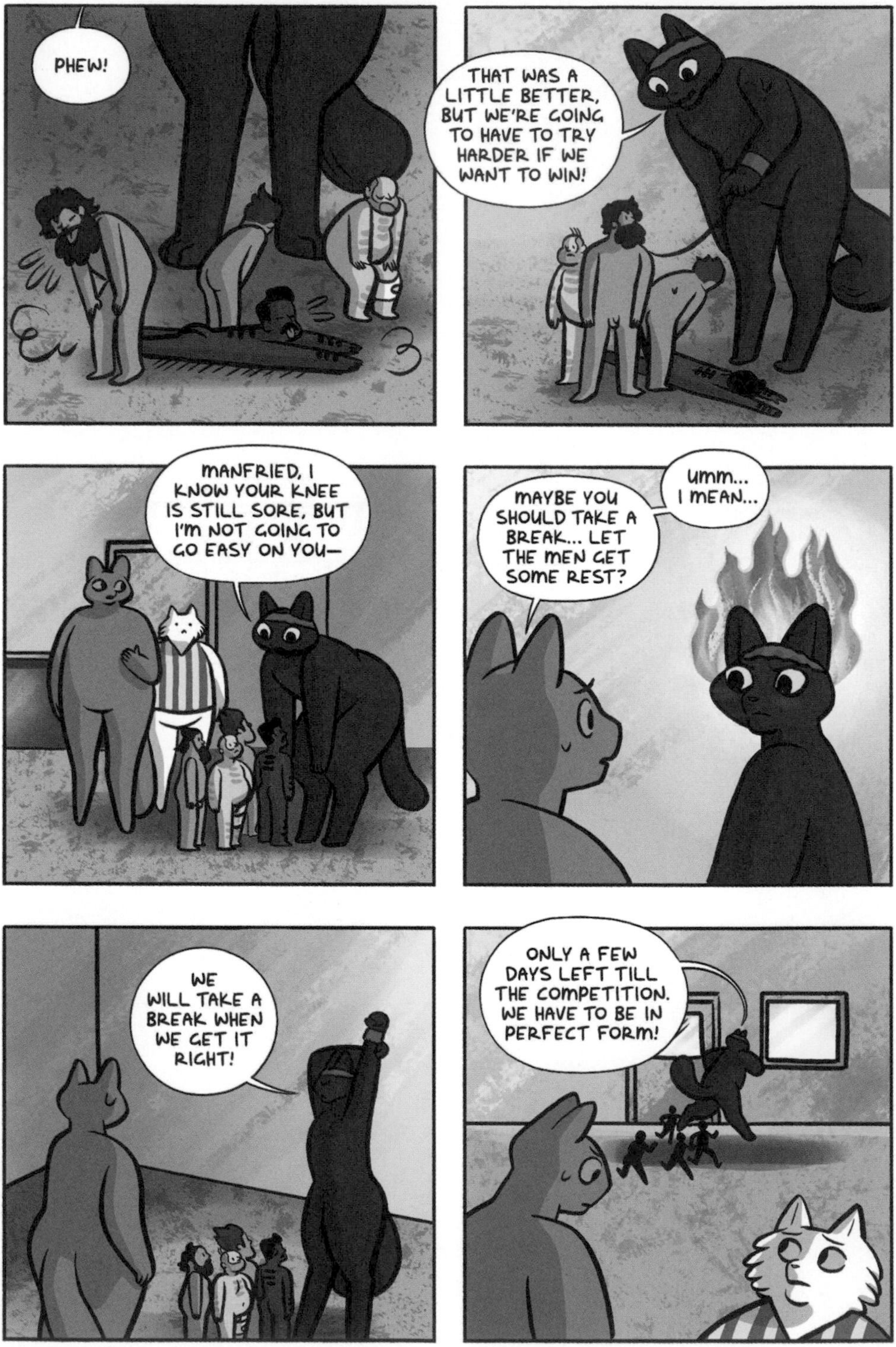
PHEW!
THAT WAS A LITTLE BETTER, BUT WE'RE GOING TO HAVE TO TRY HARDER IF WE WANT TO WIN!
MANFRIED, I KNOW YOUR KNEE IS STILL SORE, BUT I'M NOT GOING TO GO EASY ON YOU—
MAYBE YOU SHOULD TAKE A BREAK... LET THE MEN GET SOME REST?
UMM... I MEAN...
WE WILL TAKE A BREAK WHEN WE GET IT RIGHT!
ONLY A FEW DAYS LEFT TILL THE COMPETITION. WE HAVE TO BE IN PERFECT FORM!

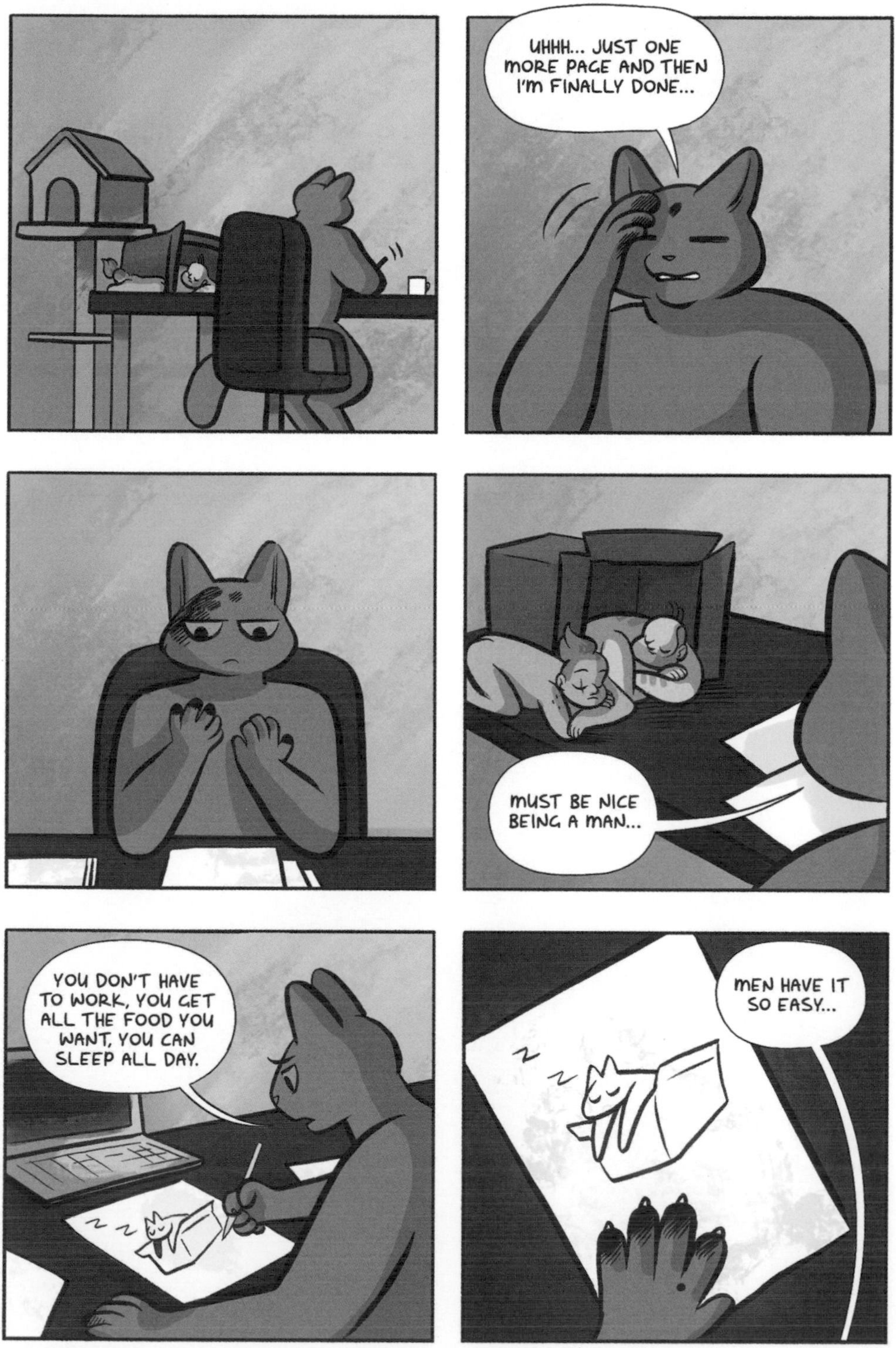
UHHH... JUST ONE MORE PAGE AND THEN I'M FINALLY DONE...
MUST BE NICE BEING A MAN...
YOU DON'T HAVE TO WORK, YOU GET ALL THE FOOD YOU WANT, YOU CAN SLEEP ALL DAY.
MEN HAVE IT SO EASY...

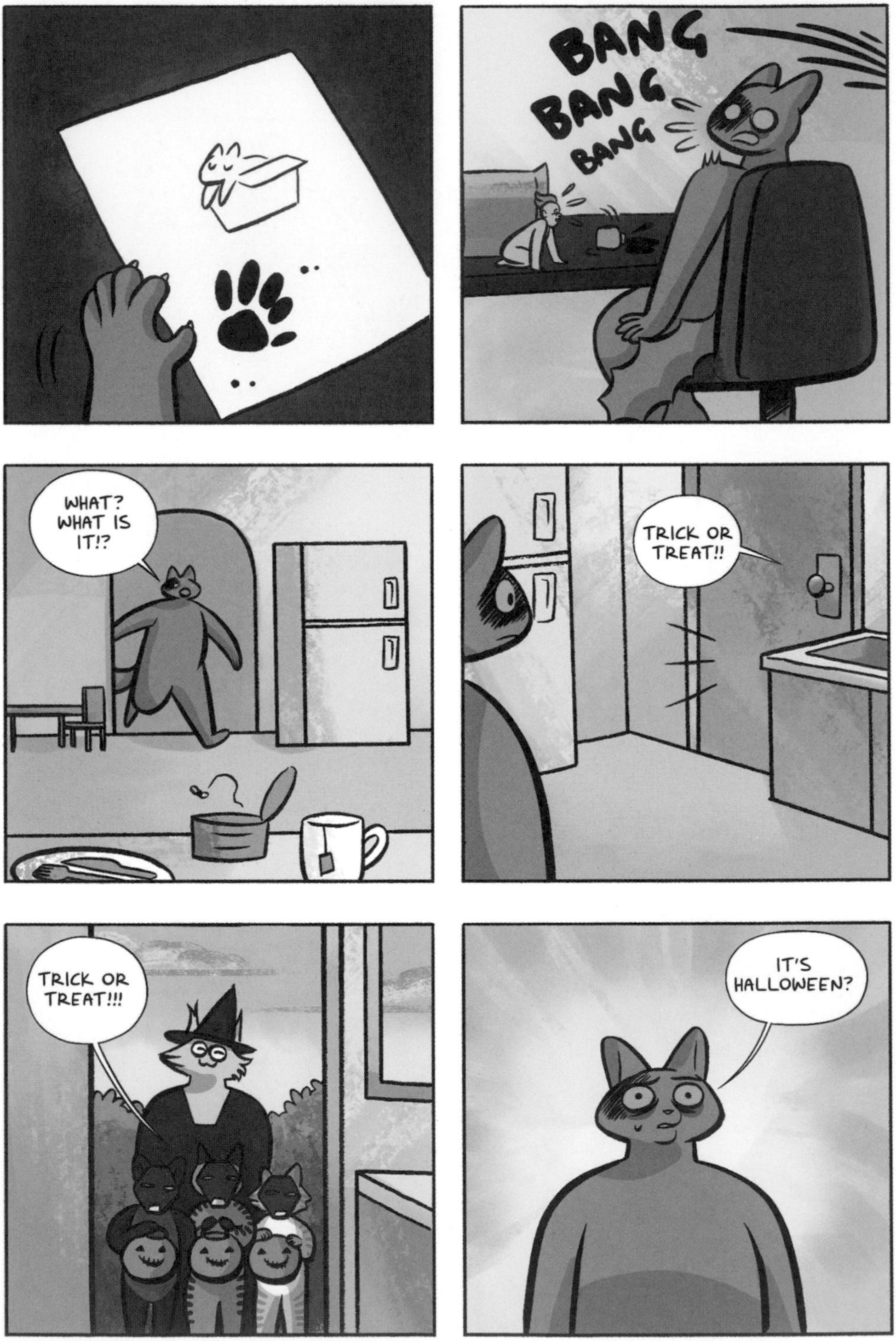
BANG
BANG
BANG
WHAT? WHAT IS IT!?
TRICK OR TREAT!!
TRICK OR TREAT!!!
IT'S HALLOWEEN?

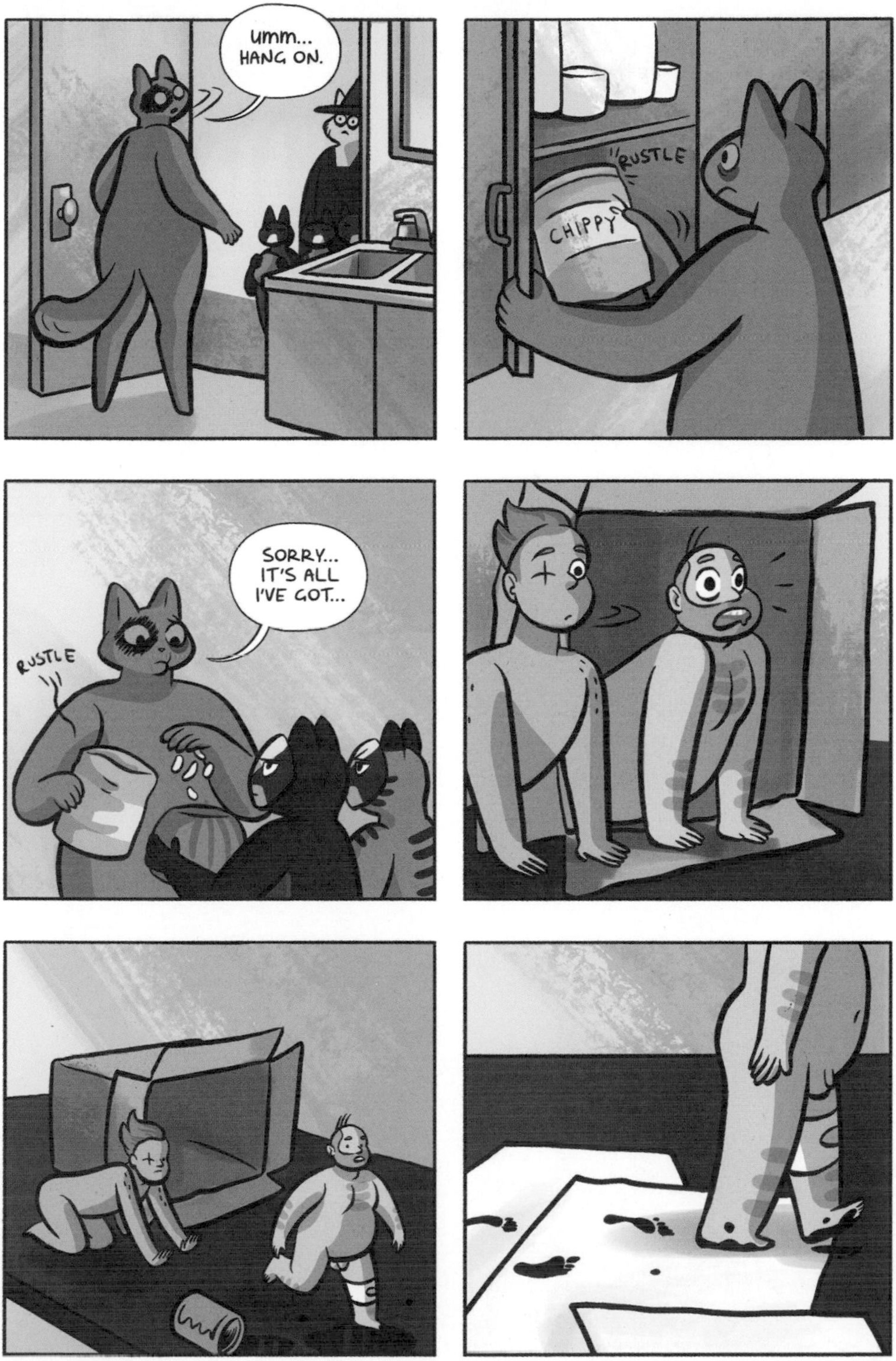
UMM... HANG ON.
RUSTLE
CHIPPY
SORRY... IT'S ALL I'VE GOT...
RUSTLE

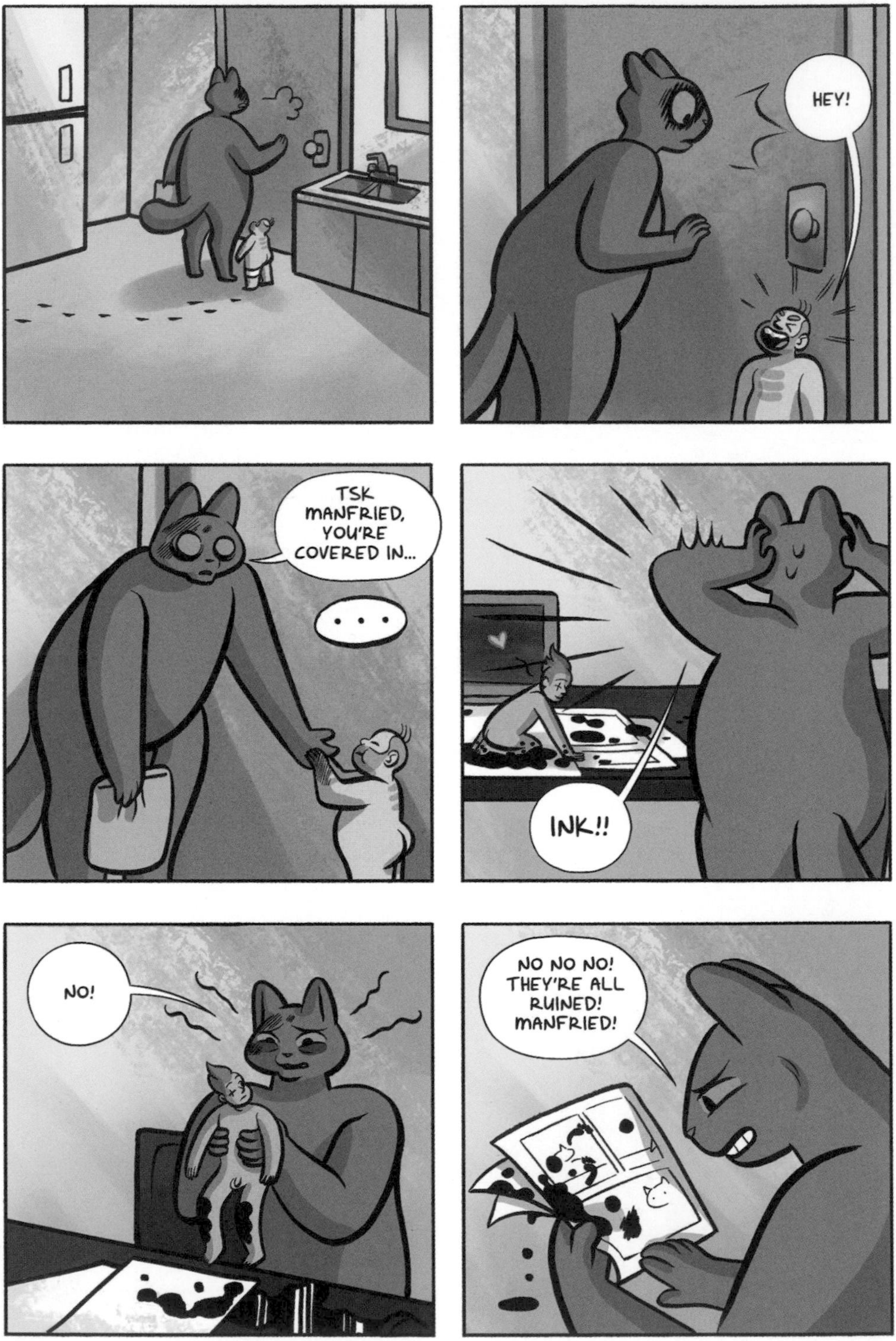
HEY!
TSK MANFRIED, YOU'RE COVERED IN...
...
INK!!
NO!
NO NO NO! THEY'RE ALL RUINED! MANFRIED!

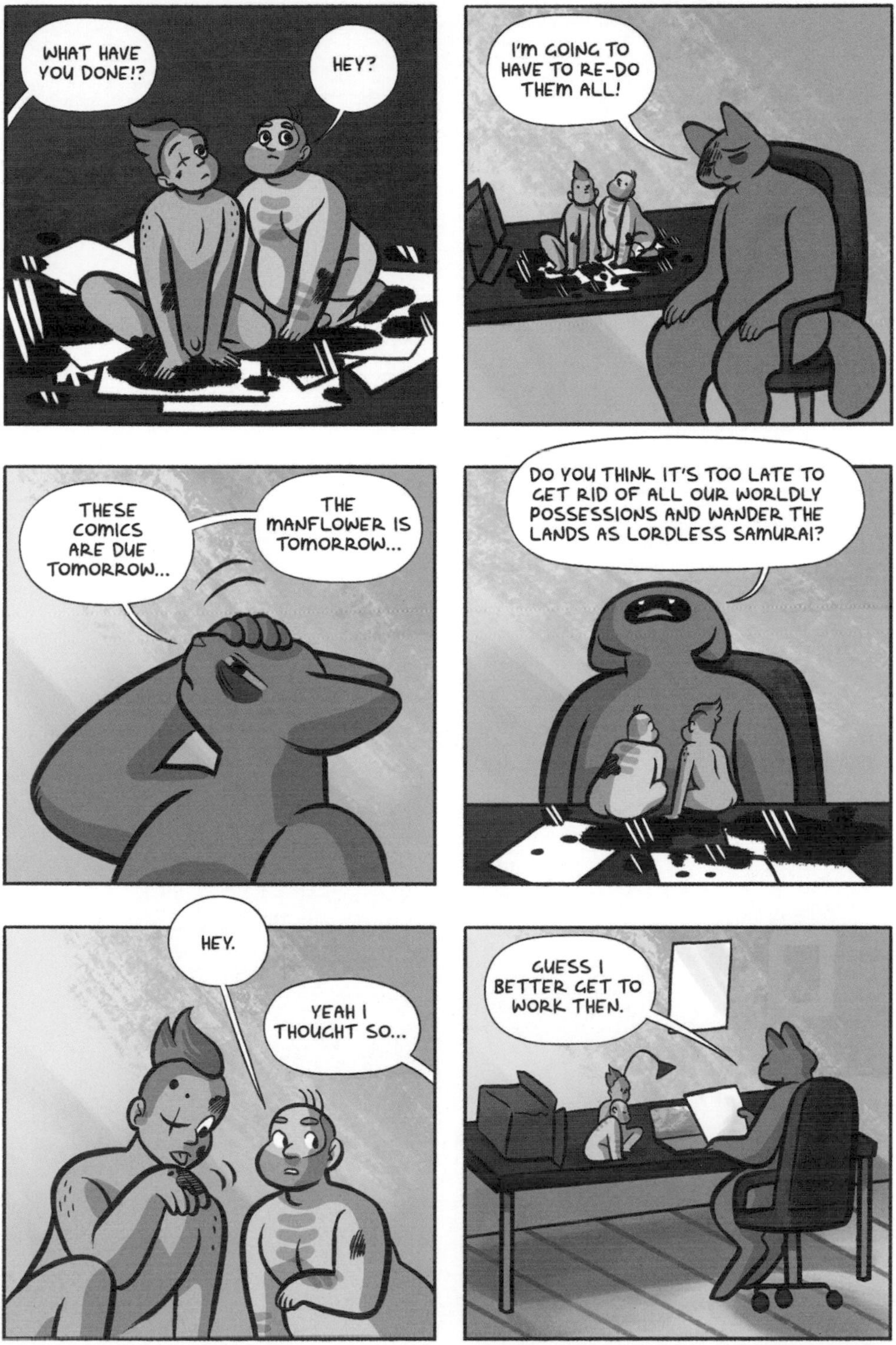
WHAT HAVE YOU DONE!?
HEY?
I'M GOING TO HAVE TO RE-DO THEM ALL!
THESE COMICS ARE DUE TOMORROW...
THE MANFLOWER IS TOMORROW...
DO YOU THINK IT'S TOO LATE TO GET RID OF ALL OUR WORLDLY POSSESSIONS AND WANDER THE LANDS AS LORDLESS SAMURAI?
HEY.
YEAH I THOUGHT SO...
GUESS I BETTER GET TO WORK THEN.

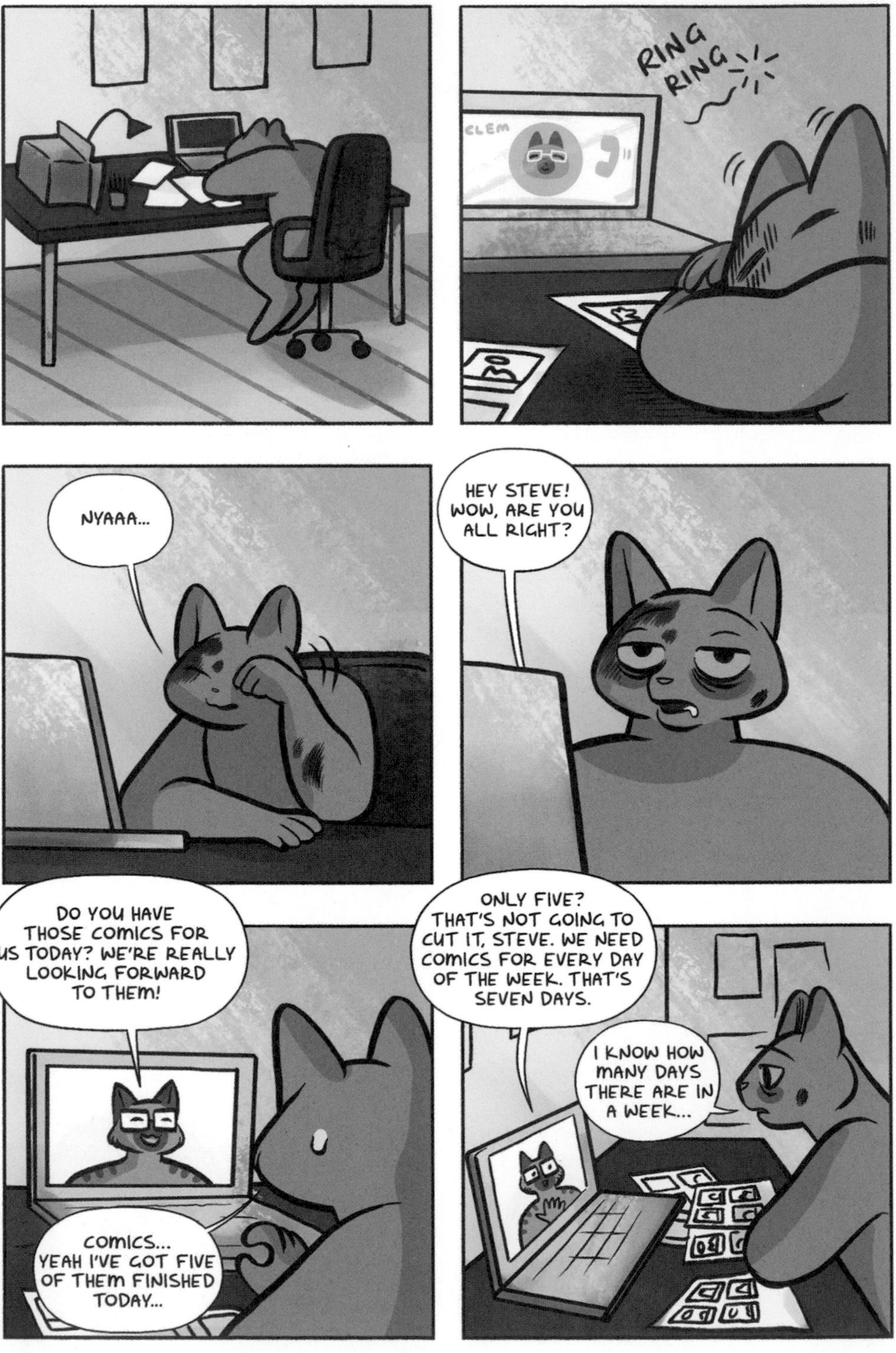
RING RING
CLEM
NYAAA...
HEY STEVE! WOW, ARE YOU ALL RIGHT?
DO YOU HAVE THOSE COMICS FOR US TODAY? WE'RE REALLY LOOKING FORWARD TO THEM!
COMICS... YEAH I'VE GOT FIVE OF THEM FINISHED TODAY...
ONLY FIVE? THAT'S NOT GOING TO CUT IT, STEVE. WE NEED COMICS FOR EVERY DAY OF THE WEEK. THAT'S SEVEN DAYS.
I KNOW HOW MANY DAYS THERE ARE IN A WEEK...

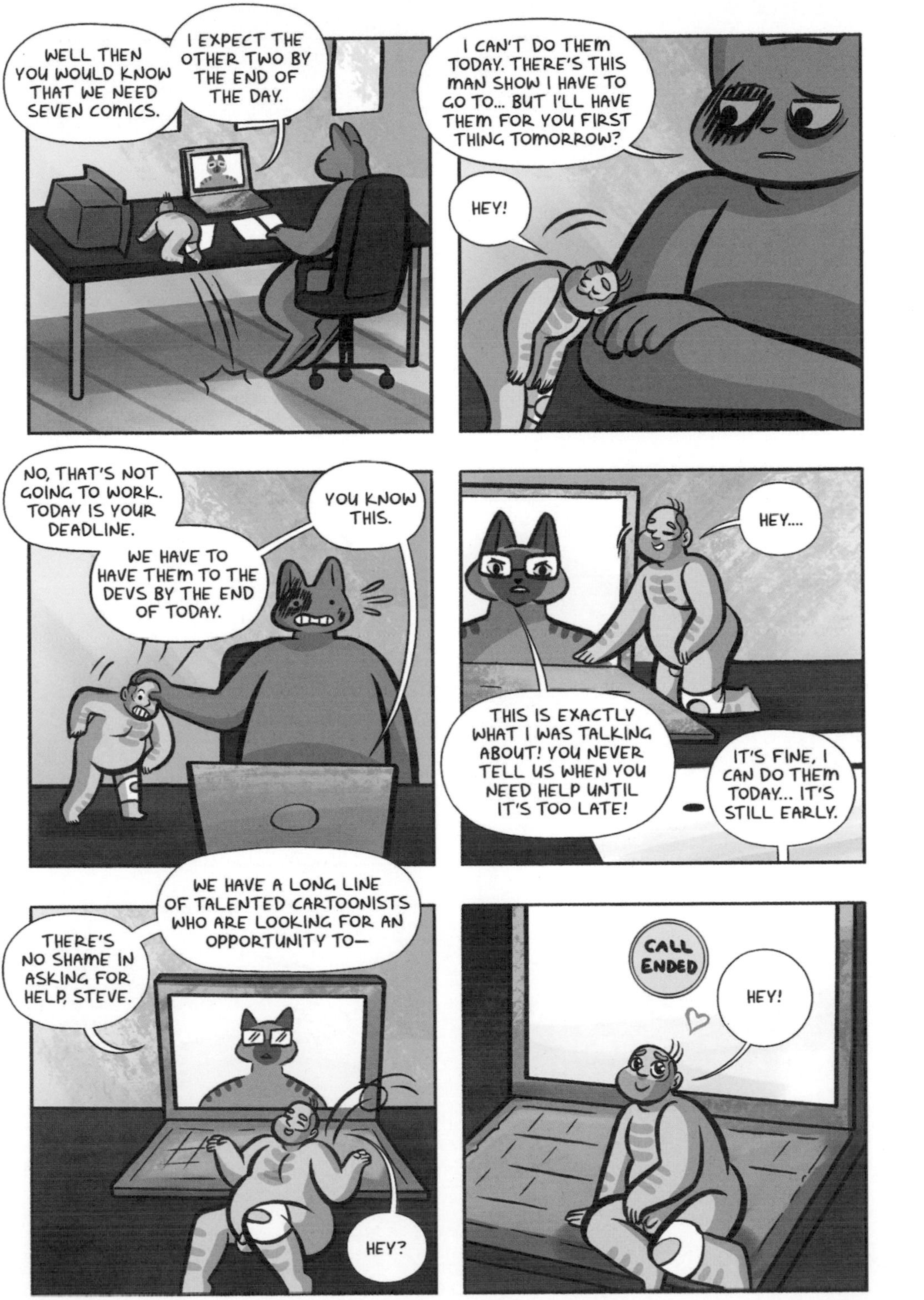
WELL THEN YOU WOULD KNOW THAT WE NEED SEVEN COMICS.
I EXPECT THE OTHER TWO BY THE END OF THE DAY.
I CAN'T DO THEM TODAY. THERE'S THIS MAN SHOW I HAVE TO GO TO... BUT I'LL HAVE THEM FOR YOU FIRST THING TOMORROW?
HEY!
NO, THAT'S NOT GOING TO WORK. TODAY IS YOUR DEADLINE.
WE HAVE TO HAVE THEM TO THE DEVS BY THE END OF TODAY.
YOU KNOW THIS.
HEY....
THIS IS EXACTLY WHAT I WAS TALKING ABOUT! YOU NEVER TELL US WHEN YOU NEED HELP UNTIL IT'S TOO LATE!
IT'S FINE, I CAN DO THEM TODAY... IT'S STILL EARLY.
THERE'S NO SHAME IN ASKING FOR HELP, STEVE.
WE HAVE A LONG LINE OF TALENTED CARTOONISTS WHO ARE LOOKING FOR AN OPPORTUNITY TO—
HEY?
CALL ENDED
HEY!

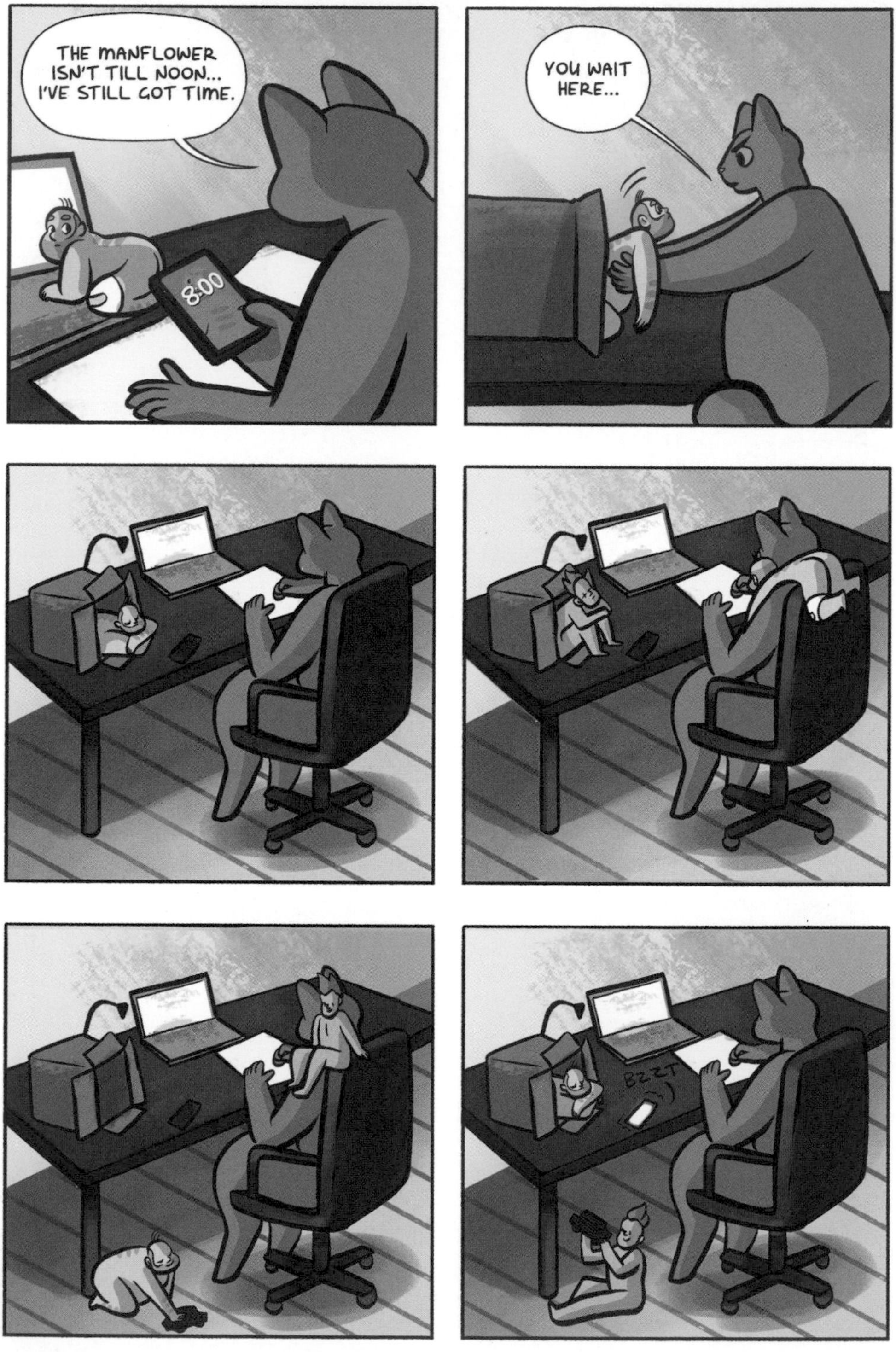
THE MANFLOWER ISN'T TILL NOON... I'VE STILL GOT TIME.
8:00
YOU WAIT HERE...
BZZT

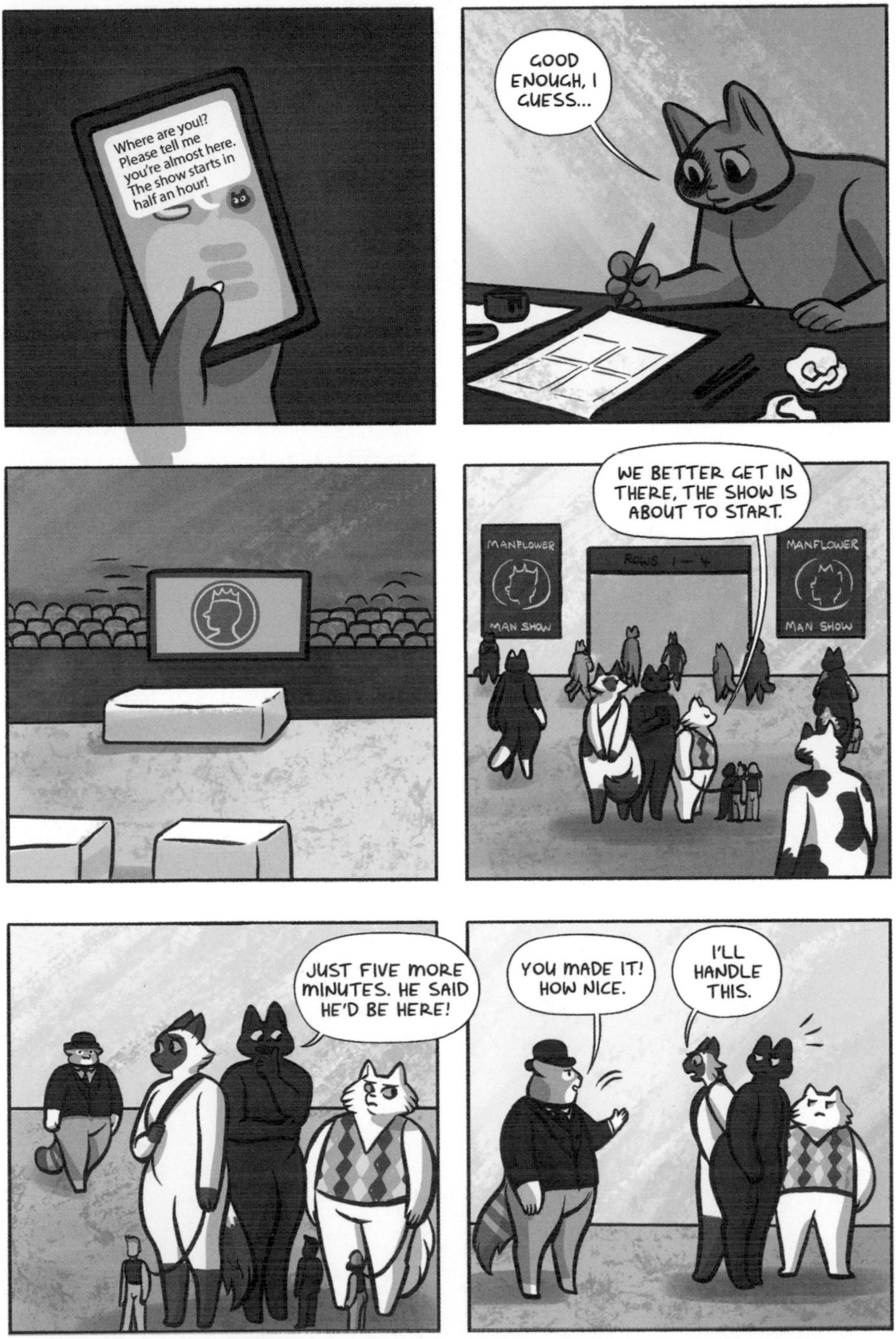
Where are you!? Please tell me you're almost here. The show starts in half an hour!
GOOD ENOUGH, I GUESS...
WE BETTER GET IN THERE, THE SHOW IS ABOUT TO START.
MANFLOWER
MAN SHOW
ROWS 1 — 4
MANFLOWER
MAN SHOW
JUST FIVE MORE MINUTES. HE SAID HE'D BE HERE!
YOU MADE IT! HOW NICE.
I'LL HANDLE THIS.

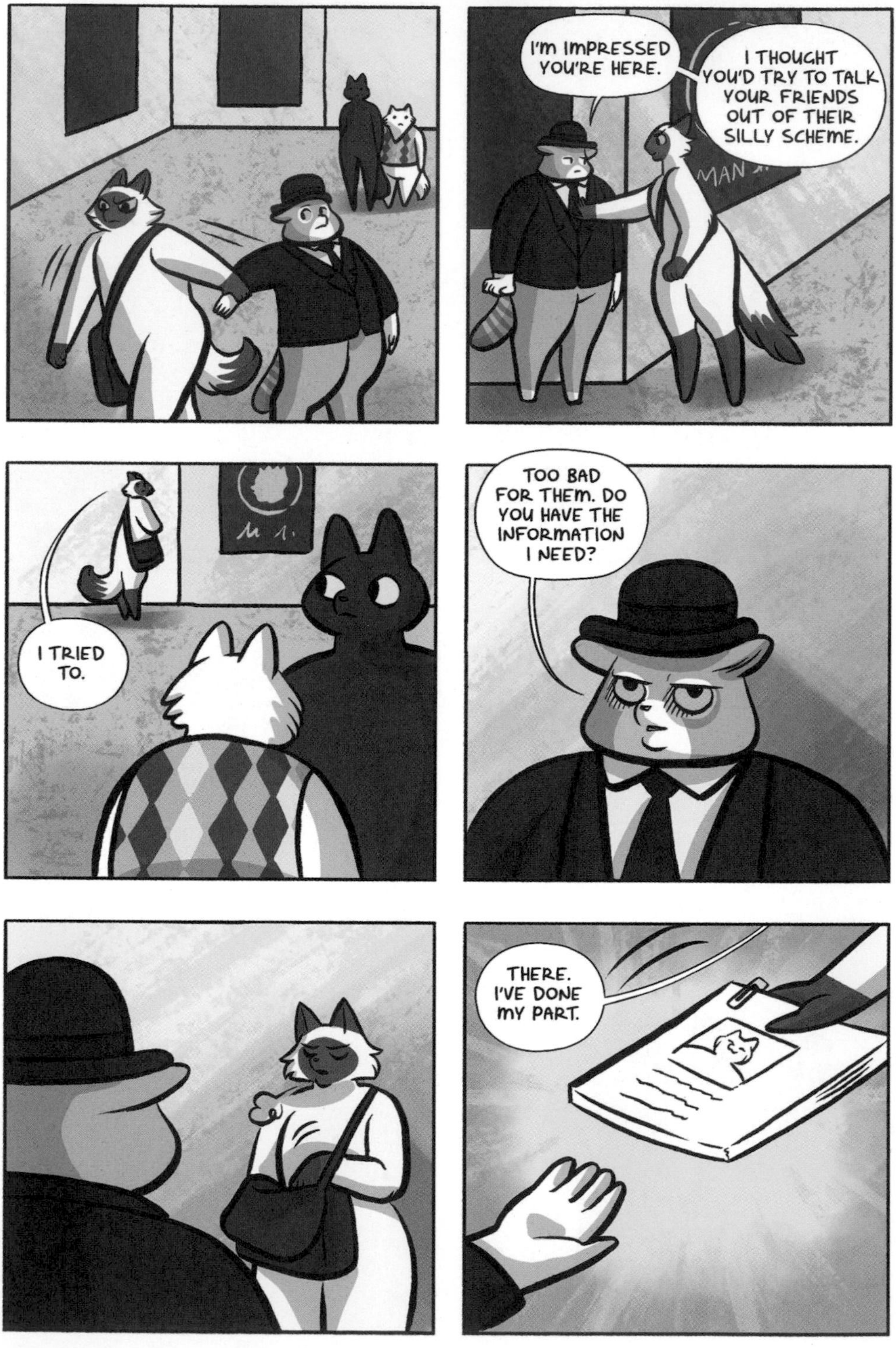
I'M IMPRESSED YOU'RE HERE.
I THOUGHT YOU'D TRY TO TALK YOUR FRIENDS OUT OF THEIR SILLY SCHEME.
I TRIED TO.
TOO BAD FOR THEM. DO YOU HAVE THE INFORMATION I NEED?
THERE. I'VE DONE MY PART.

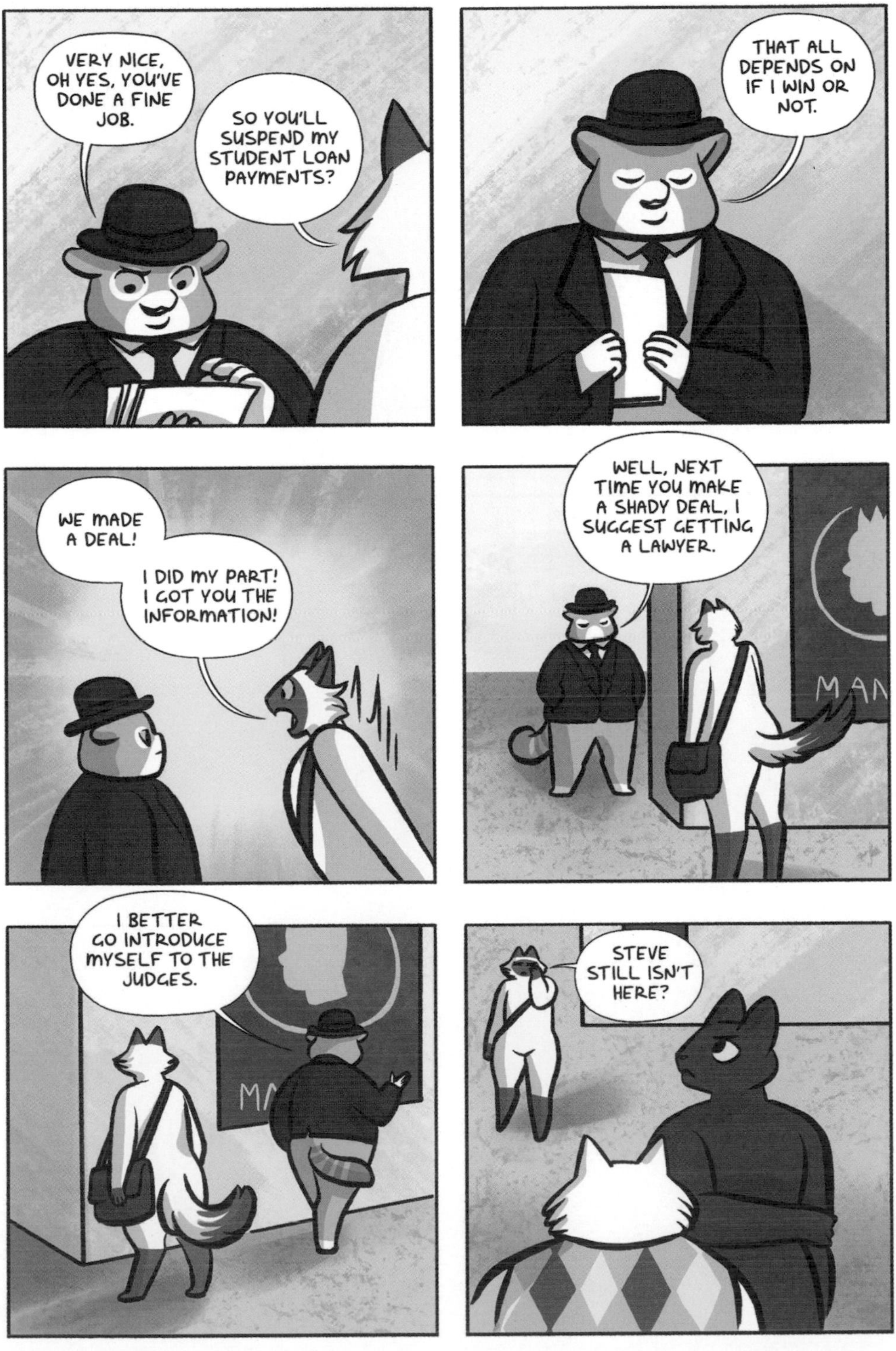
VERY NICE, OH YES, YOU'VE DONE A FINE JOB.
SO YOU'LL SUSPEND MY STUDENT LOAN PAYMENTS?
THAT ALL DEPENDS ON IF I WIN OR NOT.
WE MADE A DEAL!
I DID MY PART! I GOT YOU THE INFORMATION!
WELL, NEXT TIME YOU MAKE A SHADY DEAL, I SUGGEST GETTING A LAWYER.
MAN
I BETTER GO INTRODUCE MYSELF TO THE JUDGES.
MA
STEVE STILL ISN'T HERE?

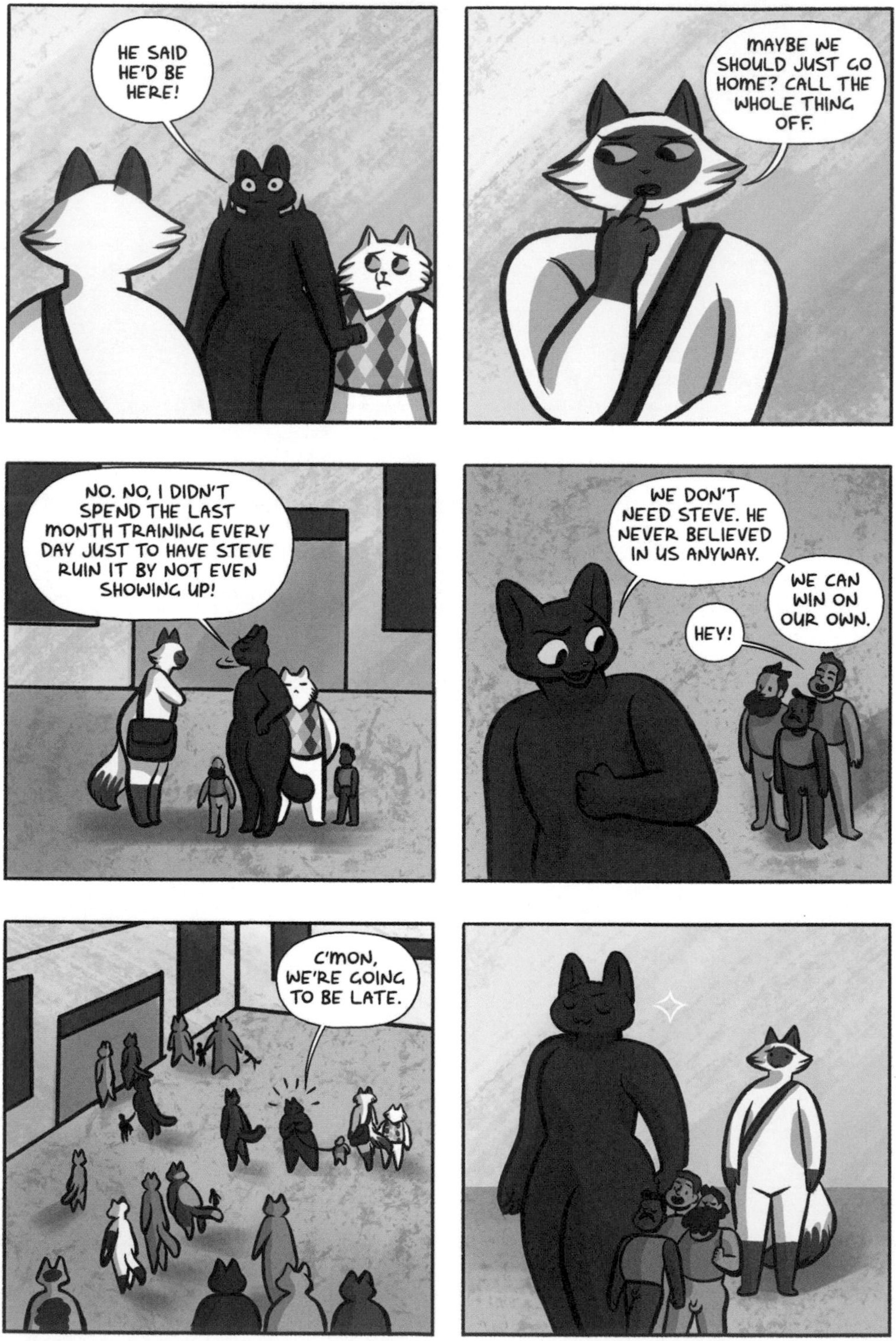
HE SAID HE'D BE HERE!
MAYBE WE SHOULD JUST GO HOME? CALL THE WHOLE THING OFF.
NO. NO, I DIDN'T SPEND THE LAST MONTH TRAINING EVERY DAY JUST TO HAVE STEVE RUIN IT BY NOT EVEN SHOWING UP!
WE DON'T NEED STEVE. HE NEVER BELIEVED IN US ANYWAY.
WE CAN WIN ON OUR OWN.
HEY!
C'MON, WE'RE GOING TO BE LATE.

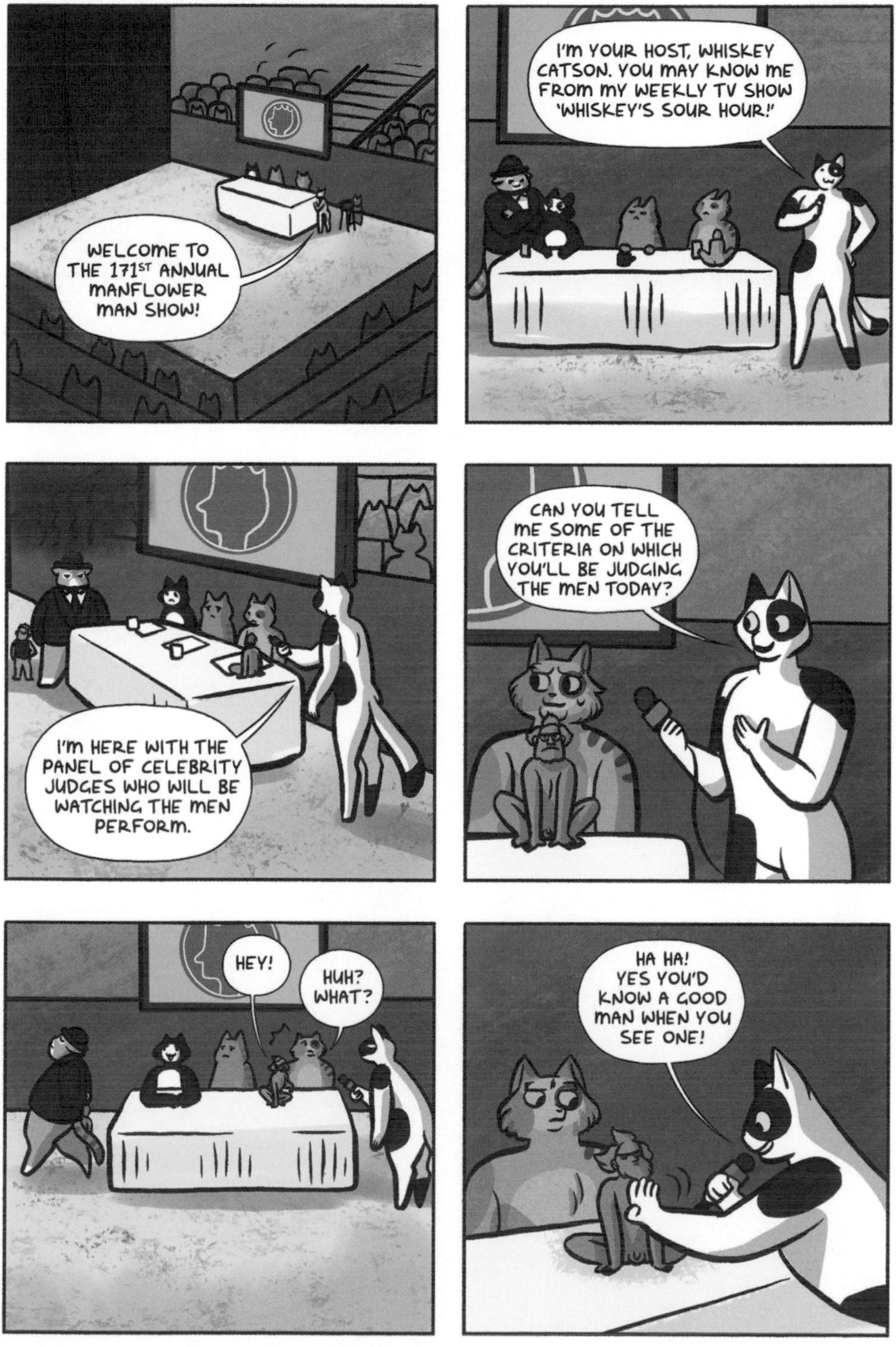
WELCOME TO THE 171ST ANNUAL MANFLOWER MAN SHOW!
I'M YOUR HOST, WHISKEY CATSON. YOU MAY KNOW ME FROM MY WEEKLY TV SHOW 'WHISKEY'S SOUR HOUR!'
I'M HERE WITH THE PANEL OF CELEBRITY JUDGES WHO WILL BE WATCHING THE MEN PERFORM.
CAN YOU TELL ME SOME OF THE CRITERIA ON WHICH YOU'LL BE JUDGING THE MEN TODAY?
HEY!
HUH? WHAT?
HA HA! YES YOU'D KNOW A GOOD MAN WHEN YOU SEE ONE!

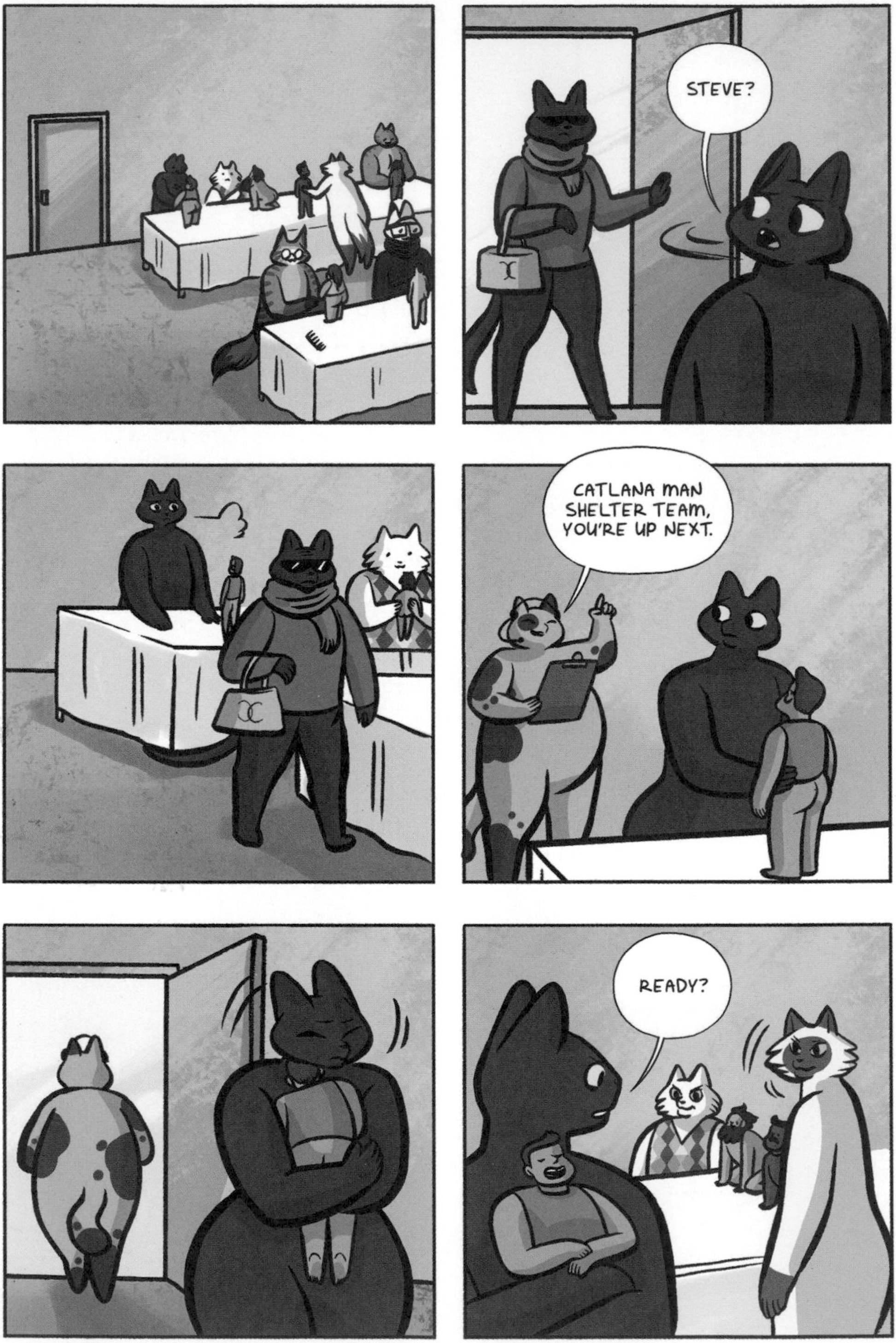

STEVE?
CATLANA MAN SHELTER TEAM, YOU'RE UP NEXT.
READY?

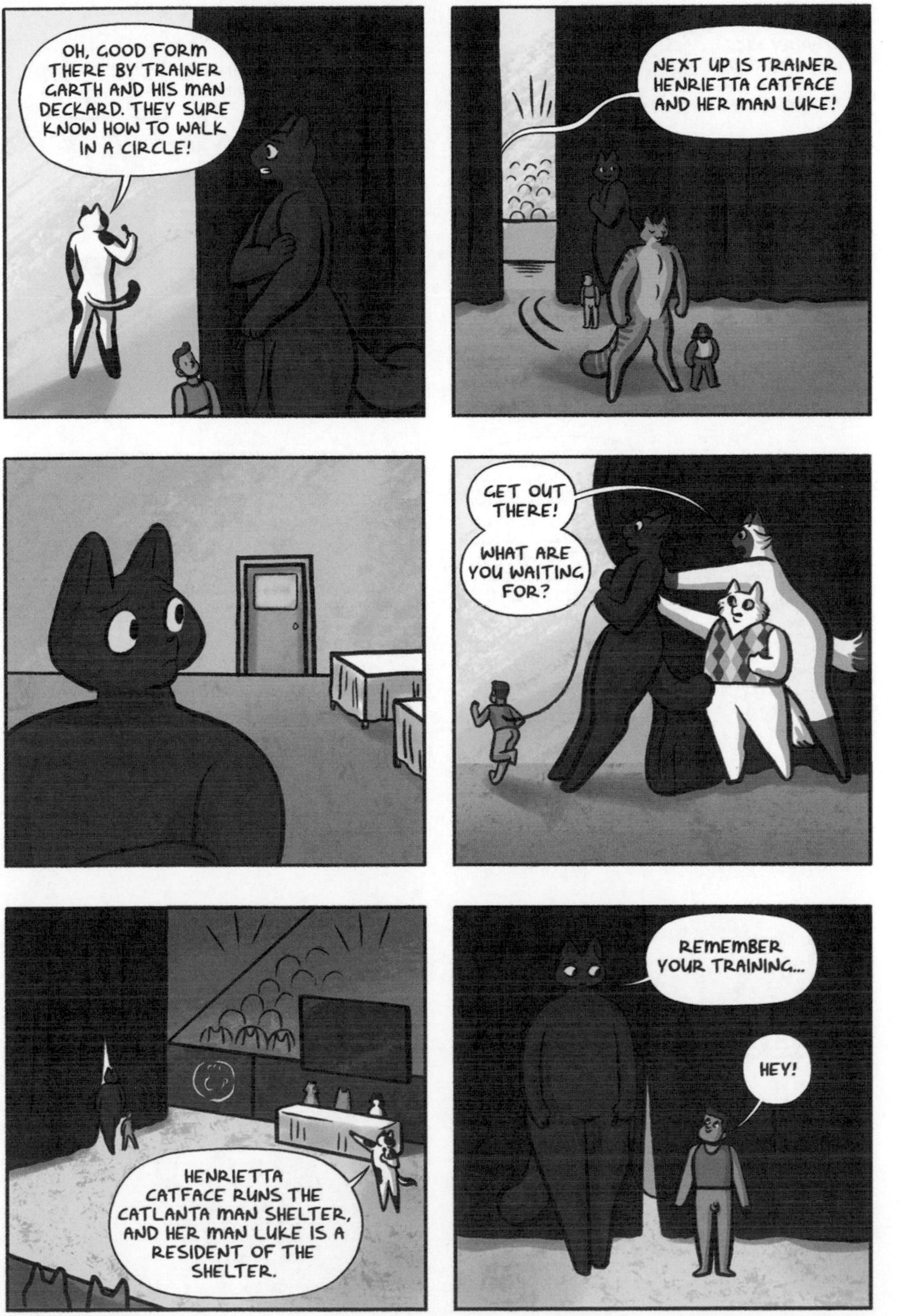
OH, GOOD FORM THERE BY TRAINER GARTH AND HIS MAN DECKARD. THEY SURE KNOW HOW TO WALK IN A CIRCLE!
NEXT UP IS TRAINER HENRIETTA CATFACE AND HER MAN LUKE!
GET OUT THERE!
WHAT ARE YOU WAITING FOR?
HENRIETTA CATFACE RUNS THE CATLANTA MAN SHELTER, AND HER MAN LUKE IS A RESIDENT OF THE SHELTER.
REMEMBER YOUR TRAINING...
HEY!

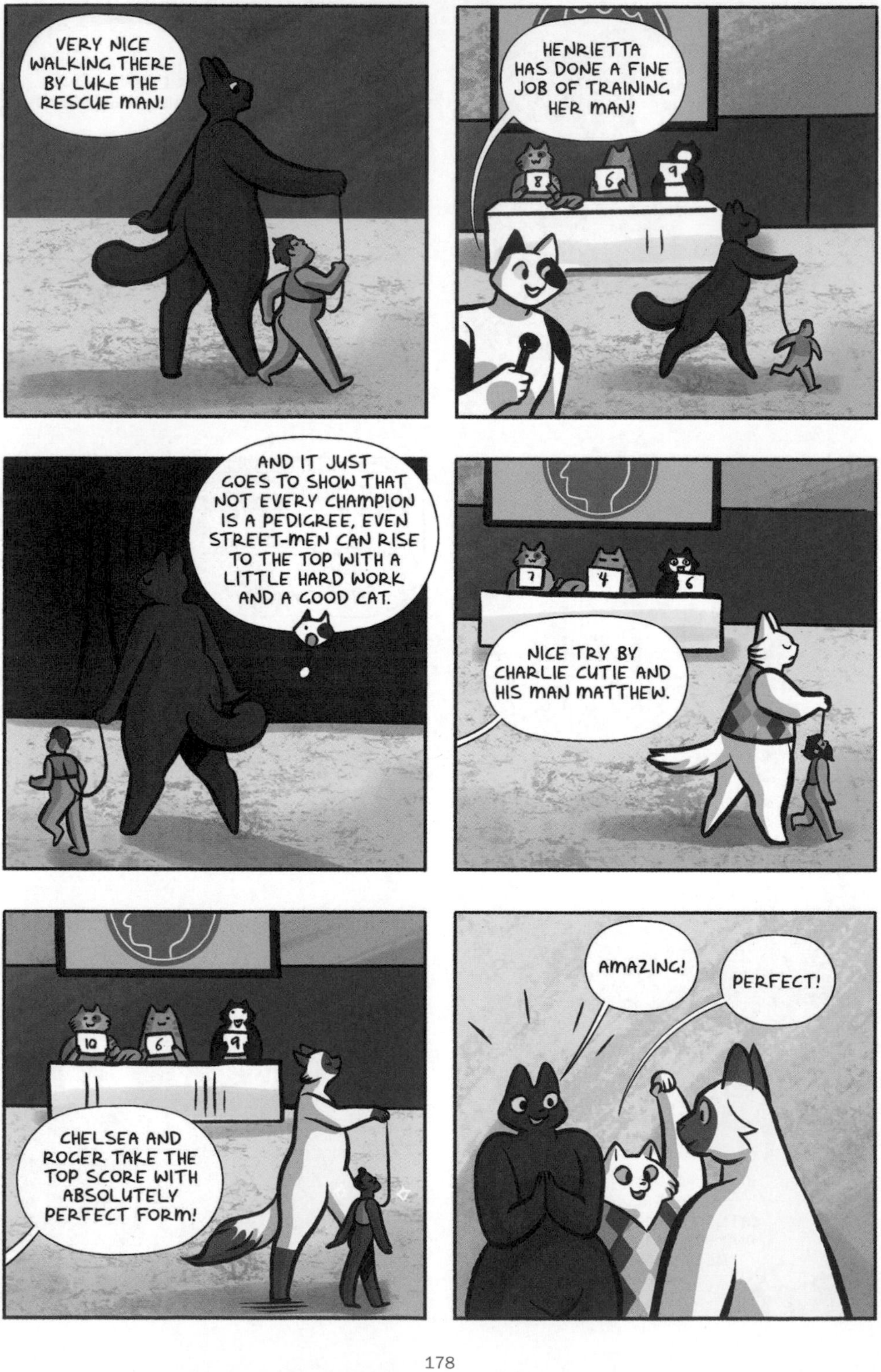
VERY NICE WALKING THERE BY LUKE THE RESCUE MAN!
HENRIETTA HAS DONE A FINE JOB OF TRAINING HER MAN!
8
6
9
AND IT JUST GOES TO SHOW THAT NOT EVERY CHAMPION IS A PEDIGREE, EVEN STREET-MEN CAN RISE TO THE TOP WITH A LITTLE HARD WORK AND A GOOD CAT.
7
4
6
NICE TRY BY CHARLIE CUTIE AND HIS MAN MATTHEW.
10
6
9
CHELSEA AND ROGER TAKE THE TOP SCORE WITH ABSOLUTELY PERFECT FORM!
AMAZING!
PERFECT!

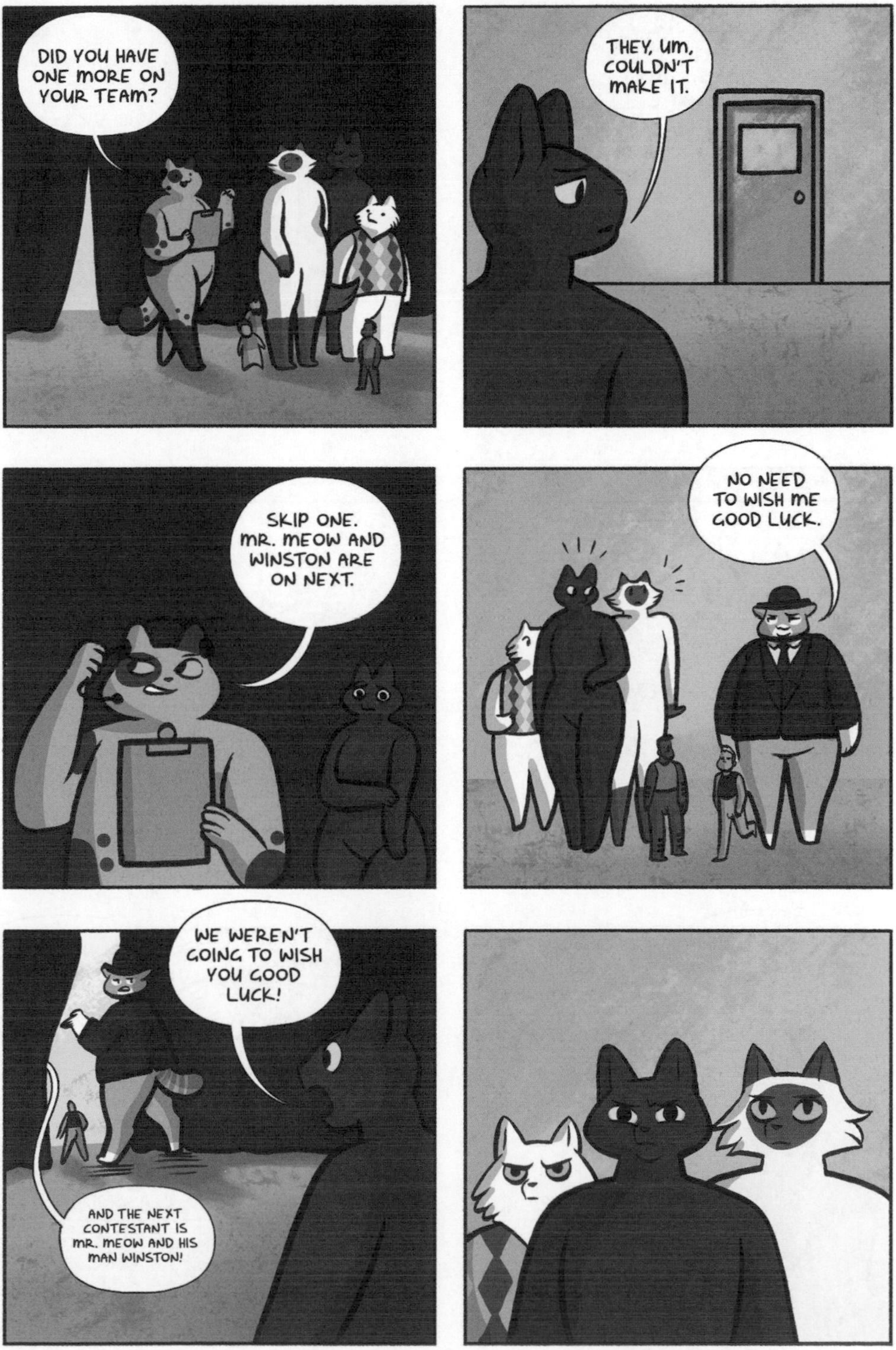
DID YOU HAVE ONE MORE ON YOUR TEAM?
THEY, UM, COULDN'T MAKE IT.
SKIP ONE. MR. MEOW AND WINSTON ARE ON NEXT.
NO NEED TO WISH ME GOOD LUCK.
WE WEREN'T GOING TO WISH YOU GOOD LUCK!
AND THE NEXT CONTESTANT IS MR. MEOW AND HIS MAN WINSTON!

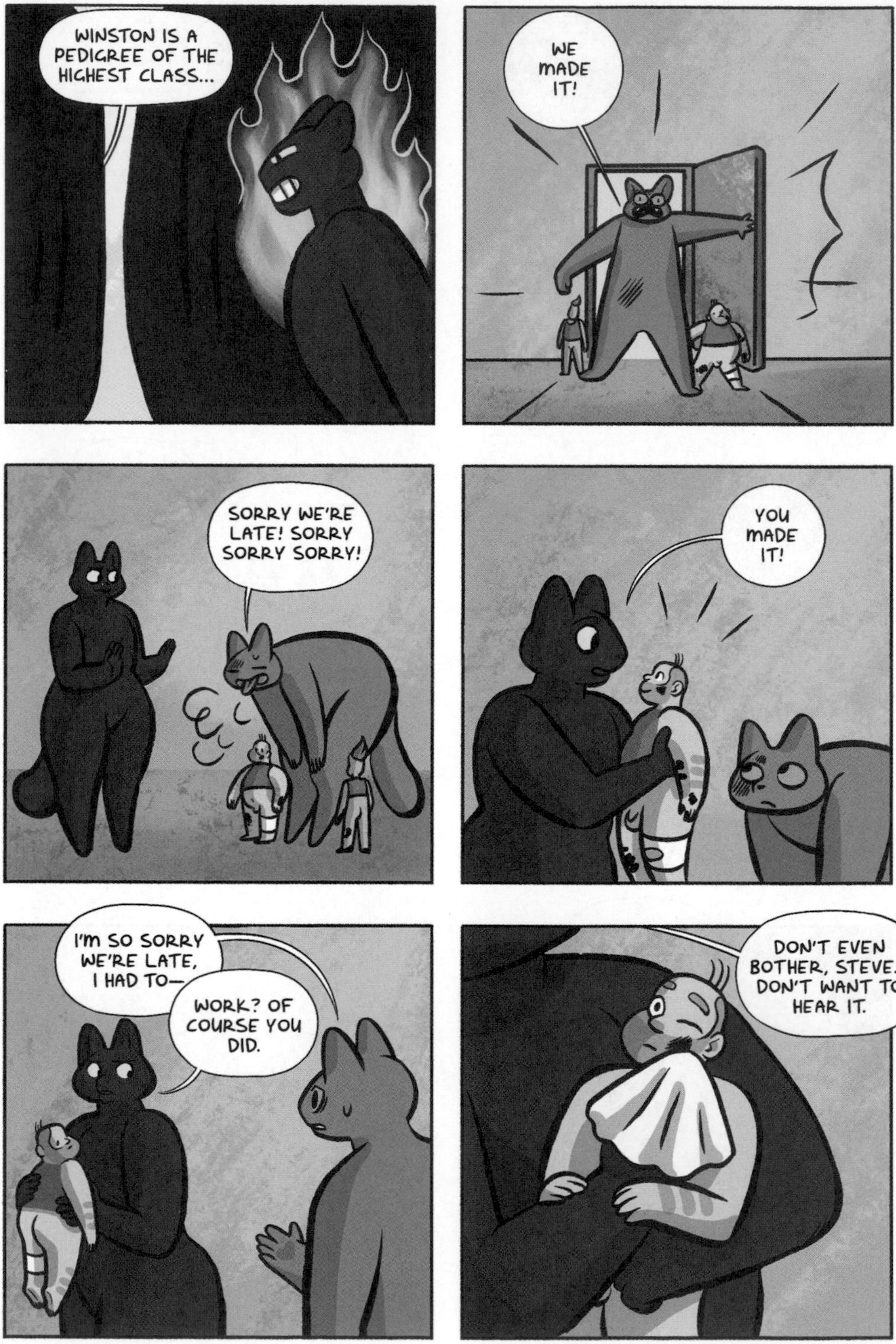
WINSTON IS A PEDIGREE OF THE HIGHEST CLASS...
WE MADE IT!
SORRY WE'RE LATE! SORRY SORRY SORRY!
YOU MADE IT!
I'M SO SORRY WE'RE LATE, I HAD TO—
WORK? OF COURSE YOU DID.
DON'T EVEN BOTHER, STEVE. I DON'T WANT TO HEAR IT.

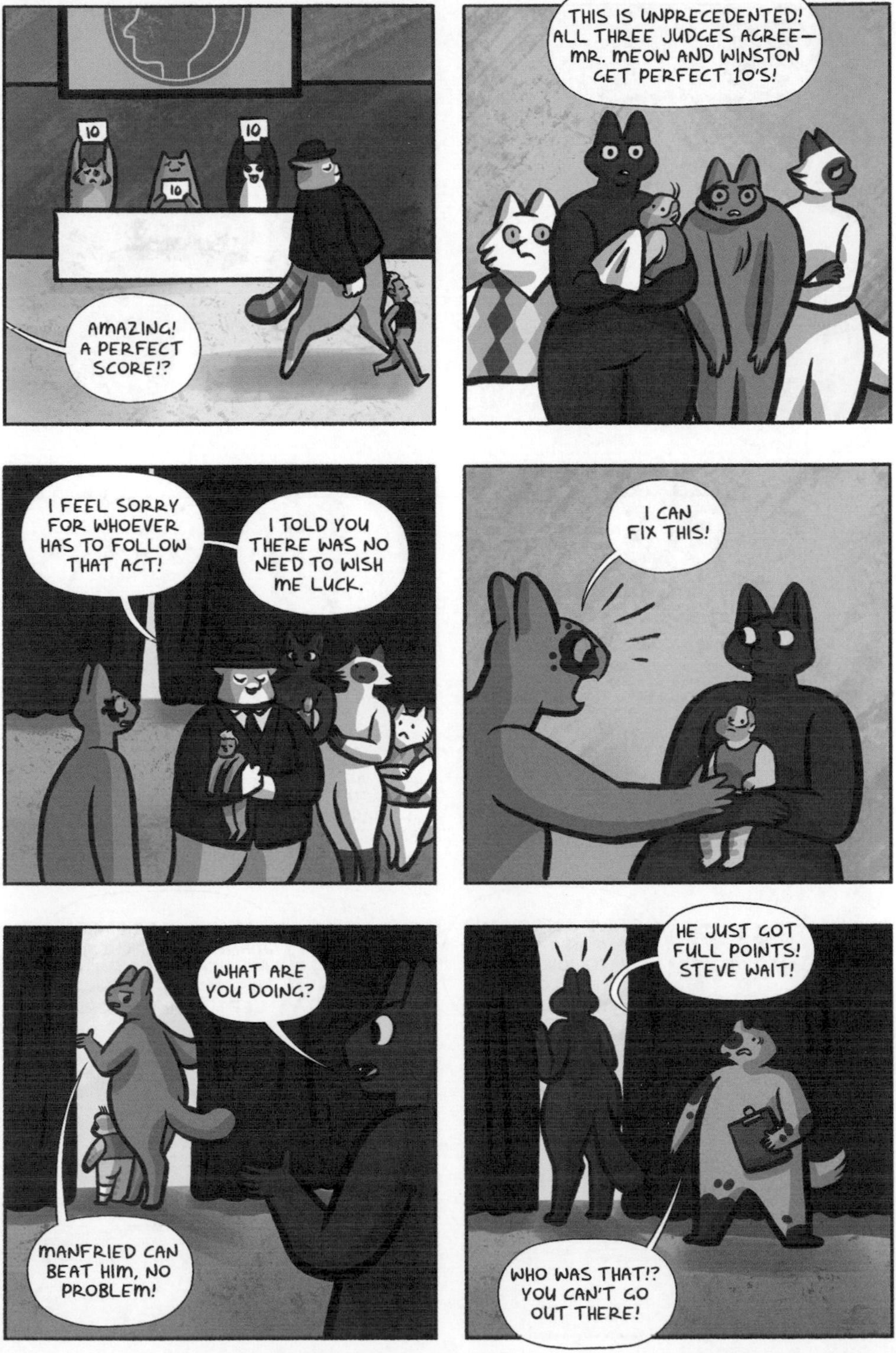
10
10
10
AMAZING! A PERFECT SCORE!?
THIS IS UNPRECEDENTED! ALL THREE JUDGES AGREE— MR. MEOW AND WINSTON GET PERFECT 10'S!
I FEEL SORRY FOR WHOEVER HAS TO FOLLOW THAT ACT!
I TOLD YOU THERE WAS NO NEED TO WISH ME LUCK.
I CAN FIX THIS!
WHAT ARE YOU DOING?
MANFRIED CAN BEAT HIM, NO PROBLEM!
HE JUST GOT FULL POINTS! STEVE WAIT!
WHO WAS THAT!? YOU CAN'T GO OUT THERE!

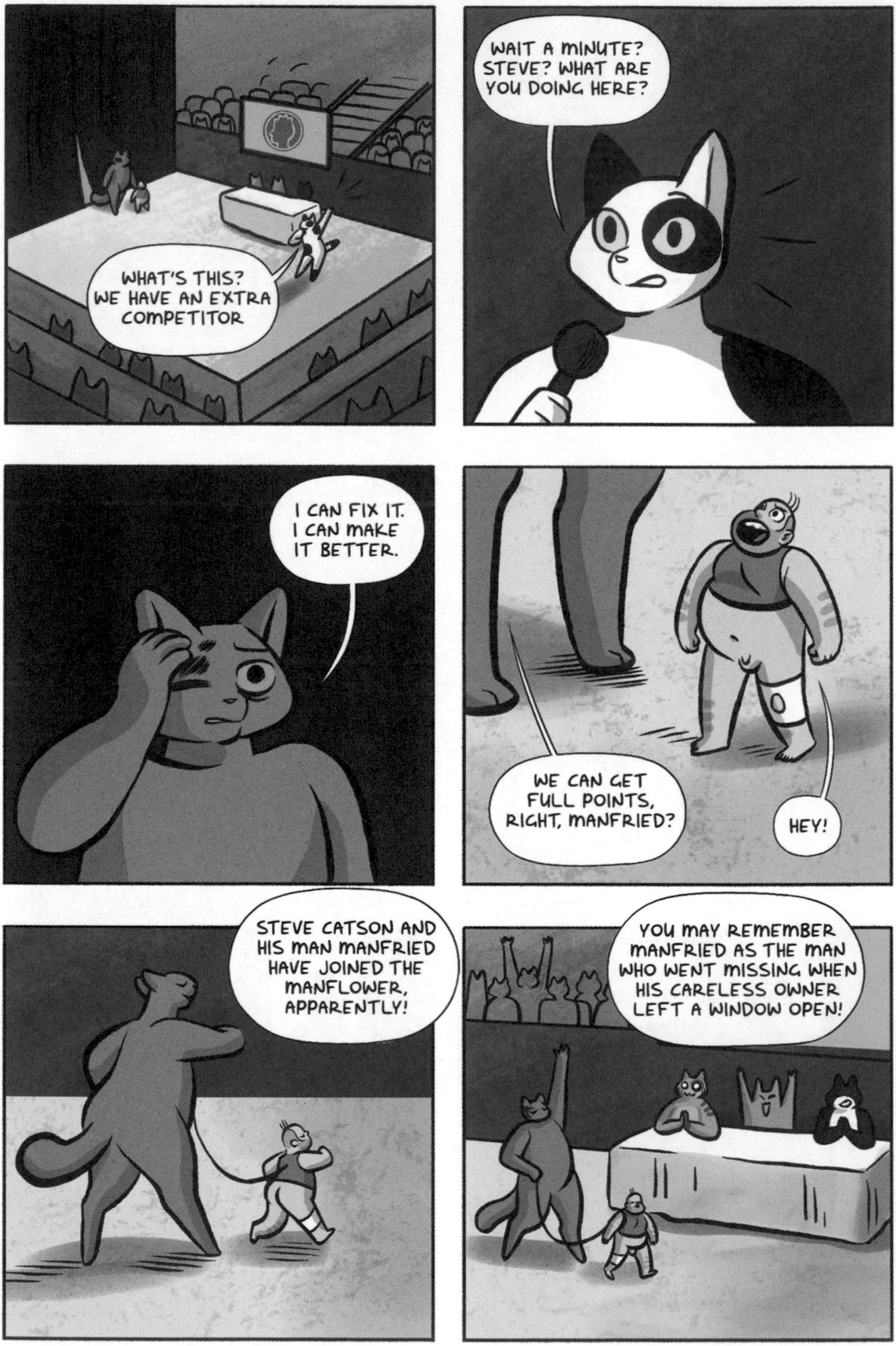
WHAT'S THIS? WE HAVE AN EXTRA COMPETITOR
WAIT A MINUTE? STEVE? WHAT ARE YOU DOING HERE?
I CAN FIX IT. I CAN MAKE IT BETTER.
WE CAN GET FULL POINTS, RIGHT, MANFRIED?
HEY!
STEVE CATSON AND HIS MAN MANFRIED HAVE JOINED THE MANFLOWER, APPARENTLY!
YOU MAY REMEMBER MANFRIED AS THE MAN WHO WENT MISSING WHEN HIS CARELESS OWNER LEFT A WINDOW OPEN!

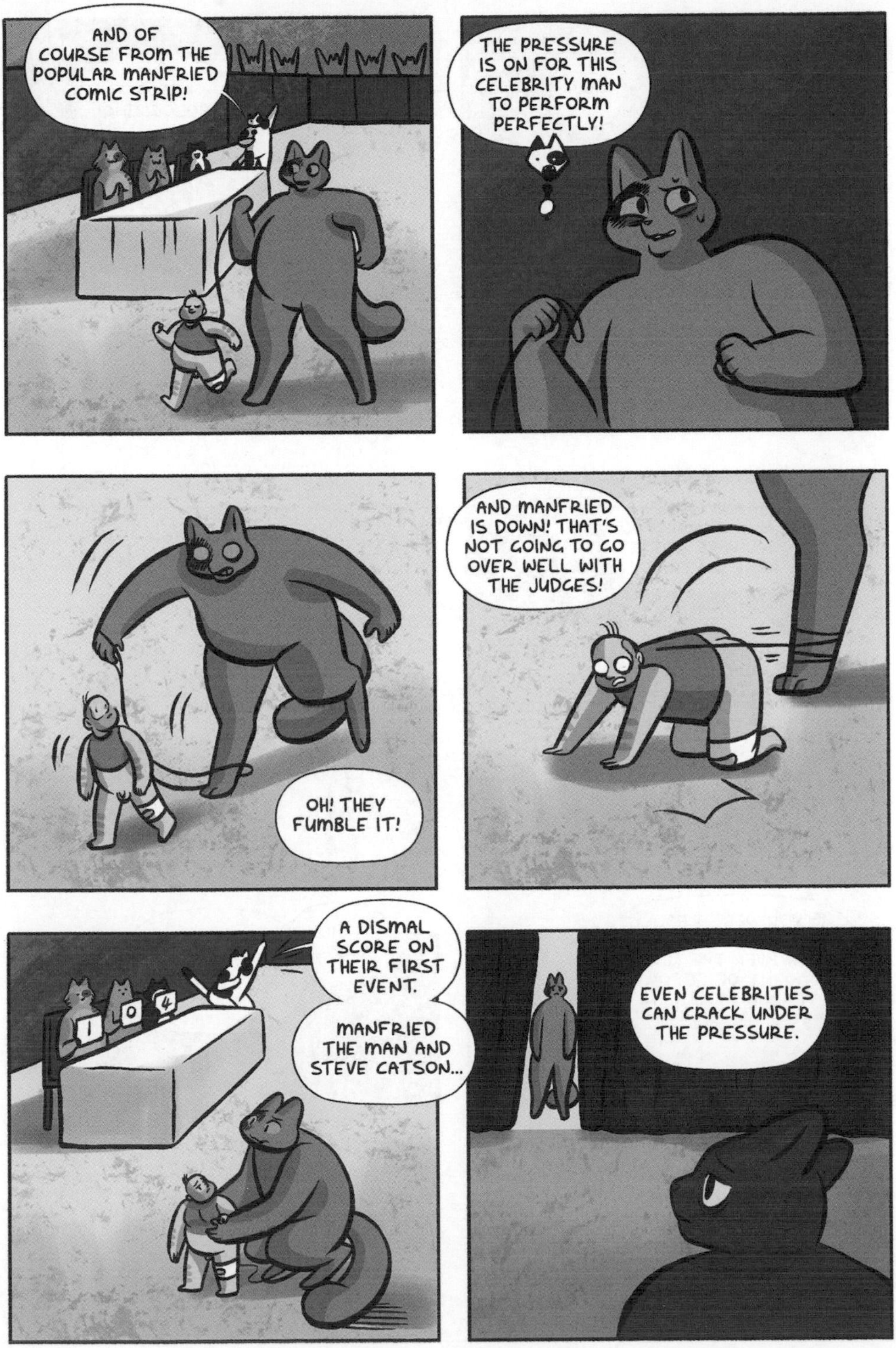
AND OF COURSE FROM THE POPULAR MANFRIED COMIC STRIP!
THE PRESSURE IS ON FOR THIS CELEBRITY MAN TO PERFORM PERFECTLY!
OH! THEY FUMBLE IT!
AND MANFRIED IS DOWN! THAT'S NOT GOING TO GO OVER WELL WITH THE JUDGES!
1 0 4
A DISMAL SCORE ON THEIR FIRST EVENT.
MANFRIED THE MAN AND STEVE CATSON...
EVEN CELEBRITIES CAN CRACK UNDER THE PRESSURE.

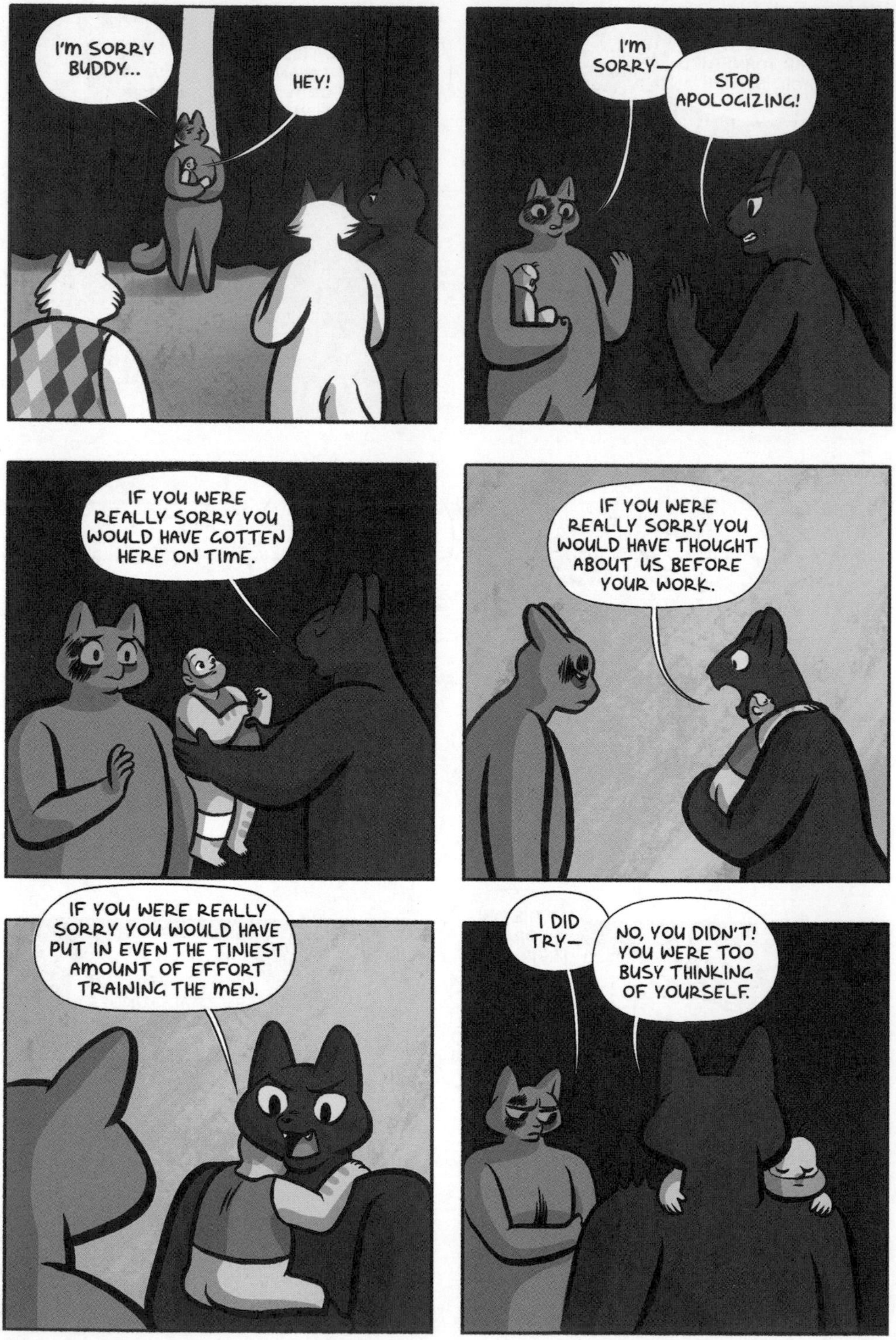

I'M SORRY BUDDY...
HEY!
I'M SORRY—
STOP APOLOGIZING!
IF YOU WERE REALLY SORRY YOU WOULD HAVE GOTTEN HERE ON TIME.
IF YOU WERE REALLY SORRY YOU WOULD HAVE THOUGHT ABOUT US BEFORE YOUR WORK.
IF YOU WERE REALLY SORRY YOU WOULD HAVE PUT IN EVEN THE TINIEST AMOUNT OF EFFORT TRAINING THE MEN.
I DID TRY—
NO, YOU DIDN'T! YOU WERE TOO BUSY THINKING OF YOURSELF.

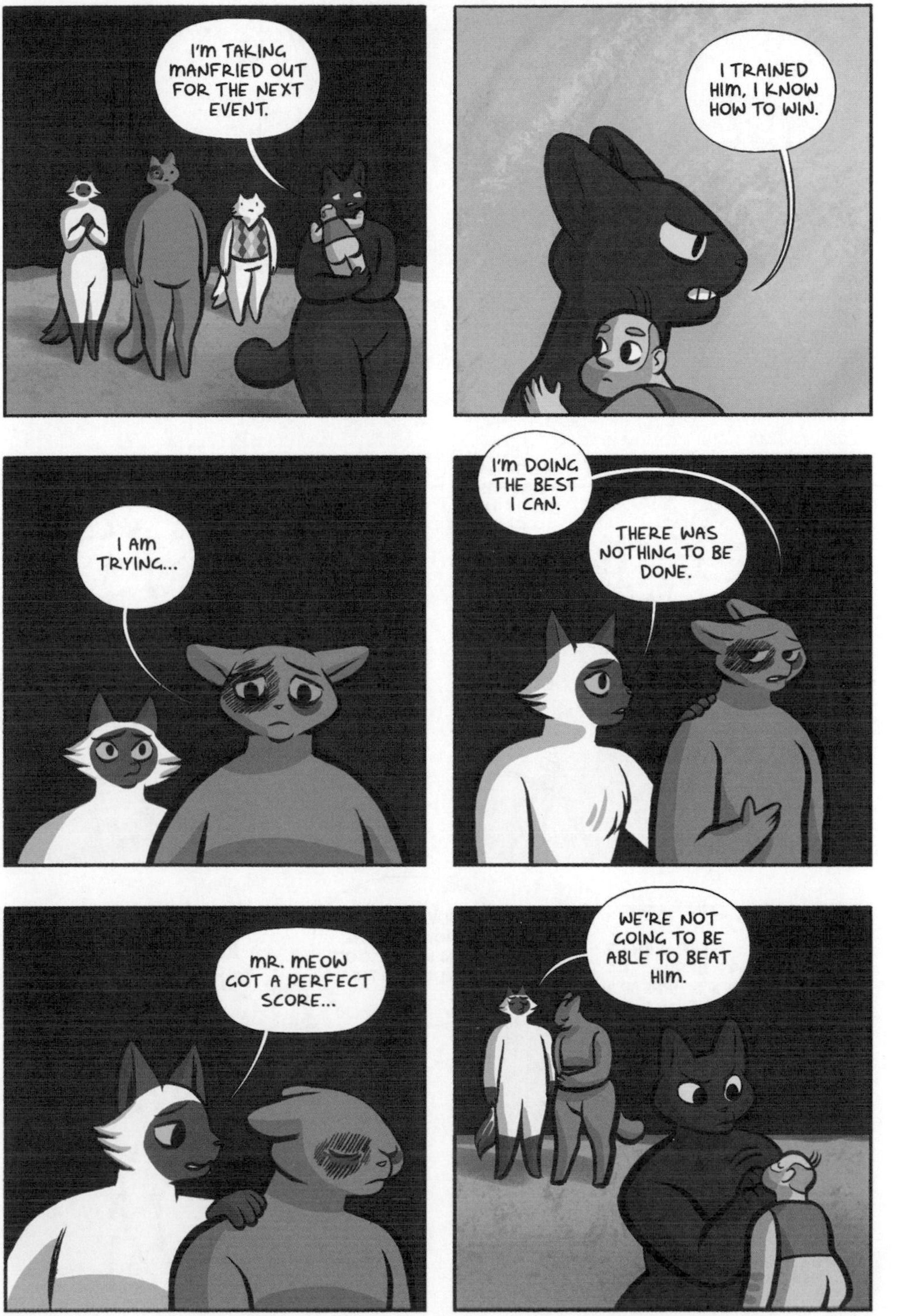
I'M TAKING MANFRIED OUT FOR THE NEXT EVENT.
I TRAINED HIM, I KNOW HOW TO WIN.
I AM TRYING...
I'M DOING THE BEST I CAN.
THERE WAS NOTHING TO BE DONE.
MR. MEOW GOT A PERFECT SCORE...
WE'RE NOT GOING TO BE ABLE TO BEAT HIM.

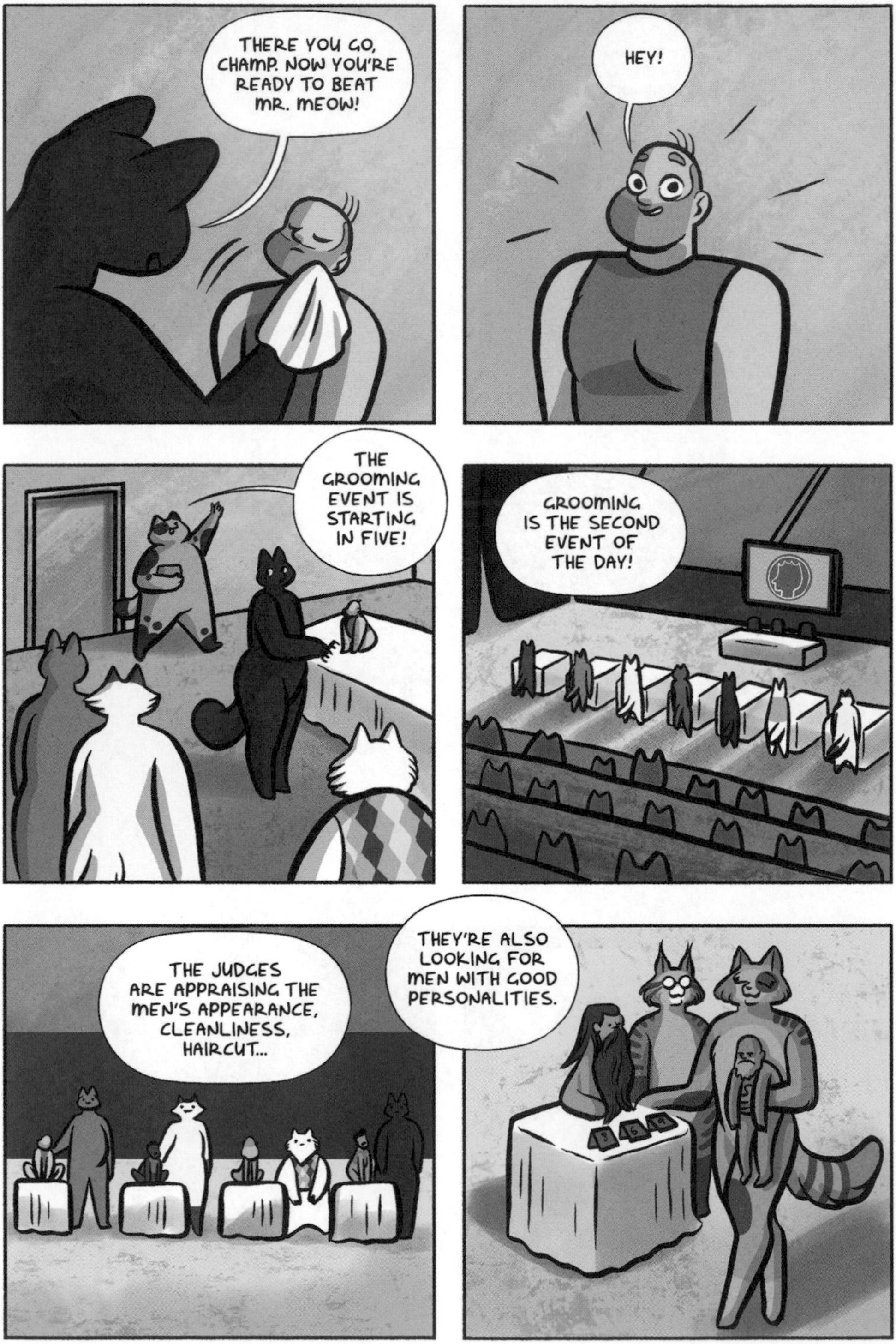
THERE YOU GO, CHAMP. NOW YOU'RE READY TO BEAT MR. MEOW!
HEY!
THE GROOMING EVENT IS STARTING IN FIVE!
GROOMING IS THE SECOND EVENT OF THE DAY!
THE JUDGES ARE APPRAISING THE MEN'S APPEARANCE, CLEANLINESS, HAIRCUT...
THEY'RE ALSO LOOKING FOR MEN WITH GOOD PERSONALITIES.

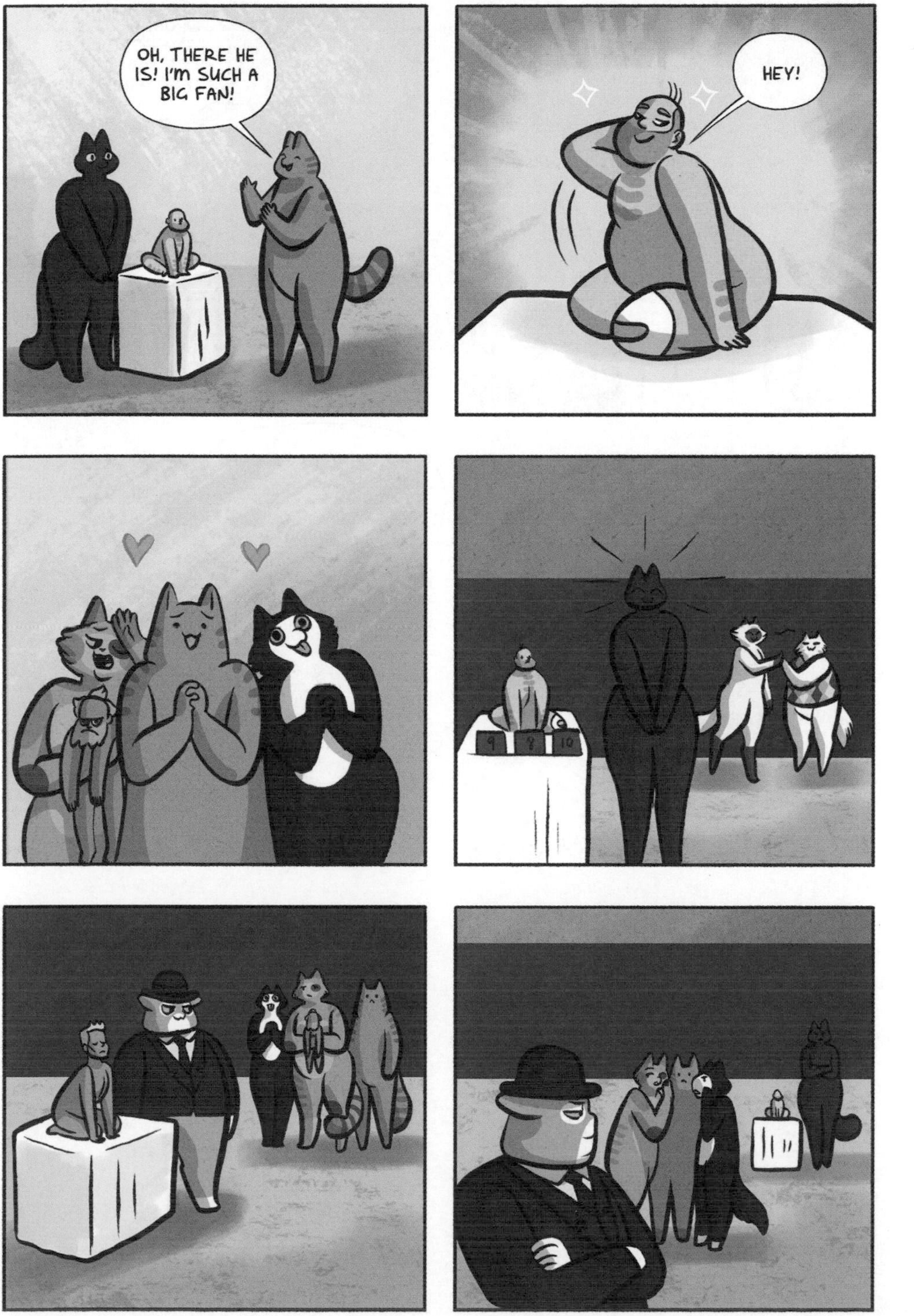
OH, THERE HE IS! I'M SUCH A BIG FAN!
HEY!
9
8
10

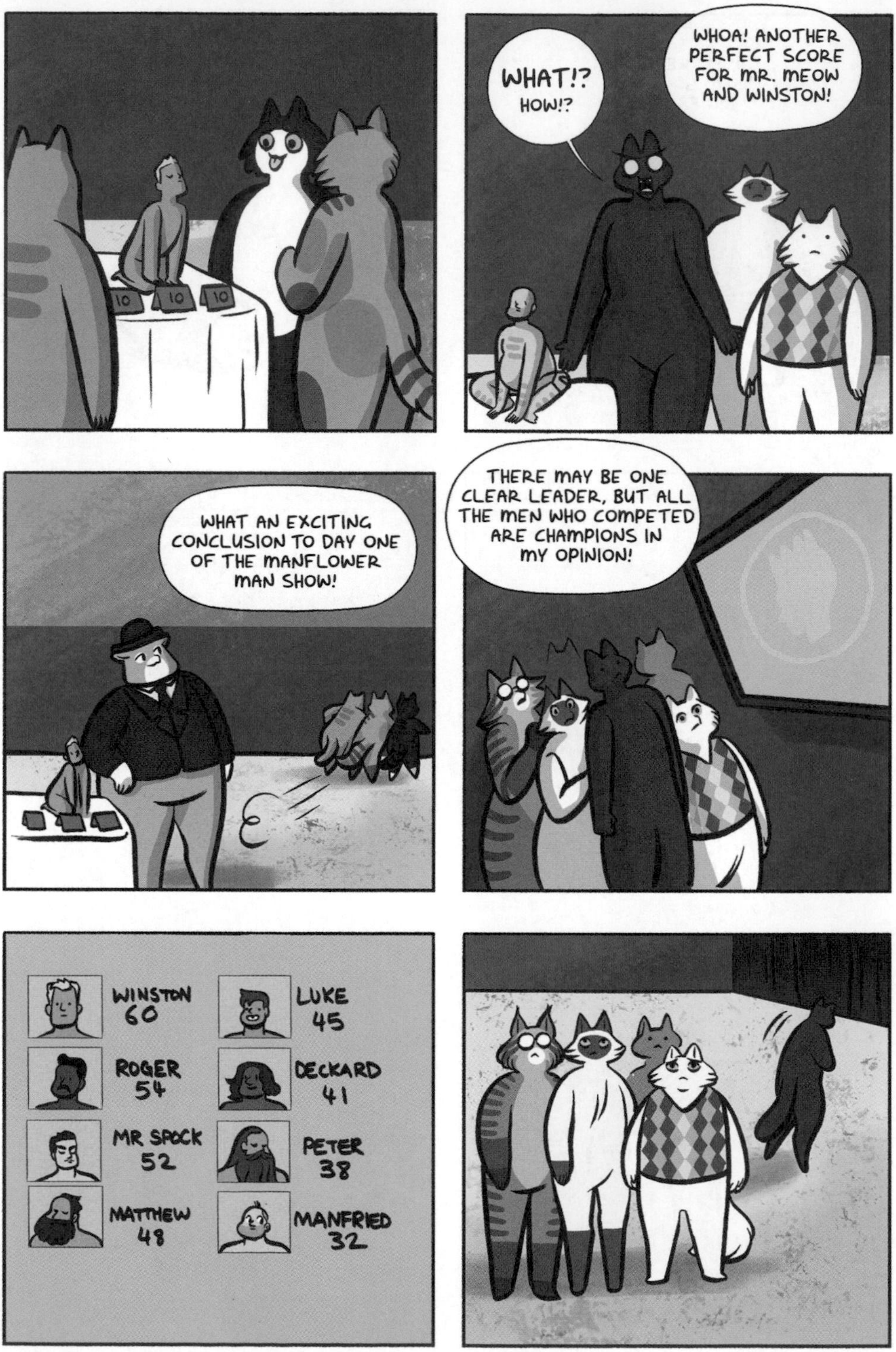
WHAT!? HOW!?
WHOA! ANOTHER PERFECT SCORE FOR MR. MEOW AND WINSTON!
WHAT AN EXCITING CONCLUSION TO DAY ONE OF THE MANFLOWER MAN SHOW!
THERE MAY BE ONE CLEAR LEADER, BUT ALL THE MEN WHO COMPETED ARE CHAMPIONS IN MY OPINION!
WINSTON 60
LUKE 45
ROGER 54
DECKARD 41
MR SPOCK 52
PETER 38
MATTHEW 48
MANFRIED 32

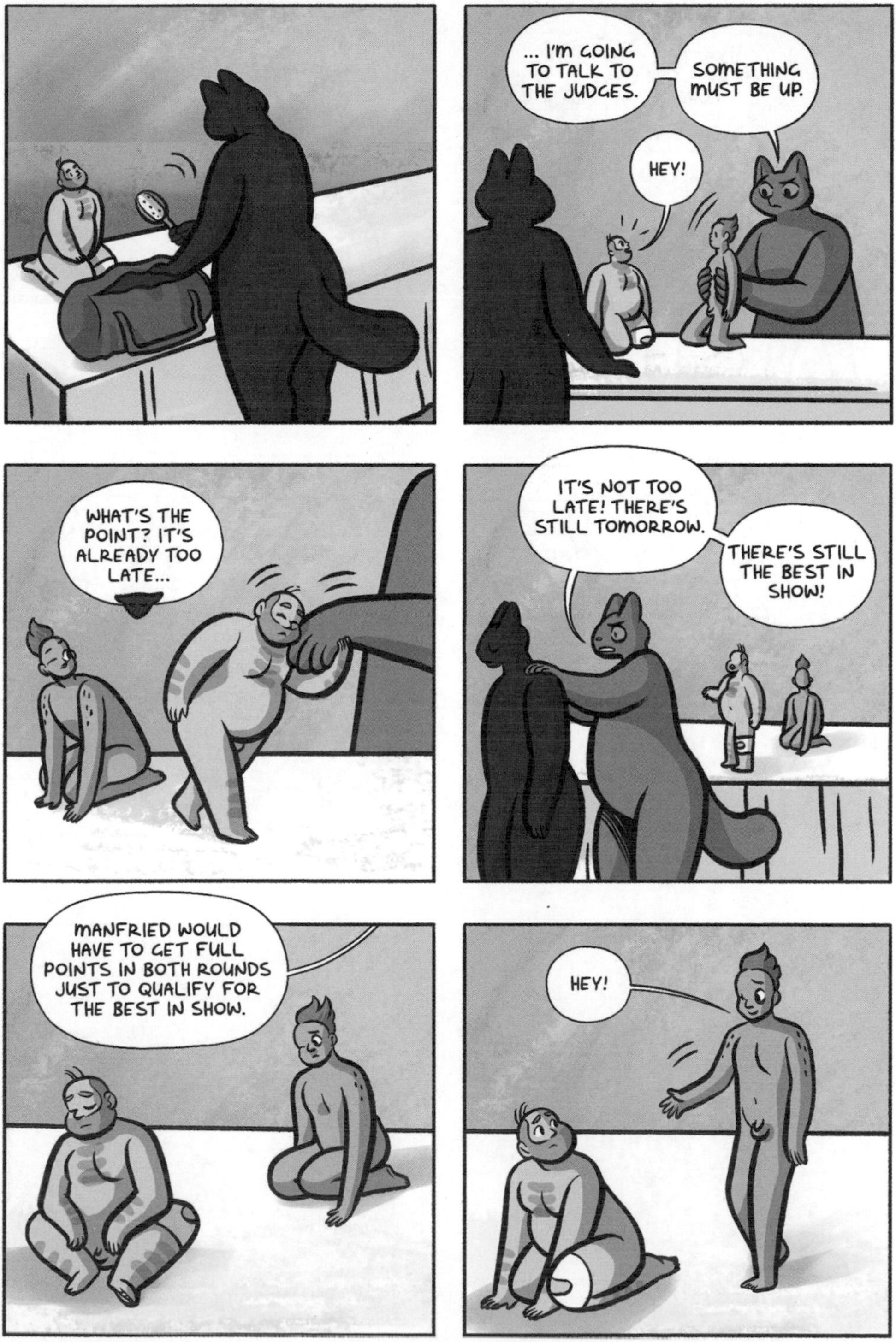
... I'M GOING TO TALK TO THE JUDGES.
SOMETHING MUST BE UP.
HEY!
WHAT'S THE POINT? IT'S ALREADY TOO LATE...
IT'S NOT TOO LATE! THERE'S STILL TOMORROW.
THERE'S STILL THE BEST IN SHOW!
MANFRIED WOULD HAVE TO GET FULL POINTS IN BOTH ROUNDS JUST TO QUALIFY FOR THE BEST IN SHOW.
HEY!

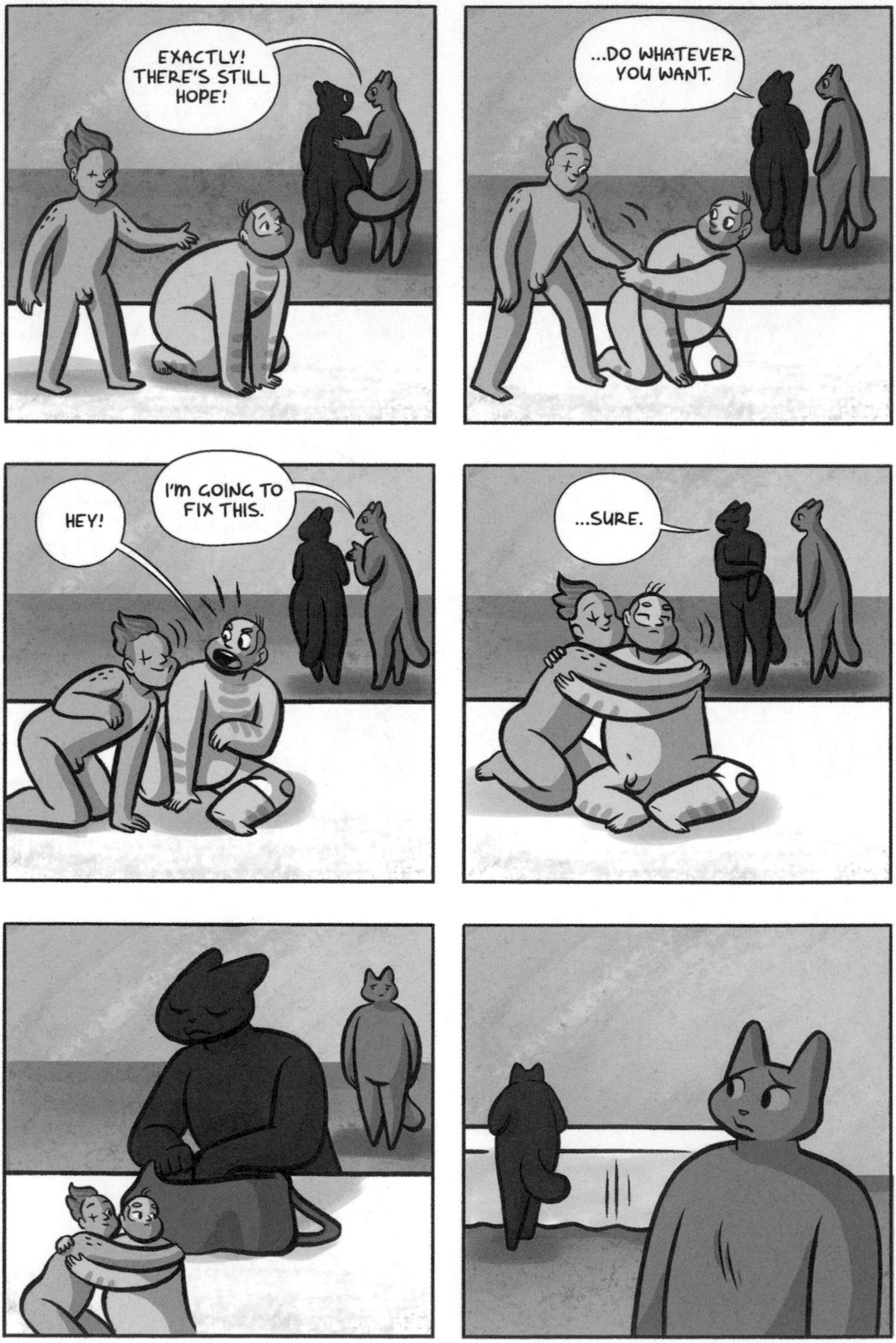
EXACTLY! THERE'S STILL HOPE!
...DO WHATEVER YOU WANT.
HEY!
I'M GOING TO FIX THIS.
...SURE.

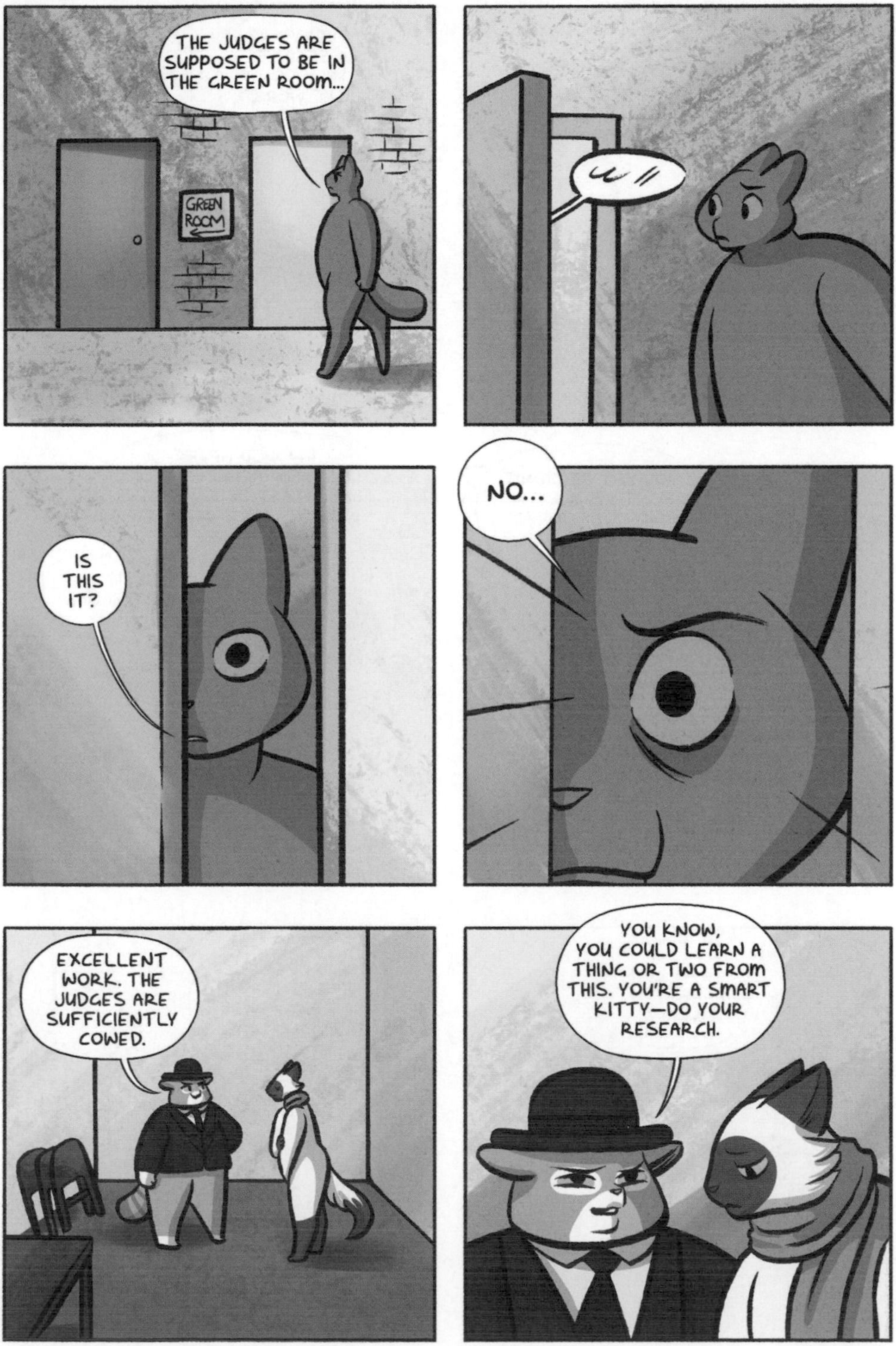
THE JUDGES ARE SUPPOSED TO BE IN THE GREEN ROOM...
GREEN ROOM
IS THIS IT?
NO...
EXCELLENT WORK. THE JUDGES ARE SUFFICIENTLY COWED.
YOU KNOW, YOU COULD LEARN A THING OR TWO FROM THIS. YOU'RE A SMART KITTY—DO YOUR RESEARCH.

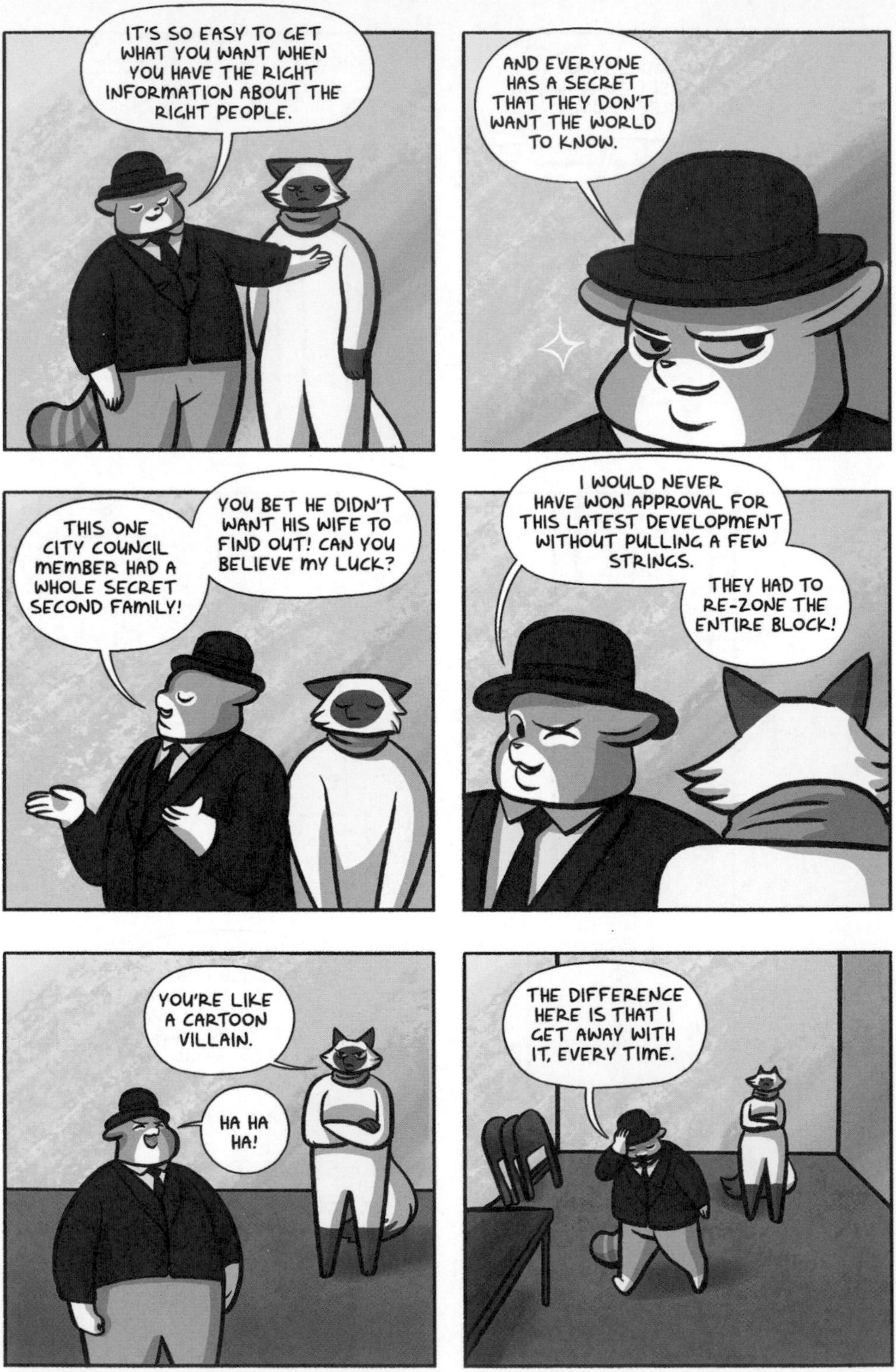
IT'S SO EASY TO GET WHAT YOU WANT WHEN YOU HAVE THE RIGHT INFORMATION ABOUT THE RIGHT PEOPLE.
AND EVERYONE HAS A SECRET THAT THEY DON'T WANT THE WORLD TO KNOW.
THIS ONE CITY COUNCIL MEMBER HAD A WHOLE SECRET SECOND FAMILY!
YOU BET HE DIDN'T WANT HIS WIFE TO FIND OUT! CAN YOU BELIEVE MY LUCK?
I WOULD NEVER HAVE WON APPROVAL FOR THIS LATEST DEVELOPMENT WITHOUT PULLING A FEW STRINGS.
THEY HAD TO RE-ZONE THE ENTIRE BLOCK!
YOU'RE LIKE A CARTOON VILLAIN.
HA HA HA!
THE DIFFERENCE HERE IS THAT I GET AWAY WITH IT, EVERY TIME.

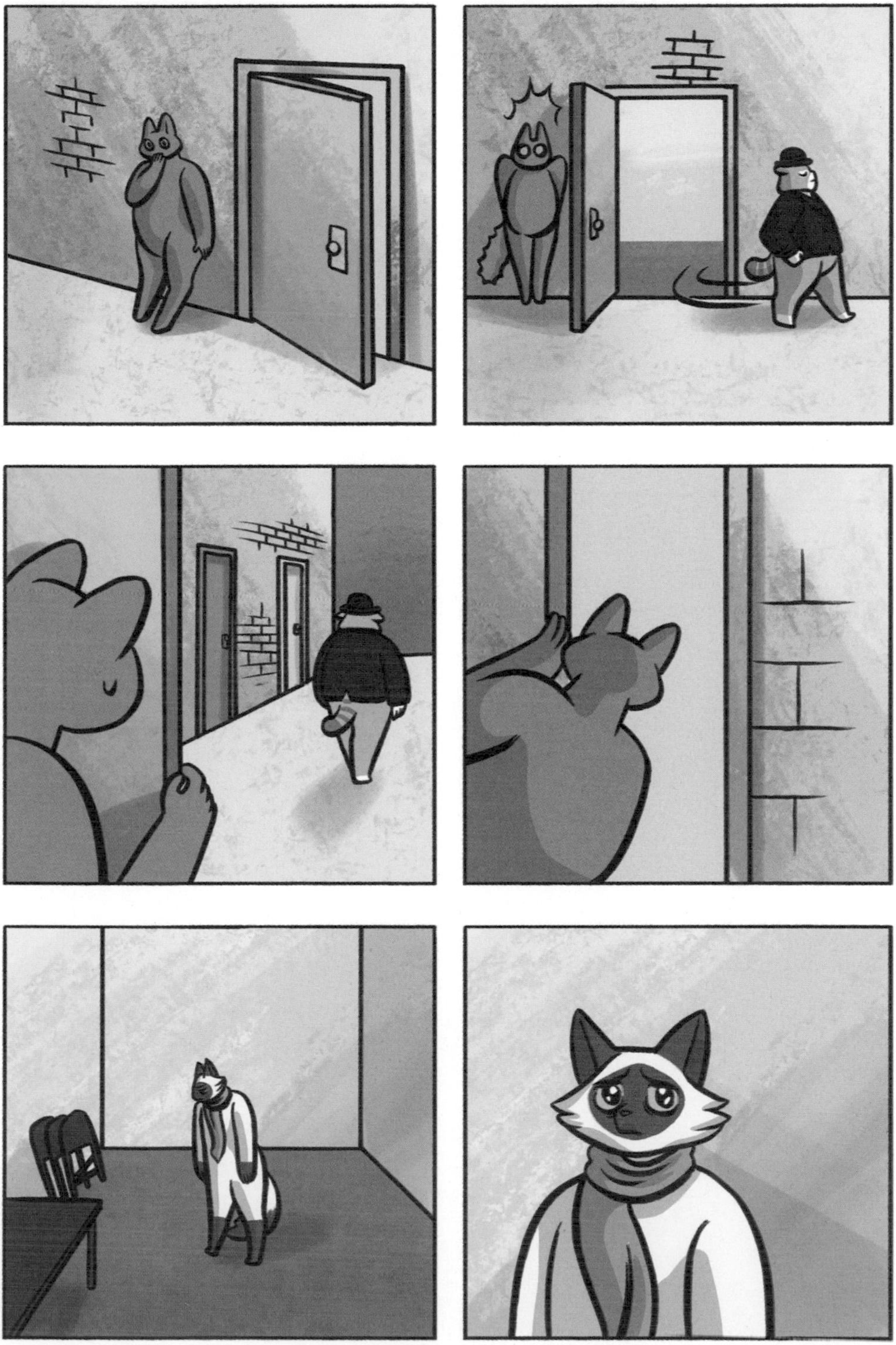

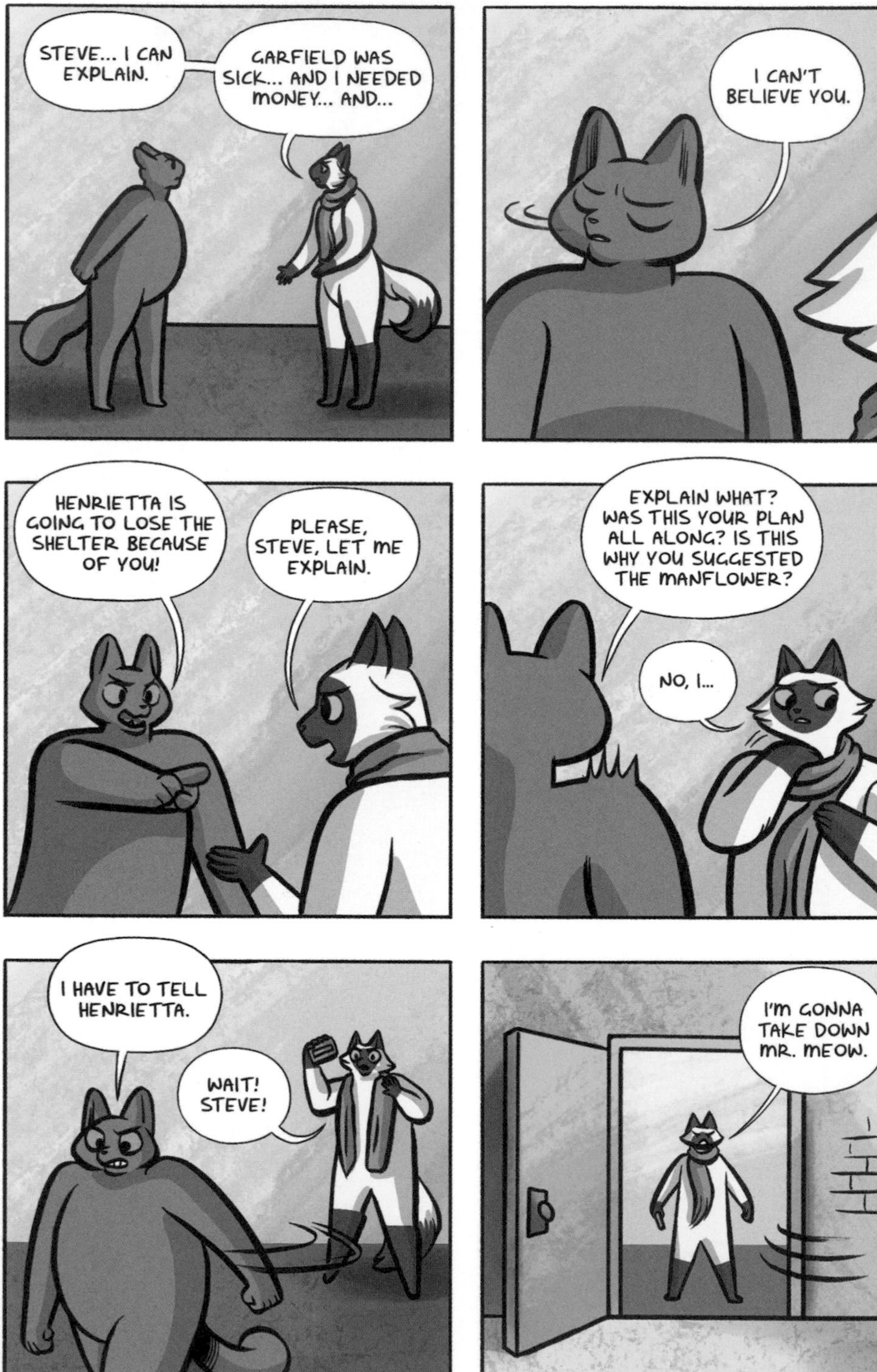

STEVE... I CAN EXPLAIN.
GARFIELD WAS SICK... AND I NEEDED MONEY... AND...
I CAN'T BELIEVE YOU.
HENRIETTA IS GOING TO LOSE THE SHELTER BECAUSE OF YOU!
PLEASE, STEVE, LET ME EXPLAIN.
EXPLAIN WHAT? WAS THIS YOUR PLAN ALL ALONG? IS THIS WHY YOU SUGGESTED THE MANFLOWER?
NO, I...
I HAVE TO TELL HENRIETTA.
WAIT! STEVE!
I'M GONNA TAKE DOWN MR. MEOW.

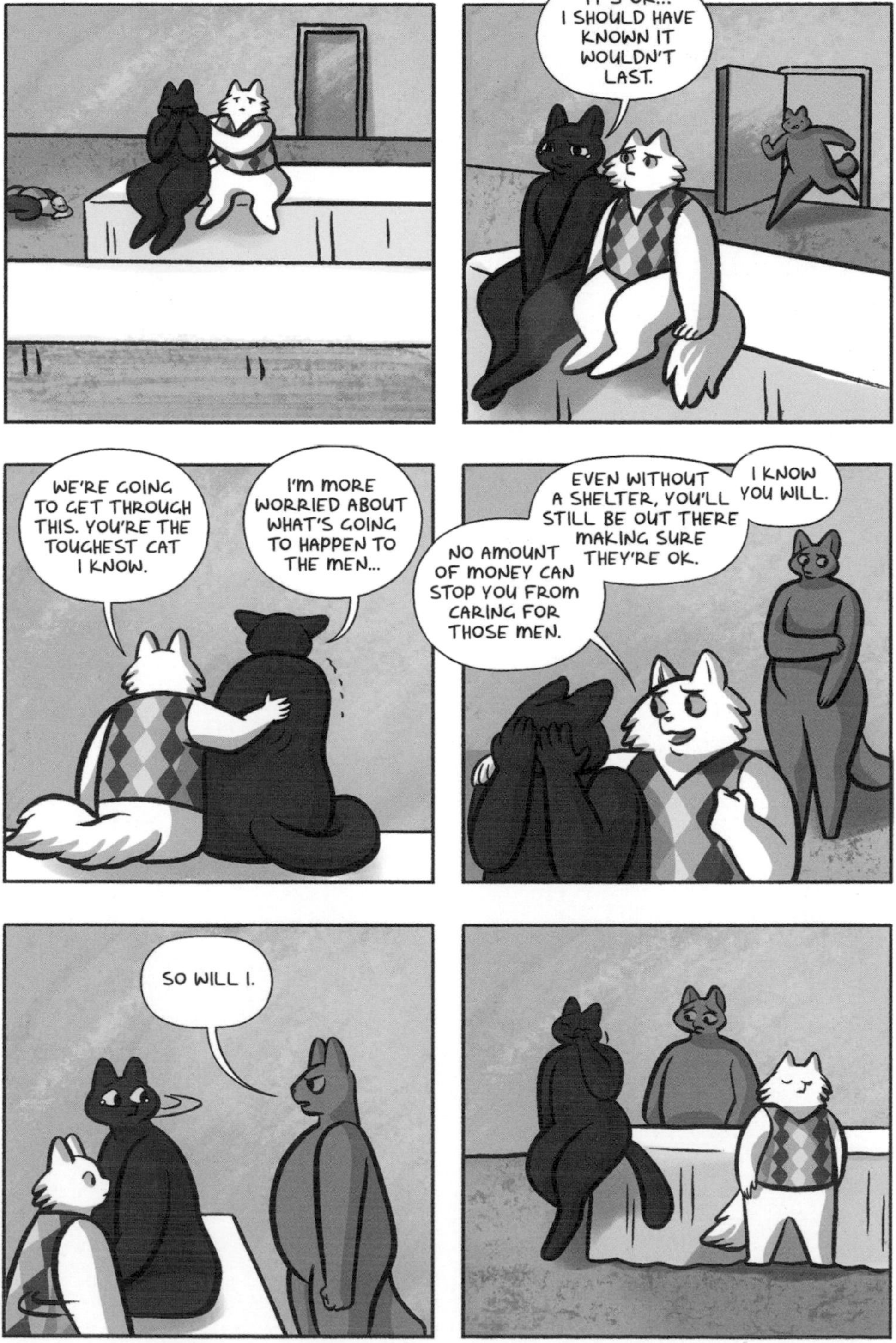
IT'S OK... I SHOULD HAVE KNOWN IT WOULDN'T LAST.
WE'RE GOING TO GET THROUGH THIS. YOU'RE THE TOUGHEST CAT I KNOW.
I'M MORE WORRIED ABOUT WHAT'S GOING TO HAPPEN TO THE MEN...
NO AMOUNT OF MONEY CAN STOP YOU FROM CARING FOR THOSE MEN.
EVEN WITHOUT A SHELTER, YOU'LL STILL BE OUT THERE MAKING SURE THEY'RE OK.
I KNOW YOU WILL.
SO WILL I.

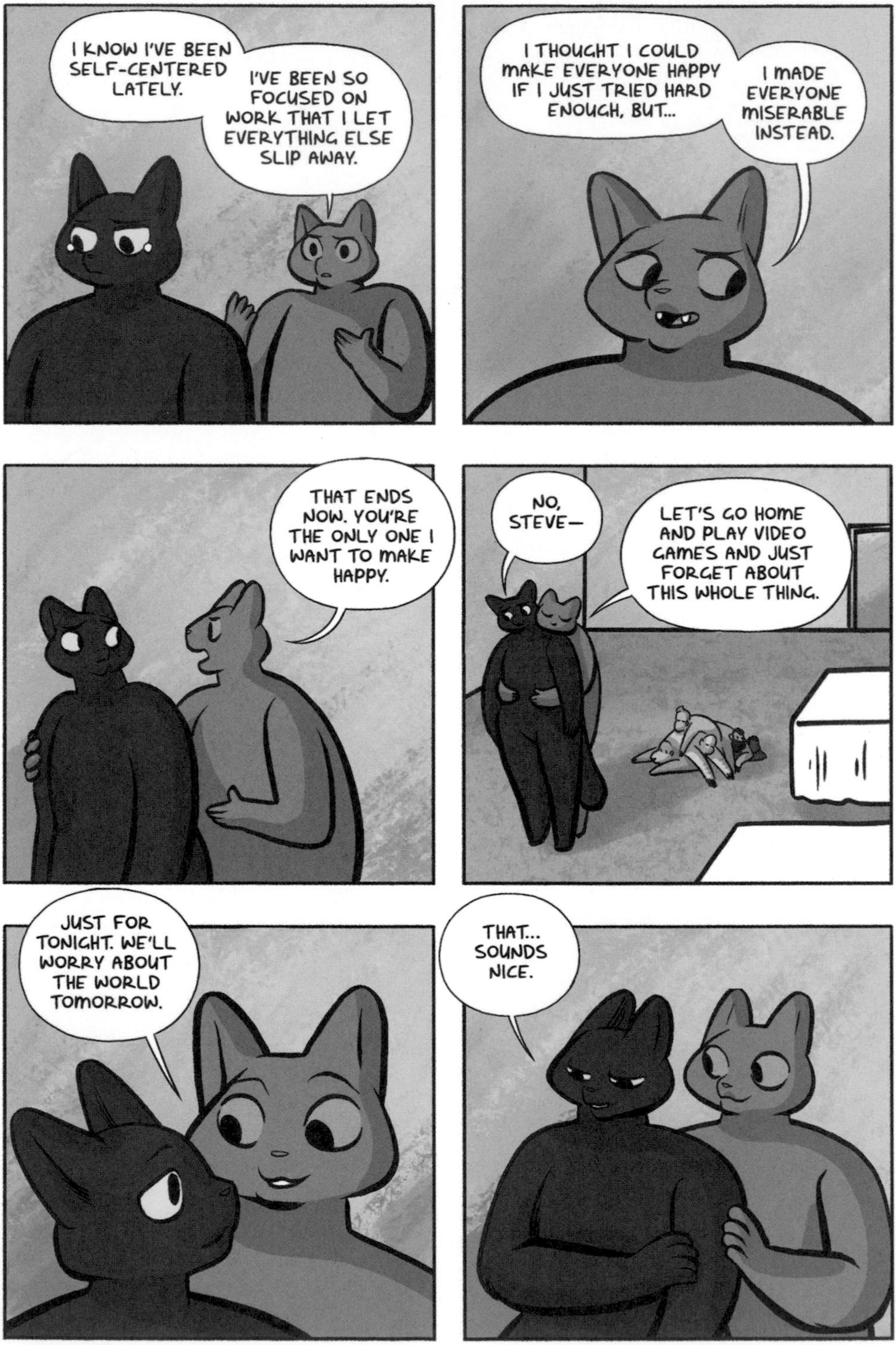
I KNOW I'VE BEEN SELF-CENTERED LATELY.
I'VE BEEN SO FOCUSED ON WORK THAT I LET EVERYTHING ELSE SLIP AWAY.
I THOUGHT I COULD MAKE EVERYONE HAPPY IF I JUST TRIED HARD ENOUGH, BUT...
I MADE EVERYONE MISERABLE INSTEAD.
THAT ENDS NOW. YOU'RE THE ONLY ONE I WANT TO MAKE HAPPY.
NO, STEVE—
LET'S GO HOME AND PLAY VIDEO GAMES AND JUST FORGET ABOUT THIS WHOLE THING.
JUST FOR TONIGHT. WE'LL WORRY ABOUT THE WORLD TOMORROW.
THAT... SOUNDS NICE.

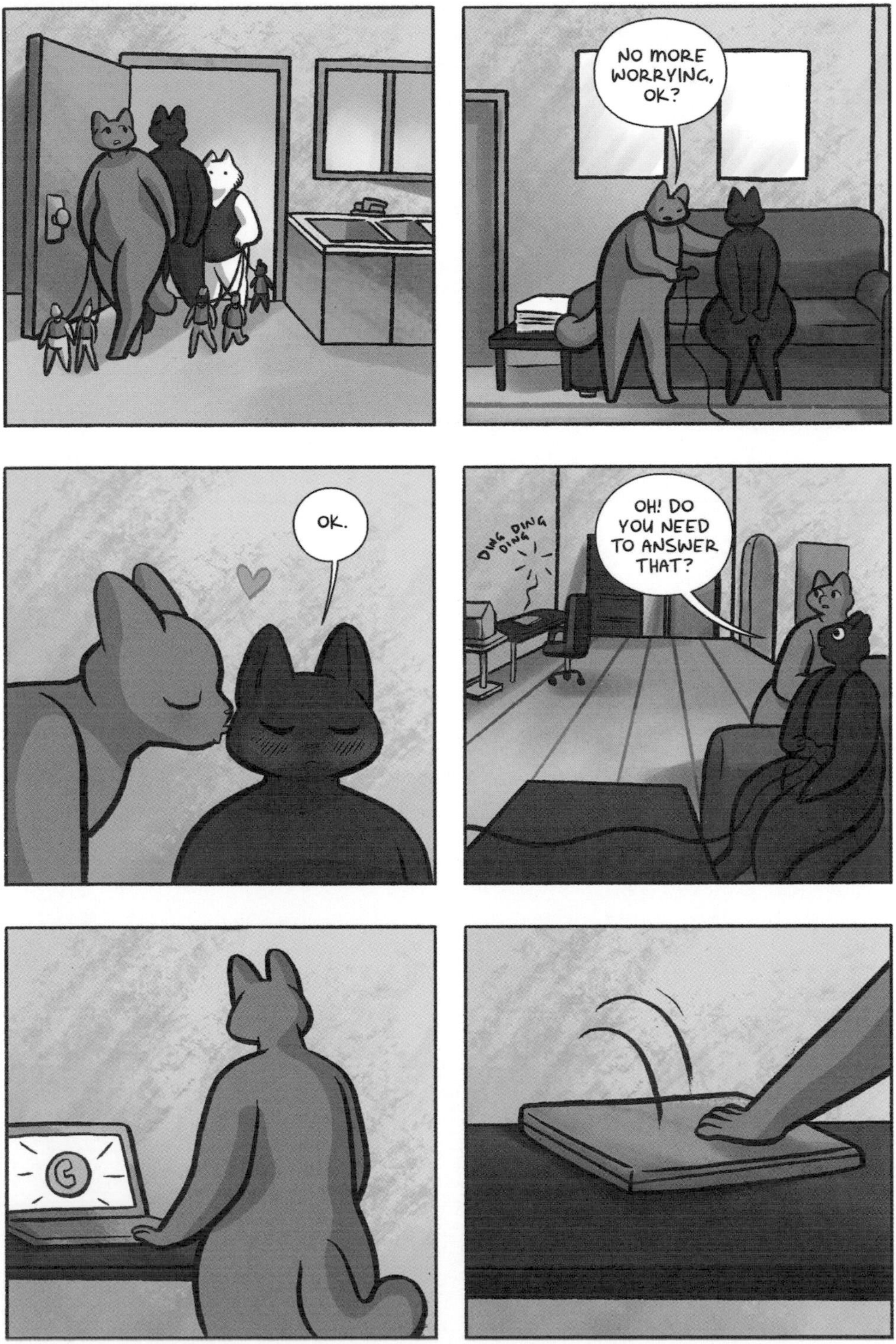
NO MORE WORRYING, OK?
OK.
DING DING DING
OH! DO YOU NEED TO ANSWER THAT?

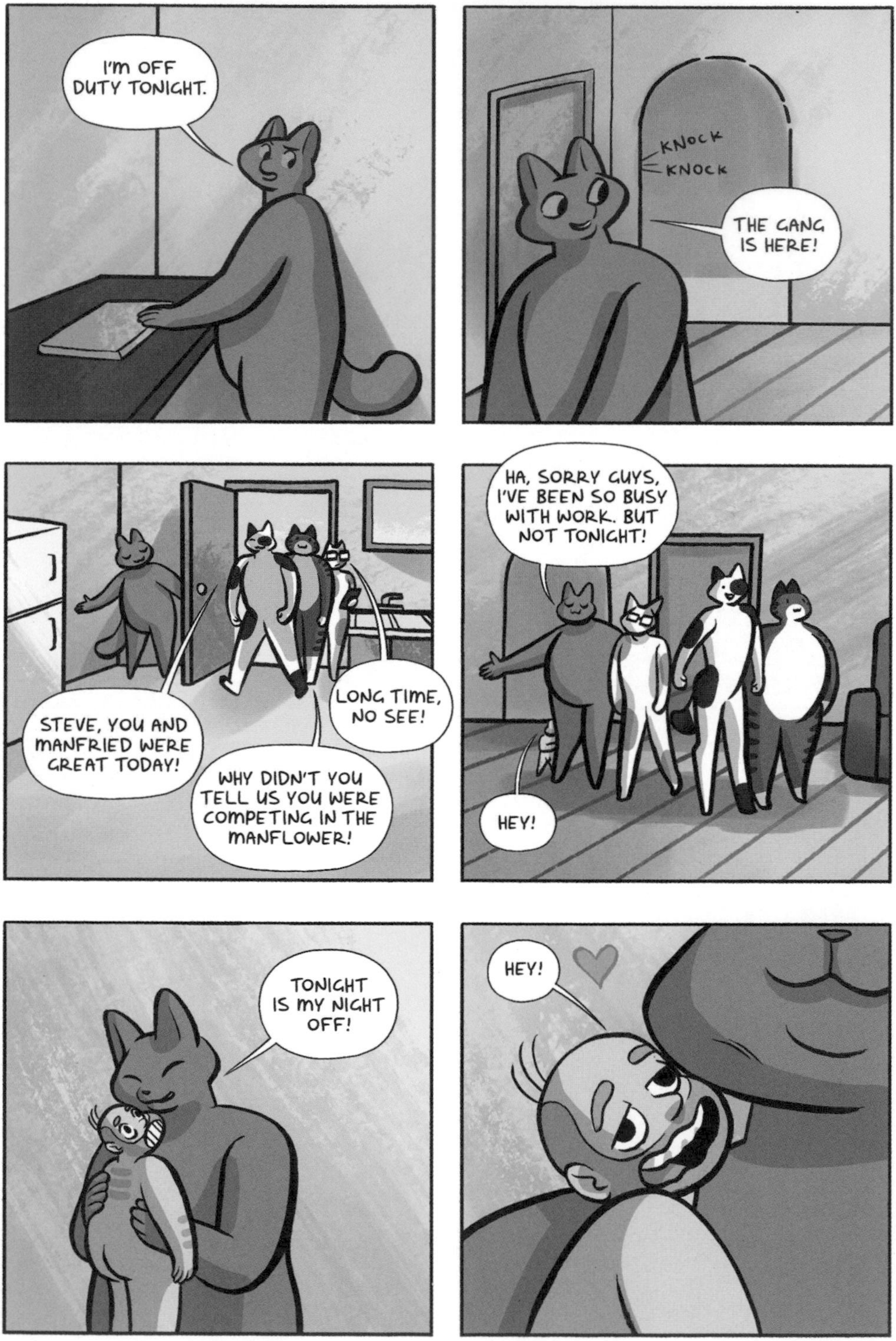

I'M OFF DUTY TONIGHT.
KNOCK
KNOCK
THE GANG IS HERE!
STEVE, YOU AND MANFRIED WERE GREAT TODAY!
WHY DIDN'T YOU TELL US YOU WERE COMPETING IN THE MANFLOWER!
LONG TIME, NO SEE!
HA, SORRY GUYS, I'VE BEEN SO BUSY WITH WORK. BUT NOT TONIGHT!
HEY!
TONIGHT IS MY NIGHT OFF!
HEY!

I am contacting you regarding a contestant at the Manflower Man Show who is subjecting the judges to blackmail. I have audio and written evidence to show that Mr. Meow of Meow Construction Co. and manager at the First Bank of Catlanta is blackmailing the judges at the Manflower Man Show. Mr. Meow and his man Winston are contestants in this year's Manflower Man Show and are currently set to win the grand prize of $500,000. I also have audio and photographic evidence, as well as personal testaments, that Mr. Meow has engaged in blackmailing members of the Catlanta city council...

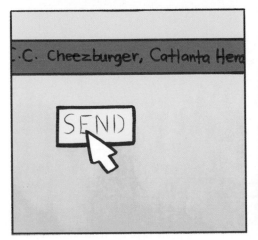

C.C. Cheezburger, Catlanta Hera

SEND

PART SEVEN

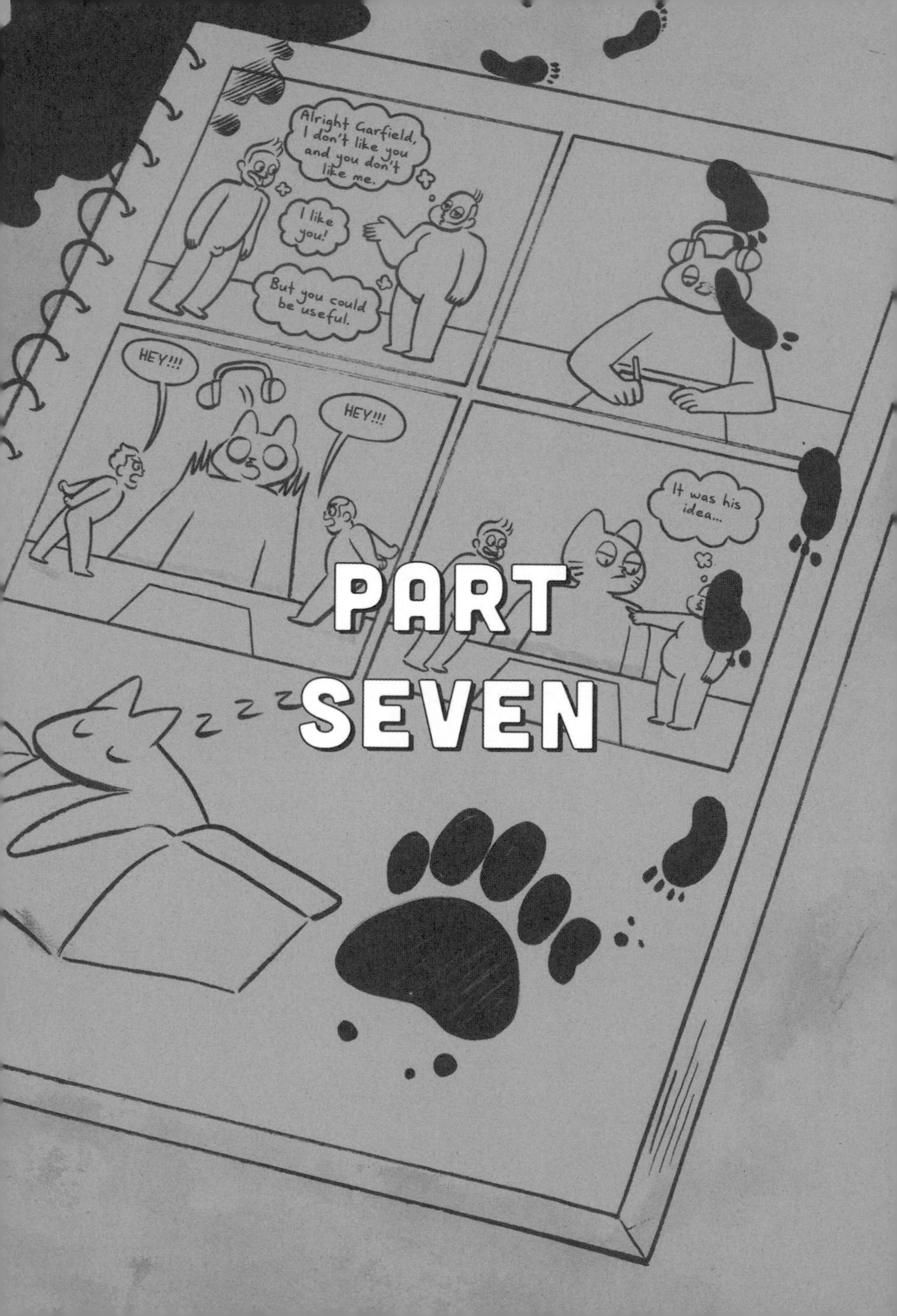
Alright Garfield, I don't like you and you don't like me.
I like you!
But you could be useful.
HEY!!!
HEY!!!
It was his idea...
ZZZ

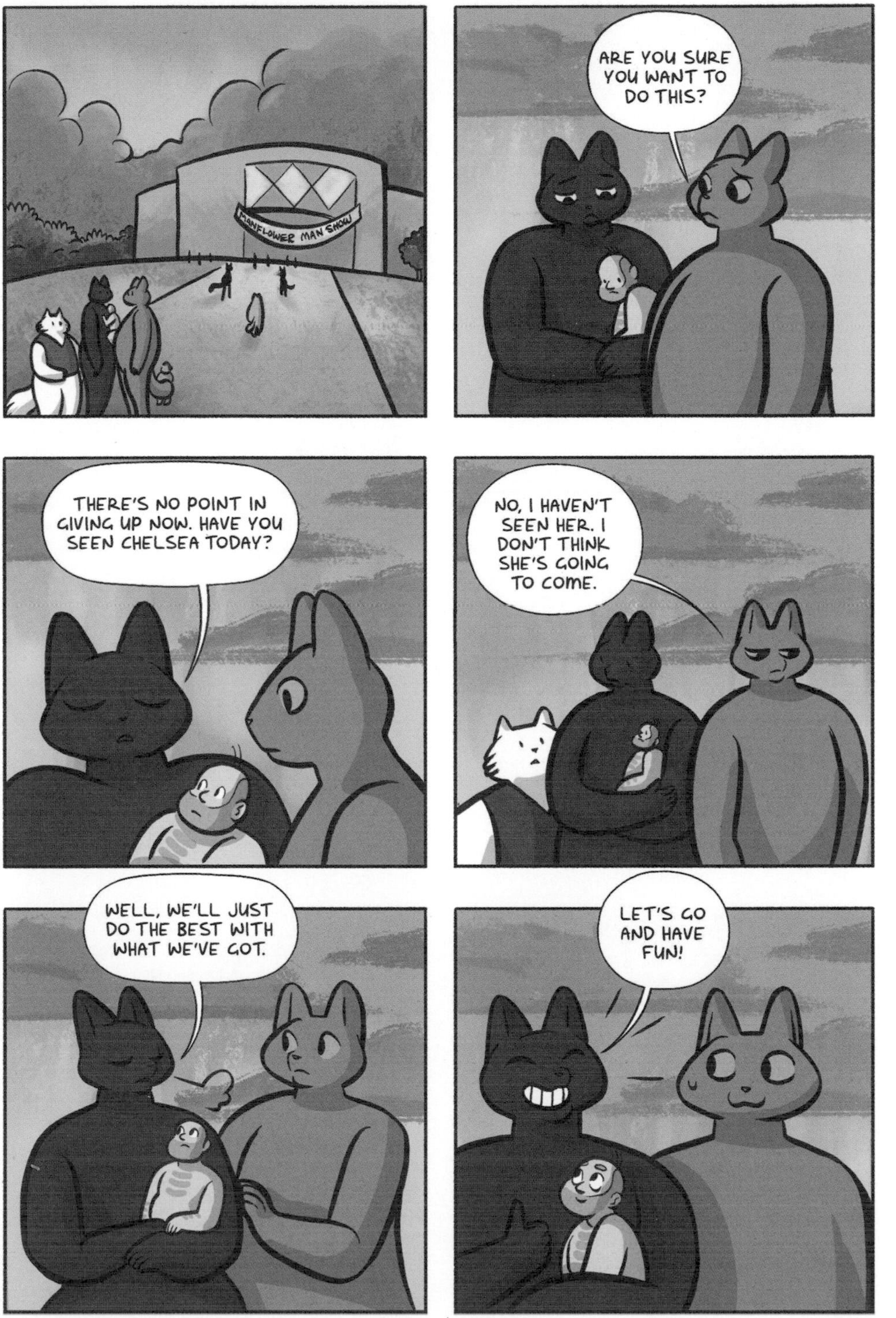
MANFLOWER MAN SHOW
ARE YOU SURE YOU WANT TO DO THIS?
THERE'S NO POINT IN GIVING UP NOW. HAVE YOU SEEN CHELSEA TODAY?
NO, I HAVEN'T SEEN HER. I DON'T THINK SHE'S GOING TO COME.
WELL, WE'LL JUST DO THE BEST WITH WHAT WE'VE GOT.
LET'S GO AND HAVE FUN!

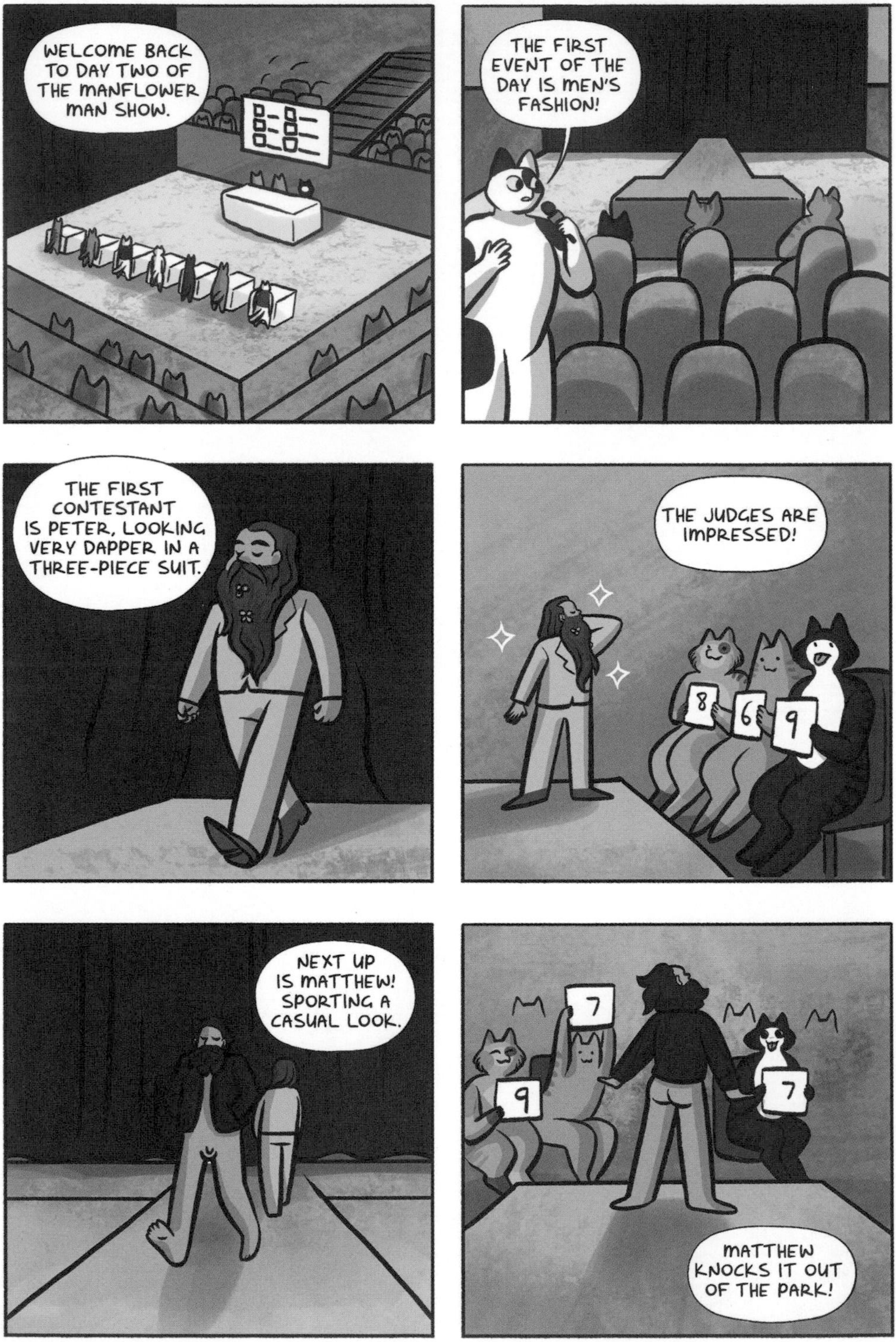
WELCOME BACK TO DAY TWO OF THE MANFLOWER MAN SHOW.
THE FIRST EVENT OF THE DAY IS MEN'S FASHION!
THE FIRST CONTESTANT IS PETER, LOOKING VERY DAPPER IN A THREE-PIECE SUIT.
THE JUDGES ARE IMPRESSED!
8
6
9
NEXT UP IS MATTHEW! SPORTING A CASUAL LOOK.
7
9
7
MATTHEW KNOCKS IT OUT OF THE PARK!

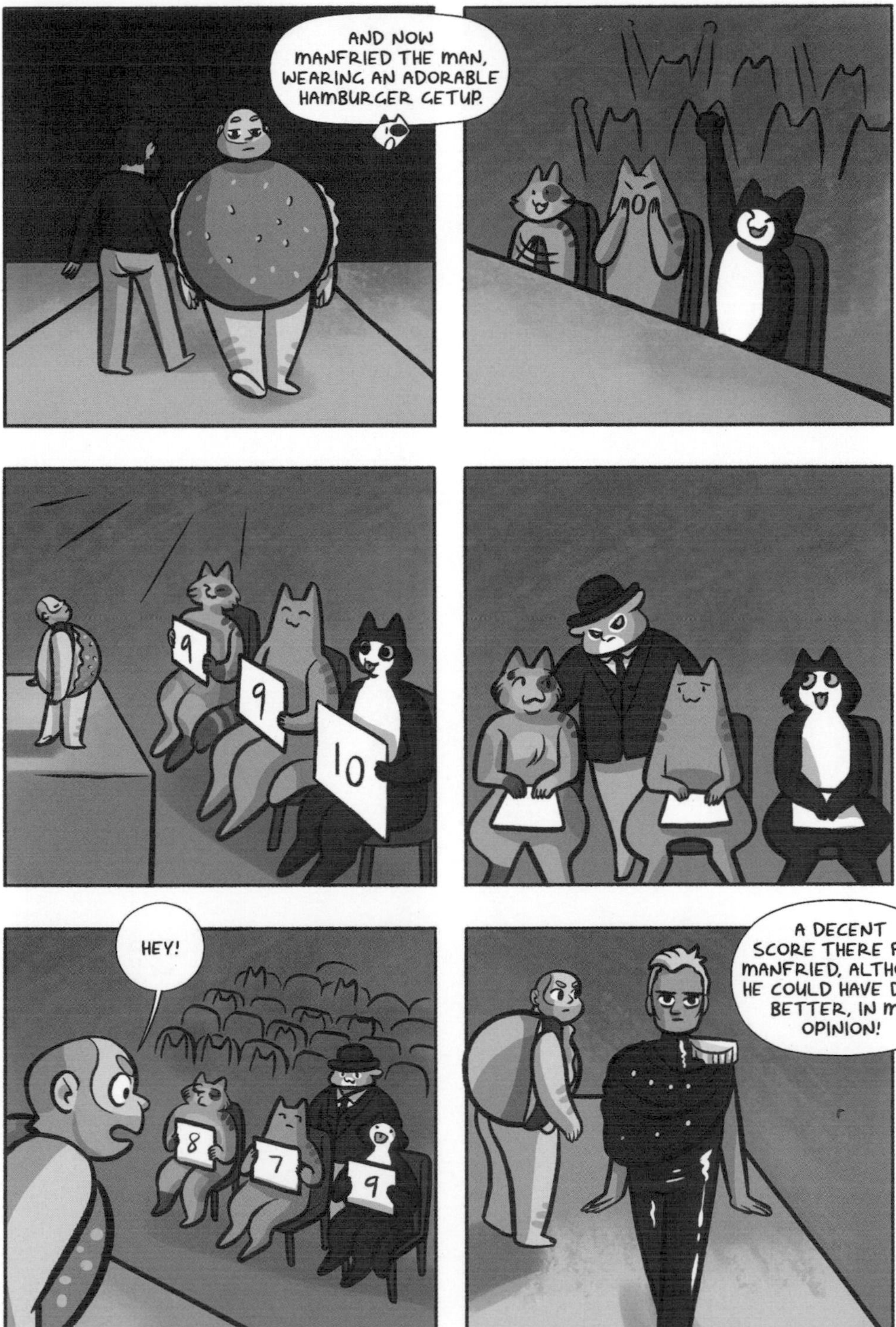
AND NOW MANFRIED THE MAN, WEARING AN ADORABLE HAMBURGER GETUP.
9
9
10
HEY!
8
7
9
A DECENT SCORE THERE FOR MANFRIED, ALTHOUGH HE COULD HAVE DONE BETTER, IN MY OPINION!

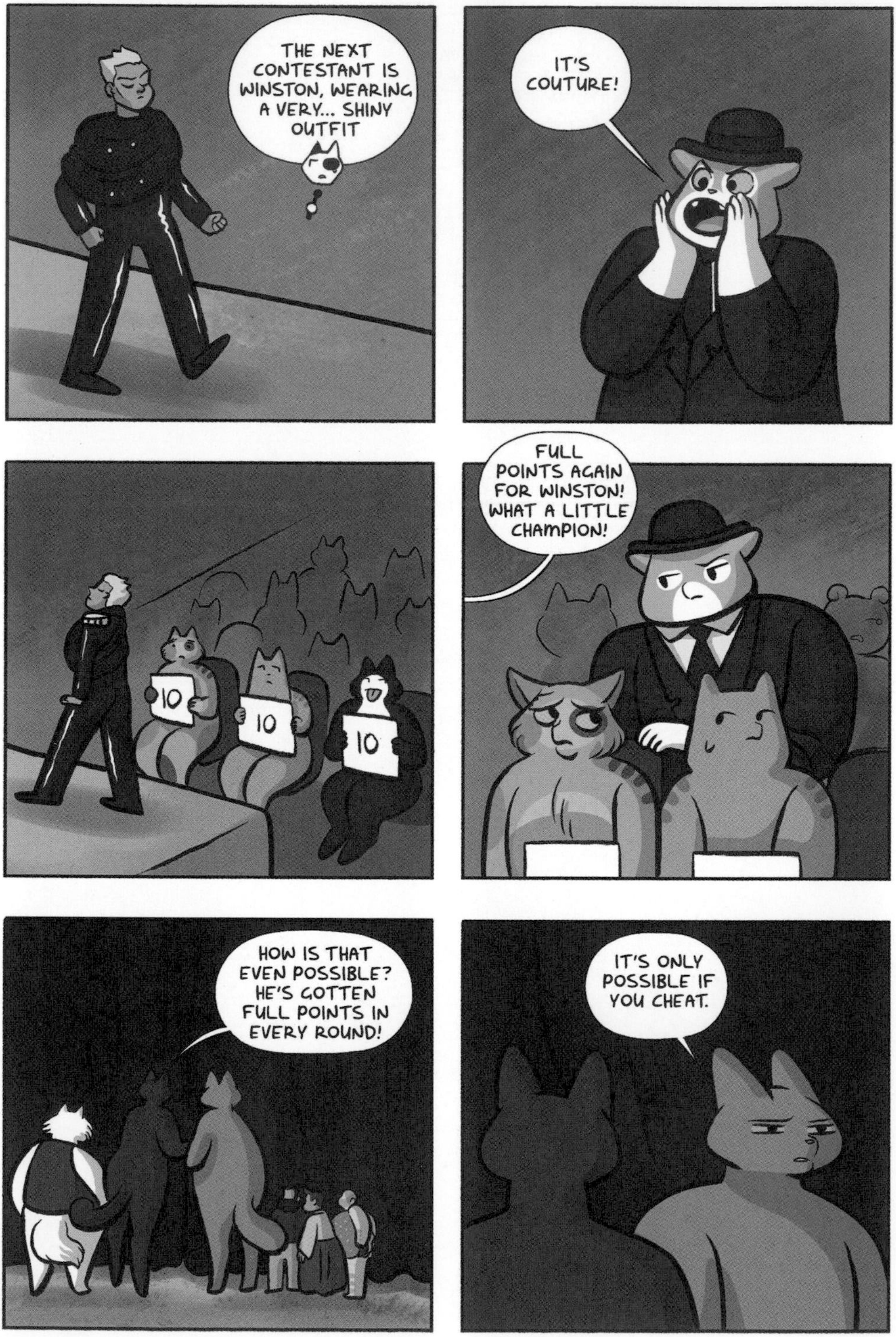
THE NEXT CONTESTANT IS WINSTON, WEARING A VERY... SHINY OUTFIT
IT'S COUTURE!
10
10
10
FULL POINTS AGAIN FOR WINSTON! WHAT A LITTLE CHAMPION!
HOW IS THAT EVEN POSSIBLE? HE'S GOTTEN FULL POINTS IN EVERY ROUND!
IT'S ONLY POSSIBLE IF YOU CHEAT.

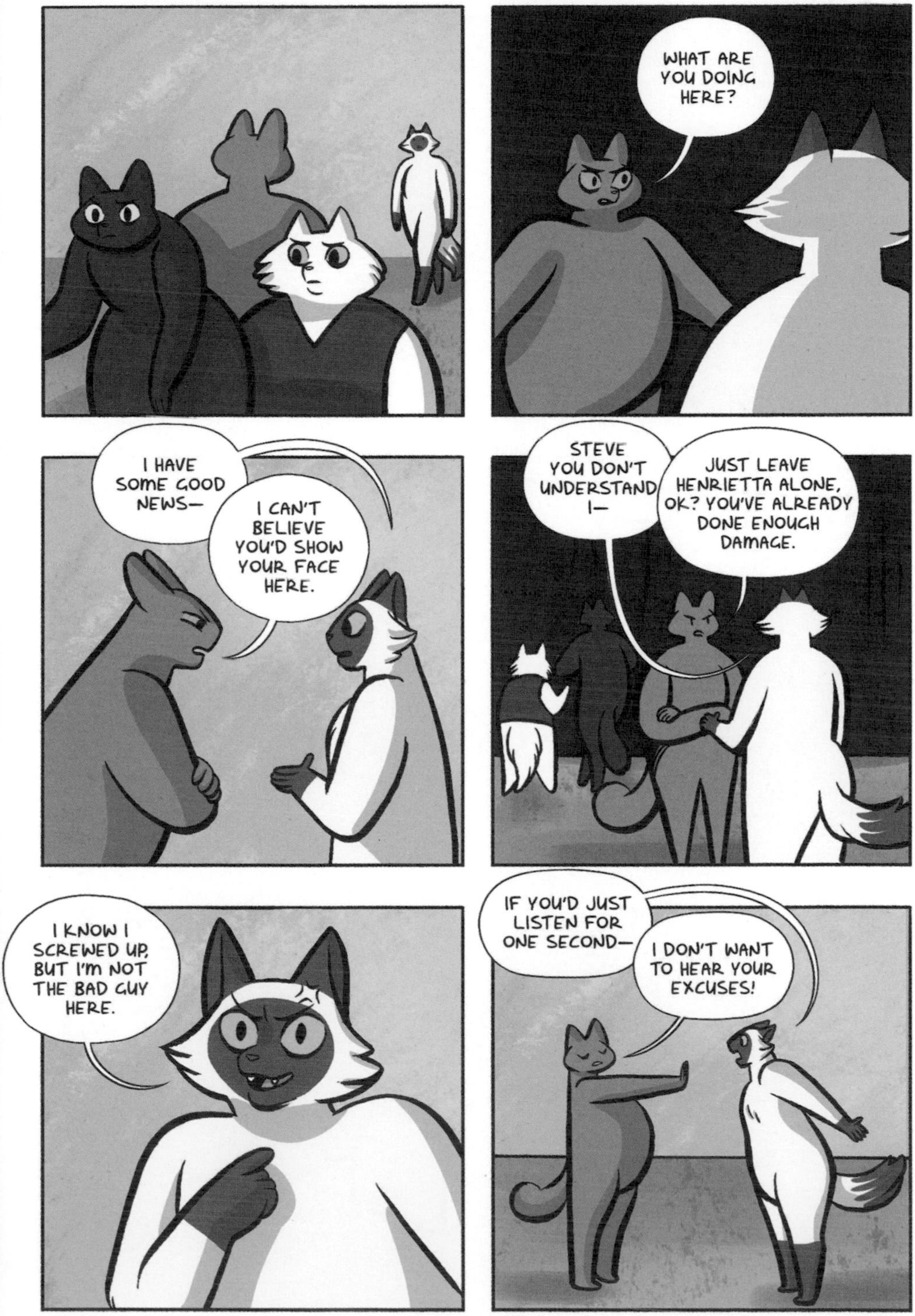
WHAT ARE YOU DOING HERE?
I HAVE SOME GOOD NEWS—
I CAN'T BELIEVE YOU'D SHOW YOUR FACE HERE.
STEVE YOU DON'T UNDERSTAND I—
JUST LEAVE HENRIETTA ALONE, OK? YOU'VE ALREADY DONE ENOUGH DAMAGE.
I KNOW I SCREWED UP, BUT I'M NOT THE BAD GUY HERE.
IF YOU'D JUST LISTEN FOR ONE SECOND—
I DON'T WANT TO HEAR YOUR EXCUSES!

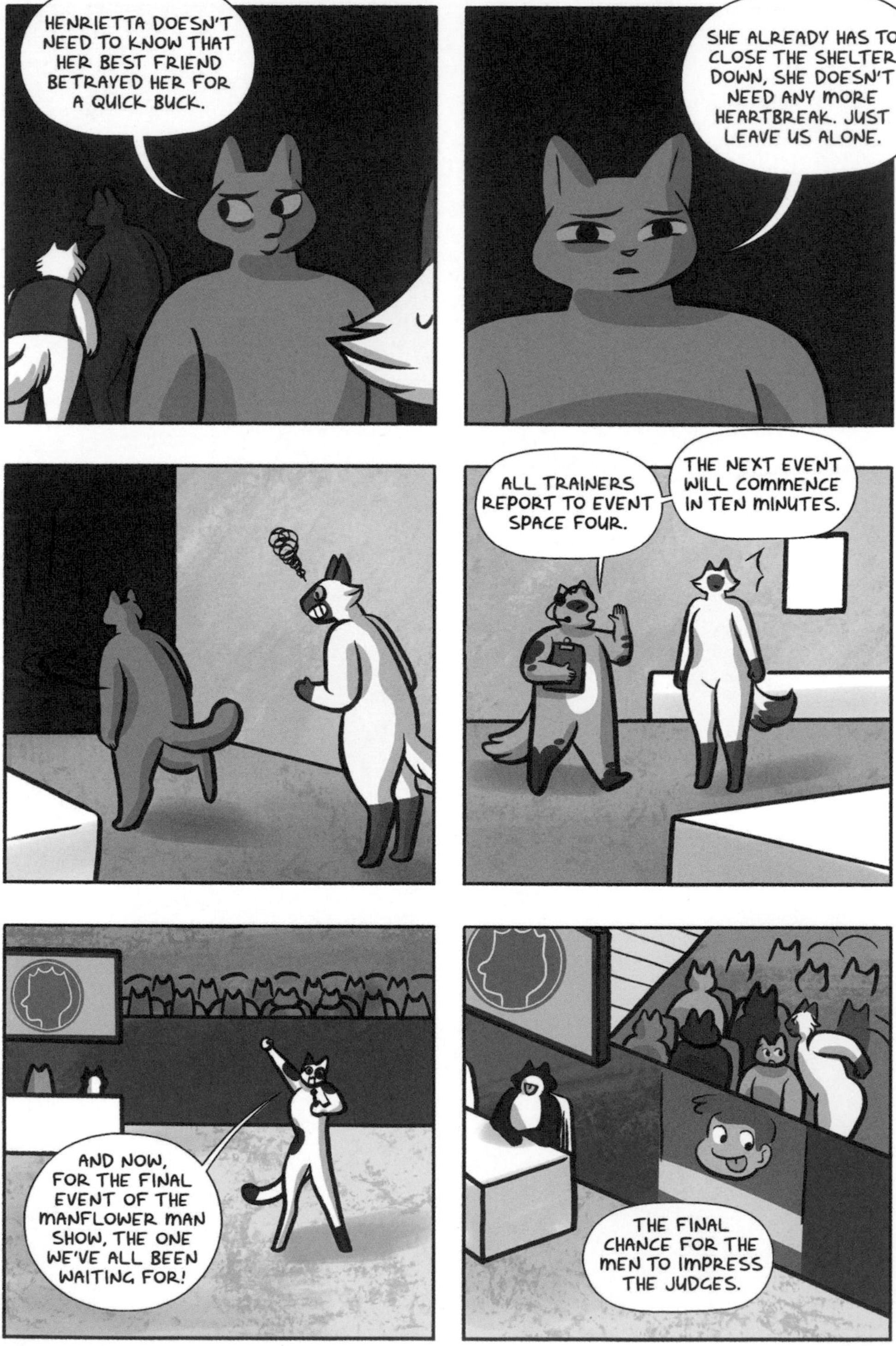
HENRIETTA DOESN'T NEED TO KNOW THAT HER BEST FRIEND BETRAYED HER FOR A QUICK BUCK.
SHE ALREADY HAS TO CLOSE THE SHELTER DOWN, SHE DOESN'T NEED ANY MORE HEARTBREAK. JUST LEAVE US ALONE.
ALL TRAINERS REPORT TO EVENT SPACE FOUR.
THE NEXT EVENT WILL COMMENCE IN TEN MINUTES.
AND NOW, FOR THE FINAL EVENT OF THE MANFLOWER MAN SHOW, THE ONE WE'VE ALL BEEN WAITING FOR!
THE FINAL CHANCE FOR THE MEN TO IMPRESS THE JUDGES.

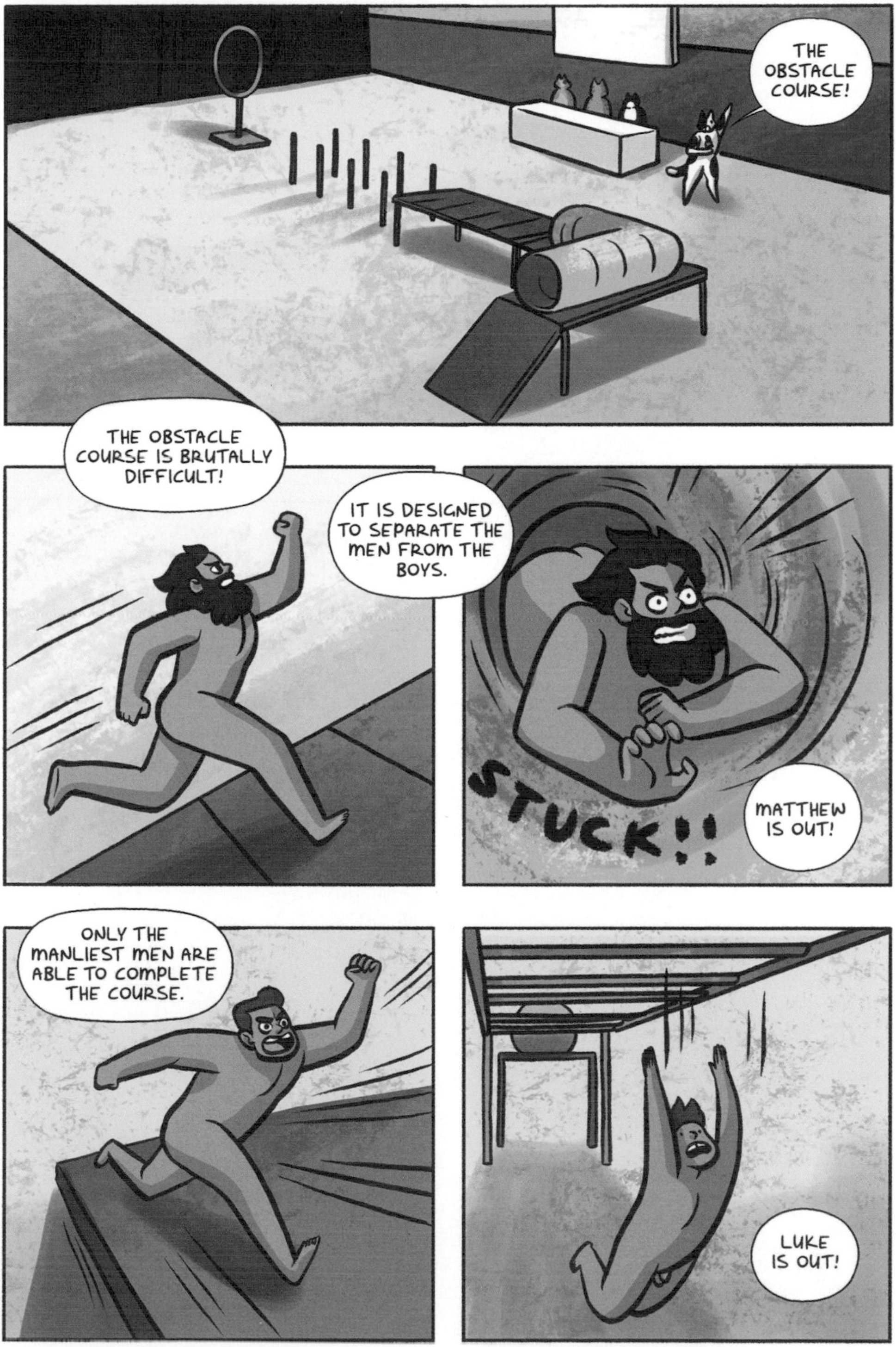
THE OBSTACLE COURSE!
THE OBSTACLE COURSE IS BRUTALLY DIFFICULT!
IT IS DESIGNED TO SEPARATE THE MEN FROM THE BOYS.
STUCK!!
MATTHEW IS OUT!
ONLY THE MANLIEST MEN ARE ABLE TO COMPLETE THE COURSE.
LUKE IS OUT!

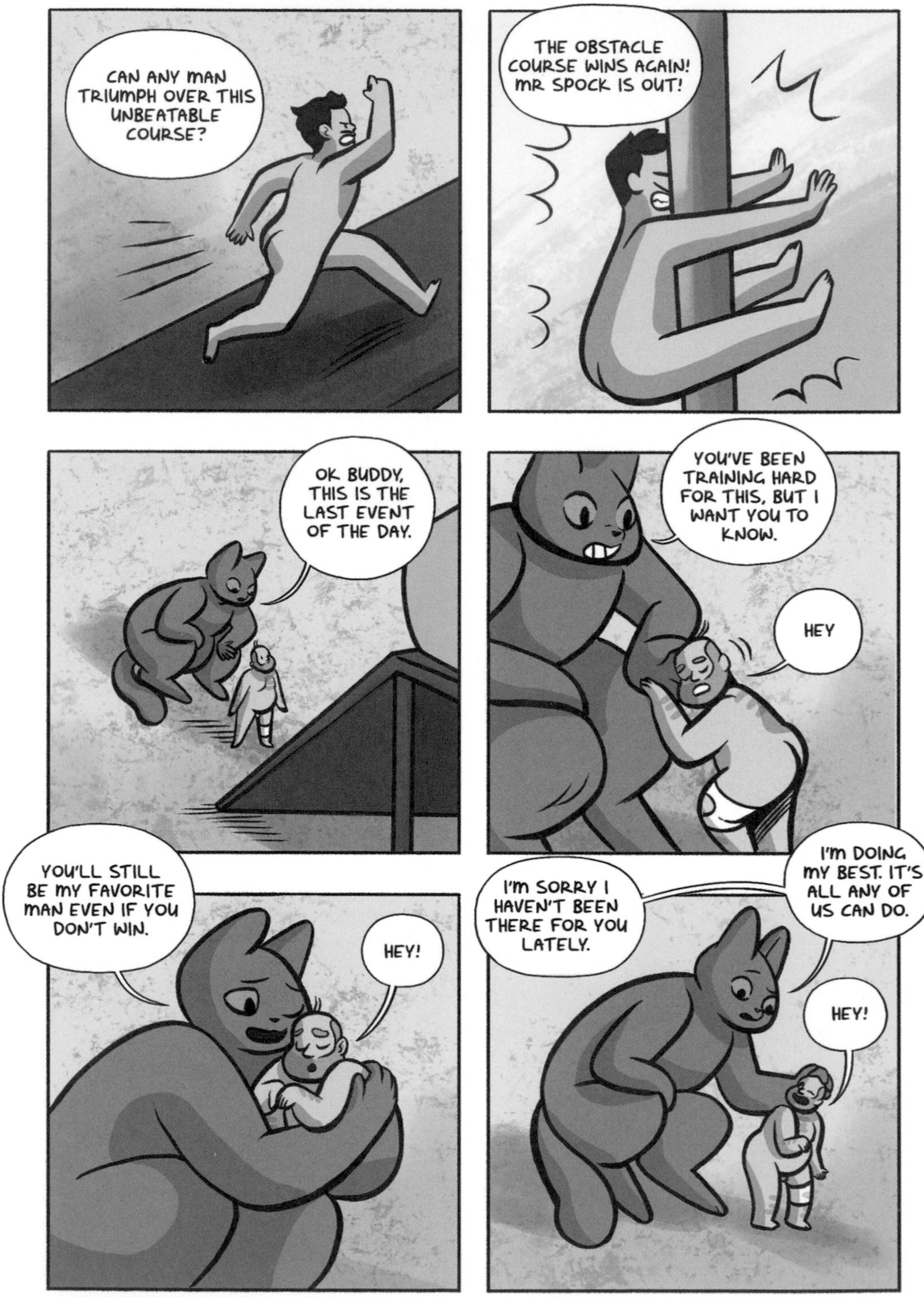
CAN ANY MAN TRIUMPH OVER THIS UNBEATABLE COURSE?
THE OBSTACLE COURSE WINS AGAIN! MR SPOCK IS OUT!
OK BUDDY, THIS IS THE LAST EVENT OF THE DAY.
YOU'VE BEEN TRAINING HARD FOR THIS, BUT I WANT YOU TO KNOW.
HEY
YOU'LL STILL BE MY FAVORITE MAN EVEN IF YOU DON'T WIN.
HEY!
I'M SORRY I HAVEN'T BEEN THERE FOR YOU LATELY.
I'M DOING MY BEST. IT'S ALL ANY OF US CAN DO.
HEY!

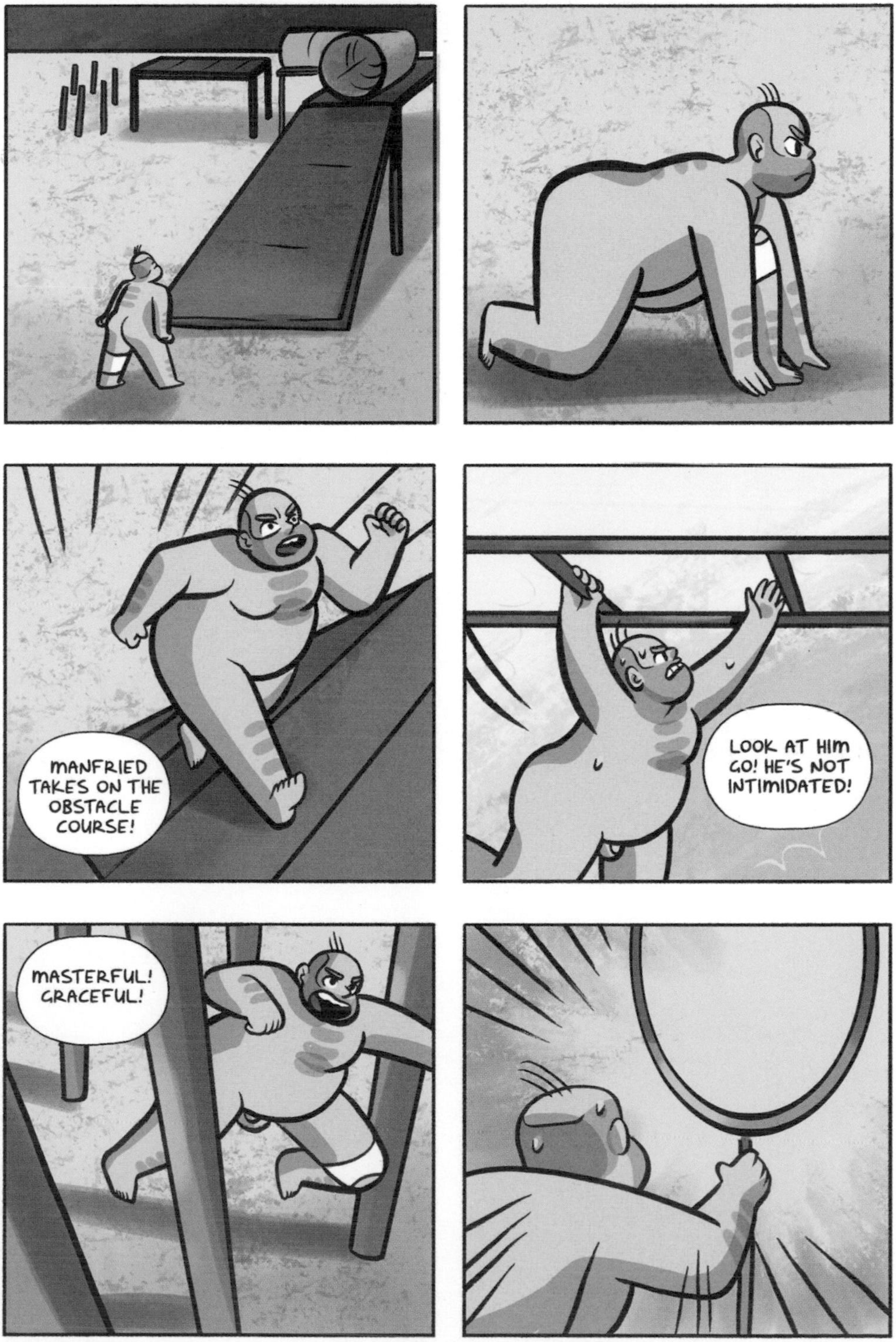
MANFRIED TAKES ON THE OBSTACLE COURSE!
LOOK AT HIM GO! HE'S NOT INTIMIDATED!
MASTERFUL! GRACEFUL!

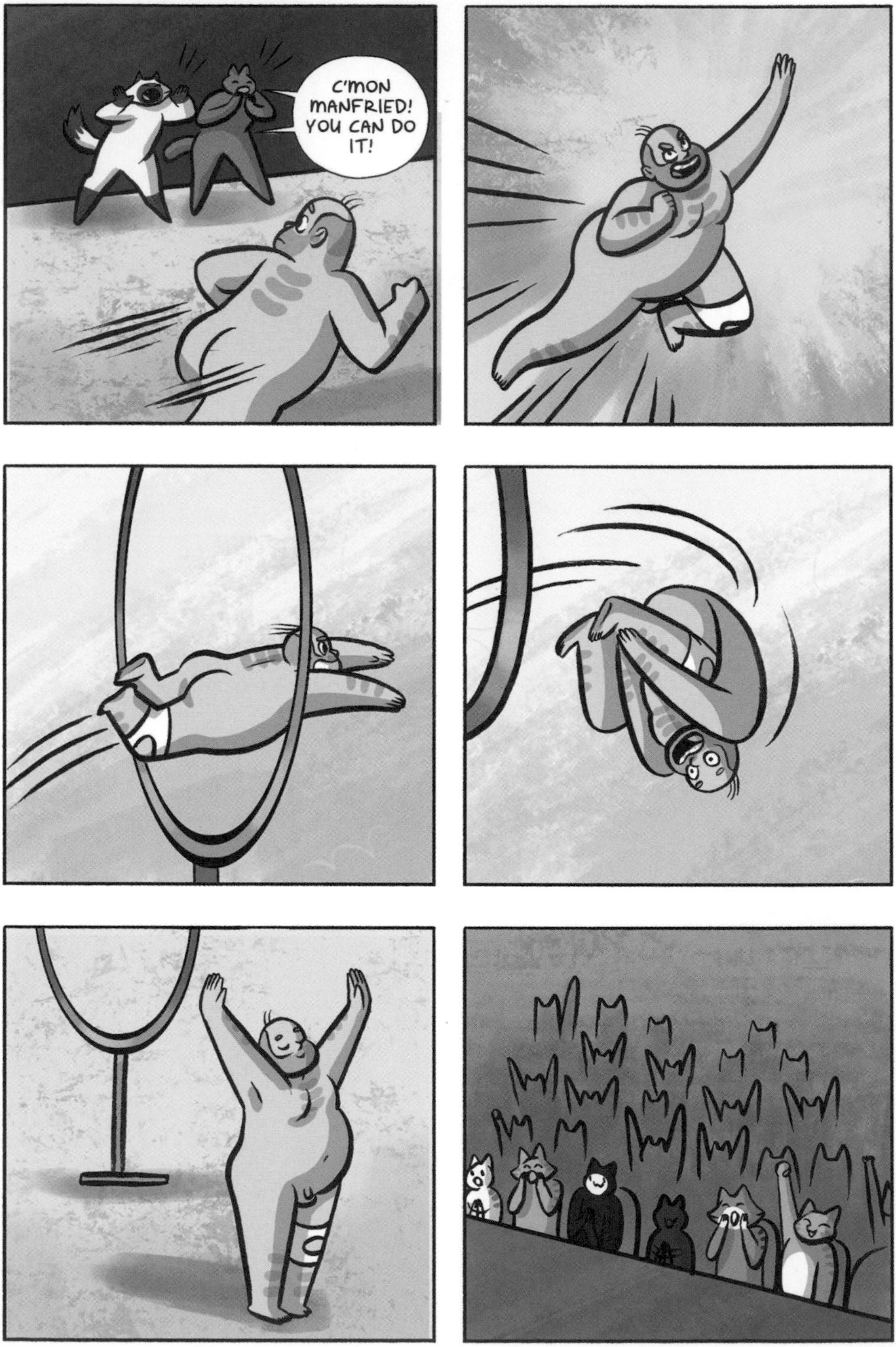
C'MON MANFRIED! YOU CAN DO IT!

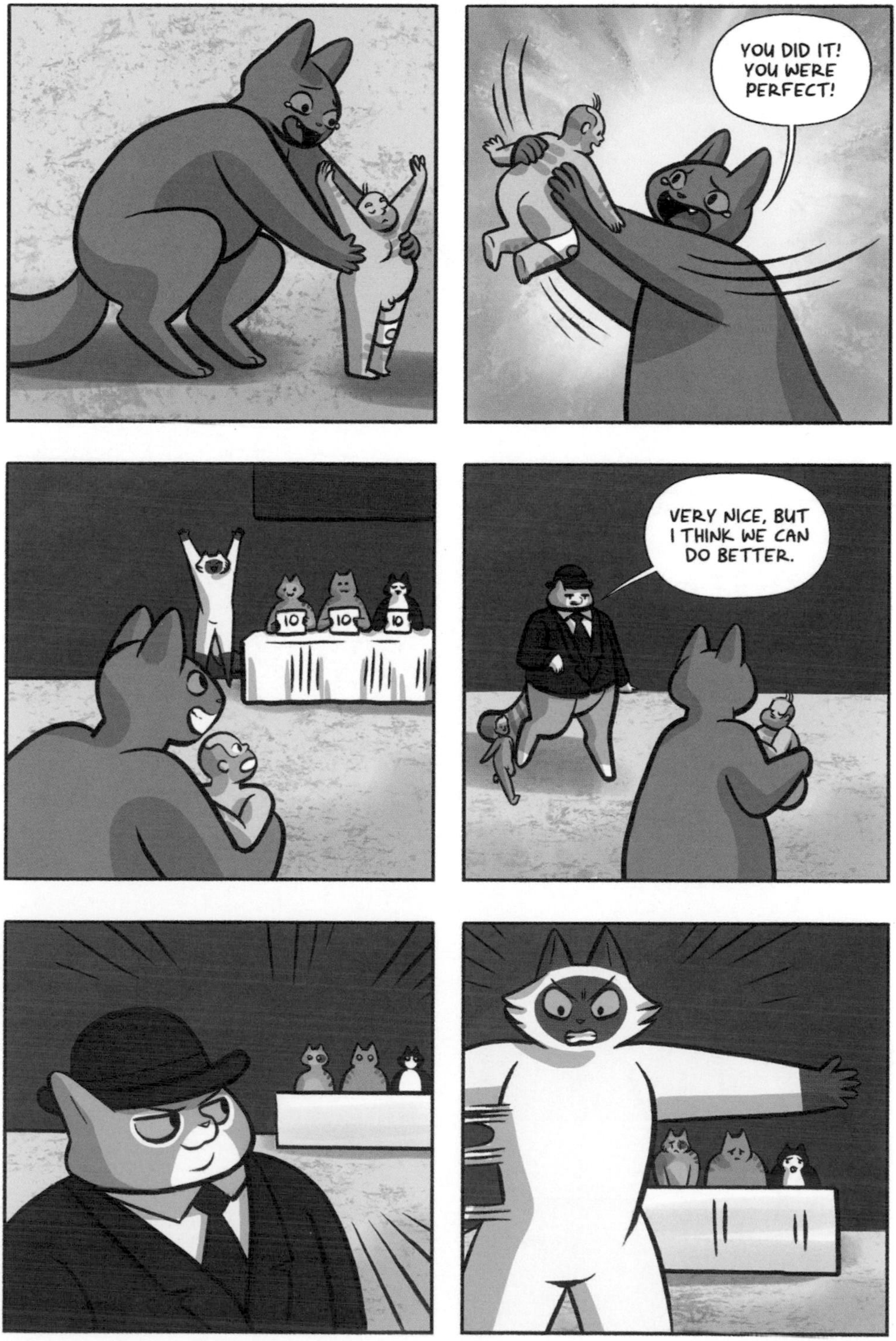
YOU DID IT!
YOU WERE
PERFECT!
10
10
10
VERY NICE, BUT
I THINK WE CAN
DO BETTER.

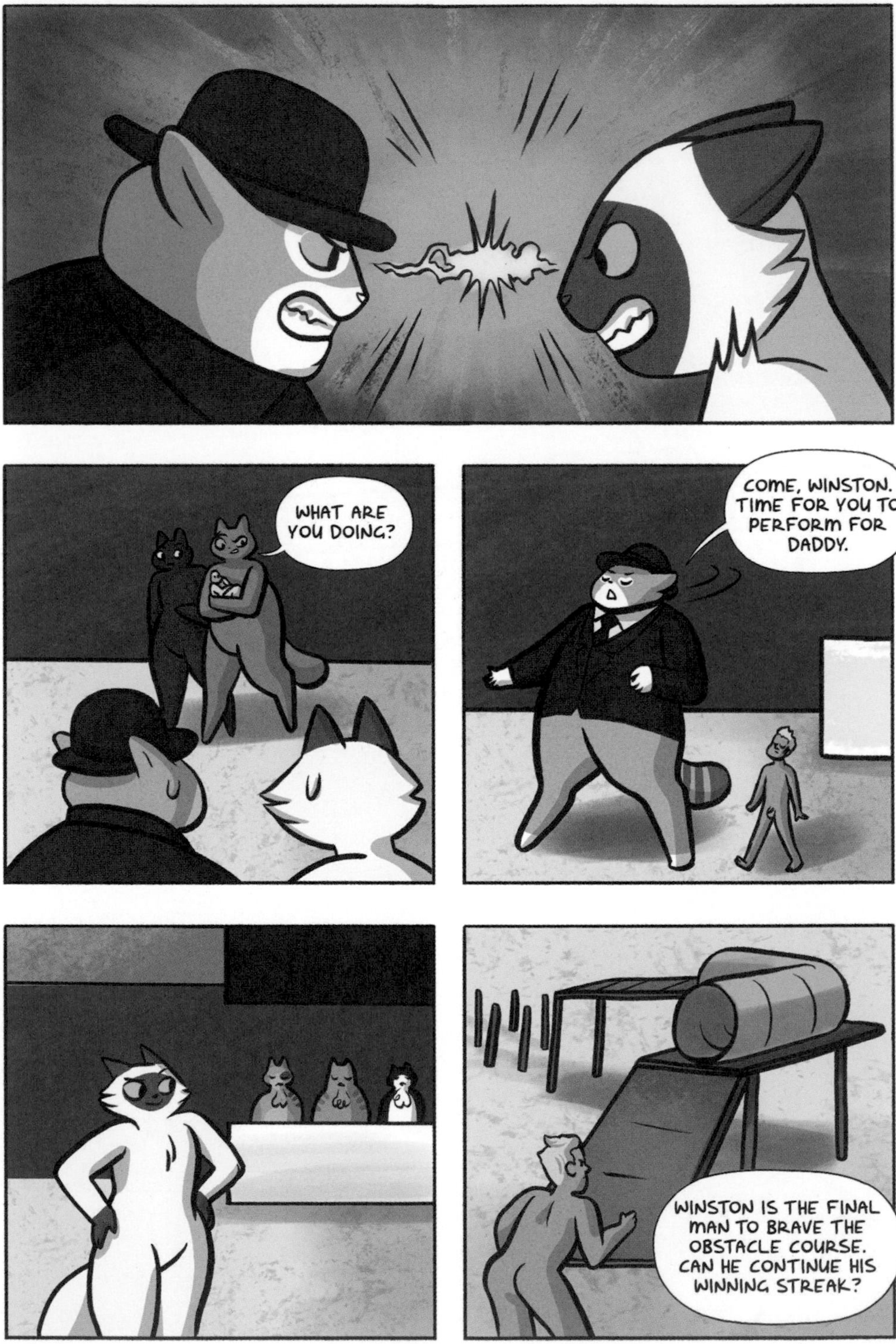
WHAT ARE YOU DOING?
COME, WINSTON. TIME FOR YOU TO PERFORM FOR DADDY.
WINSTON IS THE FINAL MAN TO BRAVE THE OBSTACLE COURSE. CAN HE CONTINUE HIS WINNING STREAK?

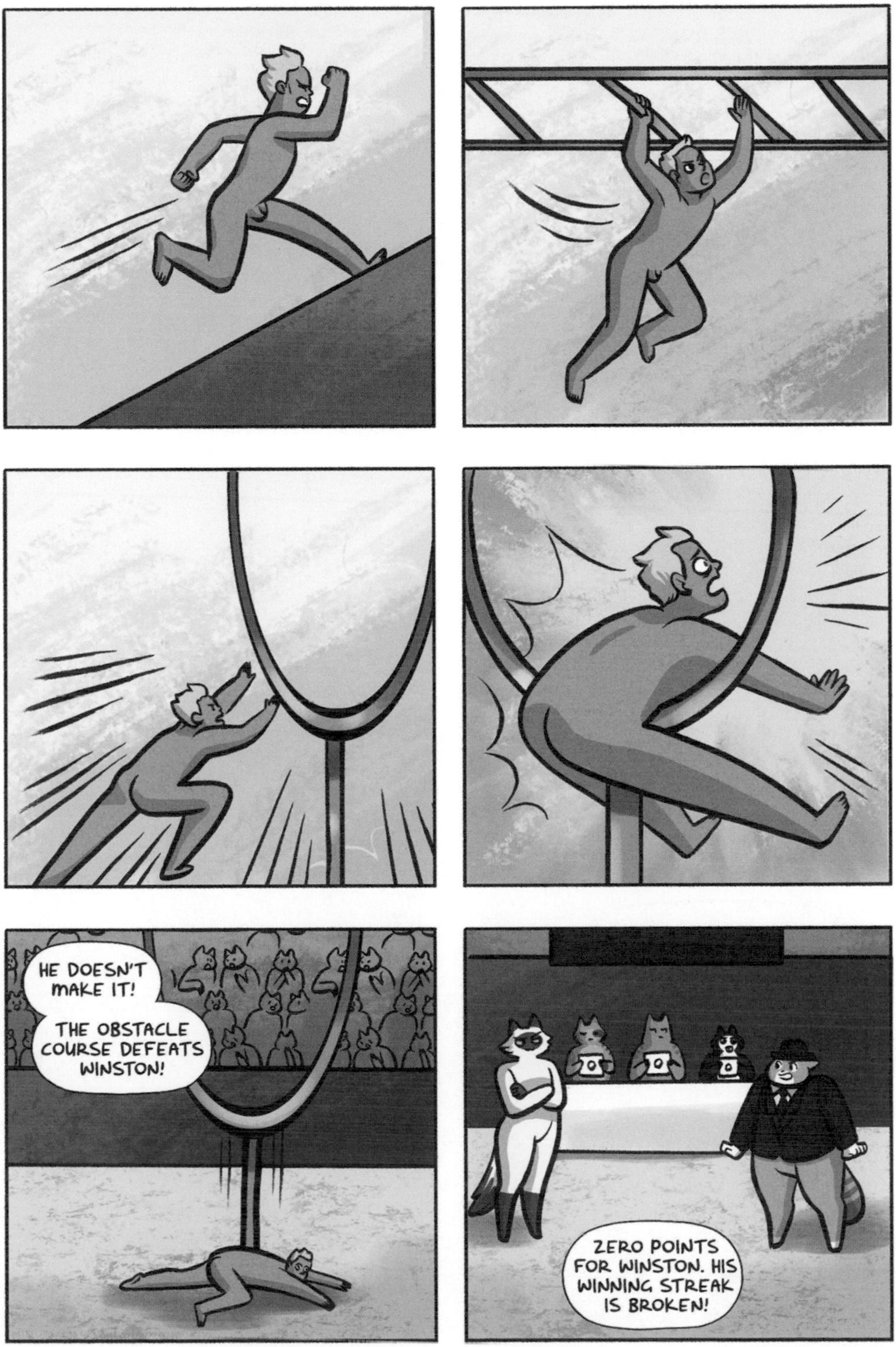
HE DOESN'T MAKE IT!
THE OBSTACLE COURSE DEFEATS WINSTON!
ZERO POINTS FOR WINSTON. HIS WINNING STREAK IS BROKEN!

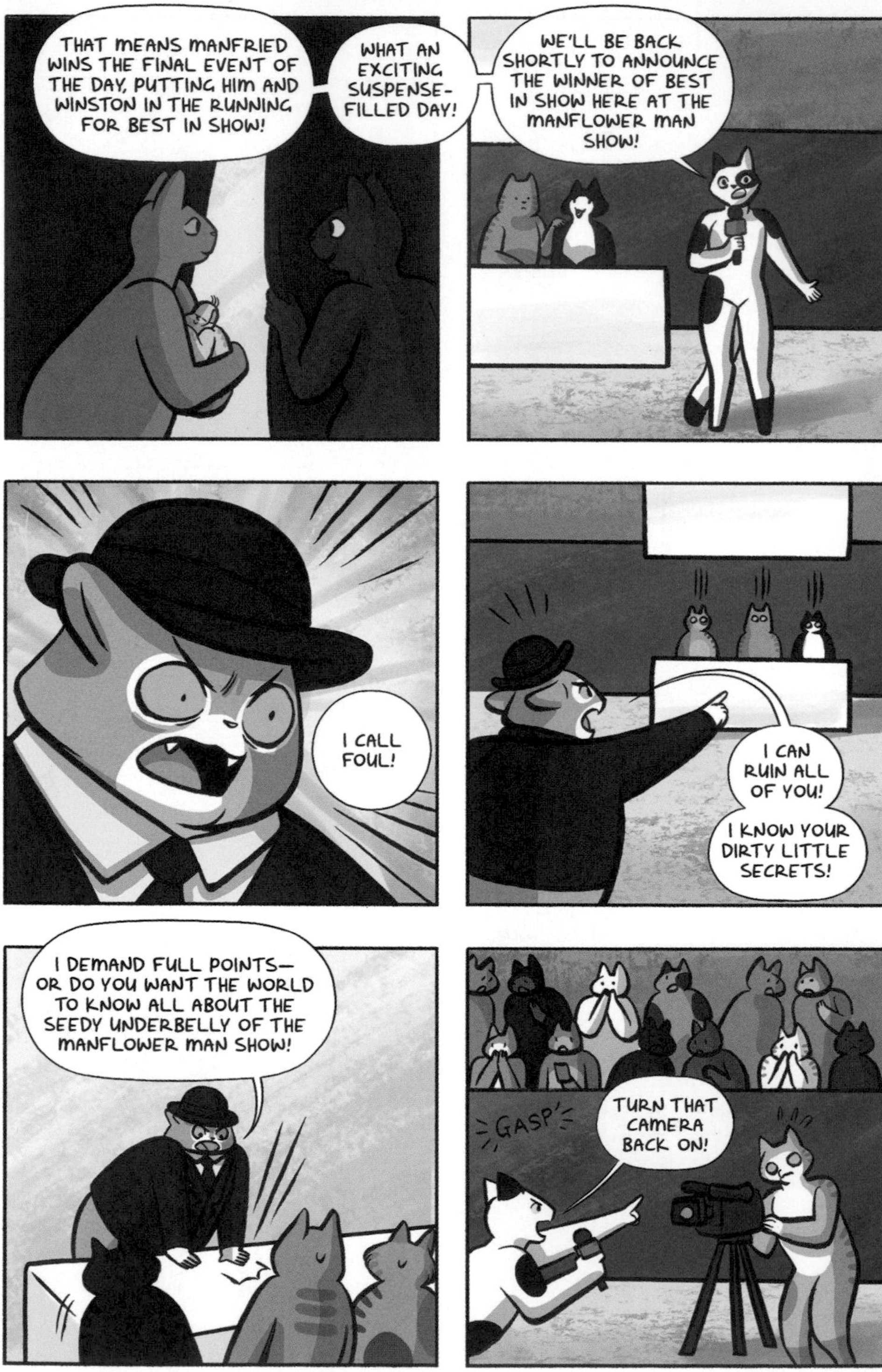
THAT MEANS MANFRIED WINS THE FINAL EVENT OF THE DAY, PUTTING HIM AND WINSTON IN THE RUNNING FOR BEST IN SHOW!
WHAT AN EXCITING SUSPENSE-FILLED DAY!
WE'LL BE BACK SHORTLY TO ANNOUNCE THE WINNER OF BEST IN SHOW HERE AT THE MANFLOWER MAN SHOW!
I CALL FOUL!
I CAN RUIN ALL OF YOU!
I KNOW YOUR DIRTY LITTLE SECRETS!
I DEMAND FULL POINTS— OR DO YOU WANT THE WORLD TO KNOW ALL ABOUT THE SEEDY UNDERBELLY OF THE MANFLOWER MAN SHOW!
GASP
TURN THAT CAMERA BACK ON!

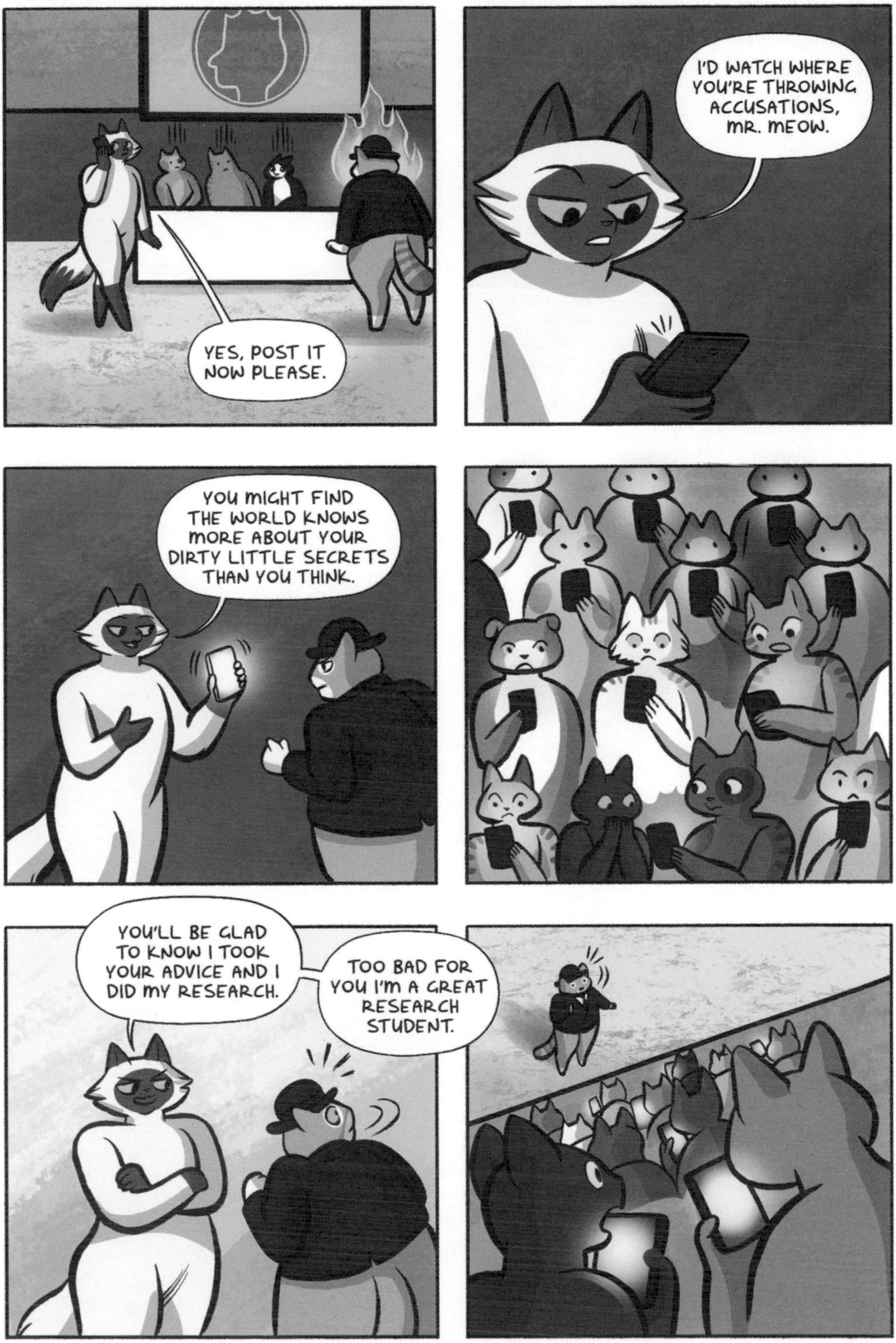
YES, POST IT NOW PLEASE.
I'D WATCH WHERE YOU'RE THROWING ACCUSATIONS, MR. MEOW.
YOU MIGHT FIND THE WORLD KNOWS MORE ABOUT YOUR DIRTY LITTLE SECRETS THAN YOU THINK.
YOU'LL BE GLAD TO KNOW I TOOK YOUR ADVICE AND I DID MY RESEARCH.
TOO BAD FOR YOU I'M A GREAT RESEARCH STUDENT.

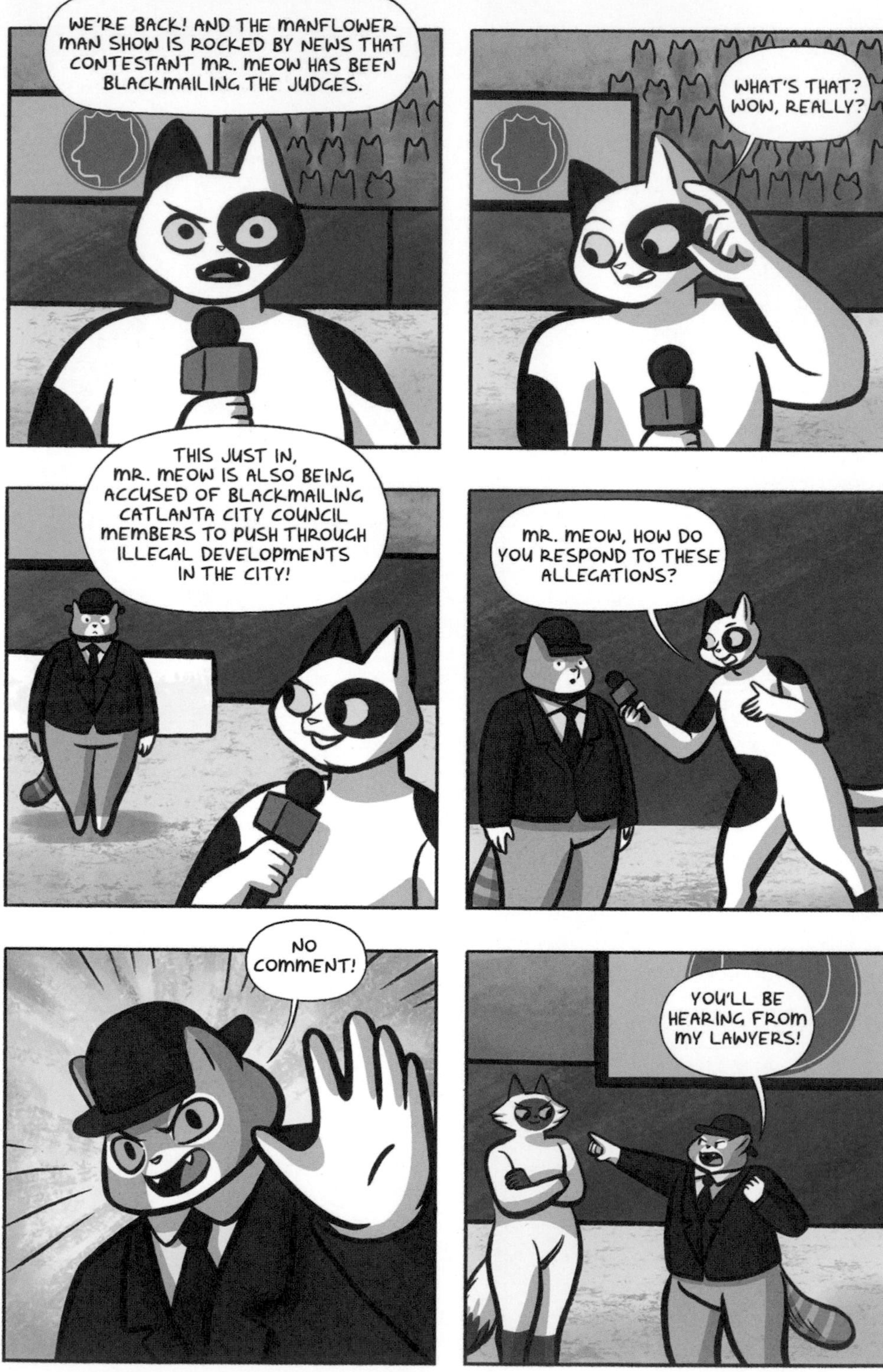
WE'RE BACK! AND THE MANFLOWER MAN SHOW IS ROCKED BY NEWS THAT CONTESTANT MR. MEOW HAS BEEN BLACKMAILING THE JUDGES.
WHAT'S THAT? WOW, REALLY?
THIS JUST IN, MR. MEOW IS ALSO BEING ACCUSED OF BLACKMAILING CATLANTA CITY COUNCIL MEMBERS TO PUSH THROUGH ILLEGAL DEVELOPMENTS IN THE CITY!
MR. MEOW, HOW DO YOU RESPOND TO THESE ALLEGATIONS?
NO COMMENT!
YOU'LL BE HEARING FROM MY LAWYERS!

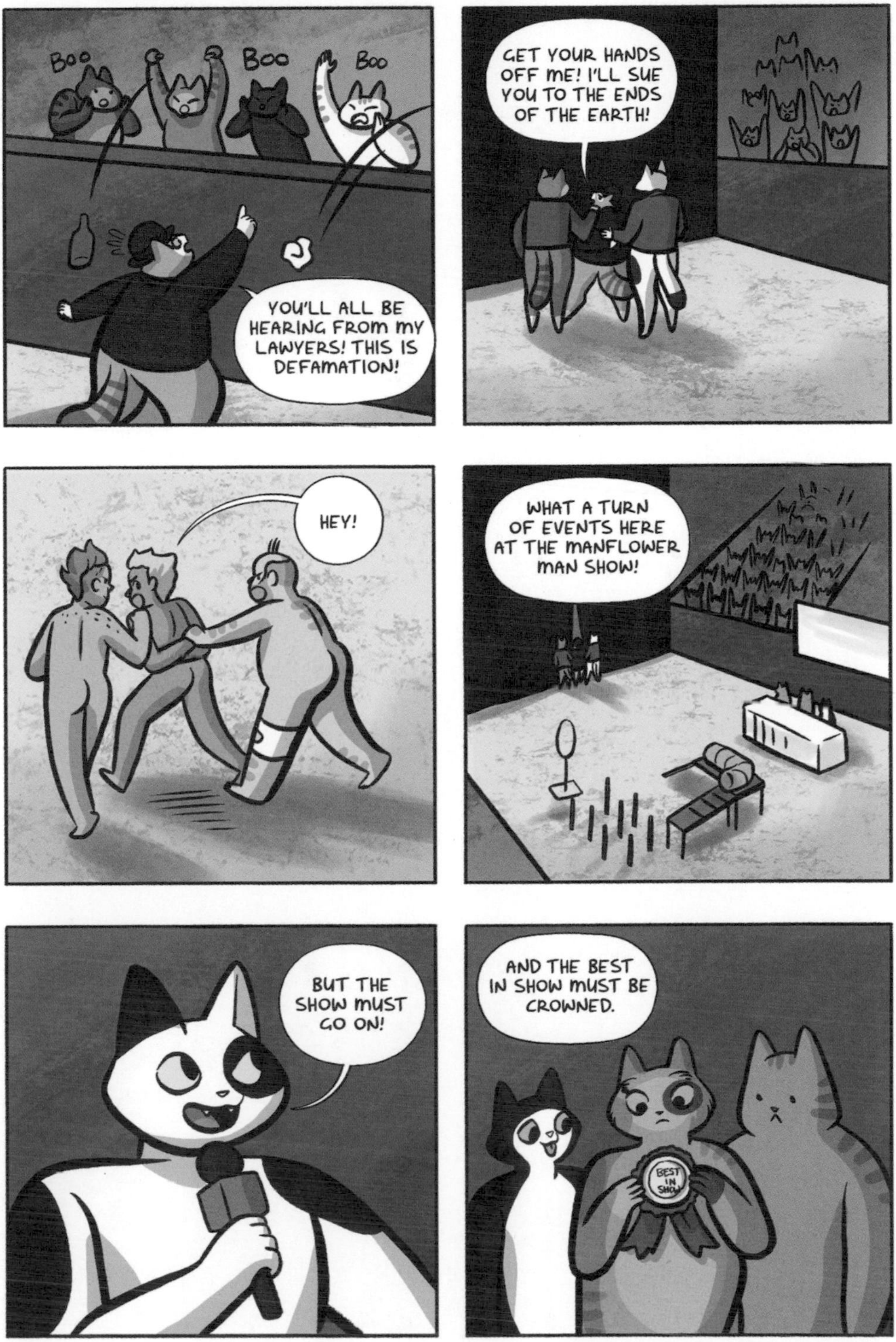
BOO
BOO
BOO
YOU'LL ALL BE HEARING FROM MY LAWYERS! THIS IS DEFAMATION!
GET YOUR HANDS OFF ME! I'LL SUE YOU TO THE ENDS OF THE EARTH!
HEY!
WHAT A TURN OF EVENTS HERE AT THE MANFLOWER MAN SHOW!
BUT THE SHOW MUST GO ON!
AND THE BEST IN SHOW MUST BE CROWNED.
BEST IN SHOW

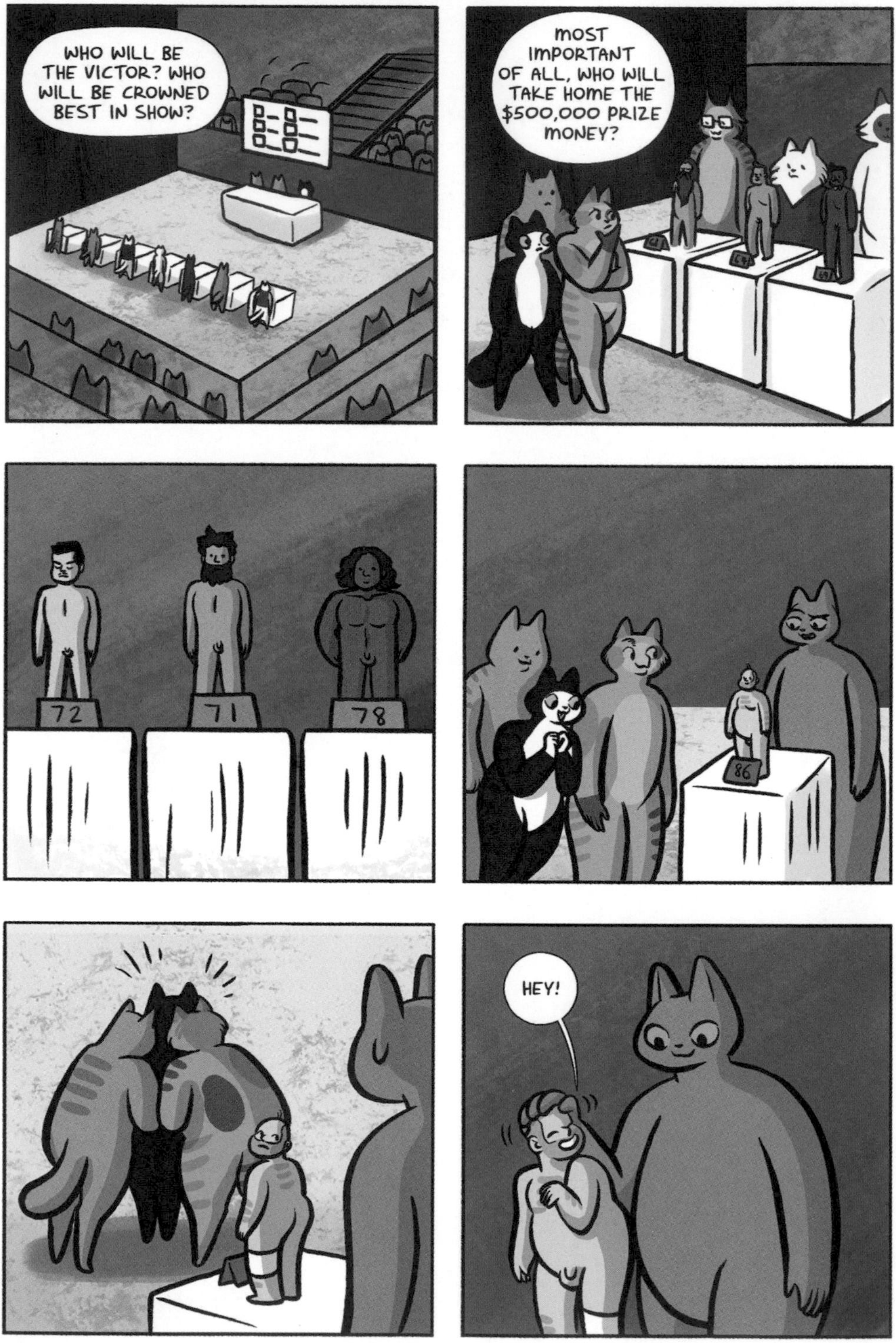
WHO WILL BE THE VICTOR? WHO WILL BE CROWNED BEST IN SHOW?
MOST IMPORTANT OF ALL, WHO WILL TAKE HOME THE $500,000 PRIZE MONEY?
72
71
78
86
HEY!

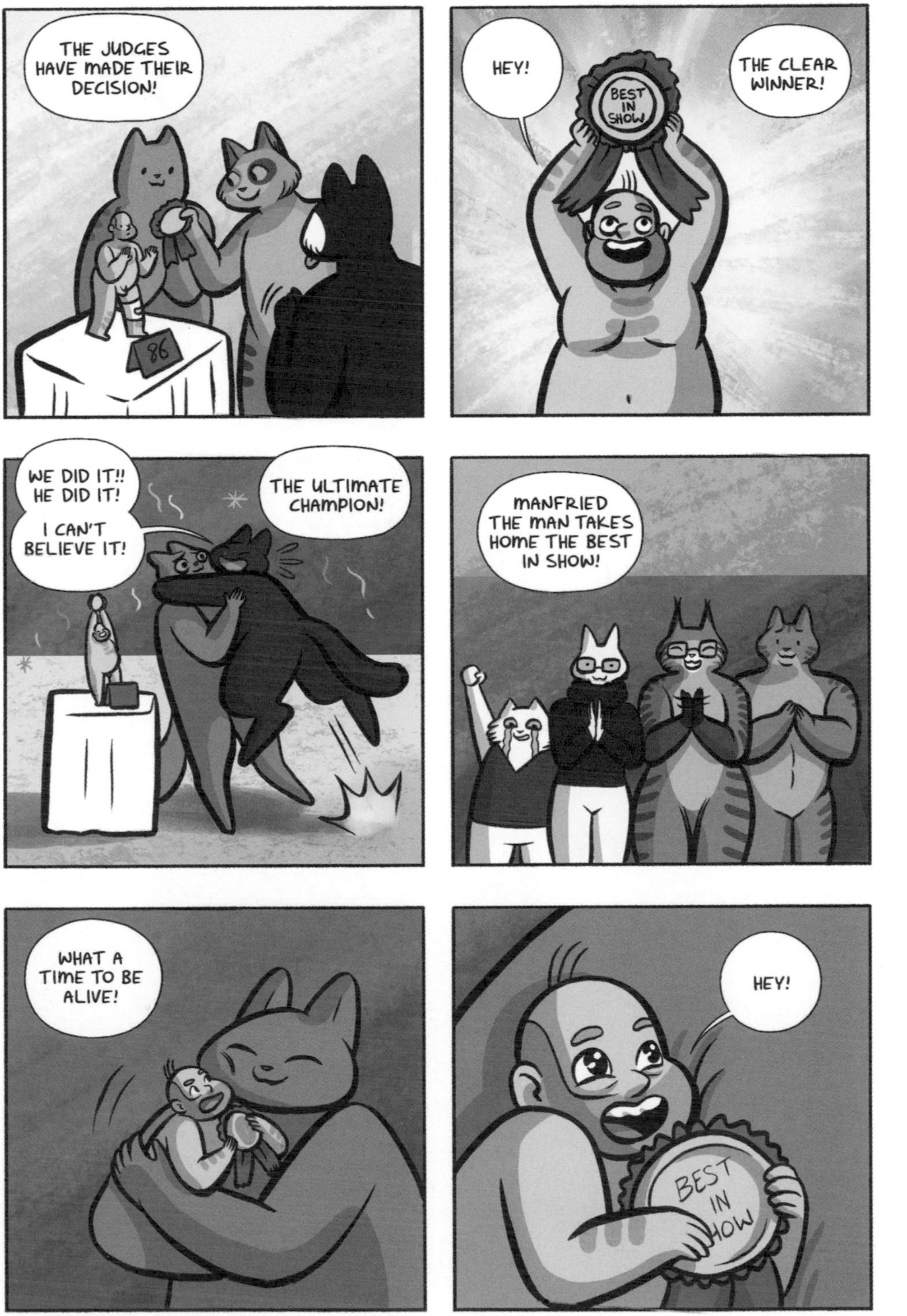
THE JUDGES HAVE MADE THEIR DECISION!
86
HEY!
BEST IN SHOW
THE CLEAR WINNER!
WE DID IT!! HE DID IT!
I CAN'T BELIEVE IT!
THE ULTIMATE CHAMPION!
MANFRIED THE MAN TAKES HOME THE BEST IN SHOW!
WHAT A TIME TO BE ALIVE!
HEY!
BEST IN SHOW

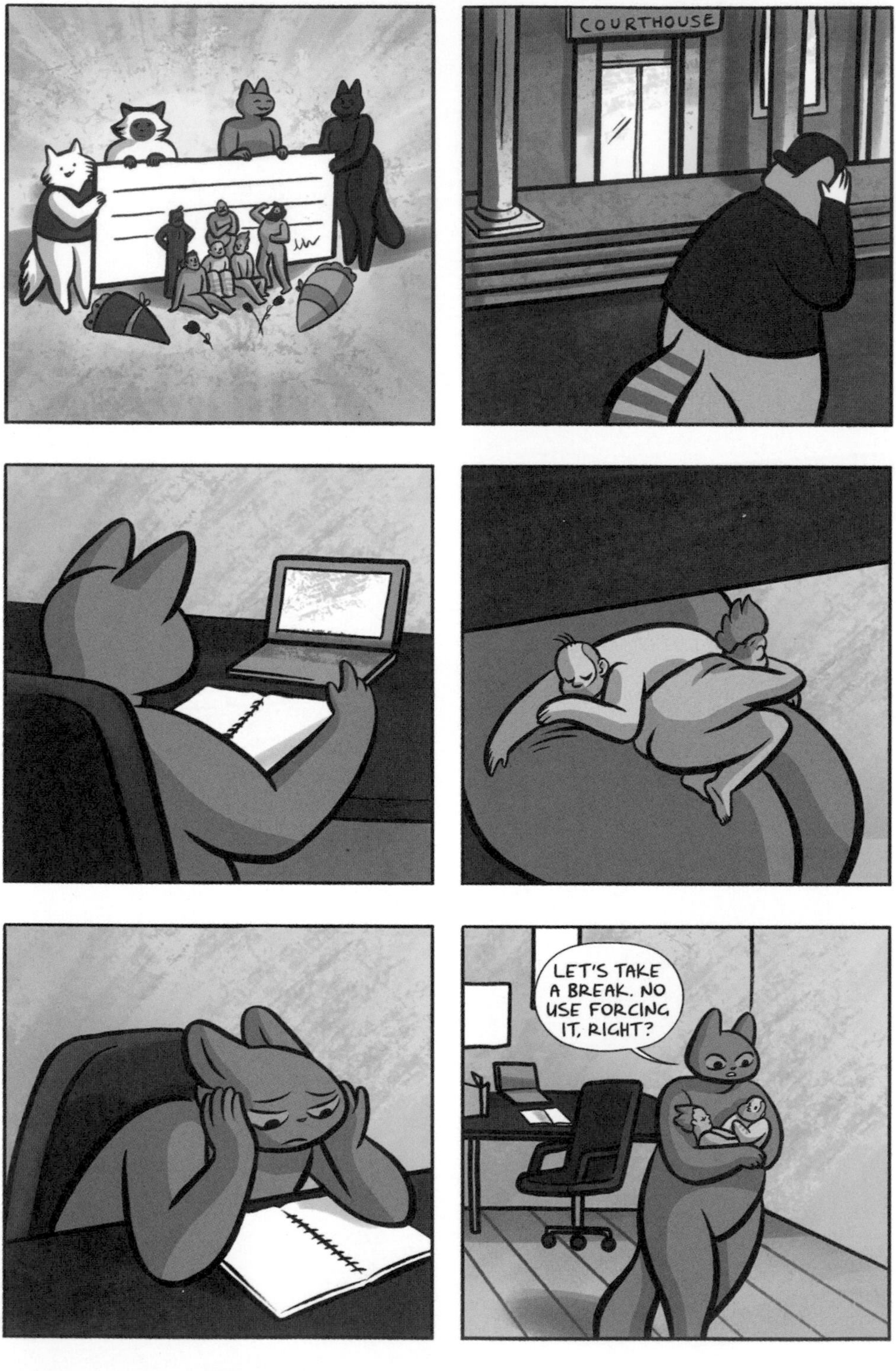
COURTHOUSE
LET'S TAKE A BREAK. NO USE FORCING IT, RIGHT?

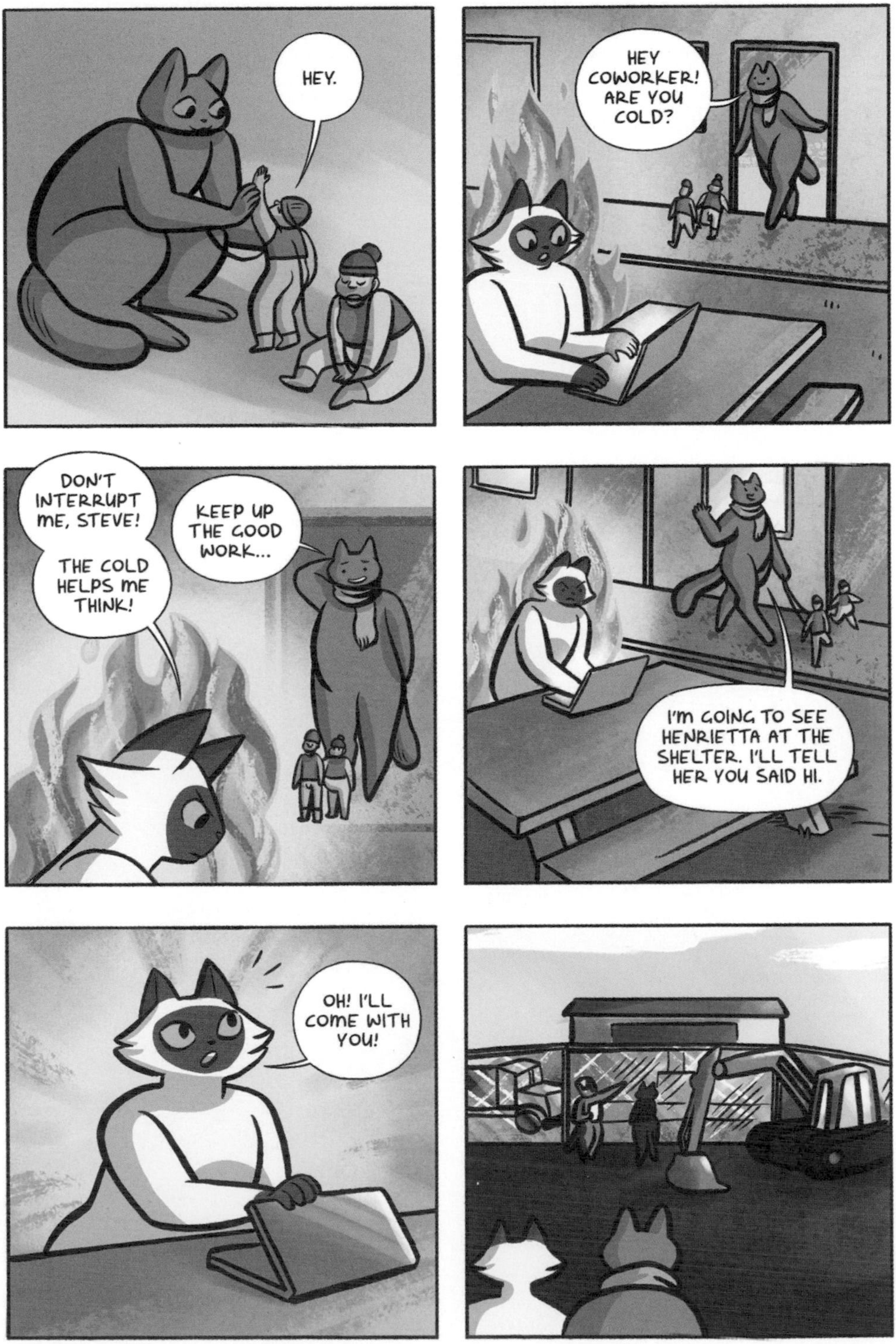
HEY.
HEY COWORKER! ARE YOU COLD?
DON'T INTERRUPT ME, STEVE!
THE COLD HELPS ME THINK!
KEEP UP THE GOOD WORK...
I'M GOING TO SEE HENRIETTA AT THE SHELTER. I'LL TELL HER YOU SAID HI.
OH! I'LL COME WITH YOU!

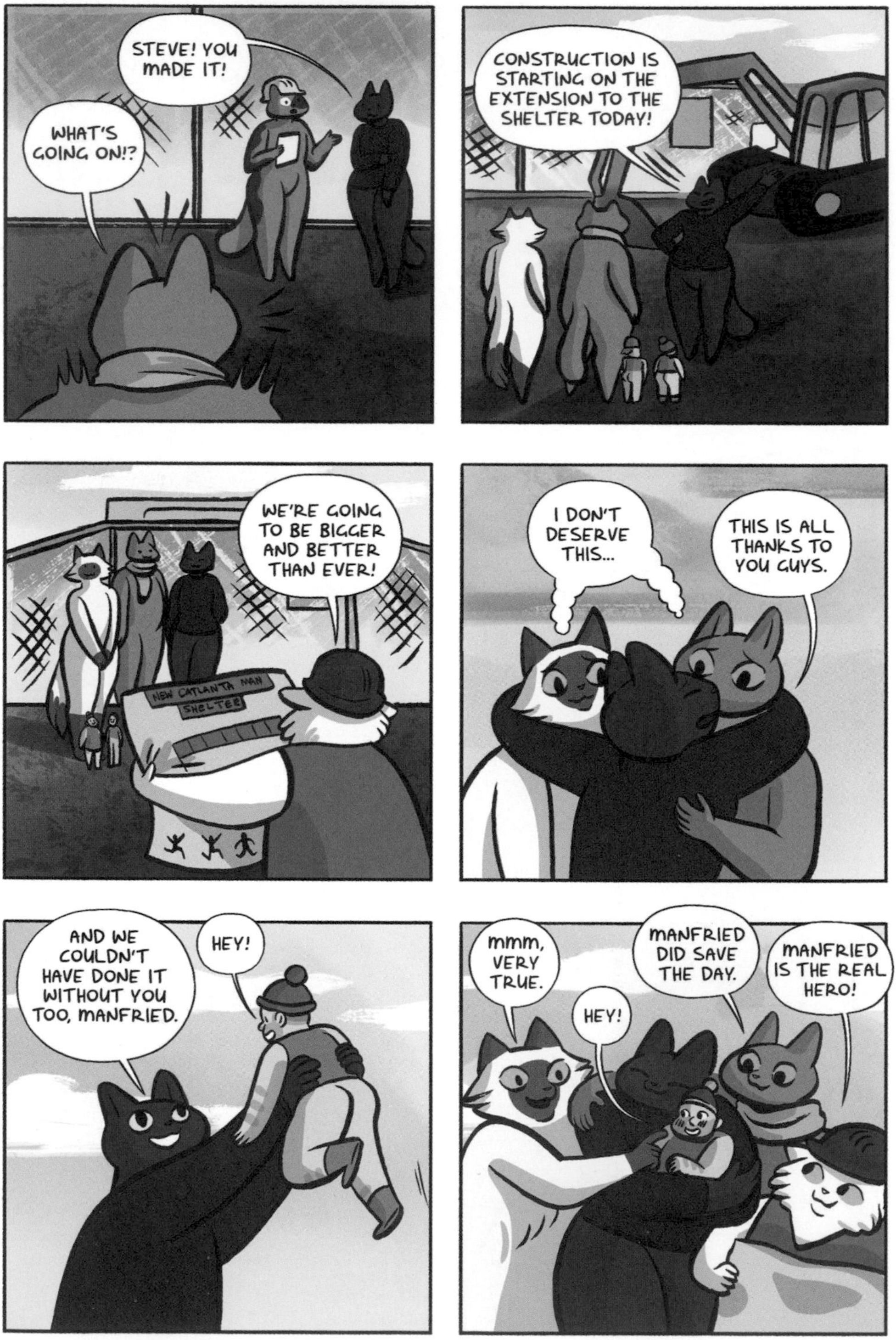
STEVE! YOU MADE IT!
WHAT'S GOING ON!?
CONSTRUCTION IS STARTING ON THE EXTENSION TO THE SHELTER TODAY!
WE'RE GOING TO BE BIGGER AND BETTER THAN EVER!
NEW CATLANTA MAN SHELTER
I DON'T DESERVE THIS...
THIS IS ALL THANKS TO YOU GUYS.
AND WE COULDN'T HAVE DONE IT WITHOUT YOU TOO, MANFRIED.
HEY!
mmm, VERY TRUE.
HEY!
MANFRIED DID SAVE THE DAY.
MANFRIED IS THE REAL HERO!

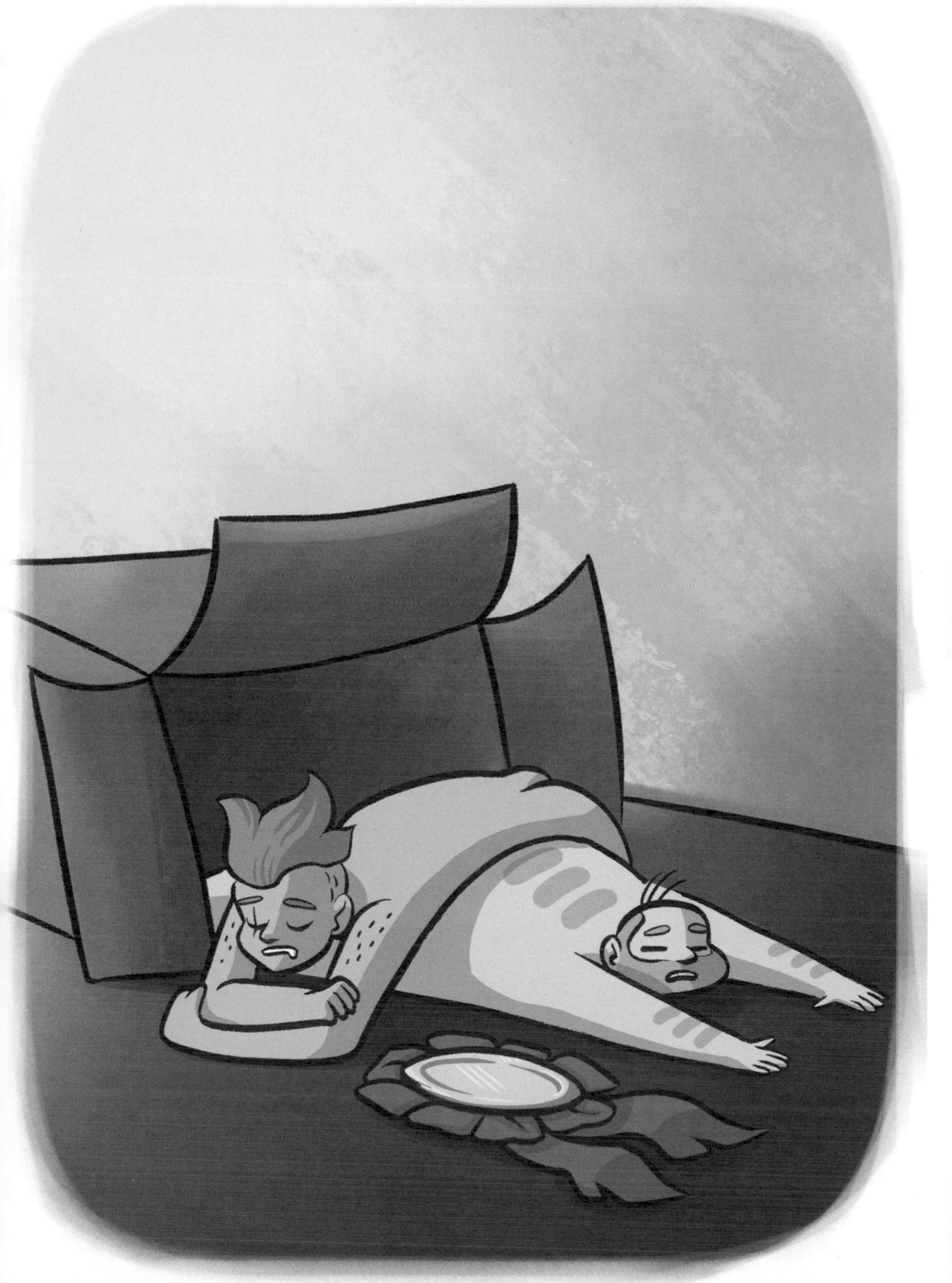

Acknowledgments

I'd like to thank Rick, Andie, Ivy, Nicole, and the rest of the Quirk crew for believing in Manfried and getting him out into the world. Thank you to Kelly for not giving up, even though it was a slog. Thank you to Matt and Meaghan for helping finish the book; you saved my bacon. Thank you to Brett and Morghan for having my back always, and for feeding me when I clearly couldn't look after myself.

—Caitlin

Once again, thank you to Luke for providing me with endless support, cracking my back when I needed it, and bringing me hundreds of cups of tea. Thanks to Caitlin for being easy-going and positive even when I thought the workload and stress would destroy her. Thanks to Matt and Megan for helping out when things got dire, and thanks to Rick and the Quirk team for giving Manfried your blessings and giving us such fantastic opportunities.

—Kelly